LAUNCHING THE "EXTENDED REPUBLIC"

The Federalist Era

UNITED STATES CAPITOL HISTORICAL SOCIETY
Clarence J. Brown, President

PERSPECTIVES ON THE AMERICAN REVOLUTION
Ronald Hoffman and Peter J. Albert, Editors

Diplomacy and Revolution: The Franco-American Alliance of 1778

Sovereign States in an Age of Uncertainty

Slavery and Freedom in the Age of the American Revolution

Arms and Independence: The Military Character of the American Revolution

An Uncivil War: The Southern Backcountry during the American Revolution

Peace and the Peacemakers: The Treaty of 1783

The Economy of Early America: The Revolutionary Period, 1763–1790

Women in the Age of the American Revolution

To Form a More Perfect Union: The Critical Ideas of the Constitution

Religion in a Revolutionary Age

Of Consuming Interests: The Style of Life in the Eighteenth Century

*The Transforming Hand of Revolution:
Reconsidering the American Revolution as a Social Movement*

Launching the "Extended Republic": The Federalist Era

Launching the "Extended Republic"

The Federalist Era

Edited by RONALD HOFFMAN
and PETER J. ALBERT

Published for the

UNITED STATES CAPITOL HISTORICAL SOCIETY

BY THE UNIVERSITY PRESS OF VIRGINIA

Charlottesville and London

THE UNIVERSITY PRESS OF VIRGINIA
Copyright © 1996 by the Rector and Visitors
of the University of Virginia

First Published 1996

⊗The paper used in this publication meets the minimum
requirements of the American National Standard for Information
Sciences—Permanence of Paper for Printed Library Materials, ANSI Z39.48-1984.

Library of Congress Cataloging-in-Publication Data

Launching the "Extended Republic" : the Federalist Era / edited by
Ronald Hoffman and Peter J. Albert.
    p. cm.—(Perspectives on the American Revolution)
    Includes index.
  ISBN 0-8139-1624-0 (cloth : alk. paper)
    1. United States—Politics and government—1789–1809.
    I. Hoffman, Ronald, 1941– . II. Albert, Peter J. III. Series.
E310.L38 1996
973.4—dc20   95-46657
                                     CIP

Printed in the United States of America

Contents

CONTENTS

Preface

FOLLOWING THE ADOPTION of the Constitution, the United States entered the 1790s both buoyantly optimistic about its prospects and deeply divided by unresolved questions concerning ideology, regional differences, and social structure. Thus, it was not long before the factional turmoil upon which James Madison had predicated his "extended republic" hardened into an intensely polarized political struggle with a wide variety of groups contending passionately against each other in an effort to determine the character of the new nation. To the dismay of state and national leaders, the Constitution, in correcting some of the Confederation era's problems, had also created a national forum that brought into sharp focus many conflicts that the former less centralized system of governance had diffused. Complicating matters further was the necessity that the United States present a unified response to the challenge posed by the French Revolution, an event that threatened to deepen the fissures already apparent in the young American republic.

The essays in this volume consider the years from 1790 to 1800 from a number of perspectives. The variety of subjects alone—domestic politics, westward expansion, Indian dispossession, slavery, the role of the courts, and the evolving legal system—offers a persuasive indication of the formidable challenges that confronted the newly formed republican polity. Gary J. Kornblith's examination of New England artisans and John L. Brooke's analysis of the Masonic movement draw attention to the ideological assumptions that informed political debate and to the complex interweaving of political and social history. James H. Kettner, Thomas P. Slaughter, and Maeva Marcus focus on different dimensions of the early national legal experience. Kettner explores tangled notions of slavery,

PREFACE

property, manumission, and court action, while Marcus traces
the evolution of judicial review and Slaughter the construction of the concept of treason. Paralleling the factional politics
and judicial acrimony of the 1790s were the young republic's
expansionist impulses, which drove its borders westward. Andrew R. L. Cayton's examination of the Blount conspiracy un-
derscores how the image of a western vacuum spurred
conflict and fed expansionist expectations. In detailing
George Washington's views on western expansion, John
Lauritz Larson shows how sharply ideals diverged from the
conditions that prevailed on the ground. Bernard W. Sheehan places the policies adopted toward the Native American
nations within a web of competing eastern and western
agendas. Gordon S. Wood's essay, which opens the volume,
sweeps the decade, effectively elucidating the soaring hopes
and bitter disappointments that comprised the first decade of
the national experience under the United States Constitution.

The editors wish to express their appreciation for the valuable contributions made by the other participants at the U.S.
Capitol Historical Society's symposium "Launching the 'Extended Republic': The Federalist Era," Steven R. Boyd, Car-
ville V. Earle, Richard E. Ellis, Owen Ireland, Harry N.
Scheiber, the late Mary K. Bonsteel Tachau, and Sean Wilentz. We would also like to extend our thanks to Diane P.
Koch and Mary C. Jeske for their assistance in the preparation of this manuscript.

LAUNCHING THE "EXTENDED REPUBLIC"

The Federalist Era

GORDON S. WOOD

Launching the "Extended Republic"

The Federalist Era

THE NATIONAL GOVERNMENT created by the Constitution was inaugurated in 1789 with more optimism and more consensus among the American people than at any time since the Declaration of Independence. A common enthusiasm for the new Constitution momentarily obscured the deep differences that existed among the national leaders and the states and sections they represented. The unanimous election of Washington as the first president gave the new government an immediate respectability it otherwise would not have had. A sense of beginning anew, of putting the republican experiment on a new and stronger foundation, ran through communities up and down the continent. By 1789 even the leading opponents of the Constitution, the Antifederalists, had come to accept it, though of course with the expectation that it would soon be amended. In fact, none of the Antifederalists in 1787 had been opposed to some sort of strengthening of the national government; they simply had not anticipated as strong a central government as the Constitution had created. Consequently, the former opponents of the Constitution were really in no position to oppose the new national government without giving it a chance.

It was a liberal, humanitarian, and cosmopolitan age. The country's leaders saw America's "rising empire" fulfilling at long last the promises of the Enlightenment. Freemasonry flourished, as John L. Brooke suggests, and orators everywhere promised an end to ignorance and superstition and the beginnings of a new era of reason, benevolence, and fraternity. It was a heroic age in which men talked of the aristocratic

1

passions—of greatness, honor, and the desire for fame. It was a neoclassical age, an Augustan age, as Linda K. Kerber has called it, an age of stability following a revolutionary upheaval in which art and literature would thrive.[1] Never in American history have the country's leaders voiced such high expectations for the cultural achievements of the nation as did Americans in the 1790s. The arts and sciences were inevitably moving across the Atlantic to the New World and bringing America into a golden age.

By whatever term the Federalist age might be called, it was in fact a very brief one. It disappeared so fast that we have a hard time recovering or understanding it. The consensus and optimism of 1789 quickly evaporated, and the decade that had begun so hopefully turned into one of the most passionate and divisive periods of American history. By the end of the 1790s the United States was on the verge of civil war, and the "whole system of American Government," in the opinion of the British ambassador, was "tottering to its foundations."[2]

The decade of the 1790s—the Federalist era—is the most awkward in American history. It seems unrelated to what preceded or followed it, a fleeting moment of heroic neoclassical dreams that were unsupported by American reality. The self-conscious, self-molded, self-controlled character of George Washington was the perfect symbol for the age; for, like Washington himself, the entire Federalist project was a monumental act of will in the face of contrary circumstances. The Federalists stood in the way of popular democracy as it was emerging in the United States, and thus they became heretics opposed to the developing democratic faith. Everything seemed to turn against them. They thought they were creating a classically heroic state, and they attempted everywhere to symbolize these classical aims. Instead they left only a legacy of indecipherable icons, unread poetry, antique place-names, and a proliferation of Greek and Roman temples. They despised political parties, but parties nonetheless

---

[1] Linda K. Kerber, *Federalists in Dissent: Imagery and Ideology in Jeffersonian America* (Ithaca, N.Y., 1970), pp. 1–22.

[2] British minister, quoted in Bernard Bailyn et al., *The Great Republic: A History of the American People*, 3d ed. (Lexington, Mass., 1985), p. 251.

emerged to shatter the remarkable harmony of 1789. They sought desperately in the 1790s to avoid conflict with the former mother country to the point where they appeared to be compromising the independence of the new nation, only to discover in end that the war with Great Britain they had avoided was to be fought anyway in 1812 by the subsequent administration of their opponents. By the early nineteenth century Alexander Hamilton, the brilliant leader of the Federalists, who more than anyone pursued the heroic dreams of the age, was not alone in his despairing conclusion "that this American world was not meant for me."[3]

The Federalist age was awkward because so many of America's leaders were heroically confident they were in control of events. No generation in American history was so acutely conscious that what it did would affect future generations, or, in the common phrase of the day, "millions yet unborn." The leaders felt an awesome responsibility not only for America's governments and political institutions but for its art, literature, and manners, indeed, for the entire culture.

But of course they were never in charge of events or circumstances. Everything was moving and changing much too fast. Indeed, it is the gap between the leaders' pretensions of control and the dynamic reality of the forces they were attempting to deal with that accounts for the strangeness and awkwardness of the decade. Subsequent generations of American leaders usually have had a much less heroic attitude about themselves. Mid-nineteenth-century leaders always had a sense of being caught up by forces larger than themselves, of being carried along by inevitable elements—whether called providence, progress, public opinion, or simply the popular masses. But most American leaders of the 1790s still clung to an older hierarchical-gentry world that assumed that a few men at the top could control and manipulate events and shape circumstances. The decade of the 1790s was the last gasp of an American eighteenth-century patrician world quickly lost and largely forgotten—a world of aristocratic as-

[3] Alexander Hamilton to Robert Morris, Feb. 29, 1802, Harold C. Syrett et al., eds., *The Papers of Alexander Hamilton*, 27 vols. (New York, 1961–87), 25:544.

sumptions, heroic leadership, and powdered wigs and knee breeches. It was a world soon to be overwhelmed by the most popular, most licentious, and most commercially ridden society history has ever known.

Rarely in American history has there been a greater separation between the expectations of the society's leaders and the reality of what eventually happened. The history of the 1790s is largely one of unfulfilled expectations, of high hopes smashed, of dreams gone awry. Most of what happened in the period was unanticipated and unwanted by the Founding Fathers. Nearly all the public leaders, both Federalists and their opponents, the Republicans, were overwhelmed by events, and little of what they intended worked out in quite the way they expected. The sudden transformation of the electoral college in the election of the president, which had been the consequence of complicated and painstaking compromises by the Philadelphia Convention, was only the most graphic example of the best-laid plans gone amiss.

It may be hard for us today to see how much in the decade turned out differently from what the leaders at the time expected; for many of their hopes and dreams did eventually get realized, even if decades or centuries after being formulated. Consequently, we tend to give the Federalists and other leaders of the decade credit for foresight and for laying the proper foundations for the future even if they were unable to bring about much in their own lifetimes. The city of Washington, D.C., is a good example. The plans for it were truly monumental, but the implementation of those plans was a long time coming. For a good part of the nineteenth century the national capital remained the butt of jokes, a city of open spaces and long distances, "bearing," as one observer said, "the marks of partial labour and general desertion."[4] Only after midcentury or perhaps only at the beginning of the twentieth century—some might say only in the past thirty years—did the federal city begin to resemble what Pierre Charles L'Enfant and others originally had hoped for it. Other dreams of the 1790s have likewise been gradually real-

---

[4]James Sterling Young, *The Washington Community, 1800–1828* (New York, 1966), p. 41.

ized in time. But the fact that many of the hopes and aspirations of the Federalist era have eventually come to pass should not obscure the extent of disillusionment and unfulfilled expectation that dominated that bizarre and stormy decade.

Most of the papers in this volume reveal to one degree or another the gap that existed between the leaders' plans and purposes on one hand and the reality of dynamic social circumstances on the other. Few of the public decision-makers, whether Federalist or Republican, clearly understood the complicated historical forces they were dealing with, or if they did, were able to control or manipulate those forces.

The problem can be most fully seen in the ways in which the national government was created in the 1790s. Certainly the political leaders had high hopes for the launching of the ship of state. But though they commonly resorted to the nautical image, they also realized that in 1789 much of their ship existed only on the drawing boards. Not only was the ship of state largely unbuilt, but the plans and blueprints for it were general and vague enough that the size and shape of the ship still remained uncertain. It was not even clear what the ship would be designed to do. Everyone realized that the nature, purposes, and strength of the new national government all had to be worked out, and beneath the outward consensus of 1789 nearly everyone had his own ideas about what these ought to be.

Because the government was so unformed and the future so problematical, the stakes were high, and men knew that precedents were being set. Consequently, every issue, no matter how trivial, seemed loaded with significance. Many members of the Senate did not think they were wasting their time in spending a month debating the proper title for addressing the president. From that title, whether "His Highness" or simply "Mr. President," might flow the very character of the future government and state.

In such uncertain circumstances the advantage lay with those whose vision was clearest, whose purposes were most certain, and this meant the Federalist leaders, and in particular Alexander Hamilton, the secretary of the Treasury. From 1787 the most nationally minded of the Federalists had wanted the United States to be no mere confederation of disparate states but a republican government in its own right with the power to act energetically in the public sphere. In building such an integrated national state, the Federalist leaders saw their principal political problem as one of adhesion: how to keep people in such a large sprawling republic from flying apart in pursuit of their partial local interests. This of course, as Montesquieu had said, was the central problem for any republic, but it was especially a problem for a huge extended republic like the United States. Unlike monarchies, republics lacked unitary authority, kingly honors and patronage, hereditary aristocracies, established national churches, and standing armies to help hold themselves together. Instead, republics were supposed to rely for cohesion on the moral qualities of their people—their virtue and their natural sociability. They had to be held together from below, by their natural affection and benevolence and by their willingness to sacrifice their partial and private interests for the sake of the public good. In light of recent events in Eastern Europe, we today are perhaps in a better position than some previous generations of Americans to appreciate the weaknesses of republics and the advantages of monarchies and authoritarian governments in holding peoples of diverse backgrounds, interests, and ethnicities together.

By 1789 many of Federalists, particularly Hamilton, had no confidence whatsoever left in the virtue or the natural sociability of the American people as adhesive forces: to rely on such wild schemes and visionary principles to tie the United States together, they said, was to rely on nothing.[5] Hence the Federalist leaders believed that they had to find things other than republican virtue and natural sociability to make the American people a single nation.

Tying people together, creating social cohesiveness, making

[5] In Hamilton's opinion, the Republican view that government eventually "will become useless, and Society will subsist and flourish free from its shackles" as "human nature shall refine and ameliorate by the operation of a more enlightened plan" based on the operation of a common moral sense and the spread of affection and benevolence was a "wild and fatal . . . scheme," even if its Republican "votaries" like Jefferson did not immediately push such a program to its fullest (Morton J. Frisch, ed., *Selected Writings and Speeches of Alexander Hamilton* [Washington, D.C., 1985], p. 415).

a single nation out of disparate sections and communities without relying on idealistic republican adhesives—this was the preoccupation of the Federalists, and it explains much of what they did—from Washington's proposals for building canals to Hamilton's financial program. Many of the Federalists actually thought in terms of turning the government of the United States into a surrogate monarchy, of devising substitutes for traditional monarchical ligaments and placing them within a republican framework. Maybe it was a true Augustan age after all, for had not Augustus sought to incorporate elements of monarchy into the Roman Empire while all the time talking about republicanism?

In place of the impotent confederation of separate states that had existed in the 1780s, the Federalists envisioned a strong, consolidated, and prosperous national state, united, as Hamilton said, "for the accomplishment of great purposes" and led by an energetic government composed of the best and most distinguished men in the society.[6] They aimed to bolster the dignity of this government by adopting some of the ceremony and majesty of monarchy. The Senate actually agreed that all American coins would bear the head of the president, as was the case with the European monarchs. Although the high-toned Federalists eventually lost this proposal, as they did the presidential title of "His Highness" (much to the relief of Washington himself), they did attempt to surround the new government with some of the trappings of monarchy. They established insufferably formal levees where the president, as one critic said, could be seen "on Stated times like an Eastern Lama," and they drew up elaborate monarchlike rules of etiquette at what soon came to be called the "American court," first in New York and after 1790 in Philadelphia.[7] They sought to make the celebration of Washington's birthday rival that of the Fourth of July. And they sent Washington on royal tours of the country in which the president was welcomed

[6] Hamilton, speech in New York ratifying convention, June 28, 1788, Syrett et al., eds., *Papers of Hamilton*, 5:118.

[7] Kenneth R. Bowling and Helen E. Veit, eds., *Documentary History of the First Federal Congress*, vol. 9, *The Diary of William Maclay and Other Notes on Senate Debates* (Baltimore, 1988), p. 21.

with triumphal arches, ceremonies, and acclaim befitting a king, including signs proclaiming "Long Live George Washington!" With Yale students debating the advantages of an elective over a hereditary king, suggestions of monarchy were very much in the air. Some people even referred to Washington's inauguration as a "coronation," and more than one commentator expressed relief that he had no heir.[8]

Many of the Federalists, in short, aimed to make the United States in time a grand illustrious nation and a rival of the great nation-states of Europe. Hamilton especially envisioned the new national government in traditional European fashion as a great military power. The federal government for him was not to be, as it was for James Madison, simply a republican remedy for republican ills. Hamilton and some other Federalists dreamed of making the United States "something noble and magnificent" and the equal of the European monarchies on their own terms—terms that, as Washington said, were "characteristic of wise and powerful Nations."[9] This meant a strong central government that reached to all parts of an integrated nation with a powerful army and navy that commanded the respect of all the world.

Hamilton's model was England, and he consciously set out to duplicate the great English achievement of the eighteenth century. England had emerged from the chaos and civil wars of the seventeenth century that had killed one king and deposed another to become the most dominant power in the world. That this small island on the northern edge of Europe with a fifth to a third of the population of France was able to

[8] David W. Robson, *Educating Republicans: The College in the Era of the American Revolution, 1758–1800* (Westport, Conn., 1985), p. 149; Thomas E. V. Smith, *The City of New York in the Year of Washington's Inauguration, 1789* (1889; reprint ed., Riverside, Conn., 1972), pp. 217–19; Winfred E. A. Bernhard, *Fisher Ames: Federalist and Statesman, 1758–1808* (Chapel Hill, 1965), p. 92; Barry Schwartz, *George Washington: The Making of an American Symbol* (New York, 1987), pp. 31–38.

[9] Hamilton, quoted in Thomas K. McCraw, "The Strategic Vision of Alexander Hamilton," *American Scholar* 63 (1994): 40; George Washington to Henry Knox, Feb. 28, 1785, quoted in John Lauritz Larson, "'Wisdom Enough to Improve Them': Government, Liberty, and Inland Waterways in the Rising American Empire," in this volume.

build the biggest empire since the Fall of Rome was the miracle of the century, even surpassing the astonishing achievement of the Netherlands in the previous century. The English "fiscal-military" state, in John Brewer's apt term, could mobilize wealth and wage war as no state in history ever had. Its centralized administration had developed an extraordinary capacity to tax and borrow from its subjects without impoverishing them.[10] Hamilton saw that the secret of England's success was its system of funded debt together with its banking structure and its market in public securities. He aimed to do for the United States what English ministers had done for the former mother country. His financial program followed directly from this aim.

Hamilton was undoubtedly concerned with the commercial prosperity of the United States—with furthering "the interests of a great people"—but he was scarcely the capitalist promoter of America's emerging business culture that is often described. He was a traditional eighteenth-century statesman, willing to allow ordinary people their profits and property, their interests and their petty pursuits of happiness, but wanting honor and glory for himself and his country. He was very much the mercantilist who believed deeply in the "need" in government for "a common directing power." He had only contempt for those who believed in laissez-faire and thought that trade and interests could regulate themselves. "This," he said, "is one of those wild speculative paradoxes which have grown into credit among us, contrary to the uniform practice and sense of the most enlightened nations. . . . It must be rejected by every man acquainted with commercial history."[11]

Of course, he accepted the prevalence of interests—indeed, he thought there could be no other tie but interest between most people in the society. He himself, however, was extraordinarily scrupulous as secretary of the Treasury in maintaining his personal disinterestedness and freedom from

[10] John Brewer, *The Sinews of Power: War, Money, and the English State, 1688–1783* (New York, 1989).

[11] Hamilton, speech in the New York ratifying convention, June 27, 1788, and *Continentalist* No. 5, Apr. 18, 1782, in Syrett et al., eds., *Papers of Hamilton,* 5:96, 3:76.

corruption. Let others, including congressmen, become "speculators" and "peculators," but not him: he would be, as he put it in one of his sardonic moods, one of those "public fools who sacrifice private to public interest at the certainty of ingratitude and obloquy." He would stand above all the interested men and try to harness and use them. He agreed with the eighteenth-century British economic philosopher Sir James Steuart that "self-interest . . . is the main spring, and only motive which a statesman should make use of, to engage a free people to concur in the plans which he lays down for their government." Although he later and rather defensively denied that he had ever made interest "the weightiest motive" behind his financial program, there is no doubt that he thought the debt and other financial measures would strengthen the national government "by increasing the number of ligaments between the Government and the interests of Individuals." [12]

In effect, in the opposition language of the eighteenth-century Anglo-American world, Hamilton set out to "corrupt" American society, to use monarchical-like governmental influence to tie existing commercial interests to the government and to create new hierarchies of interest and dependency that would substitute for the absence of virtue and the apparently weak republican adhesives existing in America. In local areas Hamilton and the Federalist leaders built up followings among Revolutionary war veterans and members of the Society of the Cincinnati. They appointed important and respectable local figures to the federal judiciary and other federal offices. They exploited the patronage of the Treasury Department and its seven hundred or more customs officials, revenue agents, and postmasters with particular effectiveness. By 1793 or so the Federalists had formed groups of "friends of government" in most of the states. Their hierarchies of patronage and dependency ran from the federal executive

[12] Hamilton to Robert Troup, Apr. 13, 1795, ibid., 18:329; Sir James Steuart (1767), quoted in Stephen Copley, *Literature and the Social Order in Eighteenth-Century England* (London, 1984), p. 120; Hamilton, The Defence of the Funding System, July 1795, Syrett, et al., eds., *Papers of Hamilton*, 19:1–73.

through Congress down to the various localities. It was as close to monarchy and a Walpolean system of influence as America was ever to have.

At same time the Federalists sought to wean the people's affections away from their state governments and to get them to feel the power of what they hoped would become a consolidated national government. The Constitution had attempted to reduce drastically the power of the states. Article I, Section 10, among other things, had forbidden the states from levying tariffs or duties on imports or exports and had barred them from issuing paper money or bills of credit. As these were the principal means by which premodern governments raised money, their prohibition cut deeply into the fiscal competency of the state governments. Some Federalists hoped to go further and eventually reduce the states to mere administrative units of the national government. Washington thought that the states might in time have no occasion for taxes and "consequently may abandon all the subjects of taxation to the Union." The federal excise taxes, especially that on whiskey, were designed to make people feel the authority of the national government. In a like way the raising of nearly fifteen thousand militia by the national government to put down the Whiskey Rebellion flowed from Hamilton's assumption voiced in 1794 that "government can never [be] said to be established until some signal display, has manifested its power of military coercion."[13]

But the national government could not rely on military force to keep people in line. Other more subtle and more ostensibly republican means were needed to control the surging passions of the people. As Maeva Marcus and several other authors in this volume make clear, the Federalists found one answer in the judiciary. They were eager to make judges a bulwark against the unruly democratic consequences of the Revolution. Since the 1780s those concerned about rampag-

[13] Washington, quoted in Leonard D. White, *The Federalists: A Study in Administrative History* (New York, 1948), p. 404n; Hamilton, quoted in Richard H. Kohn, *Eagle and Sword: The Federalists and the Creation of the Military Establishment in America, 1783–1802* (New York, 1975), p. 171.

ing state legislatures and their abuses of private property and minority rights, particularly those of creditors, had conducted a propaganda campaign to strengthen the judiciary.

Judges in colonial America had been relatively insignificant members of government; they had been viewed largely as appendages or extensions of the royal governors or chief magistrates, who usually appointed them at the pleasure of the Crown. At the time of the Revolution, Americans had done little to change this negligible status of the judiciary. In their Revolutionary state constitutions of 1776 they had taken away the appointment of judges from the governors and had given it to the state legislatures, and through codification schemes they had tried further to reduce the importance of judges by turning them into what Thomas Jefferson called "a mere machine."[14]

In the following decades all this was reversed. Suddenly in the 1780s and 1790s the judiciary in America emerged out of its earlier insignificance to become a full-fledged partner in what was now defined as the tripartite system of American government—sharing power equally with legislatures and executives. Many in fact thought that the judiciary had become the principal means for controlling popular legislatures and protecting private rights. The most dramatic institutional transformation in the early republic was this rise of what was commonly referred to as an "independent judiciary." It is a fascinating story still not told.

It is not surprising therefore that the Federalists should have been concerned with creating strong judiciaries, not only in the states but especially in the new federal government. No institution of the new national government would be less susceptible to popular democratic pressure and yet would touch the lives of ordinary people in their localities more than a federal court system. Thus the Federalists fought hard to create a separate national court structure in which, they hoped, the common law of crimes would run. The Judiciary Act of 1789, which gave concurrent original jurisdiction

[14] Thomas Jefferson, quoted in Gordon S. Wood, *The Creation of the American Republic, 1776–1787* (Chapel Hill, 1969), p. 161.

to the state courts, was scarcely satisfactory for the more nationally minded Federalists, and throughout the 1790s they struggled to expand the power and jurisdiction of the federal courts. The Judiciary Act of 1801 and the broadened and constructive interpretations of national law by federal judges in the 1790s, including that of treason discussed in this volume by Thomas P. Slaughter, were manifestations of these efforts. The actions of the John Marshall court in subsequent years, as its limited definition of treason in the Aaron Burr trial shows, far from being extensions of national power, were in fact retreats from the advanced and exposed positions that the Federalists of the 1790s attempted to stake out for the national judiciary.[15]

All these grand and grandiose aims of the Federalist leaders, particularly of the high-toned Federalists, are a measure of their fears and their disillusionment with what the Revolution was doing to American society. The fears and disillusionment had been widely shared among America's gentry leadership in 1787 and had helped create the Constitution. But the degrees of fear and disillusionment were vastly different among even fervent supporters of the Constitution. Madison, for example, certainly shared Hamilton's misgivings about democracy and his desire to reduce popular state power; and he surely wanted a commercially strong mercantilist national government that would be able both to pass navigation acts and protect minority creditor rights in the several states. But he and others who had created and supported the Constitution, particularly in the southern and Mid-Atlantic states, did not share Hamilton's vision of the United States becoming a consolidated European-like "military-fiscal"

---

[15] For two recent revisionist interpretations of the origins of judicial review see Jack M. Sosin, *The Aristocracy of the Long Robe: The Origins of Judicial Review in America* (New York, 1989), and Robert L. Clinton, *Marbury v. Madison and Judicial Review* (Lawrence, Kans., 1989). For an attempt to describe the judicial climate out of which judicial review arose see Gordon S. Wood, "The Origins of Judicial Review," *Suffolk University Law Review* 22 (1988):1293–1307, and Wood, "Judicial Review in the Era of the Founding," in Robert Licht, ed., *Is the Supreme Court the Guardian of the Constitution?* (Washington, D.C., 1993).

power. Nor did they ever really doubt the popular basis of America's governments.[16] Indeed, Madison, Jefferson, and the Republicans never accepted the newly emerging European idea of the modern state, with its elaborate administrative structures, large armies and navies, high taxes, and huge debts. The Republicans' rejection of this modern state had immense implications for America's future.

The High Federalists' attempts to impose such a modern state on America eventually divided the gentry leaders of the nation and led to passionate factional splits throughout the country. Jefferson and the Republicans came to believe quite sincerely that Hamilton and the Federalists were out to create a monarchy in America. Although Hamilton with equal sincerity denied that that was ever his aim, popular Republican resistance to his projects only made him and the High Federalists more desperate. By the end of the decade the Federalists had become truly frightened by the popular direction of events and felt compelled to pass alien and sedition acts and to make plans for war involving the creation of armies in the tens of thousands and the calling of Washington back into uniform as commander of these troops. Hamilton even toyed with the idea of dismantling the states.

We know how it all turned out—with Jefferson's election in 1800 and peaceful accession to power in 1801—and consequently we find it hard to take the fears of either the Federalists or the Republicans very seriously. But both had good reason to be frightened, for there were forces at work in the 1790s that neither the Federalists nor the Republicans fully understood or could control. The consequence was that many of their best intentions went awry.

The men who wrote the Constitution had expected to attract to the national government the best people, "men who possess the most attractive merit and the most diffusive and established characters," in Madison's words, or "men of discernment and liberality," as Washington described them.[17] They knew whom they meant even if we have a hard time

---

[16] This is the gist of Lance Banning's new book, *The Sacred Fire of Liberty: James Madison and the Founding of the Federal Republic* (Ithaca, N.Y., 1995).

[17] *Federalist* No. 10.

defining such people. They meant men pretty much like themselves, gentlemen of talent and distinction, with all that the term *gentlemen* implied in the eighteenth century. Such gentlemen should ideally be educated in the liberal arts at a good college like Harvard or Princeton, or if not, at least self-cultivated and with sufficient wealth and independence that they did not have to earn a living in too blatant or mercenary a fashion. Madison was apprehensive that the First Congress was going to be composed of the same sorts of illiberal and narrow-minded men who had sat in the state legislatures, and he was relieved at the character of most of the congressmen he met. But it soon became evident that his elevated republic was not going to be high enough to keep out permanently the middling and other ordinary and interested people who had caused so much difficulty in the state legislatures in the 1780s. In the northern parts of America at least, all levels of government were steadily being democratized and occupied by people with interests to promote. By the Second Congress, even William Findley, an ex-weaver from Pennsylvania and a prototype of the plebeian Antifederalist, made it into the elevated national government that was designed to keep his type out.

The problem was that Washington's "men of discernment and liberality" were hard to find, and even when found lacked sufficient income to behave as disinterested gentlemen in government were supposed to behave. By 1795 President Washington was having trouble recruiting proper men for the highest federal offices, including the cabinet. Federalists in the House of Representatives charged that Jefferson, Hamilton, and Henry Knox had all resigned from the cabinet "chiefly for one reason, the smallness of the salary."[18] Although this was not the case with Jefferson, both Knox and Hamilton did have trouble maintaining a genteel standard of living on their government salaries. There were of course plenty of claimants for the middle and lower offices of the government, but these were lesser sorts of men who were quite openly seeking the offices in order to make a living from them.

[18] White, *Federalists*, p. 301.

The truth was that the entire Federalist scheme rested on a false understanding of America's gentry. Washington, like other Federalists, conceived of his "men of discernment and liberality" in classically republican terms, as gentlemen of leisure and independence who were generally free of direct market interests and who therefore could take up the burden of public office as a disinterested obligation of their social rank. By proposing in the Philadelphia Convention that all members of the executive be barred from receiving any salaries or fees, Benjamin Franklin was simply expressing an extreme version of this classical republican view of officeholding. But the fact of the matter was that members of the American aristocracy, with the exception of a few wealthy individuals like Franklin and many southern gentry like Washington and Jefferson, were incapable of living up to the classical image of a leisured patriciate serving in public office without compensation.

God knows many of them tried to live up to the classical image, often with disastrous consequences for themselves and their families. Merchants who wanted to hold high public office usually had to ennoble themselves and put their property into a rentier form—John Hancock and Robert Morris being notable examples. The goal was to get enough wealth, preferably in the form of land, so that one did not have to work at accumulating money on a regular basis and in an acquisitive manner. All the desperate efforts of men like Morris, Knox, and James Wilson to find genteel independence for themselves through land speculation—efforts that ended in ruin and debtors' prison—are measures of the power of that classical image of a leisured patriciate. For it was evident to the eighteenth-century gentry, even if not to us, that one could not acquire real independence of the marketplace without having that independence based on what historian George V. Taylor, in reference to eighteenth-century France, calls "proprietary wealth."[19] Such proprietary wealth was composed of

[19] George V. Taylor, "Noncapitalist Wealth and the Origins of the French Revolution," *American Historical Review* 62 (1967):469–96; William Doyle, *Origins of the French Revolution* (Oxford, 1980), pp. 17–18.

static forms of property—"unearned income," as we might call it: rents from tenants, bonds, interest from money out on loan—that allowed its holders sufficient leisure to assume the burdens of public office without expecting high salaries. These kinds of proprietary propertyholders were those Washington had in mind when he used the term, quoted by John Lauritz Larson in his paper, *the monied gentry*.[20] These monied gentry with their static proprietary wealth were of course vulnerable to inflation, which is why the printing of paper money was so frightening to them. Although these proprietary gentry, like their counterparts in England, were often involved in various commercial ventures, they were not risk-taking entrepreneurs or businessmen in any modern sense. Instead, they were social leaders whose property was the source of their personal authority and independence; inflation therefore threatened not simply their livelihood but their very identity and social position. Until we grasp this point, we will never appreciate the depth of moral indignation behind the gentry's outcry against paper money and other debtor-relief legislation in the 1780s.

Of course, not only was this kind of proprietary wealth very hard to come by in America where, compared to England, land was so plentiful and tenantry so rare, but commerce and trade were creating new forms of property that gave wealth and power to new sorts of people. This new property was anything but static: it was risk-taking, entrepreneurial capital—not money out on loan, but money borrowed. It was in fact all the paper money that enterprising people clamored for in these years. It was not "unearned income" that came to a person, as Adam Smith defined the rents of the English landed gentry, without exertion, but "earned income" that came *with* exertion, indeed, came with labor, production, and exchange. This was the property of businessmen and protobusiness-

[20] Washington to Thomas Johnson, July 20, 1770, John C. Fitzpatrick, ed., *The Writings of George Washington*, 39 vols. (Washington, D.C., 1931–44), 3:18. On the efforts of some Boston gentry to set themselves up as country farmers, georgic style, see Tamara Platkins Thornton, *Cultivating Gentlemen: The Meaning of Country Life among the Boston Elite, 1785–1860* (New Haven, 1989).

men—of commercial farmers, artisan-manufacturers, traders, shopkeepers, and in fact all who labored for a living and produced and exchanged things, no matter how poor or wealthy they might be.

The increasing distinctions drawn in these years between, in the words of the uneducated New England farmer William Manning, "those that labour for a Living and those that git a Living without Bodily Labour," which included all gentry-professionals, expressed the rise of this new kind of property.[21] Unlike proprietary wealth, this new kind of dynamic, fluid, and evanescent property could not create personal authority or identity; it was, said Joseph Story, "continually changing like the waves of the sea."[22] Hence it was meaningless to rely on it as a source of independence. Once this was understood, then property qualifications for participation in public life either as voters or officeholders lost their relevance and rapidly fell away. The William Mannings and the William Findleys who spoke for these new kinds of entrepreneurial and labor-produced property—for "earned income"—were precisely the sorts of illiberal and parochial men that gentry like Madison in the 1780s had condemned.

But Madison, Jefferson, and other southern gentry leaders of the Republicans no more understood what was happening to American society and to property than did Hamilton and the Federalists. Nor did Hamilton and Jefferson understand very clearly the direction the American economy was taking. Both thought the future prosperity of the United States lay with foreign trade, and they were both wrong: it lay essentially with domestic or internal trade, with the United States becoming "a world within themselves."[23] Eighteenth-century

[21] Samuel Eliot Morison, ed., "William Manning's *The Key of Libberty*," *William and Mary Quarterly*, 3d ser. 13 (1956):202–54.

[22] Merrill D. Peterson, ed., *Democracy, Liberty, and Property: The State Constitutional Conventions of the 1820s* (Indianapolis, 1966), pp. 79–82. On the new democratic understanding of property as the product of labor see Alan Taylor, *Liberty Men and Great Proprietors: The Revolutionary Settlement on the Maine Frontier, 1760–1820* (Chapel Hill, 1990), pp. 25, 28.

[23] Cathy D. Matson and Peter S. Onuf, "Toward a Republican Empire: Interest and Ideology in Revolutionary America," *American Quarterly* 37

leaders had difficulty putting great value on internal trade because of their lingering zero-sum mercantilist assumption that a nation's wealth as a whole could grow only at the expense of another nation; that is, the country as a whole could prosper only by selling more abroad than it bought.[24]

Domestic trade was thought to benefit only individuals or regions but not the country as a whole; it simply moved wealth about without increasing its total. Those involved in domestic commerce, however, had a different sense of where the future prosperity of the country lay, but they needed paper money to carry on their internal trading, lots of it. Article I, Section 10, of the Constitution had prohibited the states from printing bills of credit, but the needs and desires of all the protobusinessmen and domestic traders were too great to be stymied by a paper restriction. So the states under popular pressure got round the constitutional prohibition by chartering banks, hundreds of them, which in turn issued the paper money people wanted. Hamilton no more predicted or wanted this proliferation of banks and paper money than did Jefferson; he in fact had thought his Bank of the United States would absorb the state banks and have a monopoly on banking and the issuing of currency.

Both Hamilton and Jefferson equally underestimated the importance of artisan manufacturing. As Joyce Appleby has

---

(1985):496–531. Fanny Wright, in her *Views of Society and Manners in America*, ed. Paul R. Baker (Cambridge, Mass., 1963), p. 208, used the same phrase to describe American society a generation later. Although Hamilton's Report on Manufactures suggests that he understood the importance of domestic trade, in fact, as John R. Nelson has argued, he never fully appreciated nor supported the interests of manufacturers and those involved in domestic commerce. In so far as he supported manufacturing, it was the manufacturing of goods for export. John R. Nelson, Jr., *Liberty and Property: Political Economy and Policymaking in the New Nation, 1789–1812* (Baltimore, 1987), pp. 37–51.

[24] As John E. Crowley has shown, Americans were not very good students of Adam Smith: they tended to ignore his support for domestic trade over foreign trade and remained mercantilists a lot longer than the British; that is to say, they "slight[ed] or countermand[ed] the imperatives of market relations in the name of political imperatives" (*The Privileges of Independence: Neomercantilism and the American Revolution* [Baltimore, 1993], pp. xii–xiii, 133, 207).

told us, Jefferson and the Republican party benefited from artisan and business support in the Mid-Atlantic states, but Jefferson never fully grasped this point; he never in fact appreciated the nature of the popular commercial forces he was presumably leading.[25] Hamilton's biggest political mistake was to ignore the interests of the artisan-manufacturers. Despite his 1791 Report on Manufactures, which recognized the importance of domestic commerce, Hamilton, as John R. Nelson has told us, never had his heart in manufacturing and never pushed to implement his report; instead, his program favored moneyed men and import merchants at the expense of domestic producers and traders.[26] Consequently, artisans in the Mid-Atlantic states who had been fervent Federalists in 1787–88 were eventually driven into the ranks of the Republican party. As Gary J. Kornblith points out in this volume, this did not happen in New England. Too many of the New England artisans were too closely tied into patron-client relationships with wealthy merchants in New England's port cities to develop as sharp a sense of their separate interests as that possessed by Mid-Atlantic artisans. From 1793 to 1807 New England's interests and prosperity were almost entirely absorbed in overseas trade. As a result, the emphasis Hamilton's program placed on the import trade skewed Federalist support toward New England and helped to mask the fact that the future prosperity of the United States lay largely in the development of domestic commerce.

In other areas as well, gentry leaders of all sections and both parties misunderstood the realities of American society. Many leaders in the 1790s, for example, thought that slavery was on its way to ultimate extinction. The American Revolution had unleashed enlightened principles of liberty that seemed to make the disappearance of slavery just a matter of time. Liberal opinion everywhere in the world condemned the institution. When even southerners like Jefferson, Patrick Henry, and Henry Laurens deplored the injustice of slavery,

[25] Joyce Appleby, *Capitalism and a New Social Order: The Republican Vision of the 1790s* (New York, 1984).

[26] John R. Nelson, "Alexander Hamilton and American Manufacturing: A Reexamination," *Journal of American History* 65 (1979):971–95.

from "that moment," many believed, "the slow, but certain, death-wound was inflicted upon it."[27]

Of course, as we know, such predictions could not have been more wrong: far from being doomed, slavery in the United States in the 1790s was on the verge of its greatest expansion. But such self-deception, such mistaken optimism among the Revolutionary leaders was understandable, for they wanted to believe the best, and there was some evidence that slavery was dying away. The northern states, where slavery was not inconsequential, were busy trying to eliminate the institution; and by 1804 all had done so. There were indications, as James H. Kettner's paper shows, that the same thing was happening in the southern states. More antislavery societies existed in the South than in the North, and manumissions in the South were becoming more frequent; in Virginia alone the number of free blacks increased from 3,000 in 1780 to 13,000 by 1790. Between 1790 and 1810 the free black population in the United States grew faster than the slave population. By the 1790s all the states, including South Carolina, had ended the international slave trade. Many hoped that abolishing the importation of slaves from abroad would eventually kill off the institution of slavery. But faith in the future was not enough: the Founding Fathers had simply not counted on the remarkable demographic capacity of the old slave states themselves, especially Virginia, to produce slaves for the expanding areas of the Deep South and Southwest.

Perhaps we can muster some sympathy for the Founding Fathers' difficulty in predicting the future when we take into account the breathtaking speed of events and complexity of circumstances in the 1790s. Nowhere was this speed and complexity more obvious than in the settlement of the West, and nowhere was the gap between the leaders' illusions and reality more conspicuous than in the way they dealt with the West.

The Federalists were at least not mistaken in their sense of the fragility of the United States. It was the largest republic since ancient Rome, and as such it was continually in danger

---

[27] E. H. Smith, *A Discourse Delivered April 11, 1798*. . ., quoted in Duncan J. MacLeod, *Slavery, Race, and the American Revolution* (Cambridge, 1974), p. 29.

of falling apart. Indeed, fear for the integrity of the United States lay behind the Continental Congress's passage of the Northwest Ordinance of 1787. Despite its progressive promises, this plan for the colonization of American territories was actually quite reactionary. Its proposals for garrison governments with authoritarian leadership for new western colonies resembled nothing so much as those failed seventeenth-century English efforts at establishing military governments over the obstreperous colonists. The Ordinance was an indication of how fearful eastern leaders were of the unruly westerners' leaving the union, lured away perhaps by one European power or another.

These fears that westerners could be separated from the United States by European powers were not entirely illusory—not when popular societies were toasting the right of everyone to "remove out of the limits of these United States" at will.[28] There were indeed conspiracies involving Britain and Spain on the western borders. These fears account in part at least both for the hasty admission into the union in the 1790s of Vermont, Kentucky, and Tennessee and for the later violations of the Northwest Ordinance's procedures for orderly territorial advancement to statehood. Britain was regarded as by far the more dangerous power, which helps explain the early organization of the northwestern territory that Andrew R. L. Cayton talks about. Spain, on the other hand, was thought to be so decrepit, its hold on its empire so weak, that its southern and southwestern territories could be left to fall into American hands like so many ripe fruit. Natural demographic pressures would see to that, it being a common assumption in the 1790s that most western migrants would come from the burgeoning southern states. This was one of several mistaken ideas that American leaders had about the future of the West.

The Federalists' western policy, including the working of the Northwest Ordinance and treatment of the Indians, rested on the assumption that settlement of the western territories would be neat and orderly. As Bernard W. Sheehan

[28] Eugene Perry Link, *Democratic-Republican Societies, 1790–1800* (New York, 1942), pp. 136–37.

demonstrates, many of the Federalist leaders were scrupulously concerned for the fate of the Indians; indeed, the statements of Secretary of War Henry Knox about the need for just treatment of the Native Americans a modern anthropologist might even deem politically correct. But purchasing the Indians' rights to the land and assimilating or protecting them in a civilized manner depended on an orderly and steady pace of white settlement.

So too did both the hopes for governmental revenue from the land and the plans of land speculators depend on gradual, piecemeal, and well-regulated settlement of the West. The federal government hoped to gain steady revenues by selling its western land to land companies and speculators. The speculators in turn counted on the settlers slowly filling in the territory surrounding the land they held, which would raise its value and bring them the promised returns on their investments.

Everything was built on illusions. The people moving west ignored the federal government's Indian policies and refused to buy land at the expensive prices at which it was being offered. They shunned the speculators' land, violated Indian treaty rights, and moved irregularly, chaotically, and unevenly, jumping from place to place and leaving huge chunks of unsettled land and pockets of hemmed-in Indians behind them. The government responded, and continued to respond until the Homestead Act of 1863, in a series of desperate efforts to keep up with popular pressures. It continually lowered the price of land, increased the credit it offered, and reduced the size of the parcels of land people had to buy, and still people complained and ignored the laws. Eventually the government recognized the rights of squatters to preempt the land, and finally it just gave the land away. It took more than a half century for governmental leaders to come to terms with the reality of popular settlement in the West.

For the Federalists of the 1790s it took less than that for most of their heroic plans and dreams to be exploded. Even if Jefferson had been somehow technically denied the presidency in 1800, most of the Federalists' blueprints for America were already doomed. They were too out of touch with the surging popular and commercial realities of American life.

The demographic and economic forces at work were too powerful for any gentry leadership to overcome or any election to reverse. The secret of Jefferson's success, in so far as he had any, was his unwitting surrender to these popular commercial forces. He abandoned the Federalist goals of creating a strong mercantilist European-like state, reduced the power of the national government in a variety of ways, and in effect left everyone free to pursue his happiness as he saw fit. It remained for later generations of Americans, in some cases even the generation following World War II, to fulfill many of the dreams and schemes of the Federalists of the 1790s.

Perhaps our history since 1800 has been one long effort to do in two centuries what the Federalists unsuccessfully tried to do in a decade—bring under control the powerful and unruly popular and commercial forces unleashed by the Revolution and create a strong integrated nation. So that when we look at the huge, prosperous, and unitary fiscal-military state that we have built—the most powerful state the world has ever known—we might conclude that Hamilton and the Federalists of the 1790s have had the last laugh after all.

MAEVA MARCUS

Judicial Review in the Early Republic

CONSTITUTIONAL HISTORIANS and legal scholars, when discussing the origins of judicial review, have typically begun with the question of whether the Founding Fathers intended to establish that power in the Constitution. The question must be answered, in their view, because the Constitution contains no explicit provision giving to the federal judiciary the authority to declare acts of Congress null and void if they exceed the powers granted to the national government in that document. In the search for precedents to prove that the Framers either did or did not believe in judicial review, reams of paper have been expended examining the same state court cases and the same statements of individuals involved in the drafting or ratifying of the Constitution.

Because few legal precedents exist,[1] and because many members of the founding generation favored judicial review while a significant number opposed it,[2] this evidence is inconclusive. Yet I have no hesitation in asserting my belief that the Framers of the Constitution, and those who supported ratification as well as those who opposed it, fully understood that if the new government was to work as intended, federal judges would have to exercise the power of judicial review. Indeed, when the federal government commenced, the judiciary, Congress, and the president were united in the expectation that this power formed an integral part of the judges' task. Whether the federal judiciary could successfully imple-

---

[1] See the discussion in Leonard W. Levy, *Original Intent and the Framers' Constitution* (New York, 1988), pp. 89–99.

[2] See, for example, a review of evidence of this nature in Raoul Berger, *Congress v. The Supreme Court* (Cambridge, Mass., 1969), pp. 47–143.

ment this expectation and take its place beside the national executive and legislature as a coequal branch of government was the issue of real concern to the Framers.

The power of judicial review, which is invoked to preserve the Constitution as the supreme law of the land, involves two different missions. One, arguably required by the supremacy clause of the Constitution,[3] is directed toward the states and implicates principles of federalism; the other addresses acts of the executive and legislative branches of the federal government and raises questions regarding the application of the doctrine of separation of powers. Both rely on a crucial premise—that the Constitution, in the words of Gerald Gunther, "is to be considered a species of law and accordingly cognizable in courts of law," and, therefore, that the American constitutional system implicitly confers on judges the duty to enforce constitutional limits.[4] None of this appeared to be subject to great controversy during the 1790s.

The passage of the Judiciary Act in September 1789 constitutes the earliest evidence we have of the general agreement that, if national interests were to be safeguarded, federal courts would have to review state court decisions to ensure that federal law was interpreted uniformly and that federal prerogatives were upheld by the states.[5] The supremacy clause of the Constitution obligates state judges to consider as the supreme law of the land the "Constitution, and the Laws of the United States which shall be made in Pursuance thereof; and all Treaties made, or which shall be made, under the Authority of the United States."[6] The clause does not say anything about federal courts being the enforcer of this provision. Yet in Section 25 of the Judiciary Act of 1789, a section that apparently inspired no debate in the houses of Congress,

[3] Article VI, clause 2.

[4] Gerald Gunther, "Judicial Review," in Leonard W. Levy, ed., *Encyclopedia of the American Constitution*, 4 vols. (New York, 1986), 3:1055. See also Gordon S. Wood, *The Creation of the American Republic, 1776–1787* (Chapel Hill, 1969), pp. 291–92.

[5] "An Act to establish the Judicial Courts of the United States" (hereafter, the Judiciary Act of 1789), Sept. 24, 1789, in U.S. *Statutes at Large*, 1:73–93.

[6] Article VI, clause 2.

the Supreme Court of the United States was charged with this task in cases that denied the validity of assertions of federal rights.[7] Moreover, in cases within the jurisdiction of the federal circuit courts as provided for in other sections of the Judiciary Act,[8] the question of the conformity of state statutes with the United States Constitution would undoubtedly arise and give federal judges the opportunity to strike down state laws. Indeed, during the first decade of the new government, a number of such cases were brought to the federal courts. While the decisions in these cases—involving such questions as repayment of British debts contracted before the Revolution—may not have pleased everyone, the authority of the federal courts to adjudicate them was not questioned.[9]

The state of Rhode Island's reaction to the federal court decision in the case of *Champion & Dickason* v. *Casey et al.*, heard at the June 1792 term of the United States Circuit Court for the district of Rhode Island by Chief Justice John Jay and District Judge Henry Marchant, is instructive.[10] The case, in simplified terms, involved the plea of the defendants that a resolve of the Rhode Island General Assembly granting them an extension of three years' time to pay their debt to Champion and Dickason excused them from the immediate payment demanded in the current suit. According to newspaper reports of the decision, the judges declared that the resolution of the General Assembly was in direct conflict with the contracts clause of the Constitution because the resolution impaired the obligation of the contract that was the subject of

[7] U.S. *Statutes at Large*, 1:85–87.

[8] Ibid., sections 11, 12, and 22, pp. 78–80, 84–85.

[9] Maeva Marcus et al., eds., *The Documentary History of the Supreme Court of the United States, 1789–1800*, vol. 2, *The Justices on Circuit, 1790–1794* (New York, 1988), pp. 8, 8n, 122–23, 123n, 124, 124n, 236, 236n, 338–39, 339n, 441, 441n, 472, 477–78, 478n; vol. 3, *The Justices on Circuit, 1795–1800* (New York, 1990), p. 90. See also Julius Goebel, Jr., *Antecedents and Beginnings to 1801*, The Oliver Wendell Holmes Devise History of the Supreme Court of the United States, vol. 1 (New York, 1971), pp. 590–91.

[10] The case is discussed in Goebel, *Antecedents and Beginnings*, pp. 589–90. It is also examined in Charles Warren, "Earliest Cases of Judicial Review of State Legislation by Federal Courts," *Yale Law Journal* 32 (1922): 26–28.

the suit. The court, therefore, gave judgment to the plaintiff creditors. Not only was there no public outcry after this decision but the Rhode Island legislature declared by a formal vote that, to comply with the federal court ruling, it would not pass any similar resolutions with regard to any individual in debt.[11]

Cases that came to the Supreme Court for review under its Section 25 jurisdiction also caused no great uproar. With one notable exception—*Calder* v. *Bull,* in which the meaning and scope of the term *ex post facto* law was decided[12]—these cases are virtually unknown.[13] Their adjudication seemed to be a routine matter in the sense that the cases were argued on the merits; the jurisdiction of the Court was not challenged. Not until the second decade of the nineteenth century did the Supreme Court's Section 25 jurisdiction come under fire. Thus it is not too much to say that in the 1790s the power of the federal courts to exercise judicial review to assure the conformance of state laws to the Constitution and U.S. laws was widely accepted.

So, too, was the federal courts' power to exercise judicial review with regard to acts of Congress. In a charge to the jury in a circuit court case involving the constitutionality of a state law,[14] Justice William Paterson enunciated a theory of judicial review that is worth quoting in full because it represents so well the principles upon which that power rested:

> What is a Constitution? It is the form of government, delineated by the mighty hand of the people, in which certain first principles of fundamental laws are established. The Constitution is certain

[11] Warren, "Earliest Cases of Judicial Review," pp. 27–28.

[12] 3 *United States Reports* (3 *Dallas*) 386 (1798).

[13] *Olney* v. *Arnold,* ibid., 308 (1796); *Olney* v. *Dexter* (1796) unreported; *Clerke* v. *Harwood,* 3 *United States Reports* (3 *Dallas*) 342 (1797); *Court* v. *Van Bibber* (1797) unreported; *Court* v. *Wells* (1797) unreported; and *Court* v. *Robinson* (1797) unreported. See Manuscript Case Papers, series 21, Records of the Supreme Court of the United States, Record Group 267, National Archives, Washington, D.C.

[14] *Vanhorne's Lessee* v. *Dorrance,* decided in the circuit court for the district of Pennsylvania in April 1795 (2 *United States Reports* [2 *Dallas*] 304 [1795]).

and fixed; it contains the permanent will of the people, and is the supreme law of the land; it is paramount to the power of the Legislature, and can be revoked or altered only by the authority that made it. The life-giving principle and the death-doing stroke must proceed from the same hand. What are Legislatures? Creatures of the Constitution; they owe their existence to the Constitution: they derive their powers from the Constitution: It is their commission; and, therefore, all their acts must be conformable to it, or else they will be void. The Constitution is the work or will of the People themselves, in their original, sovereign, and unlimited capacity. Law is the work or will of the Legislature in their derivative and subordinate capacity. The one is the work of the Creator, and the other of the Creature. The Constitution fixes limits to the exercise of legislative authority, and prescribes the orbit within which it must move. In short, . . . the Constitution is the sun of the political system, around which all Legislative, Executive and Judicial bodies must revolve. Whatever may be the case in other countries, yet in this there can be no doubt, that every act of the Legislature, repugnant to the Constitution, is absolutely void.[15]

Although announced in a case concerning the constitutionality of a state statute, Paterson's principles apply equally well to the power of federal courts to consider the constitutional validity of acts of Congress and even of the president. From a survey of perceptions prevailing among congressmen and of the actions taken by federal courts during the 1790s, it becomes evident that Paterson's views were commonplace among government officials in that decade.

During the course of the First Congress's deliberations over the numerous acts passed to get the new government under way, questions concerning Congress's or the president's power surfaced time and again. And, routinely, congressmen stated that Congress need not worry about such a question because the federal judiciary was established to answer it. In the long debate on the bill creating a Department of Foreign Affairs, for example, one of the topics that consumed the most time was the authority of the president to remove an officer who had been appointed with the advice and consent of the

[15] Ibid., p. 308.

Senate. To the House of Representatives this appeared to be a constitutional issue of great importance. The bill, after delineating the title and duties of the secretary of foreign affairs, included the words "to be removable from office by the President of the United States,"[16] and the debate centered on whether those words should be struck from the bill. In arguments filled with diverse views of the constitutional powers of the legislature and the executive, one point seemed to have general approval: that in the final instance it was the duty of the judiciary to decide whether and where the Constitution had lodged the removal power. Representative William Loughton Smith of South Carolina urged that "the words should be struck out, and the question of right, if it is one, left to the decision of the Judiciary. It will be time enough to determine the question when the President shall remove an officer in this way. I conceive it can properly be brought before that tribunal; the officer will have a right to a mandamus to be restored to his office, and the judges would determine whether the President exercised a Constitutional authority or not."[17] Smith chastised those in the House who thought no harm would be done if the legislature included in the bill its opinion on where the removal power lay:

> Gentlemen have said that it is proper to give a legislative construction of the Constitution. I differ with them on this point. I think it an infringement of the powers of the judiciary. It is said, we ought not to blend the legislative, executive, or judiciary powers, further than is done by the Constitution; and yet the advocates for preserving each department pure and untouched by the others, call upon this House to exercise the powers of the judges in expounding the Constitution. What authority has this House to explain the Law? . . . A great deal of mischief has arisen in the several States, by the Legislatures undertaking to decide Constitutional questions. Sir, it is the duty of the Legislature to make laws; your judges are to expound them.[18]

[16] *Annals of Congress,* 1st Cong., 1st sess., p. 455.

[17] Ibid., p. 459.

[18] Ibid., p. 470.

Those who wanted to make a legislative determination on the removal question believed it was necessary for various reasons, one of which was that it would serve as a "rule of conduct" for the president. If the legislative declaration was unconstitutional, it would be revised by the judiciary.[19] Others believed that the judges would never strike down a law as unconstitutional when Congress had made a determination where the Constitution was silent on the matter. As Representative John Laurance asserted: "If the laws shall be in violation of any part of the Constitution, the judges will not hesitate to decide against them; where the power is incident to the Government, and the Constitution is silent, it can be no impediment to a Legislative grant; I hold it necessary in such cases to make provision."[20] Another reason for the legislature to make its views known was that it would be inconvenient to wait for a judicial resolution of the matter.[21] But James Madison went even further by saying that he thought it would be impossible to obtain a judicial decision—a conclusion that was only incidental to the primary thrust of Madison's enunciation of his departmental theory of constitutional interpretation.[22]

As Madison understood the speakers before him in the House debate to have said, "The Legislature itself has no right to expound the Constitution; that wherever its meaning is doubtful, you must leave it to take its course, until the Judiciary is called upon to declare its meaning." Madison then admitted "in the *ordinary course of Government,* that the exposition of the laws and Constitution devolves upon the Judiciary [emphasis added]." But, he continued, he wanted to know

> upon what principle it can be contended, that any one department draws from the Constitution greater powers than another, in marking out the limits of the powers of the several depart-

[19] See statement by Fisher Ames, ibid., p. 477.

[20] Ibid., p. 486.

[21] See, for example, Representative Elias Boudinot's statement, ibid., p. 470.

[22] Ibid., p. 501. See also remarks of Theodore Sedgwick, ibid., p. 523.

ments? The Constitution is the charter of the people to the Government; it specifies certain great powers as absolutely granted, and marks out the departments to exercise them. If the Constitutional boundary of either be brought into question, I do not see that any one of these independent departments has more right than another to declare their sentiments on that point.[23]

Madison observed that there was no government on earth, including the United States, "in which provision is made for a particular authority to determine the limits of the Constitutional division of power between the branches of the Government." As this is the case, Madison concluded that "while the Government is not led by passion," and "while there is a desire in all to see and be guided by the benignant ray of truth," the decision of where the Constitution lodged the power to remove an executive officer would best be made by the legislature.[24]

I admit to being somewhat confused by Madison's thoughts on the function of judicial review in the new American republic. In this debate it seems to me that he concedes that it is the duty of the federal judges to expound the laws and the Constitution "in the ordinary course of Government." But what does that mean? Is Madison merely restating Article III of the Constitution, that the judicial power extends only to cases and controversies, and that the judiciary is the final expositor only when a case comes before it? Is Madison claiming that the departmental theory comes into play only when there is no possibility that a case can reach the Supreme Court, for he states in this debate on the president's removal power that he does not see how a case "could come before the judges, to obtain a fair and solemn decision?" But that does not appear to be Madison's claim, because he goes on to say that even if a case could be brought, he believes the legislature should make the decision. His reason for that belief, the absence of faction in the government, however, lacks theoretical rigor, to say the least.[25] And Madison's actions during the remainder

[23] Ibid., p. 500.

[24] Ibid., pp. 500–501. Madison reiterates this point, ibid., p. 547.

[25] Ibid., p. 501.

of the decade demonstrate his own confusion with regard to the function of judicial review.[26]

In any event, Madison's colleagues in the House were quick to refute his theory. Elbridge Gerry asked "if the judges are not *ex officio* judges of the law; and whether they would not be bound to declare the law a nullity, if this clause is continued in it, and is inconsistent with the Constitution?"[27] At another point in the debate, Gerry worried that if Congress really had the power to declare constitutional interpretations, the whole constitutional system would be subverted. What, he pondered, was the purpose of Article V of the Constitution, which contains the procedures to be used in seeking amendments, if Congress can declare on its own authority a point on which the Constitution is silent?[28] Others, like Representatives Abraham Baldwin and Peter Silvester, agreed with Madison that the House should declare its sentiments but admitted that it was the duty of the judiciary to expound the laws and that if the judges found this law unconstitutional they should not "hesitate to declare it so."[29] The frequency with which members of the House brought up the duty of the judges to examine and decide on the constitutional propriety of acts of Congress and the president during this June 1789 debate makes clear that the idea of judicial review was hardly a new one. And bear in mind that this debate took place before a federal judicial system had even been established.

Throughout the decade, in the course of considering legislation, congressmen again and again pointed to the safeguard of judicial review. In discussing a Quaker memorial on slavery and the House report on it, Representative Baldwin of Georgia declared he had no fear that the rights of his constituents would be harmed by any bill passed by the House, because it

[26] For example, when he wrote the Virginia Resolutions in 1798, Madison claimed that a state could "interpose" to stop the evil an unconstitutional act produces (Merrill D. Peterson, "Virginia and Kentucky Resolutions," in Levy, ed., *Encyclopedia of the American Constitution,* 4:1974).

[27] *Annals of Congress,* 1st Cong., 1st sess., p. 504.

[28] Ibid., pp. 536–37.

[29] Ibid., pp. 560, 562.

would need approval by the Senate and the president before it could become law. But even if, after all that careful review, a question remained as to the constitutionality of the act, it must receive "the approbation of the Supreme Court of the United States, composed of six of our most venerable sages, who, from the independence of their situation, and from the long experience we have had of their wisdom, possess our highest confidence, and is probably one of the most respectable Courts on earth."[30]

The debate in the House of Representatives in February 1791 over the establishment of a Bank of the United States elicited many similar comments. Representative Laurance parried the objection of some of his colleagues that the House should not pass a "problematical bill, which is liable to a supervision by the Judges of the Supreme Court" by observing that there was "no force" in such an idea because the "Judges are invested by the Constitution with a power to pass their judgment on all laws that may be passed."[31] Elias Boudinot joined Laurance in pointing out that he felt no uneasiness in favoring a bill that had to undergo the scrutiny of the Supreme Court. Boudinot did not controvert this right of the judiciary; rather,

> it was his boast and his confidence. It led him to greater decision on all subjects of a constitutional nature, when he reflected that if, from inattention, want of precision, or any other defect, he should do wrong, that there was a power in the Government which could constitutionally prevent the operation of such a wrong measure from effecting his constituents. He was legislating for a nation, and for thousands unborn; and it was the glory of the Constitution that there was a remedy even for the failures of the supreme Legislature itself.[32]

Representative Smith of South Carolina joined the chorus by urging that it was the duty of Congress, after careful delibera-

[30] Speech of Mar. 18, 1790, in the House of Representatives, quoted in the *Georgia Gazette* (Savannah), Apr. 8, 1790.

[31] *Annals of Congress*, 1st Cong., 3d sess., p. 1916.

[32] Ibid., p. 1927.

tion, to adopt a measure that enabled the powers granted to the government to be put into effect, as long as the measure was not forbidden by the Constitution and did not violate the rights of individuals or of any state. But, Smith continued, "it was still within the province of the Judiciary to annul the law, if it should be by them deemed not to result by fair construction from the powers vested by the Constitution."[33]

The judges who would exercise judicial review attested to their possession of that power, although they had not yet used it. Justice James Iredell, in a charge to the grand jury of the circuit court for the district of Georgia, observed that if there were any violations of the Constitution, "the courts of justice, in any such instance coming under their cognizance, are bound to resist them, they having no authority to carry into execution any acts but such as the constitution warrants."[34] And while preparing an opinion in a case that came before the Supreme Court in February 1792,[35] Justice Iredell went into some detail about the power of judicial review. In discussing acts of Congress, he noted:

All these must be justified under the authority granted by the Constitution. Within that authority all their acts are valid and obligatory. Beyond it none of them are so. And however painful such an occasion may be, if in any instance an Act of Congress exceeding its authority comes before a Court it must be declared to be *void:* because upon the very same principles that one Act of Congress can repeal a former Act, *the authority of the Legislature being at all times equal,* & therefore the latter Act shall supersede the former; so an Act contrary to fundamental Law, upon the

[33] Ibid., p. 1937. For comments that specified the judiciary as the organ of government that would decide questions on the constitutional division of powers, see, for example, the debate on the Post Office bill, *Annals of Congress,* 2d Cong., 1st sess., p. 306.

[34] James Iredell's Charge to the Grand Jury of the circuit court for the district of Georgia, Oct. 17, 1791, in Marcus et al., eds., *Justices on Circuit, 1790–1794,* p. 219.

[35] See minutes of the Supreme Court, Feb. 14, 1792, in Marcus et al., eds., *Documentary History of the Supreme Court,* vol. 1, part 1, *Appointments and Proceedings* (New York, 1985), p. 200. The case was tried in the Supreme Court during the February 1795 term (ibid., pp. 232–34).

basis of which the whole Government rests, and *unrepealable by any Acts of Congress acting under it.*[36]

Although these frequent statements about the role of the judiciary in the American polity evidence a belief in judicial review, the real test occurred when the judges actually declared an act of Congress unconstitutional. This unprecedented action, known as *Hayburn's Case*, took place in April 1792 in the United States Circuit Court for the district of Pennsylvania rather than in the Supreme Court; it therefore has not received as much attention as it deserves.[37] But at the time it created quite a stir.[38]

On March 23, 1792, Congress passed an Invalid Pensions Act.[39] As there was no bureaucratic apparatus in place to hear the claims of veterans injured in the Revolutionary War for benefits under the act, Congress designated the judges of the United States circuit courts for this task. (It should be understood that the circuit courts at this time were presided over by two Supreme Court justices and the district judge for the district in which the circuit court met.) The act charged the judges with the duty of determining whether the petitioner's disability was indeed a result of service in the military forces of the United States. If they found that it was, the petitioner's name and a recommendation for the amount of his pension

[36] Iredell's notes in *Oswald* v. *New York,* Feb. 11–14, 1792, Charles E. Johnson Collection, North Carolina State Department of Archives and History, Raleigh. Emphasis in original.

[37] The ramifications of this case, not specifically involving the issue of judicial review, had an important effect on the jurisprudence of the early Supreme Court. See Maeva Marcus and Robert Teir, "*Hayburn's Case:* A Misinterpretation of Precedent" *Wisconsin Law Review* (1988): 527–46; and Susan Low Bloch and Maeva Marcus, "John Marshall's Selective Use of History in *Marbury* v. *Madison,*" *Wisconsin Law Review* (1986): 301–37.

[38] See, for example, articles in the *National Gazette* (Philadelphia), Apr. 16, 1792, and the *General Advertiser* (Philadelphia), Apr. 20, 1792.

[39] "An Act to provide for the settlement of the Claims of Widows and Orphans barred by the limitations heretofore established, and to regulate the Claims to Invalid Pensions" (hereafter Invalid Pensions Act of 1792), U.S. *Statutes at Large,* 1:243.

was submitted to the secretary of war. The act instructed the secretary of war to check his records to ensure that the petitioner had actually served in the military. If the secretary found any indication of fraud, he was authorized to withhold the petitioner's name from the United States pension list and to report his action to Congress for its final determination of the matter.[40] Thus, the secretary of war and, after him, Congress, had the power to reverse a factual determination of a circuit court and to deny what the judges had found to be an entitlement of a claimant who had appeared before them.

Within weeks of the act's passage, William Hayburn appeared before the circuit court for the district of Pennsylvania claiming eligibility for a pension. On April 12 the court, composed of Supreme Court Justices James Wilson and John Blair and District Judge Richard Peters, refused to hear Hayburn's petition. The records of the court give no indication of the reasons for the judges' refusal to proceed, but the following day Elias Boudinot, on the floor of the House of Representatives, gave a full report of the judges' statements from the bench.[41] And soon after, the judges themselves wrote a letter to President Washington explaining their position in the case.[42]

Boudinot reported that the circuit court judges thought that the law that imposed on the court the duty of examining invalids was an unconstitutional one, because it allowed the secretary of war and Congress to revise a decision of the court. Under the Constitution the judiciary is independent, and neither the executive nor the legislature has "revisionary authority over the judicial proceedings of the courts of justice."[43]

In their letter to the president, the judges made clear that

[40] Ibid., pp. 243–44.

[41] *Annals of Congress*, 2d Cong., 1st sess., pp. 556–57.

[42] Letter from James Wilson, John Blair, and Richard Peters to George Washington, Apr. 18, 1792, *American State Papers: Miscellaneous*, 1:51. The letter is also printed in an unnumbered footnote in *Hayburn's Case, 2 United States Reports* (2 *Dallas*) 409, p. 411 (1792).

[43] *Annals of Congress*, 2d Cong., 1st sess., p. 556.

they had indeed declared the Invalid Pensions Act of 1792 unconstitutional. After a careful exposition of their reasons for finding that the act did not meet the requirements of the Constitution, they explained that their conduct, though necessary, "was far from being pleasant. To be obliged to act contrary, either to the obvious directions of Congress, or to a constitutional principle, in our judgment equally obvious, excited feelings in us, which we hope never to experience again."[44]

The judges of two other circuit courts, that of New York and that of North Carolina, composed of Supreme Court Justices John Jay, William Cushing, and James Iredell and District Judges James Duane and John Sitgreaves, concurred fully with the action of the circuit court for the district of Pennsylvania. But those circuit court judges did not have an actual case before them when they, too, wrote letters to Washington informing him of their belief that the Invalid Pensions Act of 1792 was unconstitutional, so their opinions were only advisory.[45]

In its letter, however, the circuit court for the district of New York introduced a novel interpretation of the statute that allowed that court to hear the claims of invalid petitioners. Jay and his brethren wrote that because "the objects of this act are exceedingly benevolent, and do real honor to the humanity and justice of Congress" and because "judges desire to manifest, on all proper occasions and in every proper manner their high respect for the national legislature,"[46] they would assume that what Congress really wanted them to do was to serve as commissioners to hear the veterans' claims. This theory was explained in the House of Representatives in some detail.

According to the report, the judges believed that Congress

---

[44] 2 *United States Reports* (2 *Dallas*) 409, p. 412.

[45] See letter from John Jay, William Cushing, and James Duane to Washington, Apr. 10, 1792, *American State Papers: Miscellaneous*, 1:49–50, and letter from Iredell and John Sitgreaves to Washington, June 8, 1792, ibid., pp. 52–53. These letters are also printed in 2 *United States Reports* (2 *Dallas*) 409, pp. 410, 412–14.

[46] 2 *United States Reports* (2 *Dallas*) 409, p. 410.

had the power to appoint commissioners for any special purpose and designate the persons whom it wanted to act as commissioners. Congress could indicate the individuals by their
proper names or by their official titles. Hence, the judges of
the circuit court for New York thought that the Invalid Pensions Act could be construed to appoint them commissioners
in their individual capacities rather than in their official roles
as judges of the circuit court. As commissioners they would
hear the petitions of the invalids after the adjournment of
each day's session of the circuit court.[47] Thus, Justices Jay,
Cushing, and Iredell, who agreed to go along with this interpretation of the statute, heard veterans' claims and made recommendations to the secretary of war, but Justices Wilson and
Blair did not.

Congress, struck by the novelty of these events, did not
know what to do. The House discussed a number of measures, including the passage of a law that would establish a
regular procedure for federal judges to notify Congress officially when a law was declared unconstitutional, but no specific action was taken in the immediate aftermath of the
refusal of the circuit court for the district of Pennsylvania to
comply with the Invalid Pensions Act of 1792.[48]

A letter from Attorney General Edmund Randolph to President Washington substantiates the idea that that refusal
amounted to striking down an act of Congress. Randolph described a meeting with Justice James Wilson on a Philadelphia
street before the circuit court met, in which he was told by
Wilson that he and Justice Blair strongly doubted the constitutionality of the Invalid Pensions Act.[49] After the circuit court
ruled, Madison wrote Henry Lee that the judges on circuit
in Pennsylvania had pronounced the law "unconstitutional &
void—perhaps they may be wrong in the exertion of their
power—but such an evidence of its existence gives inquietude
to those who do not wish congress to be controuled or

[47]*Annals of Congress*, 2d Cong., 1st sess., p. 557.

[48] Ibid.

[49] Edmund Randolph to Washington, Apr. 5, 1792, George Washington
Papers, Library of Congress.

doubted whilst its proceedings correspond with their views."[50]

Randolph, appearing as counsel for Hayburn, brought the case before the Supreme Court at its next term, in August 1792. The attorney general moved for a writ of mandamus to the circuit court for the district of Pennsylvania, ordering it to hear Hayburn's petition. After argument, the Supreme Court postponed a decision. Everyone understood that this meant that the justices wanted Congress to correct the Invalid Pensions Act before the Supreme Court embarrassed the legislature by declaring the act unconstitutional. And that is exactly what happened. During the six months before the next term of the Supreme Court, in February 1793, Congress became convinced that the judges' doubts about the constitutionality of the act were well founded, and a new law was passed stipulating a different procedure for examining the claims of Revolutionary War veterans.[51] Any decision by the Supreme Court would be moot.

Congress recognized another legal problem, however, and, in the Invalid Pensions Act of 1793, it provided for an adjudication of the matter by the Supreme Court. If the 1792 act was unconstitutional, were the pensions received by the veterans who had been examined by the judges of the circuit courts acting as commissioners illegally obtained? In the case of *United States* v. *Yale Todd,* decided at the February 1794 term of the Supreme Court,[52] Todd, an invalid pensioner, was or-

[50] James Madison to Henry Lee, Apr. 15, 1792, in William T. Hutchinson et al., eds., *The Papers of James Madison,* 22 vols. to date (Chicago and Charlottesville, Va., 1962–), 14:288.

[51] "An Act to Regulate Claims to Invalid Pensions," U.S. *Statutes at Large,* 1:324. See also *Annals of Congress,* 2d Cong., 2d sess., pp. 733–34; *General Advertiser* (Philadelphia), Nov. 10, 1792 (report of Nov. 9, 1792, debate in the House of Representatives), and *Independent Gazetteer* (Philadelphia), Dec. 22, 1792 (report of Dec. 14, 1792, debate in the House of Representatives). Besides the question of constitutionality, there were other causes for changes in the 1792 act as well.

[52] This case is not reported by Dallas in the *United States Reports* but is recorded in the minutes and docket of the United States Supreme Court (see Marcus et al., eds., *Appointments and Proceedings,* pp. 228, 494).

dered to return to the United States the money he had received and to renew his application under the act of 1793.[53]

Thus it would appear that this is the first instance of the Supreme Court declaring an act of Congress unconstitutional. The problem is that the Supreme Court provided no rationale for its decision, at least not one that has been recorded anywhere. And there are two grounds upon which the Court could have relied: One, the Court could have overturned the Invalid Pensions Act of 1792 because it conflicted with the constitutional separation of powers; or two, the Court could have ruled that Yale Todd's pension was invalid because the judges of the circuit courts wrongly interpreted the statute to allow them to act as commissioners and hear pension claims. If the Court relied on this second, narrower ground, the honor of being the first, officially, to strike down a congressional act goes to the Marshall Court in *Marbury* v. *Madison*. But if the Court in 1794 denied Todd his pension because the Invalid Pensions Act of 1792 was unconstitutional, the *Yale Todd* case becomes the first official instance of judicial review by the Supreme Court.[54]

Does it really matter which was first? I think not. What is important is that a federal circuit court in 1792 declared the statute unconstitutional. All the other Supreme Court justices made their identical views known. And Congress changed the act. This surely indicates a general belief in the competence of the federal courts to exercise judicial review. And the events surrounding the adjudication of the constitutionality of the Carriage Tax Act reinforce that position.

On June 5, 1794, an act requiring the payment of duties on

[53] The facts of the case are known because Chief Justice Roger Brooke Taney ordered a copy of the papers filed in the case appended to the report of *United States* v. *Ferreira* in 1852 (54 *United States Reports* [13 *Howard*] 40 [1851]). The original papers filed in the *Yale Todd* suit no longer exist.

[54] The fact that a year later Justice James Wilson appears to have told an attorney that the Supreme Court had never decided the issue of the constitutional power of the judiciary to declare an act of Congress void suggests that in *Yale Todd* the Court relied on statutory interpretation (Julius Goebel, Jr., and Joseph H. Smith, eds., *The Law Practice of Alexander Hamilton*, 5 vols. [New York, 1964–81], 4:325).

carriages became law.[55] Congress had debated the constitutionality of such a tax, a subject that involved the general question of Congress's taxing power and whether the specific tax imposed, a duty on carriages, was a direct or indirect tax. We need not go into the technical nature of the arguments put forth on both sides; what is important is that as soon as the Carriage Tax Act was passed, both its opponents and proponents worked to bring the question of its constitutionality before the Supreme Court.

In July, Edward Carrington, supervisor of the revenue for the district of Virginia, wrote to Tench Coxe, commissioner of the revenue, "I am apprehensive we shall meet with a pacific, or what will be called a legal, opposition to the Collection of the Duties on Carriages. A very general idea prevails in this district, that the act is unconstitutional, and numbers of very respectable Characters have signified their determination to try the point by legal decision."[56] When Alexander Hamilton, at that point still the secretary of the Treasury, learned of this communication, he instructed Coxe to urge Carrington to "give facility to a legal decision . . . taking care to secure an

[55] "An Act laying duties upon Carriages for the conveyance of Persons," June 5, 1794, U.S. *Statutes at Large*, 1:373–75.

[56] Edward Carrington to Tench Coxe, July 28, 1794, in Goebel and Smith, eds., *Law Practice of Alexander Hamilton*, 4:308–9. In December 1794 it was reported in a New York newspaper in a discussion of the carriage tax that "several eminent characters in Virginia . . . think it their duty and have accordingly determined to bring the matter before the federal judiciary" (*Daily Advertiser* [New York], Dec. 22, 1794). Madison also indicated that he looked to the federal courts for a resolution of the issue of the constitutionality of the carriage tax. Madison wrote to Edmund Pendleton that Jay had expressed an opinion on the nature of a tax on carriages when an advocate for the Constitution. "If it remains the same," Madison observed, "when he is to decide as Chief Justice, we may yet hope to see this breach in the Constitution repaired" (Madison to Pendleton, Jan. 8, 1795, James Madison Papers, Libr. Cong.). Jay resigned as chief justice before the Carriage Tax Case reached the Supreme Court. In 1798 Pendleton described the actions of Virginians regarding the carriage tax in a speech: "We brought on the question in the federal court, where it was decided against us and we paid the arrears" (*Philadelphia Aurora*, Jan. 15, 1799, extra edition).

appeal in the last resort to the Supreme Court."[57] Treasury officials and Attorney General William Bradford immediately began planning for the best way to bring a suit before the Supreme Court, and it was decided that a case should be instituted in a federal circuit court so that it could be taken on writ of error to the Supreme Court. The only problem with this strategy was that the Judiciary Act of 1789, in Section 11, limited the jurisdiction of the circuit courts to cases in which the disputed sum exceeded $500 and where the United States was a plaintiff, and, in Section 22, limited the Supreme Court to considering cases, after final judgment in a circuit court, where the amount in controversy exceeded $2,000.[58] In view of the low tax rates imposed in the Carriage Tax Act, it would require 250 carriages taxed at $8 each to reach the jurisdictional amount. No one in Virginia owned 250 carriages.

On the advice of Hamilton, the government resorted to a legal fiction, with the concurrence of the likely defendant, Daniel Hylton, who had not paid his tax, that enabled the desired suit to reach the Supreme Court.[59] The United States sued Hylton for recovery of $1,000, the tax on 125 carriages, and a similar sum in penalties for having been delinquent in the payment of the tax. But it was agreed that if judgment was given to the plaintiff, the defendant could satisfy the judgment by payment of $16, the total of the tax and penalty on one carriage. A writ of error, taken out before the argument in the circuit court, attested to the determination of the defendant to seek a definitive decision from the Supreme Court on the constitutional issue. And the agreement of the government to pay all Hylton's expenses in taking the case to the Supreme Court likewise showed its desire to obtain a final resolution of the question. The plea entered by defendant's counsel in the circuit court suit, *United States* v. *Daniel Lawrence*

[57] Alexander Hamilton to Coxe, undated, Goebel and Smith, eds., *Law Practice of Alexander Hamilton*, 4:309.

[58] U.S. *Statutes at Large*, 1:73, 78, 84.

[59] See letter from Hamilton to Coxe, Jan. 28, 1795, in Goebel and Smith, eds., *Law Practice of Alexander Hamilton*, 4:340–42.

Hylton, baldly asserted that the Carriage Tax Act was unconstitutional.[60]

The only part of the argument before the federal circuit court in Virginia that need concern us here is the statements made by counsel with regard to the power of judicial review. As the whole argument centered on the point of the constitutional validity of the Carriage Tax Act, John Taylor of Caroline, Hylton's counsel, thought it necessary to establish the federal court's authority to decide that question. Taylor declared that the Constitution of the United States was designed to protect certain rights of individuals against the tyranny of legislative majorities and that the mode of enforcing that Constitution was application to the independent judiciary to determine the limits of congressional power. John Wickham, representing the United States, replied that there was no need even to raise the issue of the judiciary's power to overturn an act of Congress, a power that he had intended to discuss until he learned from the bench that it required no argument because it had been previously established. According to Wickham, he had been told (we can assume by James Wilson, the only Supreme Court justice present at the circuit court for Virginia) that although the Supreme Court had never ruled on the issue, the individual justices on circuit had upheld the federal courts' power to exercise judicial review.[61]

The question of the constitutionality of the Carriage Tax Act finally came before the Supreme Court in February 1796, after the circuit court adjudication had resulted in a split decision, Justice Wilson upholding the tax's constitutionality and District Judge Cyrus Griffin disagreeing.[62] The government handled the entire case before the Supreme Court, with the approval of Daniel Hylton, even to the extent of hiring coun-

[60] Ibid., pp. 313–15.

[61] Ibid., pp. 315–25. The actual arguments before the circuit court were never reported and information about their substance comes from printed versions issued by the respective counsels after the case was decided.

[62] Ibid., 4:314.

sel to represent him.[63] The need to obtain an authoritative decision was apparent to all. George Washington had indicated to Alexander Hamilton, when he was still secretary of the Treasury, that the president would never acquiesce in a determination that the act was unconstitutional unless that determination came from the Supreme Court.[64] Attorney General William Bradford wrote Hamilton, after the circuit court decision, asking him to join counsel for the United States in the argument before the Supreme Court. Bradford considered the Carriage Tax Case "the greatest one that ever came before that Court; & it is of the last importance not only that the act should be supported, but supported by the unanimous opinion of the Judges and on grounds that will bear the public inspection." No one knew more than Hamilton about the subject, and Bradford and Washington wanted him to defend the act.[65] In the same letter Bradford commented that the Supreme Court was without a chief justice, John Jay having resigned, and lamented the fact that the Court had no "charms" for Hamilton. "When one considers how immensely important it is, where they have the power of paralizing the measures of the government by declaring a law unconstitutional, it is not to be trusted to men who are to be scared by popular clamor or warped by feeble-minded prejudices."[66]

What is noteworthy about *Hylton* v. *United States,* as decided by the Supreme Court in March 1796, is that each justice stated that the question before the Court was whether the carriage tax was constitutional.[67] No one made any attempt to

[63] Agreement of Daniel Hylton, Jan. 25, 1796, Appellate Case Files of the Supreme Court of the United States, Records of the Supreme Court. See also Goebel and Smith, eds., *Law Practice of Alexander Hamilton,* 4:329–31.

[64] Hamilton to Coxe, Jan. 28, 1795, Goebel and Smith, eds., *Law Practice of Alexander Hamilton,* 4:341.

[65] William Bradford to Hamilton, July 2, 1795, Harold C. Syrett et al., eds., *The Papers of Alexander Hamilton,* 27 vols. (New York, 1961–87), 18:393–97.

[66] Ibid., pp. 395–96.

[67] 3 *United States Reports* (3 *Dallas*) 171 (1796).

disguise the fact that the Court was engaged in examining an act of Congress that the judges had the power to overturn. Samuel Chase, the newest Supreme Court justice (he had joined the bench in February), was the only one of the justices who bothered to explain how he approached a question of judicial review. Chase pointed out that Hylton's counsel had gone to great lengths to prove that the tax was a direct one and therefore unconstitutional. If Chase had been convinced, he would have declared the act void. But he was not satisfied with Hylton's argument, so other things influenced Chase's determination. "The deliberate decision of the National Legislature, (who did not consider a tax on carriages a *direct* tax, but thought it was within the description of a *duty*) would determine me, if the case was *doubtful,* to receive the construction of the Legislature." Chase observed, however, that in this case he did not even harbor a doubt: he thought that "a tax on *carriages* is not a *direct* tax, within the *letter,* or *meaning,* of the Constitution."[68] Thus, judicial review was apparently an accepted part of the Court's role in 1796.

Throughout the remainder of the decade evidence exists that demonstrates a continuing belief in the judiciary's power to exercise judicial review. In debates in the House of Representatives concerning issues as different as a memorial of the Quakers regarding slavery and Congress's power to deny appropriations for the salary of foreign ministers, congressmen found reason to refer to the federal judges' authority to declare an act of Congress unconstitutional in ways that indicated wide acceptance of the idea.[69] Occasional newspaper articles discussed decisions of the federal circuit courts re-

[68] Ibid., pp. 172–73. Emphasis in original.

[69] See, for example, *Annals of Congress,* 5th Cong., 2d sess., pp. 667, 924, 945, 1221. In the debate on appropriations for salaries for foreign ministers, Representative James A. Bayard made the following interesting statement: "When the framers of the Constitution created an office, or gave a power to create one, and directed the office to be filled by the President, that they contemplated a reasonable compensation being provided for the officer. It was a thing so well understood, that it would have been folly to have expressed it, as great folly as to have provided that it should be the duty of the Judges to expound the law" (ibid., p. 1221).

specting the constitutionality of a statute and the view that the Supreme Court might take of the matter in a manner that showed that there was nothing unusual in this procedure.[70] And the judges themselves continued to proclaim their authority to exercise judicial review. In the case of *Cooper* v. *Telfair*, Samuel Chase observed: "It is, indeed, a general opinion, it is expressly admitted by all this bar, and some of the Judges have, individually, in the Circuits, decided, that the Supreme Court can declare an act of congress to be unconstitutional, and, therefore, invalid; but there is no adjudication of the Supreme Court itself upon the point. I concur, however, in the general sentiment, with reference to the period, when the existing constitution came into operation."[71] The other justices participating in the decision showed that they concurred in Chase's sentiments. Bushrod Washington noted that the presumption "must always be in favour of the validity of laws, if the contrary is not clearly demonstrated."[72] William Paterson stated that "to authorise this Court to pronounce any law void, it must be a clear and unequivocal breach of the constitution, not a doubtful and argumentative implication."[73] And William Cushing agreed with his brethren that the Supreme Court could declare a law void, but that this case did not warrant the exercise of that power.[74]

Samuel Chase gave a more detailed explanation of his theory of judicial review when he delivered a charge to the grand jury in the circuit court for the district of Pennsylvania on April 12, 1800. It is such a good exposition that it is worth quoting at length:

> If the *Federal* Legislature should, at any time, pass a Law *contrary to the Constitution of the United States, such Law* would be *void;* be-

---

[70] See, for example, *Philadelphia Gazette,* Nov. 18, 1799, discussion of *United States* v. *Hopkins et al.*

[71] 4 *United States Reports* (4 *Dallas*) 19 (1800).

[72] Ibid., p. 18.

[73] Ibid., p. 19.

[74] Ibid., p. 20.

cause that Constitution is the *fundamental* Law of the United States, and *paramount* any Act of the Federal Legislature; whose authority is derived from, and delegated by, that Constitution; [here Chase cited Justice Paterson's opinion in *Vanhorne's Lessee* v. *Dorrance,* 2 *United States Reports* (2 Dallas) 308] which imposes *certain restrictions* on the *Legislative* authority that can only be preserved through the *medium* of the Courts of Justice. The *Judicial* power of the United States is *co-existent, co-extensive,* and *co-ordinate* with, and *altogether independant* of, the *Legislature* & *the Executive;* and the Judges of the Supreme, and District Courts are bound by their *Oath of Office,* to regulate their Decisions *agreeably to the Constitution.* The Judicial power, therefore, are the only *proper* and *competent* authority to decide whether any Law made by Congress; or any of the State Legislatures is contrary to or in Violation of the *federal* Constitution.[75]

Judicial review became a focal point for partisan debate only with the passage of the Alien and Sedition Acts, and even then, it seems to me, the opponents of the acts did not initially dispute the federal judges' power to overturn a congressional statute.[76] Only when the judges upheld the constitutionality of the acts did their opponents advocate other methods for determining if a federal statute was within the limits set by the Constitution. One method that surfaced during the years that the Alien and Sedition Acts were in force was having judges share the power of judicial review with juries. Another more radical idea was that the states were the final arbiters of the

[75] Marcus et al., eds., *Justices on Circuit, 1795–1800,* p. 412. Emphasis in original.

[76] See, for example, *Annals of Congress,* 5th Cong., 2d sess., pp. 2152, 2157; 6th Cong., 2d sess., pp. 917–18. While the Alien and Sedition Acts were under discussion, another controversy involving the federal courts was brewing: the expansion of the jurisdiction of the federal courts to include common law crimes. This controversy was brought to the fore because the argument was made that the Sedition Act was unnecessary, the federal courts being able to entertain prosecutions for seditious libel under their common law jurisdiction. Republicans thought a common law jurisdiction unconstitutional and began, at the same time, to argue that the Constitution did not contemplate the exercise of judicial review either.

constitutionality of acts of Congress. Neither of these methods appeared to receive great support.[77]

The behavior of the Republican party after the election of 1800 lends support to the theory that most participants in the American polity believed that federal courts had the power of judicial review. To be sure, in the congressional debates over repeal of the Judiciary Act of 1801, Republicans and Federalists repeatedly discussed the locus of the power to declare laws unconstitutional, with Republicans denying the federal courts' authority.[78] But why, once the fight for repeal was won, did the Republicans worry so much about the Federalist Supreme Court declaring the repeal act unconstitutional? If few believed that the federal courts should exercise judicial review, a decision by the Supreme Court overturning the repeal act could be ignored by the other branches with impunity. Moreover, Congress could then initiate impeachment proceedings against the judges for exceeding their authority. The Republicans, however, were concerned enough to pass

[77] For a discussion of the idea that juries as well as judges should be able to decide the constitutionality of federal statutes, see Kathryn Preyer, "*United States* v. *Callender:* Judge and Jury in a Republican Society," in Maeva Marcus, ed., *Origins of the Federal Judiciary: Essays on the Judiciary Act of 1789* (New York, 1992). See also "From the Supporter," *American Citizen* (New York), July 1, 1800.

The Kentucky and Virginia Resolutions of 1798 and 1799 declared the Alien and Sedition Acts unconstitutional and asserted that each state could itself judge which statutes of Congress were beyond the powers of the federal government as delegated by the Constitution. Thomas Jefferson, the author of the Kentucky Resolutions, introduced this theory of nullification. Madison, who wrote the Virginia Resolutions, argued less forcefully that each state could "interpose" to stop the evil an unconstitutional act produces. But neither state took any other action with regard to the Alien and Sedition Acts. The resolutions received little support from the other states; northern state legislatures specifically repudiated the nullification theory and placed the power of judicial review with the federal courts where it had been lodged since the beginning of the government under the Constitution (Peterson, "Virginia and Kentucky Resolutions," in Levy, ed., *Encyclopedia of the American Constitution*, 4:1974–75).

[78] See, for example, *Annals of Congress*, 7th Cong., 1st sess., pp. 32–33, 48, 56, 89, 131, 166, 175, 178–82, 529–30, 532–33, 542–43, 552–54, 558, 574–76, etc.

a statute postponing a meeting of the Supreme Court until February 1803, after the repeal act went into effect. Because the repeal act required the justices to hold the fall 1802 circuit courts, they were forced to decide individually whether they would follow the act or not.[79]

Postponing the Supreme Court term until February 1803 put off another decision that held great interest for the nation, the case of *Marbury* v. *Madison*. The facts in *Marbury* are well known. Federalist William Marbury had been selected to be a justice of the peace by outgoing Federalist President John Adams. Marbury's commission had been signed and sealed just hours before Adams left office, but it had not been delivered. The case arose when Marbury petitioned the Supreme Court, in December 1801, to issue a writ of mandamus ordering the new Republican secretary of state, James Madison, to deliver the commission to Marbury. The Court granted the petition and ordered Secretary Madison, on the fourth day of the next term of court, to show cause why the mandamus should not issue.[80]

Marbury is cited as the cornerstone of the American practice of judicial review. It is the first case in which the Supreme Court, speaking unanimously through Chief Justice John Marshall, explicitly held an act of Congress unconstitutional

[79] The justices of the Supreme Court acquiesced in the repeal act and held the fall 1802 circuit courts. A case raising the question of the constitutionality of the repeal act, *Stuart* v. *Laird*, was brought in the circuit court over which John Marshall presided. Marshall upheld the repeal act, and on writ of error the case was brought before the Supreme Court in its February 1803 term. The Supreme Court also upheld the repeal act (5 *United States Reports* [1 *Cranch*] 299 [1803]). For a convincing explanation of the political nature of the fight over the repeal act, see Richard E. Ellis, *The Jeffersonian Crisis: Courts and Politics in the Young Republic* (New York, 1974), pp. 36–68.

[80] According to Ellis, it was this order of the Supreme Court in 1801 that unified the Republicans, including President Jefferson, in their determination to repeal the Judiciary Act of 1801. Previously some Republicans, including Jefferson, had doubts about the constitutionality of moving against the federal courts, but the show cause order in *Marbury* convinced them that the Federalist Court intended to exercise judicial control not only over acts of Congress but over acts of the executive. The Court had to be stopped (see Ellis, *Jeffersonian Crisis*, pp. 43–45).

and stated that the judiciary can order a cabinet officer to perform duties assigned to him by the legislature. Although *Marbury* is proclaimed for its ringing affirmation of the doctrine of judicial review, what is often overlooked is that that affirmation was enunciated as part of a political response that recognized the weakness of the Supreme Court at this moment in its history.

The Supreme Court ruled that William Marbury had a legal right to his commission and that a mandamus to the secretary of state was an appropriate remedy, thus delineating the Court's duty to examine certain actions of the executive branch. Chief Justice Marshall, however, held that the Court could not issue such an order to the secretary of state, because the act of Congress giving the Supreme Court the power to issue a mandamus (Judiciary Act of 1789, Section 13) was unconstitutional—enlarging the original jurisdiction of the Supreme Court beyond that specified in Article III.[81] The members of the Supreme Court knew full well that if they had simply ordered Madison to deliver the commission to Marbury, their order would have been ignored, thus weakening the position of the Supreme Court, and they may even have faced more dire political consequences, namely, impeachment. Marshall and his brethren had to find a way institutionally to affirm the constitutional duty of the Supreme Court without creating opportunities for it to be hurt. Marshall responded brilliantly to this challenge. By separating law and politics in *Marbury*, that is, by declaring that there are certain executive actions which are purely discretionary and political that should not be examined by the Supreme Court but that there are ministerial executive actions that do fall under the purview of the Court, and by forthrightly enunciating the doctrine of judicial review, Marshall captured for the Court supremacy among the three branches of the national government in interpreting the Constitution. While appearing to remove the Court from participation in the realm of partisan politics, the chief justice defined an area, the "law," in which it was the duty of the Court to provide the guidelines under which the federal government would function. Although

---

[81] 5 *U.S.* (1 *Cranch*) 153–80 (1803).

Marshall seemed to be eliminating controversial political issues from consideration by the Court, in reality he assumed
for the Court the power to decide which issues belonged in
the sphere of politics and which should be denominated issues of law. This was indeed a bold proposition, but he was
able to proclaim it in *Marbury* only by denying to the Court
jurisdiction in the case.

The assertion of the power of judicial review over legislative
acts in *Marbury* v. *Madison* occasioned no great surprise or reaction from Congress or the American people. What did create a stir was Marshall's attempt to tell the secretary of state
what was the right thing to do when the chief justice had declared that the Court had no power to order him to do it.[82]
Marshall's lecture on the proper behavior of executive officers
was not well received by President Jefferson and his cabinet,
but as they had not been ordered to do anything, there was
no way they could show their disdain for the Court's decision.
The chief justice had gauged the political situation correctly:
he knew the Court could not issue an order opposing the
president and his secretary of state; instead, he set down for
posterity his vision of the proper relationship between the judicial and the executive and legislative branches and established the theoretical basis for the practice of judicial review.
And few people, at the time, disputed Marshall's depiction of
the role of the Court.

Given the strength of the evidence from the 1790s of the
existence of a belief in judicial review and the many actions
taken in accord with that belief, I find it easy to answer affirmatively the question of whether the Founders intended
the federal judiciary to possess this power. The mystery lies in
why and how that generation came to think that way when
there seems to have been so little in the previous history of
America that would have prepared people to accept an une-
lected judiciary, tenured for life, as an integral part of the
democratic process.[83] Though I might speculate on how and

[82] Ellis, *Jeffersonian Crisis*, p. 66; Block and Marcus, "John Marshall's Selective Use of History," p. 319 n. 70.

[83] See Gordon S. Wood, "The Origins of Judicial Review," *Suffolk University Law Review* 22 (1988):1304–6.

why that happened, the answers are too important for speculation. They require thorough study of the exercise of judicial
power and attitudes regarding it in all the colonies and subsequent states. These studies do not yet exist, but they are necessary to any convincing attempt to explain the momentous
transformation that occurred in the role of the American judiciary between the 1780s and the 1790s.

THOMAS P. SLAUGHTER

"The King of Crimes"

Early American Treason Law,

1787–1860

ON THE MILES of library shelves occupied by studies of the
United States Constitution there is strikingly little serious
commentary about Article III, Section 3, the treason clause.
"For all practical purposes," legal historian James Willard
Hurst observes, "detailed analytical treatment of the law of
treason has not interested writers of standard texts since the
eighteenth century."[1] Explanations for this comparative inattention to such a historic statement on the nature of political
crime would certainly include the apparent clarity of the Constitution's definition of treason. The passage is so concise and
precise as seemingly to preclude credible controversy over the
intentions of the Framers and the legacy of their language for
all time. "Treason against the United States," reads Article III,
Section 3, "shall consist only in levying war against them, or,
in adhering to their enemies, giving them aid and comfort.
No person shall be convicted of treason unless on the testi-

I want to thank the late Mary Kay Bonsteel Tachau for her insightful comments on this essay, as well as William C. Jordan, Stanley N. Katz, James
Livingston, and Louis P. Masur for their readings and suggestions. I delivered a significantly shorter and more chronologically focused version of
this essay as a Walter Prescott Webb Memorial Lecture at the University of
Texas at Arlington. That essay was published as "The Politics of Treason in
the 1790s," in Elisabeth A. Cauthon and David Narrett, eds., *English Law
and the American Experience* (College Station, Tex., 1993).

[1] James Willard Hurst, *The Law of Treason in the United States* (Westport,
Conn., 1971), p. 49. See also George P. Fletcher, "The Case for Treason,"
Maryland Law Review 41 (1982):194.

mony of two witnesses to the same overt act, or on confession in open court."

Simple, straightforward, and effective, the treason clause has generally struck commentators as a testament to the Founding Fathers' success at balancing protection of the government from disloyal citizens with simultaneous expansion of individual rights against the encroachments of overzealous minions of the state. Lawrence M. Friedman's treatment of the treason clause in his *History of American Law* accurately reflects, in both its brevity and conclusions, the standard interpretation. "The federal Constitution radically restricted this king of crimes," Friedman writes. "It defined its content, once and for all, and hedged treason trials about with procedural safeguards. . . . It shrank the concept of state crime to an almost irreducible minimum." [2]

The infrequency of prosecutions, with fewer than forty federal treason trials in over two hundred years, and the existence of only one Supreme Court review of a treason case through the end of the Second World War, appear also to justify inattention to the law of treason. [3] Compared to the British, for example, over any similar period in their history, Americans have been a strikingly less treasonous people (in both frequency and degree), our government undeniably more lenient in defining and dealing with traitors, and our treason law considerably less subject to the periodic pressures of public and official paranoia. [4]

A final, and equally plausible, pair of explanations for the dearth of inquiry into the American law of treason reflects historians' usual approach to the study of law. In a similar

[2] Lawrence M. Friedman, *A History of American Law*, 2d ed. (New York, 1985), p. 292.

[3] The one case reviewed through the Second World War was *Cramer* v. *U.S.* (325 *United States Reports* 1–77 [1945]). But see also cases listed in note 118 below.

[4] Rebecca West, *The Meaning of Treason* (New York, 1947); Lacey Baldwin Smith, *Treason in Tudor England: Politics and Paranoia* (Princeton, 1986); George W. Keeton, *Trial for Treason* (London, 1959); Walter G. Simon, "The Evolution of Treason," *Tulane Law Review* 35 (1961):669–704; Charles Warren, "What Is Giving Aid and Comfort to the Enemy?" *Yale Law Journal* 27 (1918):331–47.

fashion, if to a somewhat lesser degree, than the commentators, jurists, and attorneys whom they study, legal historians often focus their research on what is orderly and evolutionary in law. In many cases, the study of past law is justified primarily by reference to the subject's significance for modern juridical concerns. This entirely legitimate search for the roots of modern law may help partially to explain both the relative paucity of writing on political crime and the limitations of much of what has been written about treason and related offenses. Legal historians have simply been uninterested, for the most part, in comprehending early American political crime on its own disorderly terms, because they find little that has left a significant legacy for either modern politics or criminal law.

Traditional legal historians have not identified evolutionary patterns toward an increasingly wiser, fairer, and more orderly standard of protections for the rights of individuals accused of crimes against the state. On the other side, revisionist scholars have not located, for treason law, a history of decline toward an ever more oppressive judiciary acting as the strong arm of corporate-capitalist central authority. Such rights have seemed to the traditionalists determined "once and for all" in the Constitution, as Friedman accurately reports it; and to the revisionists, those same rights seem still unprotected in our day, as historians Ronald Radosh and Joyce Milton argue in their analysis of the Rosenberg espionage case. According to Walter G. Simon, another revisionist, the apparently narrow definitions of treason in Anglo-American law still "serve not so much as a protector of the accused, but as a license for any number of unofficial agencies to use the term treason."[5]

[5] Ronald Radosh and Joyce Milton, *The Rosenberg File: A Search for the Truth* (New York, 1983). The charge against Julius and Ethel Rosenberg was not treason, but, according to Radosh and Milton, "the shadow of a still more serious accusation—treason—loomed over the courtroom" (p. 170; see also pp. 172–74). According to Simon, "To the Anglo-American mind all political crimes fall into the category of treason. . . . The Smith Act in the United States, the various espionage acts in both the United States and Great Britain, are treason statutes. Not only nine out of ten laymen, but nine out of ten lawyers or judges, if asked to describe the crime of the Rosenbergs would classify it as treason" (Simon, "Evolution of Treason," p. 699).

Despite such fundamental disagreements as these on the current status and history of our treason law, all seem to agree that the tale is not one of change. Even for the revisionists, evolution (or, more appropriately, devolution) is not a significant dimension of the history of American treason, and thus the story is not an important one to detail over time. The subject appears somehow outside of history to scholars of American law, and thus discordant, peripheral to the main story they have to tell. What does not fit is seen in good faith as an anomaly not worth sustained inquiry.

For whatever combination of reasons, then, there are only two important histories of federal treason law, one by Bradley Chapin and the other by James Willard Hurst. They disagree about the Constitution's role in defining treason for all times. Hurst takes the traditional position; Chapin champions the revisionist cause. Both authors seek the origins of modern doctrine in the early national period. While they disagree fundamentally about what the law of treason was in late eighteenth-century America, they agree that there has been little significant change in judicial interpretation of the treason clause between 1800 and the present day. Chapin ends his research with the Aaron Burr conspiracy cases of 1806–7 after confirming to his satisfaction that the law of treason did not alter from the administrations of George Washington and John Adams through Thomas Jefferson's presidency. Hurst shares the traditional understanding of Article III, Section 3 as clear, tightly circumscribing the potential for either legislative or judicial expansion, and in most respects unaltered by judicial interpretation over time.

The authors' treatment of antebellum nineteenth-century treason cases no doubt substantially reflects their legitimate interest in utilizing the past to the extent that it reveals useful truths about the present. Chapin anticipates no change, so, understandably, he skips over 150 years of history to link the 1790s with the 1960s; Hurst also has a presentist agenda to which the history of the antebellum period reasonably seems of secondary concern. This leaves plenty of room for another perspective on the treason law of the early republic. In light of fundamental disagreements between Hurst and Chapin in particular, and among traditionalists and revisionists in general, there seems potential for a better comprehension of the legal-political history of that era on its own terms, as well as an opportunity for contributing to new understandings of the larger sweep of American law. But first, it is necessary to set the historiographical stage more fully for the alternative presentation offered below.

Chapin, in a ringing dissent from traditional accounts and in sharp disagreement with Hurst, argues that in the heat of the Revolution and in its immediate aftermath American judges and legislatures, particularly at the national level, greatly expanded upon contemporary common-law definitions of "levying war" and reintroduced the concept of "constructive treason," which by this time had been abandoned by English courts as too broad, too open to corruption by the state, and thus extremely threatening to the rights of individuals.[6] In other words, Chapin finds that the Constitution, as it was interpreted by Federalist judges in the Whiskey Rebellion and Fries's Rebellion cases, represented a *broadening* of government power in respect to treason and a *corrosion* of hard-won rights achieved by Englishmen during the previous century. He argues that this expansion of central authority at the expense of individual rights was unchanged by the two Burr conspiracy cases—*Ex Parte Bollman and Swartwout* and

---

[6] According to *Black's Law Dictionary* (St. Paul, 1968), "Constructive treason [is] treason imputed to a person by law from his conduct or course of actions, though his deeds taken severally do not amount to actual treason. This doctrine is not known in the United States (1672)." The claim of the last sentence is historically inaccurate and is even controversial as applied to modern law. For a different perspective on modern law, see Radosh and Milton, *Rosenberg File*, and Simon, "Evolution of Treason." For the nineteenth-century American law, see below and the first American edition of Sir Matthew Hale, *The History of the Pleas of the Crown*, 2 vols. (Philadelphia, 1847), 1:158–60 n.16. See also Hale's definition for seventeenth-century England (p. 152), which is also somewhat different and more complex than the law dictionary's. Simply put, "constructive" treason requires a judicial "interpretation" to define an overt act or acts as treason. In the American case, as long as any term of the Constitution's definition seems imprecise to judges, then the door is left open to judicially "constructed" or "interpreted" treasons. During the period of American history considered in this essay, there was wide latitude taken by judges in the area of constructive levying of war.

U.S. v. *Aaron Burr*—and that "the doctrine of a constructive levying of war . . . remains good law to this day."[7]

In other respects, Chapin is more struck by continuities than changes in the law of treason. He characterizes the colonial era as encompassing a two-stage process in the evolution of treason law. Initially and into the 1690s there was little resemblance between the law of the colonies and English treason doctrine. Especially, but not exclusively, in New England, legal terms and definitions were biblically inspired. By the end of the seventeenth century, however, Chapin believes that "the process of shaping Colonial law more closely after English models began." He finds no evolution away from the English model, "no rational clarification" in the colonial treason law of the eighteenth century. By the end of the colonial era, he asserts, "the American law of treason was the law of England transferred to a new home."[8] With the important exceptions of expanded state authority to define levying war and constructive treason, Chapin finds that American legislatures and courts adhered to the trend in English law toward greater protections for the rights of individuals charged with political crime. In adopting the rigid defense for individuals embodied in the English two-witness rule, in confining treasonable offenses only to levying war and adherence to the nation's enemies, Americans enshrined English guarantees of personal liberty in the new Constitution.[9]

Hurst and Chapin are not at absolute odds in their interpretations. They share an emphasis on continuities from British-colonial antecedents through adoption of the Constitution, although Hurst sees a clearer break from the English past in both the Framers' intention to narrow the scope of government authority to prosecute for treason and in the courts' adherence to this higher valuation of individual rights.

[7] Bradley Chapin, *The American Law of Treason: Revolutionary and Early National Origins* (Seattle, 1964), p. 97.

[8] Ibid., pp. 5–6, 9.

[9] See also Bradley Chapin, "Colonial and Revolutionary Origins of the American Law of Treason," *William and Mary Quarterly*, 3d ser. 17 (1960):3–21; idem, "The American Revolution as Lese Majesty," *Pennsylvania Magazine of History and Biography* 79 (1955):310–30.

Both minimize the significance of evolution in treason law after ratification of the Constitution, although Chapin finds significant enhancement of state authority at the expense of individual rights in the Whiskey Rebellion and Fries's Rebellion cases of the 1790s, while Hurst locates important development in the opposite direction toward narrowing of governmental powers and expansion of protections for individual rights in *U.S.* v. *Hanway* (1851). Indeed, Hurst offers readers of Chapin's monograph "one substantial caveat." He doubts Chapin's "claim that there is continuing life in the idea of treason by constructive levying of war, in forcible resistance to enforcement of particular laws."[10] He questions whether a court today would permit a federal prosecutor to construe treasonable intent from mere presence or participation in a riot or other violent action aimed at one particular law. He believes, contrary to Chapin, that evidence of a wider conspiracy to bring down the entire government is necessary to convict for treason under our Constitution.

According to Hurst, the treason clause, as it was intended and enforced from the beginning, represented a clear step forward in the history of protecting individuals against malicious officials. "At the time of the adoption of the Constitution," he observes, "the treason clause was most praised for the reason that it prevented the use of treason trials as an instrument of political faction." From that time forward, Hurst avers, "judges have accordingly . . . agreed that the mere expression of beliefs cannot be deemed 'treason' within the constitutional definition."[11]

Thus, Hurst locates in the treason clause four clear breaks from English example: (1) there is no parallel to the vague, broad, and often judicially corrupted charge of "compassing or imagining" the king's death; (2) words alone, in the ab-

[10] Hurst, *Law of Treason*, p. ix.

[11] Ibid., pp. 5–6, 126. See also Harold W. Chase and Craig R. Ducat, eds., *Edward S. Corwin's The Constitution and What It Means Today* (Princeton, 1978), pp. 244–45. The authors of this standard text agree with Hurst and Lawrence M. Friedman that the terms of the treason clause have seemed quite clear in their meaning to judges: "'Overt act' means simply open act, that is to say, an act which may be testified to, and not a mere statement of consciousness" (p. 244).

sence of an overt act of violence against the state cannot be deemed a treasonous levying of war as defined by the Constitution; (3) the line between treason and riot is much more clearly drawn in the treason clause than it ever was in English common or statute law; and (4) the Constitution's two-witness rule is significantly more restrictive than its progenitor in the Treason Act of 25 Edward III. As English precedent existed in 1787, "the levying of war upon the king could consist in any effort by violence to fix or enforce public policy. . . . This amounted to saying that the line between treason and riot was unpredictable and would shift towards the more serious crime largely according to the ruthlessness or strong-mindedness of the administration."[12]

In these two regards, according to Hurst, Americans have been better protected from the government since 1787 than they had been before. He sees the history of colonial legislation as "an almost unbroken trend to put the interest in community security first in defining the types of conduct which shall be deemed treasonable." Despite respect for the two-witness rule, eighteenth-century legislators had never before limited treason prosecutions to cases where there were at least two witnesses to the same overt act; until the Constitution, Americans had rested content with two witnesses to the same general treasonous offense. It was the Revolution itself, according to Hurst, that led Americans to a heightened distrust of governmental authority, which resulted in the unprecedentedly narrow definition of treason in the Constitution.[13]

There is reason to question some of these basic contentions of Chapin and Hurst, both where they agree and disagree. Federal treason trials reveal less judicial concern for the rights of individuals in the decades immediately following adoption of the Constitution than Hurst or other traditional analysts of American constitutional law admit. Also, the early national and antebellum cases document a clearer break from English abuses of individual rights in treason prosecutions than Chapin and other revisionists allow. These cases display more development over time in this regard than either Chapin or

[12] Hurst, *Law of Treason*, p. 6.

[13] Ibid., pp. 81–83, 85, 91.

Hurst credits. The narrowing of governmental authority and the introduction of procedural safeguards for individual rights perceived by most modern legal historians were not obvious to judges and prosecutors during the first half-century of our federal courts. Nor did judges inquire into or feel in any sense bound by the intentions of those who drafted the treason clause. The meanings of "levying war" and the two-witness rule were neither so clear nor so set, "once and for all," as they have appeared in retrospect, precisely because for over sixty years after 1787 judges continued to entertain prosecutorial arguments that constructed treasonous intent from ambiguous actions. Nor was the line between riot and rebellion, between unlawful violence and treason, so obvious to judicial officials as it is now to legal historians.

It was not even certain that words—a "mere statement of consciousness"—could not be treasonous under the Constitution, which leaves room for the credible revisionist argument that the constitutional revolution of 1787 represented, in some ways at least, a step backward in the history of Anglo-American liberty, at least as that history was reported in the English legal treatises that Americans perused. These cases also provide evidence, however, that the procedural safeguards for individuals that exist today are more substantial than the revisionists argue; and, contrary to traditional accounts, these protections are the result of historical developments during the nineteenth century rather than legacies bequeathed intact by the Founding Fathers. Finally, there is reason to doubt whether Hurst or Chapin has built his analytical edifice upon a sufficient understanding of the nature, degree, and direction of change in treason law from the common law to the Constitution; and it is here, in English law, that a reconsideration of the American law of treason must begin.

Any discussion of the relationship between the English law of treason and that embodied in the United States Constitution must make a clear distinction between the reality of English law and the perceptions of that law held by the Founding Fathers. As Hurst shrewdly observes, there is little evidence that the drafters were familiar with ancient English statute or case law, but they had a wide (if in most cases shallow) acquaintance with the major common law commentaries, including those of Matthew Hale, Edward Coke, Michael Foster, and William Blackstone.[14] The commentators disagreed about some fundamental tenets of treason law, but collectively they gave American readers the impression that English prosecution of political crime was much less chaotic than even a cursory perusal of the state cases reveals. The reality is that order, rationality, and linear progression over time were not the hallmarks of treason law during the centuries of English colonization of the New World or, for that matter, thereafter.

The statute of 25 Edward III, which became the model for the Constitution's treason clause, was indeed a landmark in English history. It did attempt to delimit potential crimes chargeable as treason, paring the list down to seven categories of offense, including compassing or imagining the king's death; sexual violation of the king's consort, the wife of his eldest son, or his eldest unmarried daughter; levying war against the king within his realm; adhering to the king's enemies in the realm; counterfeiting the great or privy seal or the coin of the realm; and assassination of top government officials. This fourteenth-century law also took care to protect subjects from judicially constructed treasons, while assuring that the Crown would be safe from as yet unimaginable assaults: "And because that many other like cases of treason may happen in time to come, which a man cannot think nor declare at this present time; it is accorded, that if any other case, supposed treason, which is not above specified, doth happen before any justices, the justices shall tarry without any going to judgement of the treason till the cause be shewed and declared before the King and his

[14] Ibid., p. 8; Hale, *Pleas of the Crown;* Sir Edward Coke, *The Third Part of the Institutes of the Laws of England: Concerning High Treason, and Other Pleas of the Crown, and Criminal Causes* (London, 1644); Sir Michael Foster, *A Report of Some Proceedings . . . To Which Are Added Discourses upon a Few Branches of the Crown Law* (Dublin, 1767); William Blackstone, *Commentaries on the Laws of England*, 4 vols. (Oxford, 1766–69), vol. 4.

Parliament, whether it ought to be judged treason or other felony."[15]

Within its compass, and in comparison to the chaos that preceded it, this first statutory definition of the English law of treason was, in the short term, reasonably effective. It was now significantly less likely (unless the king in Parliament specifically decided otherwise) that someone could be tried and convicted of treason for nonappearance on a writ, as Thomas Becket had been during the twelfth century, or that either highway robbery or taking suit in the court of the French king would again be successfully prosecuted as treason.[16]

Still, the act of 25 Edward III did allow for legislative proliferation of treasonable offenses, and the process of adding to the original statutory list began within a generation of the first law. In 1381, in the wake of the peasant uprising, it became treasonous to begin a riot; in 1397, to *suggest* repeal of Parliamentary laws; in 1415, to clip or file money; in 1423, to suffer or assist accused traitors to escape; in 1429, to extort money by threat of arson; and this was just the beginning.

At one time or another between the fourteenth and nineteenth centuries the list expanded to include poisoning; execrations against the king; deflowering or marrying without royal permission any of the king's children, sisters, aunts, nephews, or nieces; solicitation of the chastity of the queen or princess; untoward solicitations by the queen or princess; marrying the king by a woman not a virgin, who failed to disclose this fact prior to the marriage; and twelve or more people assembling riotously for any purpose, who refused to

---

[15] 25 Edward III, stat. 5, cap. 2 (1350). This act also listed among treasonous offenses a servant slaying a master, a wife her husband, or a man his prelate. These crimes constitute the distinct, but related, offense of "petty treason," which is not considered in this essay.

[16] It took another act, 1 Henry IV, cap. 10, to eliminate some of the more irrational encrustations that accumulated over time. See J. G. Bellamy, *The Law of Treason in the Later Middle Ages* (Cambridge, 1970); trial of Thomas Becket (1163), in Thomas Bayly Howell, *Cobbett's Complete Collection of State Trials and Proceedings for High Treason . . .* , 33 vols. (London, 1809–26), 1:1–12. On the other treason prosecutions mentioned here, see Simon, "Evolution of Treason," pp. 669–704. For the list of treasonous crimes added by Henry VIII and others, see Blackstone, *Commentaries*, 4:86–87.

disperse when ordered. Most of these additions were the product of Tudor fears, and most of those reflected Henry VIII's particular fantasies. Generally, the succession of treason acts expired with the monarch who conceived them, making the law of treason unpredictable from reign to reign, particularly under the Tudors. In the long run, then, the treason statute of 25 Edward III had just the opposite effect of its framers' intentions. As the legal scholar Walter Simon has noted, instead of limiting the profusion of treason charges, "it furnished the King, when he could control Parliament, with a mechanism for the almost inexhaustible extension of treason."[17]

Clearly, the original treason law was not aimed chiefly at limiting the authority of the king or protecting English subjects from their monarch or Parliament. It is easy to picture what wide license could be given to prosecute subjects for imagining the king's death. Not surprisingly, the principal assaults upon the tenets of the original treason statutes came from the Crown, most often acting through Parliament, and from some of England's most energetic and unscrupulous monarchs (for example, Richard II and Henry VIII) during times of intense political turmoil. The law of treason was now legislatively rationalized for times of relative calm, but it still remained vulnerable to the periodic crises weathered by the English state.[18]

During eras of relative placidity, customary procedural protections for the accused did emerge, including a rule that, in lieu of a confession in open court, two witnesses were *generally*

[17] Simon, "Evolution of Treason," p. 699.

[18] Sir Frederick Pollock and Frederick William Maitland, *The History of English Law before the Time of Edward I,* 2d ed., 2 vols. (Cambridge, 1968), vol. 2. Leon Radzinowicz, *A History of English Criminal Law* (New York, 1948), p. 612, finds little order, evolution, or rationality in English treason law through the eighteenth century; Simon, "Evolution of Treason," pp. 699–700. Henry VIII's physicians feared, at the time of his last illness, that uttering their diagnosis would be construed as predicting the monarch's death, which would fall under a statutory expansion of the compassing clause. Therefore, they kept the seriousness of his physical condition to themselves. See also Isobel D. Thornley, "Treason by Words in the Fifteenth Century," *English Historical Review* 32 (1917):556–61.

necessary to sustain a charge of treason.[19] Over time, and again with exceptions reflecting the whims and fears of notoriously whimsical and frightened kings, the spirit of clearly defining and delimiting treasonous acts was sustained for centuries after adoption of the statute of 25 Edward III. Whatever portions of order, evolution, and rationality existed, however, were swept away in the torrent of sixteenth-century change presided over by Henry VIII, his daughters, and son.

English treason was an offense with "a vague circumference and more than one centre" in the sixteenth and seventeenth centuries, just as it had been before the first statutory definition of the crime. As a crime against the sovereign, who embodied the state, its terms were frequently subject to the capricious definitions of enraged monarchs. Frederick Pollock and Frederick William Maitland's observation for medieval times that "any one who grossly insulted the king might have found that the law of treason was expansive" was no less true during the Tudor and Stuart reigns. Infamously under the Tudors, a conviction for treason required no overt act beyond spoken words—"compassing," imagining, or prophesying the king's death was sufficient—and needed only the word of one weak-minded fool under threat or pain of torture.[20]

Trials were little more under the Tudors and Stuarts than state theater in which the fate of the accused was as certain as Hamlet's before each performance began. Elaborately orchestrated charges were often sustained by testimony extracted on the rack; hearsay, rumors, and vague opinions were routinely introduced by prosecutors; Crown lawyers freely browbeat

[19] L. M. Hill, "The Two-Witness Rule in English Treason Trials: Some Comments on the Emergence of Procedural Law," *American Journal of Legal History* 12 (1968):95–111.

[20] Pollock and Maitland, *History of English Law,* 2:503, 505, 507; Keeton, *Trial for Treason,* p. 46. Nonetheless, as Jonathan K. Van Patten points out, "most persons executed under the new [Tudor] treason laws had been apprehended in open warfare against the Crown, activity which had always been treasonable under the laws of England" ("Magic, Prophecy, and the Law of Treason in Reformation England," *American Journal of Legal History* 27 [1983]:11). So the Tudors were not just paranoid, they really were beleaguered by traitors. On this point, see also Smith, *Treason in Tudor England.*

the accused who were not entitled to professional counsel; and traditional or statutory procedural safeguards were often ignored and sometimes specifically denied to those who had the knowledge and bluster to press for their rights. Sir Walter Raleigh's insistence that two witnesses to a treasonous act were necessary to convict him, an appeal based on tradition and an expired law of 1571, were rejected. Raleigh's was, after all, a political trial, and, as one historian has observed, "legal niceties appear to have been of less importance than the elimination of a noxious element in the Stuart state." "At best," writes Tudor historian Lacey Baldwin Smith in reference to the mid-sixteenth century, "the line between historical fact and governmental fiction is cloudy; in case of treason it tends to vanish entirely."[21]

The Tudor reigns represent an almost uninterrupted story of statutory expansion of treasonous crime. The major exception to this drift of change is the legislative enactment of the two-witness rule in 1552, during the reign of Edward VI. Even here the Tudor contribution to protection of individual rights is less than it appears. Long before the sixteenth century, indeed going back to Bracton's time, the requirement that there must be two witnesses to sustain a charge of treason was normal procedure. It was not necessary that the two witnesses be to the same overt act, although it was generally assumed that they would be to the same general act of treason. By making the two-witness rule into positive law, the Tudor Parliaments confused the situation by opening the way for repeal or expiration of laws that embodied the rule. So, as in the case of Raleigh, accused traitors were probably more vulnerable to state abuse of this procedural protection than they had been before adoption of the law embodying the two-witness rule.[22]

[21] Hill, "Two-Witness Rule," pp. 107–8; Smith, *Treason in Tudor England*, p. 15; trial of Sir Walter Raleigh (1603), in Howell, *State Trials*, 2:1–60; Van Patten, "Magic, Prophecy, and the Law of Treason," pp. 1–32. In most of these ways, of course, the procedural rules for treason were little or no different than for other felonies. Nor were they peculiarly English. See Bellamy, *Law of Treason;* Simon H. Cuttler, *The Law of Treason and Treason Trials in Later Medieval France* (New York, 1981).

[22] Hill, "Two-Witness Rule," p. 111.

If the Tudor record is most remarkable for its legislative expansion of treasonous offenses, the Stuart era is most notable for an unprecedented growth in judicial intrusion into the realm of constructive treason; and judges utilized for their purposes both the clause of compassing or imagining the king's death and that of levying war. Procedural protections for the accused were never less meaningful than in Stuart courts. It was during the seventeenth century, when treason prosecutions "reached a fever pitch," that the English nation endured a judicial barbarity unprecedented in its history.[23]

Judge George Jeffreys's record in the Bloody Assizes following Monmouth's Rebellion is unmatched in English annals of judicial revenge. He sentenced 292 to death at Dorchester, found guilty 21 of 21 accused at Exeter, and ordered 139 hanged, drawn, and quartered at Taunton within a few days. The trial and conviction of Lady Alice Lisle was undoubtedly one of the gravest examples of judicial abuse on record. Lisle, a widow, had the misfortune to be visited by two suspected traitors. She sent a servant to alert a sheriff to their presence, but the king's troops arrived before the servant completed his task. Neither of the accused villains had been convicted at the time of Lisle's trial, so their guilt had yet to be established. Judge Jeffreys dismissed such legal niceties as irrelevant. He handled the prosecution personally, browbeat witnesses mercilessly, misinstructed and badgered the jury, and refused to receive their verdict of not guilty. Three times the jurors returned with the same verdict and three times the judge threatened, ridiculed, and denounced them. Three times he sent them back to reconsider under threats jurors knew full well that Jeffreys was capable of enforcing. Finally, they succumbed, Lisle stood convicted of treason, and she was executed for the crime.[24]

---

[23] Simon, "Evolution of Treason," p. 696.

[24] Trial of Lady Alice Lisle (1685), in Howell, *State Trials,* 11:198–382; Keeton, *Trial for Treason,* pp. 79–134. For a different interpretation, which implicitly defends Jeffreys's actions and explicitly doubts the traditional Whig interpretation of this trial, see the modern Tory historian J. P. Kenyon's, *The Stuart Constitution: Documents and Commentary* (Cambridge, 1966), p. 437 n.2.

Shortly after the Glorious Revolution and largely in response to the abuses of Stuart judges, among whom Jeffreys was only the most infamous, Parliament enacted several laws that attempted to secure procedural protections for those accused of treason. Most directly relevant to a consideration of the American law of treason was the act of 7 William III, which reintroduced to English law a statutory definition of the two-witness rule for treason cases. In the absence of a full confession in open court, this act required "the oaths and testimony of two lawful witnesses, either both of them to the same overt act, or one of them to one, and the other of them to another overt act of the same treason." Again, as with the earlier two-witness tradition in the common law and the sixteenth-century legislative enactments, this law had some positive effect, but in times of political turmoil it could be circumvented or ignored. In 1747, for example, Lord Simon Lovat received none of the procedural protections or privileges contained in the laws of 1696, 1702, and 1708. He was not given a copy of the indictment that charged him with treason; he was not provided a list of the witnesses against him or a copy of the jury panel ten days before the trial. He was denied counsel and was refused the right to compel witnesses to attend or to examine them under oath.[25]

Even the apparent advances for the rights of the accused that seemed to be represented in the acquittals of Thomas Hardy and John Horne Tooke in 1794 were reversed by a 1795 act of Parliament that ensured that written words sufficed as an overt act of treason.[26] Contrary to popular belief, then, the acquittals of Lord George Gordon in 1780 and Hardy, Tooke, and others in 1794, did not destroy the doctrine of constructive treason in English law. And even in the twentieth century, apparent gains in narrowing the scope of

[25] Trial of Lord Simon Lovat (1747), in Howell, *State Trials*, 18:530–858; Keeton, *Trial for Treason*, pp. 135, 144–45, 150–53, 162–63. The government utilized the procedure of "impeachment," a technical legislative variation on the treason charge, to circumvent procedural requirements in successive acts of 1696, 1702, and 1708.

[26] Radzinowicz, *History of English Criminal Law*, pp. 612–13; 36 George III, cap. 7 (1795); trial of Thomas Hardy (1794), in Howell, *State Trials*, 24:19–1384; trial of John Horne Tooke (1794), ibid., 25:1–748.

treason and ensuring the rights of the accused have been dealt blows by English courts that found mere words uttered abroad sufficient grounds for convicting Sir Roger Casement, and which denied, in the case of William Joyce, that one had to be an English citizen to be prosecuted for adhering to the king's enemies.[27]

In light of this unremitting extralegality in the enforcement of English treason law through the eighteenth century, it is difficult to sustain the charge of Bradley Chapin and other revisionists that Article III, Section 3 of the Constitution represented a step backwards in the history of individual rights. There has never been in America the sort of legislative abuse of treason propagated during the reigns of Henry VIII or even George III. There has been nothing comparable to the judicial excesses of either the seventeenth-century or even the eighteenth-century English courts. To deny progress in Article III, Section 3, to assert decline from the English example, is to misunderstand the English case, to minimize the true horror of the likes of Judge Jeffreys; it is to ignore the genuine and ongoing potential for abuse that corresponds with utilization of the treason act of 25 Edward III as a benchmark for enforcement, even when accompanied by the procedural safeguards legislated during the late seventeenth and early eighteenth centuries.

Reflecting upon the above summary of English case and statute law, the argument made by Chapin that Americans *reinstituted* the notion of constructive treason in the early federal cases seems overdrawn, if only because the English had never abandoned the potential for judicial construction of treason under any of the major clauses of 25 Edward III. English judges and the king in Parliament remained free to redefine treason under the clauses addressing the compassing of the king's death, levying war, and adhering to the nation's enemies. Even if Chapin is correct about the American law, judicial freedom to construct treasons under the levying war clause of Article III, Section 3 seems to represent a continuity

[27] Keeton, *Trial for Treason*, pp. 212–13; West, *Meaning of Treason*, pp. 8–9, 24–29, 44–45; trial of Lord George Gordon (1780), in Howell, *State Trials*, 21:485–652.

rather than a change from English example. Although American judges may have constructed new treasons or ones that had been long abandoned in English law (see *U.S.* v. *John Mitchell, U.S.* v. *Philip Vigol,* and *U.S.* v. *John Fries* below), they would be drawing on a long and continuing tradition of constructive treason in Anglo-American courts.

Part of the problem with the revisionist interpretation of the transition to American constitutional law stems from analysis of English treatises rather than case law. As Hurst rightly insists, such reliance is justifiable *if* the historian is interested in American perceptions of English law rather than the reality of treason prosecutions in Great Britain, and *if* he is careful to distinguish between reality and contemporary perceptions. The treatises must be utilized with care because of the common law jurists' penchant for rationalizing the sometimes irrational, for culling order from a chaotic case law. The commentators most often read by Americans—Hale, Coke, Foster, and Blackstone—were brilliant analysts and quite up to the task of sifting and sculpting past statutes and court decisions into an orderly system that Americans apparently accepted, at least for treason, as an accurate portrayal of English law as it existed at the times the respective treatises were written.

The commentators were not *just* apologists for the common law, and they disagreed fundamentally on several of the central issues of interpretation. But they did share an understanding of the law as progressive over time. They all saw their task as identifying patterns that lent predictability to the judicial system.

The seventeenth-century commentators—Hale and Coke—and the eighteenth-century commentators—Foster and Blackstone—agreed that the English law of treason had made great strides over time in the direction of narrowing the state's authority to prosecute for this crime and in broadening protections for the accused. According to Hale, the law of treason was "uncertain and arbitrary" before the act of 25 Edward III; but with the single exception of Richard II's "troublesome reign," clear limits and bounds had since restrained governmental abuses. Of course, Hale and Coke both wrote before Judge Jeffreys and the Bloody Assizes. At one time but no longer, Blackstone argued a century after the treatises of Coke and Hale, English judges enjoyed great latitude in determining the nature of treason, "whereby the creatures of tyrannical princes had opportunity to create abundance of constructive treasons."[28]

In the past, all four jurists agreed, mere utterances were sufficient to prosecute for treason, but over time the law had evolved toward the necessity of a better-articulated overt act. Coke identified Tudor statutes that defined spoken words as sufficiently treasonous overt acts of compassing the king's death, "but they all are either repealed or expired. And it is commonly said, that bare words may make an heretic, but not a traitor, without an overt act." Blackstone described the process of change in regard to treasonous words as comprising three steps: (1) at one time speech was enough; (2) by the late seventeenth century, as in the case of Algernon Sidney, the words had to be written down to constitute treason; (3) and in the mid-eighteenth century, when Blackstone wrote, publication was a minimal overt act in this regard, although "of late even that has been questioned."[29]

These four commentators all acknowledged that the clause of the treason act of 25 Edward III relating to compassing or imagining the king's death was almost a catchall and that it had, at least in the past, provided prosecutors a wider scope than they enjoyed under either of the other two main treason clauses—levying war and adhering to the king's enemies. Indeed, according to Foster, the standard of proof and the specificity of the charge were less clearly defined and thus weighed more heavily in the state's favor under the compassing clause than under the other two. "The law," Foster wrote in the mid-eighteenth century, "tendereth the safety of the King with an anxious, and if I may use the expression, with a concern bordering upon jealousy. It considereth the wicked imaginations of the heart in the same degree of guilt as if carried into actual

[28] Hale, *Pleas of the Crown*, 1:81. All subsequent references to Hale are to this, the first American edition. Blackstone, *Commentaries*, 4:75.

[29] Sir Edward Coke, *The Third Part of the Institutes of the Laws of England*, 4th ed. (London, 1669), p. 14. Blackstone, *Commentaries*, 4:79–81, quotation p. 81.

execution." "The words *compass* or *imagine* are of great latitude," Hale observed a century before Foster wrote. "They
refer to the purpose or design of the mind or will, tho the
purpose or design take not effect."[30]

By comparison, the clause relating to levying war seemed
to all the commentators quite specific and to leave much less
room for judicial interpretation or legislative embellishment.
According to Coke, "a compassing or conspiracy to levy war
is no treason, for there must be a levying of war in facto."
There must be an "open act . . . manifestly proved." Armed
assembly alone is not necessarily enough; nor is the bearing
of arms in a warlike manner prima facie evidence of treason.
As Blackstone understood the law, "a tumult with a view to
pull down a particular house, or lay open a particular enclosure, amounts at most to a riot; this being no general defiance
of public government."[31]

Evidence of treasonous intent seemed to all the commentators a minimal necessity for proving treason by levying war.
According to Foster, if an armed mob gathered to revenge
some private quarrel, that was no treason. Hale agreed that
the "assembling of many rioters in great numbers to do unlawful acts . . . may make a great riot, yet doth not always
amount to a levying of war." "There may be several riots of a
great and notorious nature, which yet amount not to high
treason." The law required evidence of an intention to de-
throne the king, to reform religion, to alter the laws, to remove high government officials, or to redress some other
grievances against the state by armed force in order to define
an armed assemblage as treason. The mob need not actually
wage war, it need not even commit any specific act of violence,
but it must be gathered in a warlike manner for a demonstrably treasonous purpose to be prosecuted under this clause.[32]

Such interpretations of the English law of treason are significant for several reasons. They represent the point from

[30] Foster, *Report of Some Proceedings*, p. 195; Hale, *Pleas of the Crown*, p. 106.

[31] Coke, *Third Part of the Institutes*, 4th ed., pp. 9, 12; Blackstone, *Commentaries*, 4:82.

[32] Foster, *Report of Some Proceedings*, p. 208; Hale, *Pleas of the Crown*, pp. 130, 135.

which delegates to the Constitutional Convention apparently *believed* that they were embarking on new law. In underestimating the chaos of English treason law, the commentators were thus actually helping to create law to the extent that their analyses became the basis for judicial and legislative understandings of treason's history and the dictates of precedent. The commentaries helped Americans—delegates to the Constitutional Convention and subsequent generations of lawyers and judges—define the limits of what could conceivably be treason. They played an important role in charting the possible meanings of critical concepts such as "levying war" and "overt act." And they literally gave Americans a tradition of the rule of law by which to measure their own progress or decline.

The English commentators did not, however, help Americans resolve the lingering problems that plagued English enforcement of treason law in the courts. Indeed, by minimizing the enduring problems of political intrusion, lack of clarity, and discordant precedents, the commentators obscured reality and thus misguided the Founding Fathers into institutionalizing, in Article III, Section 3, some of the limitations of English treason law. They contributed to Americans' well-intentioned but ignorant decision to try to freeze an English treason law that, with several significant alterations, appeared to them to be functioning quite well. Hale, Coke, Foster, and Blackstone played a role in ensuring that Americans would have to sort out in the courts some of the very problems that appeared, from a reading of the commentaries, to be already resolved in the language adopted for the Constitution from the treason statute of 25 Edward III. So there was a much greater interplay between the theory and reality of English treason law as it affected the development of American law than either the traditionalists or revisionists among legal historians have recognized.

If American practice, rather than either the theory or reality of English treason law, is used as the measure of change or continuity, there are good reasons for understanding the Constitution's drafters as *intending* to narrow the scope of the crime. Open-ended colonial definitions—ex post facto legislative, judicial, and executive pronouncements tailored specifically to cover particular individuals or events—had sufficed during the seventeenth century to hang convicted traitors for everything from cutting down tobacco plants to verbally questioning authorities. The Continental Congress made no effort to narrow the scope of the crime, define its terms, or provide procedural protections for individuals. Instead, Congress left details to the states, deciding only that residents "who shall levy war against any of the said colonies within the same, or be adherent to the king of Great Britain, or others the enemies of the said colonies, or any of them, within the same, giving to him or them aid and comfort, are guilty of treason against such colony." [33]

As a consequence of expansive legislative definitions and judicial constructions, treason charges became one outlet for wartime vengeance. Trials such as that of Philadelphia Quaker Abraham Carlisle reflected the blood lust endemic to the Revolutionary scene and the utility of treason trials for exacting judicial revenge. Carlisle was an elderly, prosperous carpenter who collaborated with the British during their occupation of Philadelphia. As a civilian employee of the Crown, his job was to check and distribute passes to those entering and leaving the city. He was also among those responsible for searching wagons for contraband and prohibited items in an attempt to keep salt and other valued commodities from rebel hands.

Numerous citizens testified during the trial that Carlisle had exercised his authority with gentility, compassion, and fairness. No witness saw Carlisle bear arms against his countrymen or commit any specific warlike act. Nonetheless, treason charges in the indictment were based both on levying war

[33] "Culpeper's Report on Virginia in 1683," *Virginia Magazine of History and Biography* 3 (1896):225–38; John Smith, *A True Relation of Such Occurrences and Accidents of Noate as Hath Hapned in Virginia* (London, 1608), in Philip L. Barbour, ed., *The Complete Works of Captain John Smith*, 3 vols. (Chapel Hill, 1986), 1:41; Worthington Chauncey Ford et al., eds., *Journals of the Continental Congress, 1774–1789*, 34 vols. (Washington, D.C., 1904–37), 5:475.

and adherence to the enemy. Carlisle did, according to the indictment, "with force and arms . . . falsely and treacherously . . . take a commission or commissions from General Sir William Howe." "Being armed and arrayed in a hostile manner," the indictment charged, Carlisle "with force and arms did falsely and traitorously assemble and join himself against this Commonwealth."[34]

Carlisle's attorneys argued that the indictment identified no specific act of levying war; and all evidence presented at the trial supported the defendant's claim that he was a Quaker pacifist, that he had no weapons, and that he had never intended to wage war against anyone. The prosecution produced neither a written commission of the sort mentioned in the indictment nor a witness to the existence of such a commission. So defense lawyers had a client charged with treason who had never raised or contemplated raising a weapon against the state, and who had never accepted a military commission from the enemy. It was no crime, and certainly not treason, the defense argued, for "a conquered city to join the conquerors." According to the defense lawyers' understandings of Foster, Blackstone, and Hale, the indictment would be thrown out of an English court for lack of a clearly defined overt act, because the defendant had never conspired or actually levied war, and because his adherence to the enemy had come at a time when he was not enjoying the protection of the state.[35]

At the time of Carlisle's trial in 1778, Pennsylvania's treason law was fairly open ended. Accepting a commission from the king of Great Britain, levying war against the state, and assisting enemies of the state were all acts of high treason during a period when the citizenry was profoundly divided in a bloody civil war. Procedural protections for the accused were minimal or nonexistent, at least as they were defined by legis-

[34] *Pennsylvania Archives*, 1st ser., 12 vols. (Philadelphia, 1852–56), 7:44–58; Alexander James Dallas, reporter, *Reports of Cases Ruled and Adjudged in the Courts of Pennsylvania, before and since the Revolution* (Philadelphia, 1790), pp. 35–36.

[35] *Pennsylvania Archives*, 1st ser., 7:50; Dallas, *Reports*, p. 36.

lation. Defense lawyers were forced to rely on English precedents, as described by English jurists, in phrasing their
arguments to a judge and jury deeply hostile toward most
things British and to "traitors" (that is, nonjurors, pacifists,
and overt loyalists). Indeed, attorney James Wilson was vic-
timized by a patriot mob shortly after the Carlisle trial at least
in part for his role in defending such enemies of the cause.[36]

Not surprisingly, then, the chief judge in the Carlisle trial
ruled against the defense on every point. He instructed the
jury that in lieu of specific evidence to the existence of a military commission, testimony to behavior consistent with having
accepted a commission could be accepted as sufficient proof
of that charge. He ruled also that "assembling, joining and
arraying himself with the forces of the enemy, is a sufficient
overt act of levying war," presumably even when there is neither evidence of a defendant's intention to wage war against
his fellow citizens nor any testimony that places him at the
scene of a battle or in a military posture. The jury found sufficient evidence of treason under the court's explanation of
the law, and Carlisle was accordingly convicted and hanged.[37]

---

[36] Four years later the list would be expanded to include any attempt to
erect a new government within the state or even publishing a notice calling
for the establishment of an independent state within the existing boundaries of Pennsylvania (Dallas, *Reports*, p. 37n). On James Wilson and the
Fort Wilson riot, see John K. Alexander, "The Fort Wilson Incident of
1779: A Case-Study of the Revolutionary Crowd," *William and Mary Quarterly*, 3d ser. 31 (1974):589–612; Geoffrey Seed, *James Wilson* (New York,
1978), app. B, pp. 186–87 ("The Treason Trials"); Charles Page Smith,
James Wilson: Founding Father, 1742–1798 (Chapel Hill, 1956), pp. 119–23;
William Henry Smith, ed., *The St. Clair Papers*, 2 vols. (Cincinnati, 1882), 1:
488–89n; Lyman H. Butterfield, ed., *Letters of Benjamin Rush*, 2 vols.
(Princeton, 1951), 1:240–41; and William B. Reed, *Life and Correspondence
of Joseph Reed*, 2 vols. (Philadelphia, 1847), 2:149–54, 423–28. See also, John
M. Coleman, "The Treason of Ralph Morden and Robert Land," *Pennsylva-
nia Magazine of History and Biography* 79 (1955):439–51.

[37] *Pennsylvania Archives*, 1st ser., 7:44–58. The verdict was a controversial
one and numerous pleas and petitions were forwarded to the executive and
council in Carlisle's behalf, but in vain (see Dallas, *Reports*, pp. 35–38; the
quotation is from p. 38). An incomplete bibliography of Revolutionary era
treason trials is appended to Chapin, "Origins of the American Law of Trea-

Revolutionary era trials such as Carlisle's help mark the law of treason at an extraordinary transitional moment in its history and assist in charting the nature and direction of development. Equally important, such cases provide indirect evidence of the opinions and intentions of those, such as defense attorneys James Wilson and William Lewis, who would later be instrumental in defining the national law of treason. Of course, as is the case for the entire Constitution, direct evidence of the Framers' understandings of the treason clause is revealing and significant, but more tantalizing than definitive. We must try to tease as much information as possible from a variety of imperfect sources—shorthand notes of deliberations, anonymous newspaper essays, unverifiable reminiscences, opinions circulated for public consumption and intended to affect a political outcome, and secondhand reports, in addition to a scattering of attributable private writings.

From what we can know about the Constitutional Convention itself, though, it appears that delegates resolved whatever controversy surfaced on the subject of treason quickly and, for the most part, amicably. The most significant divisions were between those who favored enhanced authority for the government to defend itself and those who sought greater protections for individuals against the state. In discussions of the first draft of the treason clause, James Madison thought unwise the Constitution's bar against legislative redefinition of the crime. He "did not see why more latitude might not be left to the legislature," and he thought the proposed definition of treason "too narrow." Like Madison, Charles Pinckney displayed no fear of legislative expansion and abuse of treason law. Adopting the same position and some of the same

---

son," pp. 20–21. The first two volumes of *Dallas* and several volumes of *Pennsylvania Archives* have information on a number of treason cases. See also, Henry J. Young, "Treason and Its Punishment in Revolutionary Pennsylvania," *Pennsylvania Magazine of History and Biography* 90 (1966):287–313; G. S. Rowe, "Outlawry in Pennsylvania, 1782–1788, and the Achievement of an Independent State Judiciary," *American Journal of Legal History* 20 (1976):227–44; and Steven Boyd, "Political Choice, Political Justice: The Case of the Pennsylvania Loyalists," in Michal R. Belknap, ed., *American Political Trials* (Westport, Conn., 1981), pp. 43–56.

language of an amendment to the Articles of Confederation proposed one year earlier, Pinckney would have granted the Senate and House of Representatives "the exclusive power of declaring what shall be treason."[38]

On the other side of this issue were delegates who harbored much greater fears than Madison or Pinckney of potential governmental tyranny through abuse of treason law. Luther Martin was perhaps the most extreme in reminding his colleagues of their recent careers as traitors to the British empire. "By the *principles* of the American Revolution," Martin proclaimed, "*arbitrary power may* and *ought* to be resisted even by *arms* if necessary." In the event of federal oppression, the people might be called upon by their states to levy war against the national government, thus putting them in the untenable position of choosing between being prosecuted for treason against the state or as traitors to the nation. He proposed, therefore, that an exception for such contingencies be added as an amendment to the treason clause. Martin later recalled that his proposal was defeated because it was "too much opposed to the great object of many of the leading members of the convention, which was by all means to leave the states at the mercy of the general government, since they could not succeed in their immediate and entire abolition."[39]

Unlike Madison and Pinckney, on the one hand, who harbored no evident fears of the federal government's capacity for oppressing its citizens through treason trials, and unlike Martin on the other hand, who anticipated the necessity for

[38] Max Farrand, ed., *The Records of the Federal Convention of 1787*, 3 vols. (New Haven, 1911), 2:345–50; Merrill Jensen, John P. Kaminski, and Gaspare J. Saladino, eds., *The Documentary History of the Ratification of the Constitution*, 10 vols. to date (Madison, 1976-), 1:166–67, 247. Both the Pinckney report and the New Jersey Plan had originally left it to Congress to define the law of treason, so the debate over the treason clause apparently preceded discussions recorded in surviving notes. See Farrand, ed., *Records*, 2:136; 3:614 n.37.

[39] Jensen, Kaminski, and Saladino, eds., *Documentary History*, 16:10–11; Herbert J. Storing, ed., *The Complete Anti-Federalist*, 7 vols. (Chicago, 1981), 2:58–60. Luther Martin recounted his role in regard to the treason clause in a speech to the Maryland Assembly on Nov. 29, 1787. No other account of Martin's amendment has to date been located.

all-out war against federal tyranny, Benjamin Franklin expressed a desire to enhance procedural protections for individuals against judicial abuse of the treason clause. Franklin supported an amendment to the original draft that inserted after the words "two witnesses," the clarifying limitation "to the same overt act." "Prosecutions for treason were generally virulent," Franklin advised, "and perjury too easily made use of against innocence." James Wilson, who apparently wrote the original draft of the treason clause, spoke in opposition to Franklin, arguing that such a limitation weighed too heavily against the interests of the government. "Treason may sometimes be practiced in such a manner," Wilson averred, "as to render proof extremely difficult." On these points, the Convention supported Franklin and voted against the wishes of Pinckney, Madison, and Wilson, and there was apparently little additional substantive discussion of Article III, Section 3.[40]

The Antifederalists' assault on the treason clause was neither so virulent nor so widespread as dissent from other portions of the proposed Constitution. But a number of critics did find fault with the treason provisions of the document, and, as was the case throughout the ratification debate, there was no systematic, shared ground among opponents of the treason clause. Opposition came both from those who saw the Constitution as precluding the possibility for state prosecutions of the same crime and those who imagined the potential for both state and federal prosecution of the same individual on the same charge, for the same act, but under two radically different sets of laws and procedures.[41]

---

[40] Farrand, ed., *Records*, 2:345–50. The various drafts of the treason clause, reflecting the substantive amendments and stylistic changes are to be found in Jensen, Kaminski, and Saladino, eds., *Documentary History*, 1:264, 270, 276, 294, 314–15. For attribution of the treason clause to Wilson, see Seed, *James Wilson*, p. 116; Smith, *James Wilson*, p. 123; James Willard Hurst, "Treason in the United States," *Harvard Law Review* 58 (1944):404n; and idem, *Law of Treason*, p. 169n.

[41] Storing, ed., *Complete Anti-Federalist*, 3:190, 193n. Both Chapin and Hurst failed to identify opposition to the treason clause either within or without the Constitutional Convention and assumed that there was none. Neither author had the benefit of Storing's *Complete Anti-Federalist* or the

Perhaps most frequently expressed were Antifederalist fears of executive abuse through the pardoning power. George Mason objected that under the proposed federal government the president had "the unrestrained power of granting pardon for treason, which may be sometimes exercised to screen from punishment those whom he had secretly instigated to commit the crime, and thereby prevent a discovery of his own guilt." Luther Martin thought that "no treason was so likely to take place as that in which the President himself might be engaged" and that in the event he and "the creatures of his ambition" were defeated in their attempt to usurp authority, exercise of the pardoning power could cover up the details and thus hinder or prevent impeachment proceedings.[42]

Other opponents of the Constitution specifically raised the question of defining the terms of the treason clause, and their statements indicate that the meanings of "overt act" and "levying war" were not entirely clear or settled once and for all in the eyes of all contemporaries. Most seriously, some believed,

---

volumes of Jensen, Kaminski, and Saladino's *Documentary History* to assist them. Publication of subsequent volumes of *Documentary History* may reveal additional information, but most likely they will add examples with perhaps nuanced differences from the speeches and essays already identified. Volume 3, on the state ratification debates in Delaware, New Jersey, Georgia, and Connecticut, contains no references to treason in its index. Volume 2 shows that the treason clause was a minor issue in Pennsylvania, and other sources document the concerns of several Virginians and Marylanders about the treason clause. It is unfortunate that these sources were not available to Chapin and Hurst because each builds his argument on a false sense of absolute consensus and shared understanding of the treason clause by Americans in 1787, and each is left to hypothesize the intentions of the drafters and the range of understandings and disagreements about the treason clause at that time. The significance of the additional information provided by the documentary volumes should not be overstated, though; debate over the treason clause, although real and essential for understanding contemporary views of the clause, does *not* reveal the treason clause to have been a major or central focus of discussion and debate over the Constitution.

[42] Storing, ed., *Complete Anti-Federalist*, 2:12; Jensen, Kaminski, and Saladino, eds., *Documentary History*, 13:349.

Article III, Section 3 left open the possibility that mere words could be prosecuted as treason under the Constitution. "A Slave," whose reservations about the Constitution were published in the *New York Journal,* feared "the severest and most intolerable of all curses—that of being enslaved by men of our own creation (as to power) and for whose aggrandizement many of us have fought and bled. Men who will, perhaps, construe our most innocent remarks and animadversions on their conduct, *treason,* misprision of treason, or high crimes and misdemeanors, which may be punished with unusual severity; we shall then be in a most forlorn and hopeless situation indeed." Clearly, this and like-minded critics did not see the Constitution's treason clause as necessarily the sort of great leap forward from English law that has impressed subsequent commentators and historians. He found less precision in the language and fewer protections for individuals than others detected in the clause, and he predicted more uncertainty and potentially graver consequences from imprecise language than supporters of the Constitution allowed.[43]

Apparently, none of the Constitution's supporters engaged the argument that mere words or a wide range of unspecified and undefined events could qualify as overt acts of levying war under Article III, Section 3. Rather than debating such concerns, Federalists generally took the high road of testifying to the brilliance of the treason clause in its balancing of individual rights with necessary protections for the government. Without fail, when Federalists mentioned the treason clause, they cited it as a prime example of the document's embodiment of the very sort of safeguards that opponents found lacking throughout.

Article III, Section 3 seemed to one member of the Pennsylvania ratifying convention to contribute toward laying a "solid foundation" of protections for individuals that precluded the necessity of a bill of rights. Benjamin Rush emphasized the Constitution's humanitarian regard for innocent relatives of

[43] Jensen, Kaminski, and Saladino, eds., *Documentary History,* 13:482–83; from the *New York Journal,* Oct. 25, 1787. For a similar objection, see "A Democratic Federalist," *Pennsylvania Herald,* Oct. 17, 1787, Storing, ed., *Complete Anti-Federalist,* 3:59.

traitors in its elimination of the harsh English penalties of corruption of blood and forfeiture of property for those convicted of treason. James Wilson, in the public forum of the Pennsylvania convention, was more impressed with the final version of the treason clause than he had originally been in the Constitutional Convention's private debates. As the author of the original draft of this clause, Wilson had opposed changes that enhanced procedural protections for those accused of the crime. The fact that the clause was amended over his objections did not prevent Wilson from proudly seeing the treason clause as "the first instance in which it has not been left to the legislature to extend the crime and punishment of treason so far as they thought proper." For the purposes of public debate, or perhaps because he had changed his mind, James Madison also found much more to praise in the treason clause than he had in the Constitutional Convention. Madison's *Federalist* No. 43 reflected the entire litany of praise and made a comprehensive case for the clause:

> As treason may be committed against the United States, the authority of the United States ought to be enabled to punish it. But as new-fangled and artificial treasons have been the great engines by which violent factions, the natural offspring of free governments, have usually wrecked their alternate malignity on each other, the Convention have with great judgment opposed a barrier to this peculiar danger by inserting a constitutional definition of the crime, fixing the proof necessary for conviction of it, and restraining the Congress, even in punishing it, from extending the consequences of guilt beyond the person of its author.[44]

Thus, it seemed to Federalists that the Constitution incorporated the best protections against legislative and judicial abuse of the treason charge that could be found in any country known to them in the present or in the past, and they discounted Antifederalist fears of presidential abuse through

[44] Jensen, Kaminski, and Saladino, eds., *Documentary History*, 2:430, 457, 483. See also ibid., 1:458, 493, 515–16, 524–25; *Federalist* No. 43 [James Madison], in Clinton Rossiter, ed., *The Federalist Papers* (New York, 1961), pp. 271–80.

the pardoning power. Unlike some other Virginians, "Marcus" thought that "the probability of the President of the United States committing an act of treason against his country is very slight; he is so well guarded by the other powers of government, and the natural strength of the people at large must be so weighty, that in my opinion it is the most chimerical apprehension that can be entertained." And, in any event, the machinery existed within the Constitution to handle even such unlikely contingencies as a traitorous president. It seemed to Alexander Hamilton, in *Federalist* No. 73, that the president's ability to pardon traitors could serve a very useful function in times of political unrest, and was, therefore, a necessary executive power. "In seasons of insurrection or rebellion," Hamilton reasoned, "there are often critical moments, when a well timed offer of pardon to the insurgents or rebels may restore the tranquility of the commonwealth; and which, if suffered to pass unimproved, it may never be possible afterwards to recall." Under the proposed Constitution, its friends argued, Americans were just as safe from executive abuse of the treason charge as they were from legislative and judicial tyranny; and in every case, they were better protected than they had ever been as subjects of the British Crown.[45]

Building upon the historical foundation provided by the English commentators, drafters of the Constitution had every reason to see their treason clause as an important stride, but not a leap, forward in Anglo-American law. Borrowing, as they did, the very language of the treason statute of 25 Edward III, they could view their labors as salvaging the best of the old while improving upon it. Furthermore, they could reasonably expect that American judges would abide by the limitations upon the language of the law identified by the most recent and most respected English commentators.

It could appear to the Federalists that they had expunged any equivalent of the ever-expandable and corruptible notion of compassing or imagining the king's death. The very act of establishing a written constitution seemingly eliminated the

---

[45] "Marcus," *Norfolk and Portsmouth Journal*, Mar. 5, 1788, Jensen, Kaminski, and Saladino, eds., *Documentary History*, 16:322–24; *Federalist* No. 74 [Alexander Hamilton], in Rossiter, ed., *Federalist Papers*, pp. 447–49.

threat of legislative and executive tyranny such as that suffered by the English under the Tudors. The potential for any
semblance of the judicial tyranny through constructive treason perpetrated by Stuart judges was to all appearances minimized by the clarity of the treason clause and its narrow
definition of the crime as limited only to levying war against
the government or adhering to its enemies. Finally, the drafters could proudly point to the Constitution's requirement of
two witnesses to the same overt act as a procedural safeguard
unprecedented in Anglo-American history, and one virtually
foolproof against conspiracies among the government's three
branches against the rights of citizens.

Federalists and Antifederalists alike were, of course, working in the realm of theory when they debated the potential
impact of the Constitution on American law. The realities of
the treason clause would be worked out on the battlefield and
in the courts, in those moments of intense political turmoil
that the Founders most feared. Whether the new federal government could respond effectively to internal threats was
partly a question of power and would be determined by force
of arms, but it was also a question of law and politics whether
the government would respect procedural safeguards for individual rights and the "narrow" definition of treason embodied in Article III, Section 3. And since there was some disagreement among Federalists and Antifederalists about the
precise meanings of some key concepts and terms of the treason clause, it should not be surprising that the debates over
definitions shifted from the legislators who drafted or opposed the clause to executive branch personnel responsible
for enforcing it and eventually to the courts. Nor should it
astound us that within the context of individual cases lawyers
and judges would try to exploit ambiguities in the treason
clause for their own ends, among which competing ideas of
justice, responsibility to clients, a historical sense of law, and
political pressures from sources external to the courtroom
would all play significant roles.

James Wilson was a key transitional figure between the theoretical world of drafting and debating the treason clause and
the real world of enforcing it. Despite Wilson's defeat in the
Constitutional Convention on amending the two-witness rule,

it seems that he was most directly responsible for the remainder of the language and content of the treason clause. As a member of the committee of detail, Wilson apparently drafted the original version of Article III, Section 3 himself. Fortunately, we have the indirect evidence of Wilson's law lectures delivered at the University of Pennsylvania between 1790 and 1792, from which we can discern his views on treason. Wilson's lectures are significant here not just for the light they shed on his role in drafting the clause but because as an associate justice of the Supreme Court shortly thereafter he played a critical role in defining the Whiskey Rebellion riots of 1794 as the first mass treasonous offenses against the federal government under the Constitution. Thus, we do have some evidence bearing on the relationship between the drafters' intentions and subsequent applications of the law.

Reflecting his reliance on the British commentators rather than a close study of English case law, Wilson found much to admire in the evolution of the law of treason from the fourteenth century. As Wilson misunderstood the history of that process, the treason statute of 25 Edward III had since served England "like a rock, strong by nature, and fortified, as successive occasions required, by the able and honest assistance of art." According to Wilson, who knew as much about British law as any American of his day, the English treason statute "has been impregnable by all the rude and boisterous assaults which have been made upon it at different quarters by ministers and by judges; and as an object of national security, as well as of national pride, it may well be styled the legal Gibraltar of England."[46]

In the eyes of its creator, the treason clause of the Constitution not only built on this solid English foundation, but improved it. Americans, like the British, were protected from the "judicial storms" associated with constructive treason. By eliminating the "monarchical parts" and securing protection from "legislative tempests," Wilson believed that the Founding Fathers had repaired the only structural defects in the English law. To Wilson, the terms of Article III, Section 3 were

---

[46] James DeWitt Andrews, ed., *The Works of James Wilson*, 2 vols. (Chicago, 1896), 2:413.

clear, and he drew his definitions from the commentaries of Hale, Coke, Foster, and Blackstone, amending them as appropriate for a republican nation lacking a monarch. Substituting "obedience" for "allegiance," Wilson paraphrased Blackstone's answer to the rhetorical question, "By whom may war be levied?" "Of obedience the antipode is treason," Wilson argued, and all who owe the United States obedience are capable of committing treason against it. All who receive its protection, Wilson reasoned, again relying on Blackstone, owe the nation obedience.[47]

Defining "levying war" seemed to Wilson a more complex problem, but again one that already had been resolved in English law as reported by the commentators. When people who owe the United States obedience are "arrayed in a warlike manner," to quote the normal form of an English indictment, this component of levying war exists. Borrowing directly from Hale, Wilson defined such an array "as where people are assembled in great numbers, armed with offensive weapons, or weapons of war, if they march thus armed in a body, if they have chosen commanders or officers, if they march with banners displayed, or with drums or trumpets: whether the greatness of their numbers and their continuance together doing these acts may not amount to being arrayed in a warlike manner, deserves consideration. If they have no military arms, nor march or continue together in the posture of war; they may be great rioters, but their conduct does not always amount to a levying of war."[48]

The *illusion* of precision here did not entirely escape Wilson, any more than it had escaped Foster, upon whom he relied for a clarification of the fuzzy line between riot and insurrection, between disturbing the peace and treason. According to Foster and Wilson, levying war to redress a private wrong, in response to a private quarrel, or to take revenge against particular persons could not be construed as treason under either English or American law. A warlike array that addressed a private claim or that aimed to rescue particular persons from incarceration did not seem treasonous to these

[47] Ibid., pp. 414–17.

[48] Ibid., p. 418.

legal scholars. On the other hand, "insurrections in order to throw down all inclosures, to open all prisons, to enhance the price of all labor, to expel foreigners in general, or those from any single nation living under the protection of government, to alter the established law, or to render it ineffectual—insurrections to accomplish these ends, by numbers and an open and armed force, are a levying of war against the United States."[49]

In the end, though, and unlike most modern legal historians, Wilson had to admit that "the line of division between this species of treason and an aggravated riot is sometimes very fine and difficult to be distinguished." He apparently recognized that one man's "warlike array" could be another's spontaneous gathering. What about a case where the "particular individual" who is a victim of mob violence is an officer of the government? Clearly, an armed array designed to "alter the established law" could be defined as treason, but what about such cases as those disagreed about by the legal historians Chapin and Hurst, where one particular law is under attack, but obedience to the remaining body of established law is not challenged? Is assemblage in "warlike array" necessary or sufficient evidence of treason; or, might mere words—spoken, written, or published—suffice as evidence not just of intent but as an "overt act" under the Constitution's definition? Wilson does not say, and thus the intentions of the drafters in these regards, if any of these questions even occurred to them, are not accessible to us. They all are, however, questions that came before federal courts during their first century. And where the answers seemed unclear, the courts did not always take Wilson's advice that "in such instances, it is safest and most prudent to consider the case in question as lying on the side of the inferior crime."[50]

[49] Ibid., pp. 419–20.

[50] Ibid., p. 420. Wilson apparently recognized that the treason clause did a better job of protecting American citizens from what he termed "legislative tempests" than from judicial constructions of treason, but he also believed that Americans were far better protected from odious judicial constructions of treason than the British were during the seventeenth century. See "Charge of the Hon. James Wilson, esq., Judge of the Federal

The Whiskey Rebellion (1794) was the first large-scale resistance to a law of the United States government under the Constitution and resulted in the largest armed conflict between the federal government and its citizens before the Civil War.[51] The resulting treason trials represented the first true test of the "levying war" component of the treason clause and thus give the earliest clues to the operative meanings of Article III, Section 3. At issue in the trials was (1) the strictness with which procedural protections for the accused would be respected by the courts; (2) the meaning of "overt act"; (3) definition of the line between riot and rebellion; and (4) the authority of the courts to engage in constructing treasons.

Most instructive in these regards are the trials of Philip Vigol and John Mitchell, the two "rebels" convicted of treason and eventually pardoned by President Washington. In each case the prosecution had fallen short of conforming to the procedures outlined by Congress for trying capital crimes. The sheriff had returned a greater number of jurors than the law authorized; the government had failed to provide at least three days in advance of the trial a copy of the caption of the indictment, which included specific information about the grand jury, the court, and the judges, and which might become the basis for challenges to the court's jurisdiction or that might reveal some technical flaw in the process; and the lists of prospective jurors neglected to include addresses and occupations of the panel.

Although the judges acknowledged the validity of defense attorneys' contentions in all regards, Judge Richard Peters found them irrelevant to the business of the court. "All the arguments founded on the inconveniences to the defendants, if in this case particularly any such exist (of which I much doubt)," Peters ruled, "weigh lightly when set against the delays and obstructions which the objection would throw in the

---

Court for the District of Pennsylvania, to the Grand Jury of said Court, Delivered April 12, 1790," [Carey's] *American Museum* 7 (1790):app. 2, Public Papers, p. 40.

[51] Thomas P. Slaughter, *The Whiskey Rebellion: Frontier Epilogue to the American Revolution* (New York, 1986).

way of the execution of the laws of the nation." Postponement for the requisite three days provided for notification of the defendants seemed to the judges a fair rectification of the mistakes.[52]

In light of the highly charged political atmosphere in which the court deliberated, it is not surprising if the judges displayed, on balance, a stronger sympathy for the prosecution. The government felt vulnerable to both domestic violence and international intrigue; and the judiciary was being asked to play an important, perhaps a decisive, role in demonstrating the new nation's strength for a large audience of dissident Americans and a hostile diplomatic corps. In the era of the French Revolution, the Washington administration had reasonable grounds to fear for the very lives of government officials and to wonder whether the administrative and judicial branches established by the Constitution could cooperate in moments of severe stress. But the army had failed to capture any of the "leaders" of the "rebellion" and had left Judges Peters and William Paterson with about twenty obscure characters in custody to shoulder the blame for 7,000 "rebels" and to justify the tremendous expense of marching an army of 12,950 men, an array larger than the average daily troop strength of the Continental forces in the American Revolution, to suppress this "treasonous" assault on federal tax collectors in western Pennsylvania.

Observers of the trials from among Philadelphia's legal profession theorized that Judge Peters authorized the detention of so many unlikely villains from political rather than strictly legal motives. They knew in advance, as Peters must have, that the overwhelming proportion could not be convicted no matter how sympathetically the judges responded to the prosecution, and in fact few were ever brought to trial. But the times demanded scapegoats, and the army, the administration, and the eastern citizenry required symbols of their victory over enemies of the state.[53]

Ultimately, all but Vigol and Mitchell were acquitted. Juries freed defendants for a variety of reasons, including mistaken

[52] 2 *United States Reports* (2 *Dallas*) 341 (1795).

[53] Slaughter, *Whiskey Rebellion*, pp. 219–20.

identity, lack of the requisite two witnesses to an overt act of any imaginable kind, and contradictory testimony. Lawyers witnessing the trials of Vigol and Mitchell reported that the verdicts were inescapable given the judges' behavior; clearly, the judges had decided that these were going to be the government's best cases and, if they were to achieve at least token convictions, it would have to be here. Paterson, who was an associate justice of the Supreme Court, instructed Vigol's jury that "with respect to the evidence, the current runs one way; it harmonizes in all its parts." Likewise, the jury was told, "with respect to [Vigol's] intention . . . there is not, unhappily, the slightest possibility of doubt. . . . The crime is proved." Dutifully, the jury agreed, and the judiciary was spared the embarrassment of total failure. The government had its examples, and the president an occasion for a magnanimous gesture, when he pardoned the two convicted traitors. Just as Hamilton had anticipated in his defense of the pardoning power in *Federalist* No. 73, a moment had arisen when political exigencies seemed best served by a combination of decisive action—arrest, trial, conviction, and sentencing—accompanied by the merciful hand of the president.[54]

The treason trials were more, though, than acts in a political theater. Enduring, or at least evolving, law was being made in regard to key elements of the Constitution's treason clause. Defining "levying war" was of particular concern and the arguments of respective counsel demonstrate that there was no universal or settled understanding of the term; the outcome of the cases reveals that the definition accepted by the court was much broader and less protective of individuals than is generally assumed. The prosecution in *U.S.* v. *Mitchell* contended that the term had the same meaning in the Constitution as in English law, a point that the defense did not contest. "What constitutes a levying of war," argued William Rawle, "must be the same in a technical interpretation, whether committed under a republican or a regal form of government, since either institution may be assailed and subverted by the same means." He trotted out Hale, Foster, and Blackstone, among other commentators, and referred to particular En-

[54] 2 *United States Reports* (2 Dallas) 346–47 (1795).

glish state trials in framing the broadest conceivable definition. "By the English authorities," Rawle contended, "it is uniformly and clearly declared, that raising a body of men to obtain by intimidation or violence the repeal of a law, or to oppose and prevent by force or terror the execution of the law, is an act of levying war." An assembly "armed and arrayed in a warlike manner" was enough to constitute treason, according to Foster. Although conspiracy is not alone enough, Rawle allowed, if any of the conspirators commit an overt act of levying war, all the conspirators, regardless of their actual presence, or even their support of the act, are equally complicit. Likewise, joining the array after the plot has been hatched is nonetheless treasonous, "for in treason all are principals."[55]

Mitchell's attorney acknowledged that an attempt to compel Congress to repeal a statute by violence or intimidation is an act of treason. Defense counsel either did not notice or did not care to engage frontally Rawle's significant embellishment of Blackstone's definition in his substitution of resistance to "a law" for the English commentator's more general requisite resistance to "law." The significance here, of course, is that it was not at all clear from the English commentators, including Foster and Blackstone, whether resistance to a single law, in a manner that did not pose a violent threat to the enacting body, constituted treason. On the general question, though, the defense did contest whether "resisting execution of a law, or attempting to coerce an officer into the resignation of a commission" amounted to treason. Here the defense was attempting to make the same broad distinction that Hale, Foster, and Blackstone made between general opposition to law (which was treason) and a specific act against a specific law (which was not). "Let it be granted," the defense argued, "that an insurrection for an avowed purpose of suppressing all the excise offices in the United States, may be construed into an act of levying war against the government . . . it does not follow that an attempt to oblige one officer to resign, or to suppress all the offices in one [tax collecting] district, will be a crime of the same denomination."[56]

[55] Ibid., p. 349.

[56] Ibid., p. 351.

Likewise, the defense and prosecution offered very different interpretations of "overt act"; and it seemed to the defense that the prosecution's more open-ended definition left room for constructive, or interpretive, treasons, which are "the dread and scourge of any nation that allows them." It could be proved by testimony of the requisite two witnesses that Mitchell attended a public meeting before the attack and burning of the tax supervisor's house. Only one witness placed Mitchell at the house-burning, "alone, at a distance of about thirty or forty rods; and it is not recollected whether he had a gun." Another witness vaguely recollected seeing him on the road to the house with the mob. The prosecution sought to define the overt act constructively to include both events—the meeting at which Mitchell, among many others, was heard to express opinions of a "treasonous" design and the burning of excise inspector Neville's house—as part of one overt act that also included a subsequent gathering at a later date, which, despite some heavy drinking and violent posturing by a legion of hostile rural folk, broke up without incident.[57]

Justice Paterson, in his charge to Mitchell's jury, accepted the prosecution's argument in toto. He instructed jurors that the object of the riots was clearly "of a general and public nature," and was, therefore, treason. Paterson drew on Foster's distinction between public and private grievances to redefine virtually all acts of public violence aimed at specific laws, regulations, or officials as treasonous. And he seemed to leave room within his definition of treason even for riots aimed at nongovernmental agencies or individuals. Indeed, Paterson's notion of "levying war" harkened back to the seventeenth century and was as expansive as any pronounced from an Anglo-American bench since the Glorious Revolution:

The first question to be considered is, what was the general object of the insurrection? If its object was to suppress the excise offices and to prevent the execution of an act of Congress, by force and intimidation, the offense in legal estimation is high treason; it is

[57] Ibid., pp. 350, 352.

an usurpation of the authority of government; it is high treason by levying of war. Taking the testimony in a rational and connected point of view, this was the object. It was of a general nature, and of national concern.

Rioters who focused their violence either against the government or in extralegal performance of a normal governmental function, what Paterson termed "usurpation of the authority of government," could ostensibly be prosecuted under the treason clause. This jury charge thus reflected not only the flexibility of Article III, Section 3 for meeting threats perceived by federal officials but also the distance between elite sanction of some urban crowd activity in the pre-Revolutionary years and the fear and intolerance of all mobs by Federalist politicians during the era of the French Revolution.[58]

Having defined "levying war" in a manner that, in Paterson's mind, inescapably described a series of events in western Pennsylvania during the summer of 1794, he next proceeded to explain "overt act" to the jurors in a way that just as surely included Mitchell's role in the rebellion. It seemed to the judge that whichever definition of a general or specific overt act the jury accepted, Mitchell was guilty of treason. If the defendant was present at the Braddock's Field assembly, as four witnesses concurred that he was, that was enough in the judge's mind to convict for treason. It was of no relevance that the armed array gathered there committed no act of violence toward the government, *if* Mitchell's *intention* in attending the assembly was treasonous. Reasoning backwards from this event to the meeting at Couche's Fort, at which multiple witnesses placed Mitchell, the judge found abundant evidence of treasonous intent and saw no reason not to draw connections between the Couche's Fort meeting, the burning of Neville's house, and the Braddock's Field assembly as a divisible, but single, overt act:

He was armed, he was a volunteer, he was a party to the various consultations of the insurgents; and in every scene of the insur-

[58] Ibid., p. 355.

rection, from the assembly at Couche's Fort to the day prescribed for submission to the government, he makes a conspicuous appearance. His attendance, armed, at Bradock's field, would of itself amount to Treason, if his design was treasonable. Upon the whole, whether the conspiracy at Couche's Fort may of itself be deemed Treason; or, the conspiracy there, and the proceedings at Gen. Neville's house, are considered as one act, (which is, perhaps, the true light to view the subject in) the prisoner must be pronounced guilty.[59]

It was of no account to Justice Paterson that the prosecution had failed to produce two witnesses to Mitchell's presence at Neville's house on the day of the only overtly violent act in the scenario, since the "overt act" encompassed all three events, transcended the time and place of any one of them, and could be fulfilled by presence at any one alone. So much for the traditional legal historians' assertion that constructive treason was eliminated from American law by the Constitution. So much for the anachronistic vision of the "narrow" definition of "levying war," the two witness rule, and "overt act" portions of the treason clause. When "overt act" can be defined as broadly as Justice Paterson construed it in *U.S.* v. *Mitchell*, the Constitution's two-witness rule represents no obvious advance over the English statute of 7 William III. If an overt act can be judicially constructed over time and place, the Constitution's language dictating that there must be two witnesses to the same overt act carries no more restrictive weight against the government's case than the English law's requirement that there must be at least two witnesses to the same general act of treason.

The trials of Vigol and Mitchell were not anomalies in the history of American law. The decisions of Judge Peters and Justice Paterson set precedents that guided subsequent jurists in their efforts to interpret the treason clause, and their definitions of "overt act" and "levying war" were particularly influential. Four years later, in 1799, Judge Peters, this time sitting with Associate Justice of the Supreme Court James Iredell, was called upon in *U.S.* v. *John Fries* to preside over a

---

[59] Ibid., p. 356.

major treason case that had striking parallels to the Whiskey Rebellion trials in its issues, judicial rulings, results, and the external political pressures under which the case was tried.

The occasion for Fries's alleged treason was again opposition to a federal tax, this time an internal tax on houses rather than whiskey; and the center of opposition was again Pennsylvania, but this time three eastern rather than four western counties of the state. "Fries's Rebellion," as the government labeled it, was also known locally and in the opposition press as the "Hot Water War," a title intended to ridicule the Adams administration's gross overreaction to what some people saw as, at worst, a humorous if overzealous expression of free speech. Granted, at least one woman had thrown a bucket of hot water from an upstairs window of her house onto a tax man who was trying to assess property values by counting panes. Other housewives (most of them German) had also "treated the invaders of their fire-sides with every species of indignity, resisting . . . the measurement of their windows by all the domestic artillery." Equally uncontested was the fact that tax collectors in Bucks, Montgomery, and Northampton counties had been harrassed, ridiculed, and threatened by men who described themselves as "sons of liberty" and "whiskey boys." Finally, and most seriously, a crowd of about one hundred persons, of which John Fries was the putative leader, did "rescue" about eighteen men from a federal marshal and his deputies. The prisoners were being housed at a tavern overnight en route to Philadelphia for trial on charges stemming from their opposition to the house tax.[60]

No shots were fired; no one was injured; and the prisoners, who apparently did not wish to be rescued, later made their way unescorted to Philadelphia where they surrendered to the law. Nonetheless, President Adams felt compelled to re-

[60] Francis Wharton, *State Trials of the United States during the Administrations of Washington and Adams* (1849; reprint ed., New York, 1970), p. 458n. The number of prisoners rescued at Bethlehem has been variously estimated in the secondary sources listed in note 61 below as three, eighteen, twenty, and twenty-three. The source of the confusion is unclear. There was undoubtedly an ethnic component to the protests, with Germans, many of whom apparently misunderstood the nature of the tax, taking the lead. John Fries himself, however, was of Welsh ancestry.

quest 500 militiamen to put down the "rebellion," at a cost of about $80,000 to the federal government. The troops met no resistance upon their arrival and had little to do save terrorizing the local people, knocking down liberty poles, posting the president's proclamation in German and English, and sweeping up "traitors" to be tried in federal courts. There was some suggestion by those unfriendly to the Adams administration that the subsequent treason trials represented an attempt to suppress political opposition in this Republican stronghold and to justify the cost of persecuting some of the president's political enemies.[61]

In any event, Fries was charged and twice convicted for treason by levying war against the United States.[62] The initial indictment charged Fries with

[61] William W. H. Davis, *The Fries Rebellion, 1798–99* (1899; reprint ed., New York, 1969); Peter Levine, "The Fries Rebellion: Social Violence and the Politics of the New Nation," *Pennsylvania History* 40 (1973):241–58; Jane Shaffer Elsmere, "The Trials of John Fries," *Pennsylvania Magazine of History and Biography* 103 (1979):432–45; Dwight F. Henderson, "Treason, Sedition, and Fries' Rebellion," *American Journal of Legal History* 14 (1970):308–17. In fact, and to the great embarrassment and disbelief of the government, Fries and several other "leaders" of the unrest were Federalists. One contemporary noted that on this issue the two political factions were united in Bucks and Northampton counties: "The *Tories* were opposed to the tax and the *Whigs* to the assessors" (cited in Davis, *Fries Rebellion*, p. 103). It appears that the Alien and Sedition Acts and the window tax were decisive in converting these prosperous eastern Pennsylvania Germans to the Jeffersonian-Republican cause (see Manning J. Dauer, *The Adams Federalists* [Baltimore, 1953], p. 280).

[62] The second trial was necessitated by a successful defense motion for a new trial. Only after the first trial ended, argued defense lawyers, had they been able to secure testimony that one of the jurors had openly and repeatedly declared a prejudice against the accused after he was on the jury. After considering the arguments of defense and prosecution attorneys, Judge Richard Peters found insufficient cause for a new trial, but Justice James Iredell was persuaded and Peters relented. See below and Thomas Carpenter, stenographer, *The Two Trials of John Fries on an Indictment of Treason, together with a Brief Report of the Trials of Several Other Persons, for Treason and Insurrection* (Philadelphia, 1800), app. 2, pp. 11–45. According to Henderson, "Treason, Sedition, and Fries' Rebellion," p. 312, there were eleven treason indictments, forty-four for conspiracy, thirty-two for conspiracy, rescue, and obstruction of process, and one for seditious expression.

not having the fear of God before his eyes, nor weighing the duty of his said allegiance and fidelity, but being moved and seduced by the instigation of the devil, wickedly devising and intending the peace and tranquility of the said United States to disturb, on the seventh day of March [1799] . . . at Bethlehem, in the county of Northampton . . . [where Fries] unlawfully, maliciously and traitorously did compass, imagine and intend to raise and levy war, insurrection and rebellion against the said United States; and to fulfil and bring to effect the said traitorous compassings, imaginations and intentions of him the said John Fries . . . with a great multitude . . . to the number of one hundred . . . and up-wards, armed and arrayed in a warlike manner, that is to say, with guns swords, clubs, staves and other warlike weapons, as well offensive as defensive, being then and there unlawfully, maliciously and traitorously assembled and gathered together, did falsely and traitorously assemble and join themselves together against the said United States.[63]

The language of the charge speaks eloquently to the continuing links between the American law of treason and its English antecedents. The verbiage relating to the fear of God and instigation of the devil is taken directly from ancient English forms of indictment. The adaptation of the antiquated term "compassing" from the eliminated phrase of the treason law of 25 Edward III to new American conditions testifies to more than linguistic connections between English and American treason law; it alerts us to much closer ties between the two systems of law than is obvious from perusal of the Constitution's treason clause.

Initially, in an opening speech that distorted both the past

At the time and since, jurists have drawn on both Fries's first and second trials for their understandings of the law of treason in the early republic. For reasons that will be discussed more thoroughly below, the first trial is actually a better guide to the range of arguments and decisions that would influence subsequent juridical understandings of Article III, Section 3. The arguments are developed more fully in the first trial, there were no defense lawyers in the second trial, and Judge Samuel Chase's behavior in the second trial is seen to be an anomaly, the most clear example of the potential for judicial abuse of treason law on American record.

[63] Carpenter, *Two Trials*, p. 17.

and present of Anglo-American treason law, the chief prosecuting attorney sought to exploit historical connections as a
means of lending credibility, a distinguished English past,
to the treason clause. He described the fourteenth-century
English treason statute as commanding "the veneration and
respect of that nation, almost equal with their great charter";
and he claimed, inaccurately, that the law of 25 Edward III
had never "undergone the least alteration amidst the most
severe scrutinies, and its adoption into the Constitution of the
United States without the least amendment are sufficient en-
comiums to prove its worth."[64]

Defense attorneys (including William Lewis, who, along
with James Wilson, had defended accused Pennsylvania traitors during the Revolution) attempted to seize a glorious
English past for their client and distance themselves from the
most odious precedents in Anglo-American treason law,
thereby correcting the prosecution's history. In the first place,
the defense argued, it is simply untrue that the treason clause
of the Constitution is identical to the treason statute of 25 Edward III. "They very materially differ," Lewis contended, and
he pointed particularly to the clauses of Article III, Section 3
relating to the overt act and two witnesses. "To me it appears
strange," he maintained, "that while the English statute is not
in force here, the English construction of that statute
should!"[65]

It seemed ironic to defense counsel that despite the apparently stronger protections for individual rights contained in
the Constitution, the prosecution of Fries was based upon an
almost unprecedented attempt to define riot and rescue as
treason: "The breaking open of prisons generally is treason,
but in no case [in English law] is the releasing of prisoners
before they are taken there. . . . It would not have been treason, therefore, if a number of persons had actually conspired
to rescue these prisoners from the marshal, nor even if they
had been confined in a gaol, instead of a room, because it was
not a general design to break open all prisons, but one only.
But, on the contrary, they were not in prison; they were only

[64] Ibid., p. 19.

[65] Ibid., p. 138.

in custody of the officer who served the process; how, then, in the name of reason and common sense, will it be made to amount to treason when it would not if they had been in gaol[?]" "I am not able," Lewis informed the jury, "except during the mandatory reign of Henry VIII, to find the trace of a single instance where rescue, under any circumstances whatever, has been found to amount to treason."[66]

Nowhere in English law, according to Fries's defense, with the single exception of the reign of Henry VIII, had there ever been an attempt to define resistance to one law, rather than law in general, as treason. The defense pointed to the writings of the English jurist Lord Mansfield, who mentioned only one circumstance in which the distinction between specific and general resistance relied upon by Foster and Blackstone may not apply. Mansfield ruled that opposition to the militia laws alone might be deemed treasonous:

> Why does the learned and experienced Lord Mansfield particularly specify militia laws and no other? Why does he not say to arrest the execution of any law? Why the militia law? For the best of all reasons—the same reason as the taking or attacking a fort or a castle belonging to the king, because that is the place where he keeps his military forces, and because the military is the strength of the kingdom, and this is resisting the military authority. Therefore, it must be allowed, that a resistance of militia laws is upon a very different footing than any others, and, in time of danger, resisting this law would prevent the militia being drawn into the field when there is occasion for them.[67]

[66] Ibid., pp. 147–48, 136. The defense counsel's history is generally accurate here, with two exceptions. In 1381, during the reign of Richard II, it did become treason to instigate a riot. Likewise, during the reign of Henry VIII it became treason for twelve or more persons riotously assembled for any purpose to refuse to disperse when ordered by an officer of the law. The latter example is actually a precedent that favored the defense, because the tax resistance, protests, and crowd actions in Bucks and Northampton counties effectively ceased in response to President John Adams's proclamation of March 12, 1799. There were also both statutory and judicial precedents for defining as treason rescues of prisoners who were charged or convicted of treason. The prisoners rescued at Bethlehem were not charged with treason and, in any event, this last English precedent was not resurrected during the trials of Fries.

[67] Ibid., p. 148.

In other words, what the federal government was attempting in Fries's case seemed to the defense a *"novel experiment"* in the history of Anglo-American law. Ignoring the clear precedent of English treason law that "the resistance of no law is treason, but the militia law," the prosecution sought to define riot and rescue, crimes covered perfectly well as misdemeanors under the sedition act recently adopted by Congress, as a combined capital offense. Relying on precedents from the trials of Vigol and Mitchell, the prosecution seemed bent on vitiating the Constitution's limiting clauses relating to the overt act and giving the courts almost unlimited potential to construct treasons from a series of less serious crimes. The defense never denied that Fries was guilty of several lesser offenses, indeed they acknowledged it; the lawyers simply asserted that their client should not be executed for treason, as that crime was described in the Constitution and understood under established Anglo-American definitions.[68]

For the most part, the defense lawyers were better historians than the prosecution, which is another way of saying that from a modern perspective the weight of history balanced in Fries's favor.[69] Nor did the defense misrepresent the government's case. Prosecution attorneys did not respond to defense contentions with a list of parallel cases from English law. Indeed, they readily acknowledged that an overt act by rescue of prisoners was a new, and thus perhaps a more sinister, method of acting out treasonous designs.[70]

---

[68] Ibid. The government did use the Sedition Act to prosecute other participants in Fries's Rebellion, but sought to make special examples of Fries and several other "leaders" of the unrest. See Henderson, "Treason, Sedition, and Fries' Rebellion," pp. 312, 314. In addition to Fries, Frederick Hearny and John Gettman were also convicted of treason. All three men were pardoned by President Adams. Stenographic notes of the other treason trials were apparently not taken.

[69] That is to say, the weight of history balanced in Fries's favor *if* one accepts the premise of lawyers on both sides that the law of treason had over its history a higher rationality than merely providing a public theater for labeling as illegitimate all threats to rulers and dispatching those so defined in what was perceived by the rulers to be the most politically efficacious manner.

[70] Carpenter, *Two Trials*, p. 160.

In other respects, the prosecution arguments were a re-hearsal of those presented in the Whiskey Rebellion cases, as one might expect given their success in the Mitchell and Vigol trials, the obvious parallels as tax resistance cases, and the presence of Judge Peters, whose views were known and who had ruled favorably on the same prosecution arguments in the previous trials. Indeed, the prosecution's definition of treason by levying war was a paraphrase of the judges' instructions to juries in the previous cases. No act of violence need be committed to satisfy the Constitution's treason clause "if the arrangements are made, and the numbers of armed men actually appear, so as to procure the object which they have in view by intimidation, as well as by actual force, that will constitute the offense." The raising of a military force "for the purpose of attaining any object with a design of opposing the lawful authority of the government by dint of arms, in some matter of public concern in which the insurgents have no particular interest distinct from the rest of the community" seemed to the prosecution to qualify as treason.[71]

Group violence aimed at any law or laws of the United States or designed for any public end that usurped the rightful prerogatives of government falls under the larger definition. It is the intention behind the action, rather than the overt act in isolation, which defines the crime. Under some circumstances riot and rescue might be deemed misdemeanors, but when the design is "to defeat the operation of the laws" then the crime is treason. In the specific case of Fries, he was known to have participated in meetings that culminated in a written document (that the prosecution could not produce) expressing animosity to the tax law. At those same meetings, Fries's statements against the tax law were "extremely violent, and he threatened to shoot one of the assessors, Mr. Foulke, through the legs, if he did proceed to assess the houses." Fries was also known to have threatened another assessor that "he should be committed to an old stable, and there fed on rotten corn." On yet another occasion, Fries was

[71] Ibid., p. 19.

heard to say that he would not submit to the law and that he could raise seven hundred men in opposition by the next morning. In a fit of anger, the defendant had also made statements to the effect that "it should soon be in this country as it was in France." Fries warned tax men that they might be injured if they continued in their line of work; and witnesses attested that Fries, armed with "a large pistol," had assembled fifty to sixty men, "the greatest part of whom were in arms," to prevent the assessors from going about their business in Bucks County.[72]

This pattern of behavior in Bucks County demonstrated, according to the prosecution, the intention behind Fries's actions in Bethlehem (Northampton County) on March 7, 1799. Government attorneys harbored no doubt that Fries was "the leading man, and he appears to enjoy the command." It was Fries himself who demanded at the behest of a crowd of about one hundred that the marshal surrender the three prisoners destined for arraignment in Philadelphia. It was Fries who declared to the marshal that "we will not go without taking the prisoners" and that any attempt to resist would result in violence.[73]

The parallels to the Whiskey Rebellion cases were so close, as the prosecution portrayed them, to preclude any doubt of the appropriate verdict here. Resistance to a law, intimidation of or assault on government officials, and assembly in martial array with the intention of subverting the law, even in the absence of overt violence, had already been determined twice in federal courts to sustain a treason charge under the Constitution. The government's case against Fries, as the prosecution (as well as the defense) well knew, was in important respects significantly stronger than those that had convicted Vigol and Mitchell. There was no problem finding two witnesses to a clearly defined overt act—the rescue of prisoners at Bethlehem on March 7—as there had been in the Mitchell case. Furthermore, the rescue was an even "more violent breach of the law than the attack on

[72] Ibid., pp. 20–24.

[73] Ibid., pp. 23–24.

Nevil's house" (to which Mitchell had been linked by only one witness) in the sense that Fries and the mob defied and abused not just a government official, but an officer of the law.[74]

Judge Peters, in his instructions to the jury, summarized the case decisively in the prosecution's favor. It is treason by levying war, he told the jurors, "for persons *who have not but a common interest with their fellow-citizens,* to oppose or prevent, by force, numbers or intimidation, a *public* and *general* law of the United States, *with intent* to prevent its operation, or compel its repeal. Force is necessary to complete the crime; but the quantum of force is immaterial." In restating his views, and those of Justice Paterson, from the Mitchell case, Peters was paraphrasing the English commentators' distinction between violence to right a private wrong and that which has a public purpose. Peters was taking Blackstone's reference to treasonous "general" opposition to law, which might fairly be restated as "general opposition to law," and recasting it into his own unique configuration of violent opposition to any "general law" as treason.[75]

This was a creative and astoundingly expansive interpretation of the English jurist's meaning, but the logic was a coherent outgrowth of the commentator's argument: "If numbers and force can render one law ineffectual, which is tantamount to its repeal, the whole system of laws may be destroyed in detail." Judge Jeffreys could not have put it better himself. There is no lesser crime where opposition to the government is concerned; the only distinctions are acts of magnanimity by the state. The practice of Parliament responding to the "public opinion" of the London mob was an act of grace (or an acknowledgment of impotence), not a recognition of right, and a dangerous precedent that had no place under the more representative form of government enjoyed in the United States. Justice Iredell implicitly sustained this reading by describing his ideas on points of treason law as "absolutely" coin-

[74] Ibid., p. 163.

[75] Ibid., p. 204.

ciding with those of Peters, to whom he deferred on such matters.[76]

Finally, there was the ugly issue of "constructive" treason that the defense had raised in the course of its argument that the government seemed bent on returning American law to the dark days of the Stuart kings. Peters admitted that "the doctrine of *constructive treason* has produced much real mischief in another country." He acknowledged that he and his fellow judges in the Whiskey Rebellion and Fries's Rebellion cases were engaged in constructive interpretations of the crime of treason. And yet to Peters it seemed "not fair and sound reasoning to argue against the necessary and indispensable *use* of construction, from the *abuses* it has produced." The appropriate lesson to be taken from former abuses is that jurists must be cautious in their constructions "but not so much alarmed about *abuses* as to restrain from the proper and necessary *use* of interpretation." In more modern parlance, Peters and Iredell were not "strict constructionists" of the Constitution. They found ample room for reasoned and reasonable amplification of the language of the treason clause; and they felt bound by neither the weight of English precedent nor the intentions of those who had drafted the clause.[77]

After the conviction, at the point of sentencing, evidence was presented by defense counsel that a juror expressed severe prejudice against Fries before the trial, and after he had been selected for the case. Judge Peters thought that insufficient cause for retrial, but relented in response to Justice Iredell's wishes. In the second trial, not surprisingly, the prosecution rested its case on the same judicial principles and logic that had prevailed the first time around. The significance of this second trial for a historical consideration of treason law rests less, then, on the judicial rationales used to reach

[76] Ibid., pp. 205, 164–65. Justice Iredell's interpretation of the treason clause in this case appears much more expansive than his general remarks to a South Carolina grand jury suggested several years before the Fries case. See [Carey's] *American Museum* 12 (1795):36.

[77] Carpenter, *Two Trials*, pp. 206–7.

the same verdict than on the behavior of the presiding judge.[78]

Fries ended up without an attorney in his second trial, and Associate Justice of the Supreme Court Samuel Chase thus served multiple roles as judge (along with District Judge Peters) and counsel to the defendant. Defense lawyers resigned when Chase presented a written opinion on the law of treason at the beginning of the trial, thereby vitiating any possibility of a defense based on the law rather than the facts of the case. In the face of a huge backlog of cases, and in the interest of saving time, Chase had provided his interpretation of the law in a manner consistent with normal practice in Maryland, his native state. Such judicial behavior was unusual, indeed in recent memory unprecedented, in Pennsylvania.

Thus it was the manner in which Chase delivered his opinion on the law—in writing—and the timing of the presentation—before defense attorneys' attempts to influence his interpretation and the jury's role in deciding the law of the case—that struck the defense counsel as novel and inappropriate. The opinion itself was not one to which his coadjudicator on the bench, Judge Peters, had any objections. "It is the opinion of the court," Chase wrote, "that any insurrection or rising of any body of people, within the United states, to attain or effect, by *force* or *violence,* any object of a great public nature, or of public and general (or national) concern, is a *levying war* against the United States, within the contemplation and construction of the Constitution of the United States." In Chase's opinion, attempts by violence or force to prevent the execution of a tax law qualified as levying war under the treason clause of the Constitution. In this regard, the central distinction made by Chase was between conspiracy to resist enforcement of a statute, which he defined as a high misdemeanor, and those cases where people "proceed to carry *such intention into execution by force,*" which was clearly treason. "The true criterion," according the Chase, "to determine whether *acts committed* are a *treason* or a *less offence* (as a riot) is the *quo animo* the people did assemble. When the intention is *universal or general,* as to effect some object of a general public nature,

[78] Ibid., app. 2, pp. 11–45.

it will be treason, and cannot be considered construed or reduced to a *riot.*"[79]

The defense lawyers resigned from the case in protest, refused to resume their places when Chase offered to withdraw his statement, and privately advised Fries not to accept court-appointed counsel. They apparently reasoned that the facts of the case were not in dispute, and since the judge had ruled on the law prior to their arguments, that Fries had no defense whatever. It was in their client's best interest, they believed, to contribute to creating a situation in which there was the appearance of an unfair trial, thus establishing grounds for appeal or, better yet, a popular uproar that would lead to a pardon of Fries after the inevitable conviction and death sentence.

The plan worked, as President Adams's change of heart on the necessity for token executions suggests. The unpopularity of the president's decision to pardon Fries (and the two others convicted of treason) within his cabinet and among his supporters in the Federalist party testify to the political atmosphere in which the trial was conducted. The clamor for pardon in Pennsylvania and from Republican politicians and newspaper editors illustrates the contending pressures under which Adams (and the judges) labored. And the president's consultation with the defense attorneys prior to his decision highlights his attempt to balance legal, humanitarian, and political concerns in this sensitive case. In retrospect, it appears that Adams was in a no-win situation. His pardon of Fries made few, if any, converts from among his detractors within the Republican camp, and he alienated further those friends and foes in the Federalist party who increasingly doubted his capacity to lead.

The case also had repercussions for Justice Chase, who was tried by the Senate for high crimes and misdemeanors in 1804. The first of eight articles of impeachment addressed his behavior on the bench during Fries's second trial. A Republican Congress charged the Federalist judge with "highly arbitrary, oppressive and unjust" conduct in the Fries case.

---

[79] Charles Evans, stenographer, *Report of the Trial of the Hon. Samuel Chase* (Baltimore, 1805), app., pp. 44–45.

Specifically, the Senate committee accused him of prejudicing the jury against Fries by delivering a written opinion on the law before defense arguments on those points, refusing defense counsel the freedom to cite English precedents where they found them relevant to the case, and barring the defense from addressing questions of law. In sum, Chase was charged with having disgraced "the character of the American bench, in manifest violation of law and justice, and in open contempt of the rights of juries, on which ultimately rest the liberty and safety of the American people."[80]

There was, of course, no questioning of Chase's interpretation of Article III, Section 3, his defense of judicially constructed treason, or his understanding of the relationship between English and American treason law. The law of treason apparently did not define one of the ideological fissures between Federalists and Republicans. More clearly, it highlighted conflict between the "outs" (Antifederalists, proto-Republicans, and others who fell outside the real and philosophical contours of power during the Washington and Adams administrations) who were attempting to define legitimate and successful methods for overturning the political status quo and the "ins" who sought, in an age that was only beginning to credit the existence of political parties, to use the courts as one means to establish and extend their rule across time and space.

The politics of this struggle became even more clearly expressed in treason law as executive- and then legislative-branch control was wrested from Federalists by the Republicans beginning in 1801. For the first time in its history the nation was faced with a judiciary that, overwhelmingly Federalist, was out of sympathy with the president *and* Congress. The impeachment and trial of Chase was one significant illustration of interbranch conflict. The primacy of Fries's treason trial in the charges against Chase reflects the symbolic and real significance of Federalist use (and, in the eyes of Republicans, abuse) of the treason charge for political ends, as well as the Republicans' eagerness to do the same with Republican

[80] Ibid., pp. 3–4.

judges. And the inability to convict Chase in the Senate on close votes testifies to the transitional and incomplete status of the transfer of power.[81]

Ironically, and at least partly as a function of this ongoing conflict among the branches of government, it would be a Federalist judge who began the process of narrowing the scope of treason law and who, for the first time, sought to define clear limits to the authority of the state and broader rights and protections for those rights as they were contested in treason trials. Only when judges began to conceive of executive and legislative behavior as oppressive in theory and practice would they start to take more literally the "narrow" definition of treason that subsequent judges and legal historians have found embodied in the Constitution. Again, ironically, it would be associates of Aaron Burr, a Republican partisan and a literal murderer of that Federalist idol Alexander Hamilton, who would be the first to benefit from a reinterpretation of the law of treason.

The government failed even to bring Erick Bollman and Samuel Swartwout, accomplices of Burr in his alleged conspiracy to dismember the United States, to trial for treason. In ex parte proceedings in February 1807, prosecutors faced difficulty defining the specific crime with which Bollman and Swartwout would be charged. Clearly the general offense alleged would be treason by levying war, but the specific overt act remained vague. "It is true," the prosecution admitted, "that we cannot at present say exactly when and where the overt act of levying war was committed," nor had the government clear evidence that such an overt act indeed even occurred. Nonetheless, prosecutors had affidavits from several

---

[81] The House of Representatives favored impeachment of Chase by a 73 to 32 vote. The Senate, in which Republicans also outnumbered Federalists by a considerable margin, failed narrowly to secure the two-thirds vote necessary for conviction. The process by which Chase narrowly escaped conviction on the impeachment charges testifies to the transitional and incomplete process of the transfer of power and to how much the Republican leadership had yet to learn about managing floor votes in the upper house. See Melvin I. Urofsky, *A March of Liberty: A Constitutional History of the United States* (New York, 1988), pp. 189–91; Richard E. Ellis, "The Impeachment of Samuel Chase," in Belknap, ed., *American Political Trials*, pp. 57–78.

people, including a copy of a proclamation signed by President Jefferson, which seemed sufficient to establish probable cause that such a crime had taken place. "No belief," the defense retorted, "of a fact tending to show probable cause, no hearsay, no opinion of any person, *however high in office,* respecting the guilt of the person accused, can be received in evidence on this examination." "The order of commitment ought also to have stated more particularly the overt act of treason," a defense lawyer contended. "It is too vague and uncertain."[82]

Chief Justice John Marshall, speaking for the court, shared the defense attorneys' concerns. Conspiracy to levy war and actual levying of war against the United States were two distinct crimes. Commitment of prisoners under a charge of treason for levying war must show probable cause that war had actually been levied, according to Marshall.

> It is not the intention of the court to say that no individual can be guilty of this crime who has not appeared in arms against his country. On the contrary, if war be actually levied, that is, if a body of men be actually assembled for the purpose of effecting by force a treasonable purpose, all those who perform any part, however minute, or however remote from the scene of action, and who are actually leagued in the general conspiracy, are to be considered as traitors. But there must be an actual assembling of men for the treasonable purpose, to constitute a levying of war.[83]

Actual assemblage with treasonable intent was necessary to complete the crime, as Marshall defined it. Planning the assembly or the assault, enlisting the soldiers, even marching to a preliminary place of rendezvous before the actual assemblage of the army, was not enough. If the prosecution could establish probable cause to believe that the defendants played a role, however minor and however distant from an actual

---

[82] 8 *United States Reports* (4 *Cranch*) 115, 109, 108 (1807). See also, Robert Faulkner, "John Marshall and the Burr Trial," *Journal of American History* 53 (1966):247–58.

[83] 8 *United States Reports* (4 *Cranch*) 126 (1807).

assemblage, in raising or supplying an army that had as its goal, *in the defendants' full knowledge,* overturning the government of the United States in New Orleans by force as an initial step toward an invasion of Mexico, *and if such an assemblage had actually taken place,* then the justices would agree that a commitment of the prisoners was warranted. Federal attorneys could not supply such evidence, and Bollman and Swartwout, to the president's fury, were therefore released.

Marshall's handling of *Ex parte Bollman and Swartwout* was more attentive to procedural safeguards for the accused than that of any previous federal judge in treason proceedings. No such care had been taken in the Whiskey Rebellion cases, where rumors and unverified accusations had sufficed to justify sweeping up suspected traitors in the dead of night, transportation at bayonet point across the state of Pennsylvania, and incarceration in dank Philadelphia jails. For Marshall and his court, the president's word that traitors stalked the land proved less convincing than such executive branch pronouncements had to other Federalist judges during the Washington and Adams administrations.

At the same time, Marshall's definition of treasonable levying of war was more comprehensive than any previously articulated from a federal bench. Not only did Marshall expand upon the language of Judges Paterson, Iredell, Chase, and Peters before him, he offered new thoughts on the subject of "constructive presence"—the doctrine by which a principal to treason need not necessarily be physically present at the overt act described in the indictment—while attempting to narrow the meaning of "levying war." Like Chase in *U.S.* v. *John Fries,* Marshall seemed to insist that force must be employed in an act of levying war, thereby narrowing the scope of the judges' language in *U.S.* v. *Mitchell,* where no such limitation was mentioned. It is not necessary, Marshall reasoned, that an entire army has to assemble to establish levying of war, "but it is necessary that there should be an actual assemblage, and, therefore, the evidence should make the fact unequivocal. The traveling of individuals to the place of rendezvous would perhaps not be sufficient. This would be an equivocal act, and has no warlike appearance. The meeting of particular bodies of men, and their marching from places of partial to a place of general rendezvous, would be such an assemblage."[84]

That Marshall's language could also be interpreted as expansion of the meaning of levying war became clear in the government's case against Aaron Burr. But Marshall's contribution to the procedural protection of accused traitors was less susceptible to misunderstanding. Throughout the proceedings against Burr, just as in *Ex parte Bollman and Swartwout,* the defendant enjoyed consistently more sympathetic rulings from the bench than any accused traitor tried in a federal court during the 1790s. On a number of occasions, Chief Justice Marshall chastised the government for its heavy-handed methods, its disregard for procedural safeguards designed to protect the rights of the accused, and its apparent pursuit of a vendetta against the defendant, a crusade to destroy Burr that apparently emanated from the highest office in the land.

The indictment charged Burr with levying war against the United States on December 10, 1806, on Blennerhassett's Island, Wood County, Virginia. The government alleged that Burr, "with force and arms, unlawfully, falsely, maliciously and traitorously did compass, imagine and intend to raise and levy war, insurrection and rebellion" against the United States; that he and an army of accomplices, "to the number of thirty persons and upwards, armed and arrayed in a warlike manner . . . did falsely and traitorously assemble and join themselves together against the said United States, and then and there with force and arms did falsely and traitorously, and in a warlike and hostile manner, array and dispose themselves against the said United States"; that this party, which was "traitorously assembled and armed and arrayed in manner aforesaid, most wickedly, maliciously and traitorously did ordain, prepare and levy war against the said United States."[85]

The problem, among others, with the government's case was that Burr was demonstrably not present on the date and at the place mentioned in the indictment. The government

[84] Ibid., p. 134.

[85] J. J. Coombs, comp., *The Trial of Aaron Burr for High Treason* (Washington, D.C., 1864), p. 141.

was attempting to utilize a notion of "constructive presence" that acknowledged Burr's physical absence from the only alleged overt act, while insisting that the defendant was a principal in a levying of war in which no weapons were fired, no American army was confronted, no specific law was resisted, and no actual assault on the territory, officers, or offices of the nation was actually made. Prosecutors were attempting to seize the language of Chief Justice Marshall in *Ex parte Bollman and Swartwout* to establish Burr's role as a "procurer" of treason, as chief conspirator, solicitor of funds, purchaser of supplies, propagandist for the enterprise, and enlister of men at distances remote from the overt act of the army's assemblage on Blennerhassett's Island. Not only had the question of constructive presence already been settled in the Bollman and Swartwout case, but it seemed to the prosecution that it was a legal absurdity to require the actual presence of a traitor at an overt act of waging war to charge and convict him of treason: "If it [the law] require actual presence at the scene of the assemblage to involve a man in the guilt of treason, how easy will it be for the principal traitor to avoid this guilt and escape punishment for ever? He may go into distant states, from one state to another. He may secretly wander like a demon of darkness from one end of the continent to the other."[86]

The Constitution specified an act of "levying," not "waging," war, the prosecutors observed. "Levy" is derived from a French word, which "when applied to soldiers . . . means raising only, not gathering, assembling, or even bringing them together, but merely raising." Since the English treason statute of 25 Edward III was originally drafted in Norman French, since in the appropriate English translation "levying" and "raising" are synonymous, it seemed to the federal attorneys that "the mere enlistment of soldiers of itself [is] an overt act of levying war." The levy seemed to them a distinct and totally different act than the war itself: "The levy is the preparation: the war is the purpose."[87]

According to the prosecution, no open deed of war is re-

---

[86] *The Federal Cases: Comprising Cases Argued and Determined in the Circuit and District Courts of the United States,* 30 vols. (St. Paul, 1894–97), 25:125.

[87] Ibid., p. 133.

quired to sustain a charge of treason, only a levy for the purpose of waging war within the realm. Had not George III been rightly accused of levying war against his colonies from 3,000 miles away? It is the monarch who declares the war, "by whose directions the troops are raised and employed. It is he who levies the war, and not his subjects, who fight the battles; his generals and soldiers, who come hither for slaughter and murder, they make the war upon us, but they do not levy it. . . . A man may, on principles of common sense, not only levy war, but make war without being present at the place where a battle is fought."[88]

The defense, not surprisingly, had a different understanding of "levying war." "The presence of the party accused is," they argued, "by the constitution of the United States, indispensably necessary to make him guilty of the fact of levying war." Granted, in England advising, procuring, or conspiring were enough under the "compassing" clause. But that clause was dropped in drafting the Constitution, and plotting or imagining the destruction of the state is not enough in America to convict for treason. "There must be an actual levying of war. . . . Proof of the intention alone would be inadmissible." And force, the defense contended, is a necessary component of levying war. If the drafters of the Constitution had meant that procuring supplies and raising troops was treasonous, they would have said so. Instead, they limited the crime to levying war or adhering to the nation's enemies. Levying war and making or waging war seemed to the defense synonymous terms. "Levying of war implies force of some kind. The idea of violence of some kind is inseparable from that of war. . . . Whatever is making war is levying it."[89]

What, they asked, is the overt act that Burr allegedly committed? Where, they demanded, are the two requisite witnesses to Burr's commission of a specific overt act of treason? If there is no overt act, there is no treason. How could Burr be convicted of procuring men and supplies for a treason that was never acted out? In his own defense, Burr argued that "gentlemen ought to come forward and say that they mean to

[88] Ibid., p. 137.

[89] Ibid., pp. 143, 146–47, 152.

charge me upon the common law: that though there was no force used in reality, yet by construction there was force used; that though I was not personally present, yet that by construction I was present; that though there really was no military array, yet by construction there was military array."[90]

So there was no evidence presented that directly connected Burr to events on Blennerhassett's Island on the date alleged in the indictment; there was, according to the defense lawyers' definition of levying war, no evidence of an overt act of treason presented at the trial. The prosecution was attempting to define the meaning of the treason clause in unprecedentedly expansive ways. Not only were they attempting to construct a treason across time and space, prosecutors argued for a concept of constructive "legal presence," distinguishable from actual presence at a physical place, and they utilized Justice Marshall's language from *Ex parte Bollman and Swartwout* to argue that force and violence were not necessary components of treason by levying war.

It rightly appeared to defense counsel that the government was effectively arguing that the compassing clause of the English treason statute was implicitly retained in the Constitution. By the prosecution's definitions, indictments for treason in federal courts could be as vague and infinitely expandable as those of the Tudor and Stuart reigns: the indictment charged Burr with levying war at a specific time and place, but the prosecution argued in court that it never intended to prove that he was actually at Blennerhassett's Island on December 10, 1806, although he was allegedly "legally present" by logical construction of his role as a procurer of treason. Should they succeed, the prosecution's arguments would establish the most elaborate and ethereal constructive treason on record in Anglo-American courts. As the defense contended, the potential existed for adding a "Will-o'-the-Wisp Treason" to the convictions in the Whiskey Rebellion and the Hot Water War.[91]

Justice Marshall's opinion fell somewhere in between the prosecution and defense, making him the first federal judge

[90] Ibid., pp. 111, 113.

[91] Ibid., p. 154.

who did not swallow whole the government's argument in a treason case. On "levying war" Marshall chose what he termed the "natural" rather than "technical" meaning of the words: "It must be a warlike assemblage, carrying the appearance of force, and in a situation to practice hostility." His language in *Ex parte Bollman and Swartwout* had seemed to suggest that "force" was not a necessary component of levying war; and, indeed, the prosecution had seized upon the literal meaning of his words to argue just that in the Burr case. Marshall contended that he had been misunderstood by prosecution lawyers, although one wonders whether he simply changed his mind in light of the unanticipated impact his language would have in enlarging the government's net for enforcing the law of treason. The problem was one of splitting legal hairs to establish that he did not intend to make new law in the Bollman and Swartwout cases, or, for that matter, in the Burr case either.[92]

Marshall insisted that he was following long-standing Anglo-American practice in ruling that "an assemblage to subvert by force the government of our country, and amounting to a levying of war, should be an assemblage in force." The law required, as it had for centuries, that an assemblage of men with the intention of waging war was necessary to establish an overt act of levying war. No shot need be fired, no officer of the state need be injured or killed, but he never intended that "the idea of force was . . . separated from this assemblage." Thus Marshall was staking out ground in between the defense contention that some overt act of force—the firing of a gun, a march on an arsenal or city, an assault on a government official—was a necessary component of levying war and the prosecution's argument that force was irrelevant where the intention to levy war was clear from spoken or written words or from deeds performed away from the purported scene of action.[93]

Marshall had no qualms about utilizing the doctrine of constructive presence at an overt act of treason; indeed, he adhered fully to Coke's adage that "in treason all be principals."

[92] Ibid., p. 165.

[93] Ibid., p. 166.

The problem for the chief justice was application of this legal truth to the particular case at hand. To Marshall's under-standing of the concept, it does not follow that an accomplice to one or more overt acts related to a general act of treason is therefore a principal to all the overt acts in the chain, includ-ing the ultimate levying of war. Evidence of a general conspir-acy to commit treason may be relevant to establishing the intent behind a particular overt act, but two witnesses must link the accused to the overt act named in the indictment. "Far from considering a man as constructively present at ev-ery overt act of the general treason in which he may have been concerned," Marshall reasoned, "the whole doctrine of the books limits the proof against him to those particular overt acts of levying war with which he is charged." The pros-ecution was unable to produce two witnesses to Burr's partici-pation, constructive or otherwise, in the assemblage at Blennerhassett's Island on December 10, 1806; therefore, ac-cording to Marshall, the treason charge as stated in the indict-ment could not be sustained under American law.[94]

The indictment was fundamentally flawed. If the govern-ment had charged Burr with constructive presence, rather than actual participation, at the assemblage on Blennerhas-sett's Island, if the indictment had alleged procuring of men and supplies at specific times and places distant from the as-semblage but contributory to it, and had provided at least two witnesses to one or more overt acts of procurement actually named in the indictment, then the prosecution would have a credible case. According to the chief justice:

> If it be said that the advising or procurement of treason is a secret transaction, which can scarcely ever be proved in the manner required by this opinion, the answer which will readily suggest itself is, that the difficulty of proving a fact will not justify convic-tion without proof. Certainly it will not justify conviction without a direct and positive witness in a case where the constitution re-quires two. The more correct inference from this circumstance would seem to be, that the advising of the fact is not within the constitutional definition of the crime. To advise or procure a trea-

[94] Ibid., pp. 170, 172.

117

son is in the nature of conspiring or plotting treason, which is not treason in itself.[95]

In other words, the "compassing" clause of the English treason statute of 25 Edward III was effectively eliminated (the Framers had only literally removed it) from the Constitution's treason clause as Marshall interpreted it here. His definition of "overt act" represented a significant narrowing of the term compared to rulings in previous cases. And Marshall enhanced procedural protections for alleged traitors. On the other hand, the concept of "constructive treason" was still viable, indeed it was specifically articulated, defined, and sustained by Marshall's dicta in the Burr case. The meaning of "levying war" remained equally broad. It could be argued that Marshall actually expanded the definition of this term in the government's favor. The line between riot and treason was no more precisely defined; the notion that opposition to one "general" statute could be treason was still good law; and the necessity for "force" as a component of levying war was sufficiently imprecise, partly as a consequence of Marshall's apparently contradictory rulings in the Burr and Bollman and Swartwout cases, that subsequent judges had no clear guide to the necessary relationship between violence and levying war.

None of these issues was resolved; none of Marshall's constructive interpretations of the treason clause was reversed during the next fifty years. His efforts to widen procedural protections for those accused of treason were reinforced and expanded in subsequent antebellum rulings. Later judges followed in Marshall's steps as they charted a direction for the federal judiciary that was more independent from executive branch pressures than had been the case under the Federalist administrations. Subsequent decisions quoted Marshall at length in defining "overt act" and "levying war" to juries, and sometimes even acknowledged the ways in which the law of treason had changed from the 1790s.

Only one year after Burr's trial, a treason case in the Vermont circuit court presented another opportunity for clarifi-

[95] Ibid., pp. 175–76.

cation or redefinition of "levying war." The decision in *U.S. v. Hoxie* (1808) contributed to the process of narrowing the Constitution's treason clause in precisely the area that the treason cases of the 1790s had expanded it. A customs officer had seized and put under guard a raft of timber that the owner attempted to float across the Canadian border in defiance of the embargo law then in effect. The indictment charged that Frederick Hoxie and an armed band of sixty men assembled and violently resisted the authority of the customs collector and federal troops who guarded the contraband goods. Hoxie and his confederates allegedly stole the raft, in the course of which shots were exchanged, and then floated it to Canada in defiance of lawful authority. The government argued that this was a clear case of treason by levying war: there was an assemblage in armed array, shots were fired, and there were multiple witnesses to the specific overt act of violence in resistance to a federal law and the authorities charged to enforce it.

Associate Justice of the Supreme Court Henry Brockholst Livingston, sitting on the Vermont circuit, presided over the case. This Republican judge recognized the definitional quagmire that "levying war" had become in the federal courts. If he could rely on a commonsense reading of the Constitution alone, Livingston reasoned that this incident was clearly not treason:

> A levying of war, without having recourse to rules of construction, or artificial reasoning, would seem to be nothing short of the employment, or at least, of the embodying of a military force, armed and arrayed, in a warlike manner, for the purpose of forcibly subverting the government, dismembering the Union, or destroying the legislative functions of Congress. These troops should be so armed, and so directed, as to leave no doubt, that the United States, or their government, were the immediate object of their attack.[96]

His common sense thus presented Livingston with a problem because, at least according to the prosecution, it was in

---

[96] *U.S. v. Hoxie* (1808), ibid., 26:398.

conflict with the applications of the treason clause in the Whiskey Rebellion and Fries's Rebellion cases, where violent opposition to a law of the United States had been found treasonous levying of war even when there was no general attempt to subvert the government, dismember the union, or destroy the legislative functions of Congress. Justice Livingston rejected the prosecution's argument and denied that previous judges had defined "levying war" so broadly. His definition was not new American law, Livingston insisted, since "no construction in England, and certainly none in America, has yet carried this doctrine the length to which we are at present expected to go." For his language and reasoning, the judge went back to Blackstone and Foster, who clearly distinguished between a riot that had private ends—"a tumult with a view to pull down a particular house, or lay open a particular enclosure," as Blackstone put it—and insurrections with general public purposes, such as overthrowing the government. "When the object of an insurrection is of a local or private nature," Livingston ruled, "not having a direct tendency to destroy all property and all government by numbers and armed force, it will not amount to treason."[97]

Livingston could not agree with unnamed "other judges," (Peters, Paterson, Iredell, and Chase) who had contended that the quantum of force, the numbers of persons arrayed against the government, was irrelevant in defining a specific incident as levying war. When the array is, as in the Hoxie case, "so very small and despicable, it furnishes strong evidence of some intent very far short of that of measuring their strength with the United States: unless we can believe that a force, if it deserve that name, scarcely competent to the reduction of a single family, were meditating hostilities and rebellion against a government defended by several millions of freemen." In this and other regards, there seemed to Livingston a decisive difference between the Whiskey Rebellion and Fries's Rebellion on the one hand and the Hoxie episode on the other. Hoxie's little band of men had a distinctly private aim, retaking a particular raft of logs belonging to the man who employed them; the size of the force reflected this limited goal. On the other hand, Vigol, Mitchell, and Fries were, according to Livingston, engaged in insurrections that "threatened the existence of government. . . . These cases cannot be considered as parallel without destroying at once every distinction between trespass, riots, and treasons."[98]

Had the prosecution been able to demonstrate that the Hoxie episode was part of a larger conspiracy to defeat the embargo law, then Livingston would have entertained the argument that it represented an overt act of a general treasonous levying of war. Like the judges in previous federal treason cases, Livingston had no problem defining armed resistance to a single law as treason, so long as evidence of such an intent was clear and there were two witnesses to an overt act consistent with carrying out such a plan. To Livingston's reading, no previous federal judge had declared that every violent act of opposition to a public law, "no matter how momentary, how slight, in what shape, or for what purpose, amounted to treason." Such a ruling would be absurd in this judge's mind, since interpreting the Constitution so broadly and flexibly would make treason indictments "as common as indictments for petit larcenies, assaults and batteries, or other misdemeanors. If every opposition to law be treason . . . who can say how many of them will in time become ranged under the class of treason."[99]

Consistently to this point in the nation's history, levying war against one particular law was defined by federal judges as potentially treasonous. Livingston did contribute toward a substantial narrowing of the potential application of the term *levying war* by insisting, contrary to previous federal judicial opinion, that the nature of an armed array must bear some reasonable relationship to the ends defined in a treason indictment. Evidence on both the intent and the capacity of the military force seemed to him essential components of a successful treason prosecution. Where the line would be drawn between riot and treason was still unclear, and perhaps further muddied in this case, in the sense that Livingston accepted the argument that approximately one hundred

[98] Ibid., p. 400.

[99] Ibid., pp. 401–2.

"rebels" under the command of John Fries was a credible force to sustain a treason charge for levying war, but ridiculed the prosecution's argument in the Hoxie case that sixty men, armed and arrayed in a warlike manner, represented a sufficiently serious threat to the government to be even potentially treasonous. Was there a point between sixty and one hundred that defined a credible threat, or had the government grown significantly more secure during the decade between the two cases?

Whatever the conscious or subconscious rationales behind Livingston's decision, in light of substantially altered perceptions of the political scene and changing relationships between the executive and judicial branches, subsequent judges would rely on the narrower definitions and expanded procedural protections afforded in the Burr and Hoxie cases. Although prosecuting attorneys would continue to cite the precedents of the Whiskey Rebellion and Fries's Rebellion cases, the law was headed in a different direction. Treason prosecutions associated with the War of 1812 continued this trend. Government prosecutors found it difficult to sustain charges of treason for adhering to the enemy in the face of the strict two-witness rule, the necessity for evidence of a precisely defined overt act, and the willingness of judges and juries to credit testimony about extenuating circumstances. For example, an attempt to prosecute William Pryor (*U.S.* v. *Pryor,* 1814) for adhering to the enemy and attempting to procure supplies for a British squadron failed, because he was a prisoner of war who claimed that his attempt to purchase goods for the enemy was part of a plan to secure the escape of himself and fellow prisoners. The judge and the jury, which found it unnecessary even to leave the bar for deliberations on Pryor's guilt, found the charges entirely without merit.[100]

In the case of *U.S.* v. *John Hodges* (1815), a jury refused with equal alacrity to convict for high treason on clear evidence that Hodges and others "adhered to the enemy" by delivering up prisoners of war in order to save their town from destruction by British troops. Government attorneys argued that

---

[100] *U.S.* v. *Pryor* (1814), ibid., 27:628–31. See also, *U.S.* v. *Lee* (1814), ibid., 26:907–8.

threatened destruction of property was insufficient justification for adhering to the enemy. Although the judge was sympathetic to the prosecution's case against Hodges, shared the government's broad interpretation of the treason clause, and found ample precedent in British and American cases to sustain the charge, he refused to offer the jury definitive and binding instructions on the law. In the face of broad disagreement among legal authorities about the law of treason, the judge found the jury's right to decide both law and fact preeminent. It was now the turn of Federalist editors to chortle about Republican assaults on the liberties of the citizenry, to denounce unsuccessful Republican attempts "to enforce the abominable doctrine of CONSTRUCTIVE TREASON." [101]

The small number of antebellum treason cases after the War of 1812 certainly reflects an improved relationship between the federal government and at least its native white citizenry since the 1790s. It no doubt also testifies to growing confidence in federal power and authority, reflecting a decline in the political paranoia suffered during the era of the French Revolution. In this same regard, it clearly demonstrates the gradual acceptance of political opposition and an acknowledgment of the legitimate role played by political parties on the national scene. And yet the decisions to permit state treason prosecutions in the cases of Thomas Dorr (1842) and John Brown (1859) suggest a lack of confidence among national officials that they were capable of securing treason convictions in light of the narrowing judicial definitions of the treason clause. Opinion was divided within the legal community about whether state prosecution of treason was an infringement of prerogatives exclusive to the federal government under the Constitution. Some legal scholars berated federal officials for not pursuing their responsibilities with greater vigor, for not protecting the nation from its internal enemies; in sum, for neglecting to defend the Constitution from both the states and traitors. [102]

[101] [John Elihu Hall], *Report of the Trial of John Hodges* (Philadelphia, 1817), p. 4.

[102] On the question of state prosecution of treason, see *American Law Magazine* 8 (1845):318–50; James Kent, *Commentaries on American Law,* 4 vols.,

In one case, however, the federal government chose to act. Indeed, the political pressure was intense from Maryland and other slaveholding states to prosecute Castner Hanway for treason by levying war in the Christiana Riot of 1851. At stake was the federal government's credibility in the South, where many questioned its commitment to enforce the fugitive slave law of 1850. The decision to prosecute for treason, rather than murder or some combination of riot, rescue, and resisting arrest, reflected such political concerns more than it represented sound legal judgment. The determination to prosecute a white man, who played no active role in the violence associated with the riot by an exclusively black crowd, reveals both racist presumptions about "leadership" and the desire to make an example of a northern white abolitionist. Indeed, according to one defense attorney, this case was primarily intended to frighten northern people, under threat of the gallows, into assisting southern masters to recapture escaped slaves; the fate of Castner Hanway was of secondary concern. The riot at Christiana was the first nationally publicized episode of armed and fatal resistance to the fugitive slave law and was reported across the nation in banner headlines such as "Civil War, First Blow Struck." The prosecution of Hanway thus became a cause célèbre, the most blatantly political trial since the Burr case, and, given the perceived stakes, a case of equal or greater significance than any of the previous alleged treasons against the federal government.[103]

12th ed. (Boston, 1896), 1:403 n.a; *Kemp* v. *Kennedy* (1808), in *Federal Cases,* 14:281–85; *The People* v. *Mark Lynch, Aspenwall Cornell, and John Hagerman, Supreme Court of New York* (1814) in William Johnson, *Reports of Cases Argued and Determined in the Supreme Court of Judicature; And in the Court for the Trial of Impeachments and the Correction of Errors of the State of New York,* 20 vols. (New York, 1811–23), 11:549–54. On the John Brown case, see Stephen B. Oates, *To Purge This Land with Blood* (New York, 1970). On the case against Thomas W. Dorr, see George M. Dennison, *The Dorr War: Republicanism on Trial, 1831–1861* (Lexington, Ky., 1976).

[103] Jonathan Katz, *Resistance at Christiana: The Fugitive Slave Rebellion, Christiana, Pennsylvania, September 11, 1851: A Documentary Account* (New York, 1974), p. 4; Paul Finkelman, "The Treason Trial of Castner Hanway," in Belknap, ed., *American Political Trials,* pp. 79–100; James J. Robbins, *Re-*

The riot occurred early on the morning of September 11, 1851, when a Maryland slaveowner by the name of Edward Gorsuch arrived at the home of a black man in Christiana, Lancaster County, Pennsylvania, with a warrant for the arrest of four of his escaped slaves and an armed posse composed of relatives, friends, a federal deputy marshal, and several men employed for the purpose by the marshal. The details of what happened next were disputed, but shots were exchanged between the posse and a crowd that perhaps ultimately numbered as many as one hundred black men and women. Gorsuch was killed in the melee and several others on both sides were seriously wounded. Hanway, a miller of Quaker descent and principles, arrived on the scene some time after the posse, but before the carnage. The marshal contended that Hanway refused requests to assist the law officers in their duty; indeed, according to the marshal, Hanway directed the mob, ordered them to fire, and obstructed the posse's attempts to withdraw from the scene.

The indictment alleged that the riot was part of a larger conspiracy, in which Hanway was engaged, to resist enforcement of the fugitive slave law and that the riot was, accordingly, an act of levying war against enforcement of a particular law of the federal government. The government charged that Hanway, with a multitude of others, assembled for a traitorous purpose "with force and arms"; that he resisted, opposed, and assaulted the marshal, preventing him from performing his duty; and that Hanway "by force and arms" liberated persons in the custody of the marshal. The prosecution accused Hanway of engaging in a conspiracy to defeat the fugitive slave law in its operations, a conspiracy that included the composition, publication, and circulation of "divers books, pamphlets, letters, declarations, resolutions, addresses, papers and writings," which he "did then and there maliciously and traitorously publish and disperse."[104]

----

port of the *Trial of Castner Hanway for Treason* (Philadelphia, 1852), p. 181; Thomas P. Slaughter, *Bloody Dawn: The Christiana Riot and Racial Violence in the Antebellum North* (New York, 1991), pp. 112–38.

[104] Ibid., pp. 18–19.

The prosecution had a basic problem establishing facts in the case. Its principal witness, Marshal Henry Kline, was a notorious liar and his account of events on the day in question changed in various retellings, all of which was exploited to dramatic effect by the defense. Another essential witness, a local black man, recanted his previous testimony, and two other black witnesses were spirited away from the jail where they had been kept in protective custody. The scene of the riot was such that other members of the posse were unable to testify authoritatively to the nature of Hanway's participation, except for one who credited Hanway with saving his life. So government attorneys were seriously handicapped in their ability to define an overt act of treason, however broadly construed, for which they had two witnesses to Hanway's participation.

The acquittal, then, represents something more than a change in the law of treason from the late eighteenth century. And yet the judicial decision to permit a series of witnesses whose sole function was to assassinate the character of the federal marshal was a controversial one that certainly would not have been decided in favor of the defense by Judge Peters or Justice Chase fifty years earlier. Nor would the previous judges have sanctioned, over outraged prosecution objections, testimony to the general environment of fear in which free blacks lived during the year before the riot. Parallel rulings in the Whiskey Rebellion and Fries's Rebellion cases favored the prosecution and denied the relevance of contextual evidence to meliorating circumstances. The judges' consistently favorable rulings in the Hanway trial on defense motions relating to procedural details were likewise a departure from judicial behavior in treason cases before the era of Chief Justice John Marshall. Cumulatively, these judicial rulings helped create an environment in which the government appeared to have something less than a monopoly on truth and in which justice rather than mercy dictated the sparing of an accused traitor's life.[105]

[105] It is also interesting to speculate on whether the judges who tried Vigol, Mitchell, and Fries would have denied prosecution attempts to present new evidence essential to their case as part of the rebuttal. The prose-

In this case, as in the major federal treason trials preceding
it, much hinged on the definition of "levying war" accepted
by the court. Never had prosecutors argued for a broader
construction of the term; never had defense attorneys construed it more narrowly. According to the government's
lawyers, "Any combination or conspiracy by force and intimidation to prevent the execution of an act of Congress, so as to
render it inoperative and ineffective, is in legal estimation
high treason." If the perpetrator's intention includes a "public," rather than simply a private end, if the *threat* of force
exists, then it matters not, according to the prosecution,
whether a shot is fired or whether the numbers involved are
fifty or fewer: "You cannot resist the stipulations and obligations of . . . [the] Constitution without treason to the government." [106]

If such an overt act of resistance is committed, the fact that
the accused wielded no weapon, or was not even on the field
of battle, is immaterial to the charge. If he uttered "treasonable language" or "traitorous words" that inspired others to
public violence, then his guilt was as great as those who fired
a gun or wielded a sword. As the charge in the indictment
relating to writings "traitorously" published suggests, the government contended that words—spoken, written, perhaps
unpublished—sufficed as overt acts of treason under the

---

cution attempted to do just that in the Hanway case, bringing forward
witnesses to testify on the existence of black gangs in the Lancaster area
before the Christiana riot. Prosecutors contended that the purpose and
function of those gangs was to thwart by intimidation and violence any efforts of southern masters to retake escaped slaves. Such testimony was critical to developing the government's argument that there was a general
conspiracy to resist the fugitive slave act, of which the Christiana riot was
only one battle in a war levied against enforcement of the law. The defense
objected on procedural grounds and the judges ruled in favor of the defense, which effectively killed any chance the prosecution had to establish
that treason had been committed at Christiana on September 11. Judge
Robert C. Grier pointed specifically to the absence of such evidence as the
major failing of the government's case in his instructions to the jury (ibid.,
pp. 159–62, 247).

[106] Ibid., pp. 45, 224.

Constitution. It did not even seem to prosecuting attorneys that the Constitution required at least two witnesses to the defendant's commission of an overt act of treason, as long as "the connection of the prisoner with the overt act may be made out by circumstances." In each detail, prosecutors drew knowledgeably upon judicial decisions in the Whiskey Rebellion and Fries's Rebellion cases and cited historical precedents from the English law.[107]

The defense contended that judicial rulings in the Whiskey Rebellion and Fries's Rebellion cases were no longer relevant:

> The government was then new, the treasury exhausted, and the nation comparatively weak. The trial of the great experiment of a constitutional republic was considered of doubtful success, and was watched with earnest solicitude by the statesmen of the day. The value of the Union was still a debatable subject. Reverence for the Constitution had not become a common sentiment. In every speck of disaffection there was danger. Every open opposition to the regular action of the government, furnished just cause for alarm. . . . Under different circumstances the law might have been, and probably would have been differently ruled; or general principles laid down less broadly.

Fifty years later, though, the United States was a nation of thirty million rather than three million people, its borders stretched from the Atlantic to the Pacific, its survival seemed to defense counsel less precarious in every way. Under such changed circumstances, it appeared ludicrous that "three harmless, non-resisting Quakers and eight-and-thirty wretched, miserable, penniless negroes, armed with corn-cutters, clubs, and a few muskets, and headed by a miller, in a felt hat, without a coat, without arms, and mounted on a sorrel nag, levied war against the United States."[108]

According to the defense, as the nation changed, so too had the law of treason. *U.S.* v. *Hoxie,* which the prosecution tried to explain away as an anomalous decision, gives Article III,

---

[107] Ibid., pp. 215–16. The prosecution presented no evidence or argument during the course of the trial that sustained the charge of traitorous publication.

[108] Ibid., pp. 187, 109.

Section 3 a "common sense construction. It does away with the idea of constructive war; of a war in a legal sense, without a war in fact; of a war by which men may become traitors without a war of which the country has ever had any knowledge; and, in short, of all microscopic wars." There must be two witnesses to an overt act of war actually levied; force, not just conspiracy to use force, is a necessary component of war and thus of treason, as the defense understood the common-sense meanings of the words and the rulings of federal judges in treason cases since the 1790s. Nothing short of a national insurrection to bring down the government, to dismember the federal union, seemed to the defense chargeable under the Constitution as the Constitution was now understood.[109]

Judge Robert C. Grier agreed with the defense that the law of treason had changed since the 1790s, but he tried his best to avoid open disagreement with any of the federal judges who had previously ruled on the question. Neither changing political winds, nor executive and public pressure on the judiciary, nor mistaken readings of the law, nor enhanced power in the hands of federal authorities seemed to him likely explanations for legal change. According to Grier, "Many of the English cases . . . considered good law [in the 1790s] and quoted by the best text writers as authorities have since been discredited if not overruled in that country." Since there had been so few treason trials in this nation since the 1790s, American judges simply had not had the opportunity to articulate the ways in which these modernizing tendencies affected interpretations of Article III, Section 3.[110]

This rationale for restating the law of treason in strikingly different terms from Paterson, Iredell, and Chase before him, helped Grier to foster the illusion of consistency and rationality in American treason law. It enabled him to avoid framing his instructions to the jury in the stark terms presented by prosecution and defense attorneys, to avoid explicit recognition that the Hoxie case represented a clear redefinition of the crime since the convictions of Vigol, Mitchell, and Fries. And, unintentionally to be sure, it gave Grier a role in hiding

[109] Ibid., pp. 190, 185–86.

[110] Ibid., p. 246.

the nature and direction of change in the law of treason from legal historians.

These new rulings in England suggested to Grier that the term *levying war* "should be confined to insurrections and rebellions for the purpose of overturning the government by force and arms." Constructive treasons, of the sort once recognized in English and American courts, "would perhaps now be treated merely as aggravated riots or felonies." In the particular case of Hanway, Judge Grier instructed the jury that in his opinion the prosecution had not presented the sort of evidence necessary to sustain the treason charge: "That the persons engaged in . . . [the Christiana affray] are guilty of aggravated riot and murder cannot be denied. . . . But riot and murder are offences against the State government. It would be a dangerous precedent for the Court and jury in this case to extend the crime of treason by construction to doubtful cases." To constitute treason, there would need to be evidence of a previous conspiracy "to make a *general and public resistance to any law* of the United States." The prosecution had presented no proof that any of the rioters even knew that there was a federal fugitive slave law on the books. "General and public" resistance to one law only sufficed in the opinion of Judges Grier and John K. Kane (the other sitting judge in the case) and the numbers involved in the crime are not clearly material to the judgment, but "public armed opposition to the execution of this law is as much treason as it would be against any other act of Congress to be found in our statute book."[111]

Judge Grier might also have drawn on the authority of American legal commentators to buttress his opinion that the law of treason had changed significantly over the previous fifty years. William Rawle, Thomas Sergeant, Joseph Story, St. George Tucker, and Francis Wharton were cited frequently during the Hanway trial by defense lawyers as counterweights to the prosecution's reliance on Blackstone, Coke, Foster, and Hale. Working with a much shorter national legal tradition, to be sure, than their distinguished English predecessors, the

[111] Ibid., pp. 246–48, 243.

American commentators rationalized and traced evolution in the law of the United States. Each of the American commentators considered the federal law of treason and attempted to clarify the meanings of Article III, Section 3 as the courts had interpreted it over time. None found this a simple task; nor would any of the commentators have agreed with modern assessments of the treason clause as clearly defined once and for all when the drafters put down their quills.[112]

Tucker, in the earliest of these commentaries, noted that "no part of the Constitution of the United States was supposed to be less susceptible of various interpretations" than the treason clause. "It is probable," Tucker observed, "that every man in America (with the exception, perhaps of half a dozen lawyers) understood the term levying war, when the Constitution was adopted." Indeed, it seemed to him that 999 out of 1,000 "plain" Americans could have come to a clear, commonsense understanding of Article III, Section 3, were it not for the "technical" men who had worked prodigiously since the ratification of the Constitution to obscure its meaning. As a result of lawyerly obfuscation, federal treason law quickly became embroiled in controversy.[113]

---

[112] William Rawle, *A View of the Constitution of the United States of America* (Philadelphia, 1829); Thomas Sergeant, *Constitutional Law: Being a Collection of Points Arising upon the Constitution and Jurisprudence of the United States Which Have Been Settled by Judicial Decision and Practice* (Philadelphia, 1822); Joseph Story, *Commentaries on the Constitution of the United States, with a Preliminary Review of the Constitutional History of the Colonies and States, before the Adoption of the Constitution*, 3 vols. (Boston, 1833); St. George Tucker, *Blackstone's Commentaries, with Notes of Reference to the Constitution and Laws of the Federal Government of the United States and of the Commonwealth of Virginia*, 5 vols. (1803; reprint ed., New York, 1969); Francis Wharton, *A Treatise on the Criminal Law of the United States . . .* (Philadelphia, 1846). Subsequent editions of Rawle, Sergeant, Story, and Wharton were revised to take into account new court decisions. These have been checked in light of the interpretive comments offered herein about the nature and direction of change in the law of treason before the Civil War, and lack of change regarding the "levying war" clause thereafter. The famous Civil War cases, including *U.S. v. Greathouse et al.*, made no substantive alteration in those critical parts of the law of treason discussed in this essay. The same is true for the World War I and World War II cases.

[113] Tucker, *Blackstone's Commentaries*, 5:11, 13, 15.

Writing several years before Marshall's decision in the Burr case, Tucker had few kind words for the judges who presided over the trials of Vigol, Mitchell, and Fries. It seemed to him that Justice Chase in particular made pronouncements in Fries's second trial that were "both *questionable* and extrajudicial." The expansive definitions of levying war that could apply to situations in which no weapons were fired or even held, to cases where the accused had not even appeared on a field of battle, no matter how loosely defined, or to expressions of dissent that were not even specifically aimed at the federal government, went well beyond what Tucker saw as the plain and intended meaning of the Constitution's Framers.[114]

To this early-nineteenth century commentator, when the Constitution said that there were "only" two ways to commit treason—levying war and adhering to an enemy—it meant just that. "Enemy" meant *the subjects of foreign powers, with whom we are at open war*"; "levying war" just as certainly necessitated "raising an army" for the purpose of challenging the federal government's existence. Surely there were no Americans who would convict the likes of Lady Alice Lisle of treason for feeding a traitor, either before or after he was accused and convicted of the crime? Tucker thought not, and yet he accurately read the implications of recent decisions as harkening back to the days of the notorious English Judge Jeffreys. The Federalist judiciary in the 1790s was just as actively engaged in the dubious process of constructing treason as the seventeenth-century English judges had been. "To infer that the courts of the United States are left to range at large in the boundless field of *construction,* in search of *other cases* of treason against the United States," seemed to Tucker, "to be a doctrine equally unfounded, awful, and dangerous," and obviously contrary to the drafters' intentions "to cut up all *constructive* treasons, root and branch."[115]

Subsequent antebellum commentators, lawyers, and fed-

---

[114] Ibid., pp. 26–27, 29.

[115] Ibid., pp. 33, 35, 39–40. None of the other commentators mentioned in note 112 above were so openly critical of judicial rulings in treason trials as Tucker; all approached the task more as synthesizers of existing law than

eral judges worked toward an understanding of the treason clause that is closer to Tucker's than to those of Federalist decisions during the 1790s. Given the range of procedural and interpretive protections for the accused defined by nineteenth-century courts, it is implausible that the likes of Vigol, Mitchell, and Fries could again be convicted of treason against the federal government. The Civil War treason cases, which might have been expected to reverse the trend, actually continued the process of narrowing the definitions of key terms in Article III, Section 3, and of broadening procedural protections for accused traitors.

A federal judge in the case of *Shortridge et al.* v. *Macon* (1867) even went so far as to declare—for apparently the first time from a federal bench—that "the word 'only' was used [in the treason clause] to exclude from the criminal jurisprudence of the new republic the odious doctrines of constructive treason." The judge's knowledge of history was certainly no worse than that contained in a modern law dictionary, and his heart was in the same place as St. George Tucker's and those Antifederalists who worried about the potential for abuse inherent in the treason clause. This and other federal judges who presided over treason cases during the 1860s accomplished their reforming ends, either intentially or in ignorance, by avoiding any reference to treason trials prior to the Burr Conspiracy. The treason convictions of the 1790s could now be "forgotten" as the narrower interpretations of "overt act," "levying war," and "enemy" became fixed in judicial pronouncements accompanying the cases of *Greiner* (1861), *Greathouse et al.* (1863), *Cathcart* (1864), *Davis* (1867–71), and others. There can be no doubt that the crime of treason in 1851, 1861, and today is much

---

as critics, and thus sought to avoid wherever possible (even to the point of distortion) any identification of areas where judicial interpretations had been overruled. Nonetheless, all recognized that the law of treason was to be found more in the cases of Aaron Burr, Frederick Hoxie, and Hanway (in revised editions that came after 1851) than in the Whiskey Rebellion and Fries's Rebellion cases.

more precisely and narrowly defined than it was in 1787, 1795, and 1799.[116]

There has been no twentieth-century treason prosecution for levying war against the United States, and thus no ruling to embellish or alter the narrow interpretation of the judges in *U.S.* v. *Hanway* and the Civil War cases. Indeed, the government's decision not to prosecute for treason in several plausible situations very well may reflect a general understanding approximating that of St. George Tucker's early nineteenth-century treatise. World Wars I and II have generated a number of treason charges (and convictions) for adhering to an enemy. Cumulatively, these decisions have furthered the process of narrowing the scope of the treason clause by adding precision to the definitions of "adhering" and "enemy" that was lacking in the antebellum cases.[117]

Still, today the possibility of convicting a "procurer" of treason—one who purchases arms, recruits soldiers, or even

[116] *U.S.* v. *Greiner* (1861), *Federal Cases,* 26:36–41; *U.S.* v. *Greathouse et al.* (1863), ibid., pp. 18–30; *U.S.* v. *Cathcart* (1864), ibid., 25:344–50; *Shortridge et al.* v. *Macon* (1867), ibid., 22:20–23; case of Davis (1867–71), ibid., 7:63–102; *Keppel* v. *Petersburg R. Co.* (1868), ibid., 14:357–75; *U.S.* v. *Cramer* (1943), *Federal Reporter,* 2d ser. 137:888–98; charges to grand juries, treason, *Federal Cases,* 30:997–1051; Frank L. Klement, "The Indianapolis Treason Trials and *Ex Parte Milligan,*" in Belknap, ed., *American Political Trials,* pp. 101–27. For the reference to the law dictionary, see note 6 above.

Although there were no federal prosecutions for treason by levying war after the Civil War, there was one state prosecution, in Pennsylvania, of several strike leaders associated with the Homestead Strike (1892). They were acquitted. See Hurst, *Law of Treason,* pp. 199–200.

[117] See *U.S.* v. *Fricke* (1919), *Federal Reporter,* 259:673–84; *U.S.* v. *Robinson* (1919), ibid., 309:685–94; *U.S.* v. *Cramer* (1943), ibid., 2d ser., 337:888–98; *U.S.* v. *Kawakita* (1950), *Federal Supplement,* 96:824–61; *Kawakita* v. *U.S.* (1952), *Federal Reporter,* 2d ser., 190:506–29, and 343 *United States Reports* 717–46; *D'Aguino* v. *U.S.* (1951), *Federal Reporter,* 2d ser., 292:338–76; *Chandler* v. *U.S.* (1948), ibid., 171:921–47; *Gillars* v. *U.S.* (1950), ibid., 182:962–84; *Best* v. *U.S.* (1950), ibid., 184:131–41; *Haupt* v. *U.S.,* 330 *United States Reports* 631–49. (1946). Francis S. Ruddy, "Permissible Dissent or Treason?" *Criminal Law Bulletin* 4 (1968):145–59; Jabez W. Loane, "Treason and Trading with the Enemy," *Military Law Review* 30 (1965):43–81; Margaret Boveri, *Treason in the Twentieth Century* (New York, 1963); Nathaniel Weyl, *Treason: The Story of Disloyalty and Betrayal in American History* (Washington, D.C., 1950); West, *Meaning of Treason.*

knowingly sells a watermelon to a putative traitor or enemy—
remains just as plausible as before. Constructive treason certainly has come under fire, and the seemingly limitless potential for its use and abuse has probably been greatly reduced.
But no judicial decision, statutory enactment, or constitutional interpretation has eliminated judges' authority to construct new and heretofore unimagined treasons within the
bounds of what has proved to be a very elastic treason clause.
The judicial interpretation of Article III, Section 3 that found
resistance to one "general" federal statute potentially treasonous is still good law. There can be no authoritative statement,
in light of the history of treason prosecutions in the federal
courts, that the threat of armed resistance to any one "general" law—say, for example, the income tax—is not potentially treasonous. Perhaps the greatest testament to both the
success of the antebellum judiciary in circumscribing the law
of treason, and to the limitations of that process of redefinition, is the government's perception in the twentieth century
that it needs and has the constitutional authority to enforce a
series of "espionage" laws to prosecute "enemies" of the
state—traitors—under another guise.[118]

[118]The watermelon was at issue in *U.S.* v. *Lee* (1814), *Federal Cases,*
26:907.

JAMES H. KETTNER

Persons or Property?
The Pleasants Slaves in
the Virginia Courts,
1792–1799

CHATTEL SLAVERY CRYSTALLIZED as a legal institution in Virginia in the mid-seventeenth century and endured down through the Civil War. During those two hundred years, the last two decades of the eighteenth century stand out as the period in which a significant challenge was first mounted to the institution, as hundreds of Virginia masters freed their slaves and organized publicly to oppose slavery.[1]

Robert Pleasants, a Virginia Quaker, was one of those who became very active in promoting the cause of emancipation, both through private and public correspondence and in his role as a founder and president of the Virginia Abolition Society.[2] In addition to his efforts in this broader public arena, he

Research for this essay was supported by a grant from the Huntington Library and the Mead Foundation. I gratefully acknowledge the generous assistance of the staffs of the Earl Gregg Swem Library, the Friends Historical Library of Swarthmore College, the Henry E. Huntington Library, the Historical Society of Pennsylvania, the Virginia Historical Society, and the Virginia State Library.

[1] For a thoughtful overview see Richard S. Dunn, "Black Society in the Chesapeake, 1776–1810," in Ira Berlin and Ronald Hoffman, eds., *Slavery and Freedom in the Age of the American Revolution* (Charlottesville, Va., 1983), pp. 49–82.

[2] A communication addressed "To the Friends of Liberty" in the *Virginia Independent Chronicle, and General Advertiser* (Richmond), Jan. 30, 1790, announced plans to establish an antislavery society, which adopted the name "Virginia Society for Promoting the Abolition of Slavery, and the Relief of

engaged in a more personal struggle to win freedom for the
slaves held by his own family. That struggle began with attempts to persuade his relatives to manumit their slaves under the provisions of a law of 1782 that he and other Friends
had lobbied for strenuously. It culminated before the bench
of the High Court of Appeals, which finally met to determine
whether the Pleasants slaves were persons or property. The
course of the controversy over the Pleasants slaves illustrates
some of the forces undergirding the opposition to slavery in
the early years of the republic as well as some of the obstacles
that opponents of the institution faced. Its outcome also poi-
gnantly reveals the Virginia courts' ambivalent response to
the conflict between the rights of liberty and the rights of
property in the post-Revolutionary era.

On the evening of August 13, 1771, John Pleasants, Sr., of
Curles plantation in Henrico County, Virginia, died.[3] Two
days earlier, he had signed and sealed his last will and testament, disposing of the considerable estate he had amassed in
his seventy-five years as a successful planter and merchant.[4]
Pleasants carefully allocated tracts of land scattered through

---

Free Negroes, and Others, Unlawfully Held in Bondage, and Other Humane Purposes." Robert Pleasants was elected president of the "Humane
Society" at its organizational meeting in April 1790.

[3] Obituary notice in *Virginia Gazette* (Purdie and Dixon), Sept. 12, 1771,
in "Personal Notices from the Virginia Gazette," *William and Mary Quarterly,*
1st ser. 8 (1899–1900):190. See also Richard Adams to Thomas Adams,
Aug..16, 1771, "Letters of Richard Adams to Thomas Adams," *Virginia Historical Magazine* 22 (1914): 383, noting the time of John's death and the fact
that the "Colony in general" was "very Sickly."

[4] The original will, signed Aug. 11, 1771, and a short codicil added the
next day were destroyed during the War for Independence. A copy was
presented to commissioners appointed to restore the county's records, May
8, 1783, and the attested copy was later submitted to the Henrico County
Court and recorded on Mar. 3, 1784. See Proceedings of Commissioners
Respecting the Records of Henrico Court Destroyed by the British, 1774–
82, pp. 63–82, Virginia State Library, Richmond; Henrico County, Orders,
1 (1781–84), p. 498, Va. St. Libr. The will, with some minor textual variations, is reprinted in Clayton Torrence et al., eds., *The Edward Pleasants Valentine Papers,* 4 vols. (Richmond, 1927), 2:1116–28.

at least five Virginia counties to his children and grandchildren, and by specific bequests of money, household goods, and slaves he distributed his valuable personal estate. Two years later, Robert Pleasants—John's eldest son and chief executor—wrote to his brother Samuel in Philadelphia that the "appraisement of the Estate is completed and the amount of the whole is £12,143.11.¾ of which £9,722.10 are Negroes."[5]

In his will the Quaker patriarch expressed his desire "to do all manner of good to my poor slaves as far as in my power and consistent to the laws of the land [do] justice to them and my family."[6] He made special provisions for fifteen of his slaves—permitting them to live with whomever they chose or allowing them at least part of the income of their own labor—then distributed the rest among his family and kin. According to Robert Pleasants, the slaves bequeathed by his father "amounted in the whole to 215."[7]

None of these bequests would have been problematic had not John Pleasants made them all conditional, requiring the legatees to renounce their property rights in the slaves at some point in the future. The crucial clause of his will read: "And my desire is respecting my poor slaves all of them as I shall die possessed of shall be free (if they choose it) when they arrive at the age of thirty years and the law of the land will admit them to be set free without their being transported out of the country. I say all my slaves now born or hereafter to be born whilst their mothers are in the service of me or my heirs to be free at the age of thirty years as before mentioned."[8] Five years later, John's son Jonathan followed his father's lead

---

[5] Robert Pleasants to Samuel Pleasants, 8 mo. [Aug.] 28, 1773, in Robert Pleasants Letterbook, 1771–89, Earl Gregg Swem Library, College of William and Mary, Williamsburg, Va. This letterbook is unpaginated.

[6] Will of John Pleasants, Torrence et al., eds., *Edward Pleasants Valentine Papers,* 2:1117.

[7] Robert Pleasants to James Pemberton, 11 mo. [Nov.] 13, 1790, in *Manuscript Collection Belonging to the Pennsylvania Society for Promoting the Abolition of Slavery, for the Relief of Free Negroes Unlawfully Held in Bondage, and for Improving the Condition of the African Race,* 8 vols. (Philadelphia, 1876), 2:221.

[8] Will of John Pleasants, Torrence et al., eds., *Edward Pleasants Valentine Papers,* 2:1117–18.

in his own will, providing that all his slaves be freed at age thirty "whenever the Law of the Country will admit absolute freedom to them." On "these express conditions and no others," Jonathan then distributed the slaves to his relatives, giving the largest share to his sister Mary and appointing Robert Pleasants—who may in fact have been responsible for the manumission clauses—as his chief executor.[9]

John Pleasants and his son Robert were devout Quakers, and it is apparent that the unusual provisions in these wills concerning the slaves reflected their religious convictions. Despite some sporadic criticisms of the system of slaveholding in earlier decades, members of the Society of Friends had largely accommodated themselves to the institution. By the mid-1760s, however, Virginia Quakers had begun moving toward a policy of disengagement from slavery.[10] In 1768 the Virginia Yearly Meeting held that none of its members "should be permitted to purchase a Negro or other Slave without being guilty of a breach of our discipline," while the Cedar Creek Quarterly Meeting requested advice as to "what measures should be taken by such friends who are burdened by keeping them in Slavery, to clear themselves and their families from them."[11] In 1772 the Yearly Meeting declared that any mem-

[9] Will of Jonathan Pleasants, May 11, 1776, ibid., 2:1130–31. This varies in some minor details from the copy recorded by the commissioners to restore the Henrico County records, in Proceedings of Commissioners Respecting the Records of Henrico Court, pp. 92–96. For the possibility that Robert Pleasants was responsible for the manumission provisions, see Robert Pleasants to Samuel Pleasants, 7 mo. [July] 8, 1776, Robert Pleasants Letterbook,

1754–97, p. 39 (microfilm [M 827], Maryland State Archives, Annapolis).

[10] For the classic survey, see Stephen B. Weeks, *Southern Quakers and Slavery: A Study in Institutional History* (Baltimore, 1896), chap. 9. See also, Kenneth L. Carroll, ed., "Robert Pleasants on Quakerism: 'Some Account of the First Settlement of Friends in Virginia . . . ,'" *Virginia Magazine of History and Biography* 86 (1978):3–16.

[11] Quoted in William C. Dunlap, *Quaker Education in Baltimore and Virginia Yearly Meetings with an Account of Certain Meetings of Delaware and the Eastern Shore Affiliated with Philadelphia. Based on the Manuscript Sources* (Philadelphia, 1936), p. 455. According to Douglas Summers Brown, Cedar Creek Friends took the lead in antislavery activities of this period. See his introduction to extracts from the Cedar Creek Monthly Meeting in William Wade Hinshaw

ber who should "purchase a negro or other slave with no other view but their own benefit or convenience" should be disowned.[12] Finally, in November 1774, the Henrico Quarterly Meeting advised "Friends who are burdened with keeping them [slaves] in Bondage to seek relief by suitable application to our next Assembly, to repeal that clause of Law, which prohibits Freeing them."[13]

The law was indeed the major obstacle preventing troubled masters from freeing their slaves. The Virginia Assembly had moved to restrict the growth of a free black population as early as 1691, providing that "no negro or mulatto be . . . set free by any person or persons whatsoever, unless such person or persons . . . pay for the transportation of such negro or negroes out of the country within six months after setting them free."[14] Controls were tightened in 1723, when the legislature banned private manumission "upon any pretense whatsoever, except for some meritorious services," the latter to be first adjudged by the governor and council, who would issue a special license to authorize the act. Slaves freed in violation of the statute were to be taken up by the churchwardens and sold "by public outcry" at the next county court, the proceeds to be applied to the use of the parish.[15] These provisions were reaffirmed by the comprehensive act of 1748, which was still in force when John and Jonathan Pleasants died.[16]

The escalating struggle with England over questions of

---

et al., comps., *Encyclopedia of American Quaker Genealogy*, vol. 6, *Virginia* (Ann Arbor, 1950), p. 225.

[12] Quoted in Dunlap, *Quaker Education*, p. 456.

[13] Entry for 11 mo. [Nov.] 27, 1774 [Society of Friends], Book of Record for Our Quarterly Meeting of Henrico County, Commenced on the 6th of 2d. Mo. 1745, Ending the 16th of the 5th Mo. 1783, p. 237, Robert Alonzo Brock Collection, BR 7, Henry E. Huntington Library, San Marino, Calif.

[14] April sess., 1691, chap. 16, William Waller Hening, comp., *The Statutes at Large; Being a Collection of All the Laws of Virginia, from the First Session of the Legislature, in the Year 1619*, 13 vols. (Richmond, 1819–23), 3:86–87.

[15] May sess., 1723, chap. 4, ibid., 4:132.

[16] October sess., 1748, chap. 38, ibid., 6:104–12.

power and right that led to war and eventually to Independence encouraged Robert Pleasants to "hope that a time may come, and perhaps its not fare distant, when we . . . may have it in our power to invest them [the slaves] with freedom."[17] In 1777 he informed then-governor Patrick Henry that many Friends, "from a full conviction of the injustice, and an apprehention of duty, have been induced to embrace the present favourable juncture, when the Representatives of the people have nobly declared *all men equally free,* to manumit," de facto, many of their slaves, despite the standing prohibition of that practice.[18] Because such people were still vulnerable to seizure by the churchwardens, Pleasants admitted that they "mostly remained under the Care & protection of their late masters, either as tenants, or servants on wages."[19]

Whatever hopes Pleasants harbored about the ultimate impact of the War for Independence, in the short run it posed immediate problems for him and his fellow Quakers. Robert himself suffered extensively for his pacifism and his refusal to aid the war effort in any way, bearing, according to one authority, "between a quarter and a half of all the fines, distraints, and seizures levied on Quakers in Henrico Monthly Meeting" between 1778 and 1783.[20] It was not just money that was at stake, either. In May 1782 the Henrico Quarterly Meeting recorded that Friends had suffered losses of £224.15.6, "including a mannumited Negro Girl about eight years old, taken from Robert Pleasants."[21]

[17] Robert Pleasants to Samuel Pleasants, 7 mo. [July] 8, 1776, Robert Pleasants letterbook, 1754–97, p. 39.

[18] Robert Pleasants to "Respected Friend" [Patrick Henry], 3 mo. [Mar.] 28, 1777, included in Robert Pleasants Letters Received, 1746–97, n.p. (microfilm [M 827], Md. St. Arch.). A manuscript copy, with slight variations, is in the Henry Family Papers, 1723–1801, MSS 1/H3968/a 1–30, Virginia Historical Society, Richmond.

[19] Carroll, ed., "Robert Pleasants on Quakerism," p. 14. A variant version, dated 8 mo. [Aug.] 10, 1786, is in Robert Pleasants Letterbook, 1754–97, pp. 93–95.

[20] Carroll, ed., "Robert Pleasants on Quakerism," p. 6 n. 12.

[21] Entry for 5 mo. [May] 15, 1782, Record for Quarterly Meeting of Henrico Co., p. 323, Brock Collection. An extract from the Henrico Monthly

Pleasants and other Virginia Friends refused to let the disruptions and animosities of war deflect them from their antislavery goals. In November 1780 they petitioned the House of Delegates to repeal the law prohibiting private manumission. Although a bill was brought in and twice read, it was postponed by a narrow vote.[22] The Quakers persisted, however, petitioning the Assembly again in May 1782, and this time the House of Delegates responded favorably, passing an act that made it lawful for any person "by his or her last will and testament, or by any other instrument of writing, under his or her hand and seal, . . . to emancipate and set free, his or her slaves." Slaves who in the court's judgment were not of sound mind and body, as well as those over forty-five years or under the age of majority (eighteen for females, twenty-one for males), were to be supported and maintained by the person liberating them. Those freed under this act were not required to leave the state.[23]

Robert Pleasants immediately took advantage of the new law. At Henrico County Court on November 4, 1782, he recorded a deed of emancipation for his seventy-eight slaves. Twenty-nine of them, ranging in age from eighteen to sixty,

---

Meeting (White Oak Swamp) and Waynoke Preparation Meeting Minute Book, 1781–1805, dated 6 mo. [June] 1, 1782, reprinted in Torrence et al., eds., *Edward Pleasants Valentine Papers*, 2:1247, reads: "Taken from Robert Pleasants by James Sharp, deputy Sheriff and bought by Robert Elam on acct. of substitute fines, Taxes etc., a negro girl named Betty about 7 years, Manumitted the 21 of 7 mo. 1777. The Sheriff was informed at the time of Seizure and the people at the sale publicly advertised that the girl had a right to Freedom on the 1st, of the 12 mo. 1792."

[22] Petition dated Nov. 29, 1780, in Legislative Petitions, Miscellaneous, Box C (1780–81), Va. St. Libr. For the legislature's handling of the petition, see *Journal of the House of Delegates of the Commonwealth of Virginia* [Oct. 16, 1780-Jan. 2, 1781] (Richmond, 1827), pp. 32, 38, 42, 49, 54. See also Robert Pleasants to Anthony Benezet, 2 mo. [Feb.] 1781, in George S. Brookes, *Friend Anthony Benezet* (Philadelphia, 1937), p. 437.

[23] May sess., 1782, chap. 21, Hening, comp., *Statutes at Large*, 11:39–40. The petition, dated May 29, 1782, is in Legislative Petitions, Miscellaneous, Box D (1782–83).

he freed immediately. The remaining forty-nine minors were to enjoy their liberty "after they shall attain to their respective lawful Ages of eighteen and twenty-one without any interruption from me or any person or persons claiming for, by, from, or under me."[24] Six months later, in a deed of emancipation signed jointly by Robert and his brother Samuel, twelve more blacks finally received in law the freedom they had been promised in the wills of John and Jonathan Pleasants.[25]

Had it been within his power, Robert Pleasants would undoubtedly have manumitted all the slaves promised freedom by his father and brother, but his status as executor did not endow him with that authority. Whether for reasons of filial loyalty or their own antislavery convictions, John's sons had done what they could to fulfill their father's wishes that the slaves be freed. His grandson, Samuel Pleasants, Jr., and his daughters and granddaughters proved more obstinate. The surviving evidence suggests very little about why Samuel Jr. refused to free the slaves he had been given. As one of the major legatees, he of course had a substantial economic interest at stake. It also seems likely that his religious convictions—a powerful source of his relatives' antislavery impulses—were not deep: his uncle Robert had pleaded with him to follow the faith and confessed disappointment in his conduct as early as 1779.[26] As for John's female descendants, the fact that they failed to comply with the terms of his will by no means proves that they were indifferent to his wishes or unsympathetic to the slaves' predicament. Once these women married, control of their slaves rested with

[24] Henrico County, Deeds, 1 (1781–85), pp. 41–42, Va. St. Libr. The deed was signed Aug. 1 and recorded on Nov. 4 (Henrico County, Orders, 1, p. 118). A certificate of emancipation of one of the minors—Lydia, who would attain her majority Jan. 1, 1789—can be found in the George Bryan Papers, Box 1, fol. 8, Historical Society of Pennsylvania, Philadelphia.

[25] Henrico County, Deeds, 1, pp. 210–11. Although it was dated May 23, 1783, the deed was not formally recorded in the county court until May 3, 1784 (Henrico County, Orders, 1, p. 534).

[26] Robert Pleasants to Samuel Pleasants, Jr., 7 mo. [July] 7, 1779, Robert Pleasants Letterbook, 1754–97, p. 52.

their husbands, who might well be more prone to calculate the economic consequences of manumission.[27]

Robert foresaw the complications that might ensue from a "bad" marriage. Writing to his brother Samuel shortly after Jonathan's death in 1776, he noted that Jonathan had "given the bulk of his Estate to his Sister Molly [i.e., Mary], who I fear, should she remain in Virginia, will be in eminent danger of becoming a prey to some designing fellow." Robert thus proposed to send Mary to the presumably safer environs of Philadelphia, where she might be watched over by Samuel and his wife.[28] Mary did remove to Philadelphia, joining a monthly meeting there in May 1777. Two years later, in July 1779, she married Charles Logan, grandson of the distinguished colonial statesman and proprietary leader James Logan.[29]

Whether Charles Logan was a "designing fellow" may be arguable, but it is clear that he was not in fact prepared to renounce the estate that marriage to the "heires[s] of the Pleasants family" brought.[30] To be sure, he did execute a manumission of the slaves—who were still in Virginia under Robert's supervision—on the very day of his marriage.[31] But

[27] For recent discussions of the limited property rights of married women in Virginia, see Suzanne Lebsock, *The Free Women of Petersburg: Status and Culture in a Southern Town, 1784–1860* (New York, 1984), chap. 2; and Joan R. Gunderson and Gwen Victor Gampel, "Married Women's Legal Status in Eighteenth-Century New York and Virginia," *William and Mary Quarterly*, 3d ser. 39 (1982):116–27.

[28] Robert Pleasants to Samuel Pleasants, 5 mo. [May] 17, 1776, Robert Pleasants Letterbook, 1754–97, p. 37.

[29] Hinshaw et al., comps., *Encyclopedia of American Quaker Genealogy*, vol. 2, *Pennsylvania* (Ann Arbor, 1938), pp. 623, 584. There are a few genealogical details in Amelia Mott Gummere, "Two Logan Letters," *Journal of the Friends' Historical Society* 9 (1912):85–87.

[30] The "heiress" reference came in a letter of introduction for Charles Logan by Isaac Zane. See Zane to Thomas Jefferson, Feb. 25, 1782, in Julian P. Boyd et al., eds., *The Papers of Thomas Jefferson*, 28 vols. to date (Princeton, 1950-), 6:160.

[31] Robert Pleasants to Jacob Shoemaker, Jr., et al., 5 mo. [May] 12, 1788, Robert Pleasants Letterbook, 1754–97, p. 146. Pemberton later informed Robert Pleasants that "the original of C Logan & wife's manumission is here

when he moved permanently to Virginia in 1782, he showed no inclination to treat that act as anything but an empty gesture. It was probably about this time that Robert consulted Edmund Randolph, then practicing law in the superior courts, about the effect of the manumission Logan had recorded in Philadelphia. Randolph's professional opinion was that "as it was done on the day of his Marriage, when his wife was under age, and at a time when the law suppos'd a man to be under perticular influence, he supposed it would be ineffectual to compel a performance." [32]

Throughout the 1780s Robert Pleasants tried to persuade Logan and the other legatees to free the slaves they held under the wills, but such efforts proved fruitless. Nor did religious sanctions have much effect. Logan had been disowned by the Quakers in 1782 for "joining himself in an association with a number of men engaged in war," and although his wife, Mary, and two children transferred their membership to the Cedar Creek Monthly Meeting when they returned to Virginia, there is no evidence that Charles ever sought to be restored to fellowship with the Society. His apparent indifference may even have eroded his wife's convictions, for within a few years, she, too, would be disowned for "nonattendance" and "inconsistent conduct." [33]

Since Robert could not persuade his relatives to free their slaves voluntarily, he turned to the state's legal institutions—

[in Philadelphia], and Recorded in one of our public office." See marginal notation in Pemberton to Robert Pleasants, 2 mo. [Feb.] 28, 1790, Pleasants Family Papers, BR Box 12 (3), Brock Collection. For a copy of the original manumission, see Manumission Book: A Record of Manumissions for Slaves Released from Bondage within the Limits of the Three Monthly Meetings of Friends of the City and Liberties of Philadelphia [1776–96], pp. 32–33, Friends Historical Library of Swarthmore College, Swarthmore, Pa.

[32] Robert Pleasants to Shoemaker, Jr., et al., 5 mo. [May] 12, 1788, Robert Pleasants Letterbook, 1754–97, pp. 146–47.

[33] [July] 26, 1782 entry, Hinshaw et al., comps., *Encyclopedia of American Quaker Genealogy*, 2:584 (Charles disowned, wife and children granted certificates of removal); [Apr.] 12, 1783 entry, ibid., 6:258 (Mary and children received by Cedar Creek Monthly Meeting); [July] 12, 1788 entry, ibid. (Mary disowned).

the legislature and the courts—for assistance. In September 1790, following customary procedure, he announced in the local newspaper that he intended to petition the legislature for a special act confirming the wills of his father and brother and directing that the slaves be manumitted as they had intended.[34] He informed his Philadelphia relative, James Pemberton, that he expected "to incur the displeasure of some of my relations, who I love, by being active in this business," but he thought there was a "fair prospect" that the legislature would confirm the slaves' right to freedom.[35]

Robert's prediction that his relatives would oppose his petition was fulfilled on November 20, when Charles Logan and Samuel Pleasants, Jr., submitted a memorial urging the legislature not to act. Noting that the law prohibited private manumission at the time the wills were made and citing legal advice to the effect that the manumission clauses in the wills were "a Mere Nullity," the memorialists contended that Robert's petition was "not a proper Subject of Legislative interference," especially since in their opinion "John Pleasants had no Legal right to some of the Slaves devised by his Will—and that there are Circumstances in respect to other gifts that would have great Weight in a Court of Judicature."[36]

The memorial apparently persuaded the Committee for Courts of Justice. Although it had earlier found the petition of Robert Pleasants "reasonable," it now urged that it "be rejected; the same involving private rights, and depending on the legal construction of several clauses in the said wills, and on other circumstances not proper for the consideration of the Legislative, but of the Judiciary authority."[37] Although Robert tried again the next year, submitting separate peti-

---

[34] *Virginia Gazette, and General Advertiser* (Richmond), Sept. 8, 1790.

[35] Robert Pleasants to Pemberton, 11 mo. [Nov.] 13, 1790, in *Manuscript Collection Belonging to the Pennsylvania Society for Abolition*, 2:220–21. The committee had agreed to a favorable report on Nov. 10, noted Pleasants, though it did not formally report back to the House until Nov. 15.

[36] Petition of Nov. 20, 1790, in Legislative Petitions, Henrico County, Box A (1778–90), Va. St. Libr.

[37] *Journal of the House of Delegates* (Oct. 18-Dec. 29, 1790), pp. 107, 126.

tions asking the legislature to enforce the wills, the House again refused to act, holding that "the subject matter of the petitions of the said Robert Pleasants . . . is properly cognizable in the courts of judicature of this commonwealth."[38]

It was probably at this point that Pleasants turned to the courts and initiated a suit against his relatives to force them to free their slaves. Although the first formal action mentioned in the published records came on March 16, 1798, when the High Court of Chancery issued an injunction ordering the various defendants not to remove the slaves in their possession from the state, a number of anomalies suggest that the first steps in the suit occurred earlier, probably in 1792 or 1793.[39] In any event, the details of the arguments presented in Robert's bill and the defendants' answers—the written complaints and defenses submitted in chancery proceedings—and the arguments advanced by counsel cannot be fully recovered, since the original suit papers were apparently destroyed when the state courthouse burned during the Confederate evacuation of Richmond in April 1865.[40] The printed reports indicate that the defendants all demurred to the jurisdiction of the High Court of Chancery and that several of them claimed to hold the slaves by titles paramount to the

[38] *Virginia Gazette, and General Advertiser* (Richmond), Aug. 10, 1791; *Journal of the House of Delegates* (Oct. 17-Dec. 20, 1791), pp. 14, 45, 63.

[39] The chancery proceedings are partly recorded in *Virginia: In the High Court of Chancery, March 16, 1798. Between Robert Pleasants . . . and Mary Logan . . .* (N.p. [Richmond], n.d. [1800]), pp. 1–7, and are followed by detailed inventories of the slaves then held by the various parties. For the report of *Pleasants et al.* v. *Pleasants* in the Court of Appeals, see Daniel Call, *Reports of Cases Argued and Adjudged in the Court of Appeals of Virginia,* 6 vols. (Richmond, 1801–33), 2:319–57. Some of Call's dates are inaccurate, and for the timing of the actions in this court I have relied on Irwin S. Rhodes, *The Papers of John Marshall: A Descriptive Calendar,* 2 vols. (Norman, Okla., 1969), 2:368–69. Robert Pleasants had initiated a suit in chancery against Charles and Mary Logan in the Powhatan County Court as early as Mar. 22, 1793 (Powhatan County, Orders, 4 [1791–94], p. 229, Va. St. Libr.). It is not clear from the formulaic Order Book entries whether this was the same suit—or perhaps one of several distinct suits against the various defendants—that finally came into George Wythe's High Court of Chancery, but the timing is plausible.

[40] Wilmer L. Hall, "The Public Records of Virginia: Their Destruction and Preservation," *Virginia Libraries* 4 (1931):12.

wills or argued that the slaves were subject to counterclaims that should take priority.

Chancellor George Wythe, himself sympathetic to the antislavery cause, overruled the demurrers to his court's jurisdiction. In a characteristically learned and somewhat pedantic decree, he held that the case involved a charitable trust properly adjudicated in the High Court of Chancery. On the main issue, Wythe ruled that the condition John and Jonathan Pleasants had annexed to their bequests—namely, that the slaves be freed when the law so allowed—was in itself lawful. It did not violate existing statutes, nor, in Wythe's view, did it violate the rule against perpetuities—a well-established legal doctrine that voided any condition that tended to render property inalienable or prevent title from vesting for a period longer than a life or lives in being, plus twenty-one years. Thus he concluded that the slaves should be freed. His decree, issued September 12, 1798, declared that all slaves aged thirty or older when the manumission act was passed in 1782 were entitled to freedom. Those born before the act would be free when they reached that age, and those born after the statute "were at their birth entitled to freedom." He directed that an inventory of the slaves be made, ascertaining "the times when, according to the foregoing opinion, any of them ought heretofore to have been and hereafter to be liberated from servitude, and stating accounts of profits, to which they who have been wrongfully detained are entitled."[41]

On September 26, 1798, the defendants prayed that an appeal from Wythe's decree in favor of the slaves be allowed, a request the chancellor routinely approved on condition of their giving bond and security.[42] Counsel engaged to argue the case on appeal included the most prominent and prestigious members of the Virginia bar. John Wickham, the "leader of that bar (or at least its most active member)," and Edmund Randolph, former state attorney general, governor, United States attorney general, and secretary of state, repre-

[41] *High Court of Chancery: Pleasants v. Logan*, pp. 2–3. For a short sketch of Wythe's career, see L. S. Herrink, "George Wythe," *John P. Branch Historical Papers of Randolph-Macon College* 3 (1912):283–313.

[42] *High Court of Chancery: Pleasants v. Logan*, pp. 3–4.

sented the appellants (the legatees). Representing Robert
Pleasants on behalf of the slaves were John Marshall, shortly
to become chief justice of the United States Supreme Court,
and John ("Old Jock") Warden, recognized as "a profound
lawyer, and the ablest conveyancer in Virginia."[43] Hearing the
case were Edmund Pendleton, president of the Court of Appeals, and his fellow appellate judges, Paul Carrington, William Fleming, and the brilliant young Spencer Roane.[44]

The first point argued by counsel when the case was heard
in early November involved the threshold procedural question of whether the High Court of Chancery had properly
exercised jurisdiction. After hearing technical discussion by
counsel, all three judges who issued opinions in the case sustained Wythe's jurisdiction. In the view of one modern authority, they "took an extraordinary, almost twentieth-century
approach to the procedural issue," upholding jurisdiction despite their "bewilderment as to the exact source of the authority for so acting."[45] Pendleton concluded that if the slaves
were "entitled to relief, at all, it is on the ground of a trust

[43] David John Mays, *Edmund Pendleton, 1721–1803: A Biography*, 2 vols.
(Cambridge, Mass., 1952), 2:281–85, provides brief sketches of John Wickham, John Marshall, Edmund Randolph, and John Warden and discusses
their place in the Virginia bar (quotations pp. 281, 284). All four were qualified to practice in the High Court of Chancery, at least as of 1800, though
it is not clear that they represented the parties in that forum as well—except for Warden, who was assigned as counsel in the companion suit of *Ned
v. Elizabeth Pleasants*. See lists of lawyers qualified in Chancery, *Annual Register, and Virginia Repository, for the Year 1800* (Petersburg, n.d. [1801]), p. 177;
and *High Court of Chancery: Pleasants v. Logan*, p. 7, for Warden's appointment.

[44] For sketches of Judges Paul Carrington, William Fleming, and Spencer
Roane, see Mays, *Edmund Pendleton*, 2:298–300. Pendleton was reputed the
equal, if not the superior, of George Wythe himself. For the long rivalry
between the two, see ibid., 1:226–31, 2:290–302. The fifth judge of the
court, Peter Lyons, was absent when arguments were made and the opinions rendered, while Fleming was present but delivered no opinion
(George H. Hoemann to author, June 14, 1983. My thanks to Dr. Hoemann, assistant editor of *The Papers of John Marshall*, for sharing the preliminary draft of his editorial note on *Pleasants v. Pleasants*).

[45] Robert M. Cover, *Justice Accused: Antislavery and the Judicial Process* (New
Haven, 1975), p. 69n.

created by the wills," and although he confessed that he was unsure of Robert's technical standing to bring the suit, yet he thought that the case "ought to be heard and decided upon, without a rigid attention to legal forms."[46]

Upholding Wythe's jurisdiction was not the same as sustaining his position on the merits, of course, and the court still had to consider the substantive issues of the case. Not surprisingly, those issues were not framed in the broad terms of religion, morality, and justice that Robert Pleasants had long been accustomed to use in his own antislavery advocacy but were now cast as technical questions of law. As John Wickham noted, "Although it may be true that liberty is to be favored, the rights of property are as sacred as those of liberty," and he insisted that "this cause should be decided on the same principles of law, that other causes are."[47]

Wickham contended that the principles of law could not sustain the slaves' claim to freedom. The statute of 1748 banning private manumission had been in effect when the wills were made, and thus the condition requiring the legatees to free the slaves was void. Moreover the condition was "contrary to the nature of the estate, for it tended to bar the alienation of the property." The bequests in his view were "in effect, but a devise of the slaves in absolute property, with a condition, that the devisee shall not alien." Citing the venerable English jurist Sir Edward Coke, Wickham observed that "a privilege, inseparable from the estate, cannot be restrained; and the right of alienation is a privilege inseparable from the right of property."[48] Moreover, the act of 1782 had established conditions restricting manumission—"such as the maintenance of the young and aged slaves"—and neither the

[46] *Pleasants et al.* v. *Pleasants,* 2 Call 319, 350.

[47] Ibid., p. 324.

[48] Ibid., p. 325, citing "Co. Litt. 224." In the passage cited, Coke was discussing certain incidents to an estate tail, observing that "if a man make a gift in tail, upon condition to restrain him of any of these incidents, the condition is repugnant and void in Law" (see Sir Edward Coke, *The First Part of the Institutes of the Laws of England, or, A Commentary upon Littleton . . .* , ed. Francis Hargrave and Charles Butler, 1st Am. ed. from the 19th London ed., corrected, 2 vols. [Philadelphia, 1853], 2:224a).

wills nor Wythe's decree made provision for this. Finally, the decree in fact did not—and in Wickham's view, ought not— "follow the testators intention." John Pleasants had "intended to erect the slaves into a distinct kind of property: that is to say, they were to be slaves till 30, and free men afterwards."[49] And this was to be the case for all those born before their mothers reached the age of thirty. To enforce this intention, in Wickham's view, "would be to allow the testator to create a new species of property, subject to rules unknown to the law. But this is what no man can do."[50]

Edmund Randolph, cocounsel for the appellants, concentrated on the argument that the condition annexed to the bequests was void because it violated the rule against perpetuities. That rule nullified any grant or limitation of an estate or interest in property that was capable of vesting at an uncertain or too remote period of time. "The period of a life, or lives, in being, and twenty one years afterwards, is the fixed rule; insomuch that it has now become a fixed canon of property; and to alter it, would be to shake titles, and unsettle property." At best, the slaves' right to freedom was not to vest until they reached the age of thirty, a period, Randolph claimed, that was "too long, and never has been allowed." Moreover, the grant of freedom was not to take place until the legislature authorized private manumission, "and when that should be was wholly uncertain." At the time of the will, that contingency would have been deemed unpredictable and hence too remote, thus the condition attached to the bequests must be deemed void.[51]

Warden and Marshall contested all of these views. The act of 1748 did not invalidate the emancipations, for they were not to go into effect at once, but only after the law had been changed to allow manumission. Nor did they think the devises violated the rule against perpetuities. Marshall discussed the "great question . . . as to the perpetuity" in some detail.

[49] *Pleasants et al.* v. *Pleasants*, 2 Call 319, 327.

[50] Ibid., p. 328.

[51] Ibid., p. 333. For a useful and succinct discussion of the history and applications of the rule against perpetuities, see R[obert] E[dgar] Megarry, *A Manual of the Law of Real Property*, 2d ed. (London, 1955), pp. 145–65.

He argued that the grants of freedom could be "construed severally" with reference to different categories of slaves. For those alive at the time of the wills the grant was surely good, because the "contingency"—the passage of a manumission act—had to occur within a "life in being"—namely, their own. The children born to those slaves before 1782 also qualified—although here Marshall's reasoning was quite strained. In their case, he argued, the contingency had to happen within a life in being—namely, their mother's—plus a "reasonable period" of thirty years—the time they would be obliged to serve. Thirty years, he insisted, was "a period not denied by any book. For the authorities are all affirmatively, that it may depend on a life in being and twenty one years afterwards; and not negatively, that it shall not depend on a longer term than a life in being, and twenty one years afterwards." He conceded that the case of subsequent generations might be different, but that Wythe's order that the ages of the slaves be ascertained was therefore appropriate.[52]

After taking the case under advisement, three judges of the court delivered separate opinions on May 6, 1799. Spencer Roane's was the most interesting in its attempt to uphold the bulk of Wythe's decree while adhering strictly to the formal rules of property law. He did so by considering the slaves not as persons claiming freedom, but rather as "ordinary remaindermen," claiming property in themselves, and testing that claim "by the rules of the common law, relative to ordinary cases of limitations of personal chattels."[53] In a complex and not altogether persuasive argument that followed some of the lines marked out by Marshall, Roane denied that the bequests violated the rule against perpetuities and thus upheld their validity. More importantly, he concluded that the right to freedom vested immediately in all the slaves living when the 1782 manumission act passed. Those who were not yet thirty at that time were "postponed as to the time of enjoyment," but their situation was that of "persons bound to service for a term of years; who have a general right to freedom, but there

[52] *Pleasants et al.* v. *Pleasants*, 2 Call 319, 331.

[53] Ibid., p. 335.

is an exception, out of it, by contract or otherwise." This meant that all children born after 1782 were born free, for the "condition" of their mothers was "that of free persons, held to service, for a term of years," and their children thus were "not the children of slaves." In this case, the "power of the testator" to require all future generations to serve until age thirty had to yield "to the great principle of natural law, which, is also a principle of our municipal law, that the children of a free mother are themselves also free." Any provision of the will requiring service of them must be considered "void, as being contrary to law; it being an attempt to detain in slavery, persons that are born free."[54]

Roane's reasoning did not carry the other judges, although they also upheld the validity of the wills. Pendleton, in particular, felt that a strict application of the perpetuities rule would have to nullify the bequests. However, to apply that rule to a case involving freedom "would be too rigid," and he proposed that a more "reasonable principle ought to be adopted" to suit the "peculiar circumstances" of this case. He suggested—and the majority of the court agreed—that the bequests be deemed valid with respect to all slaves still in possession of the legatees when the 1782 law passed, "without any change by the intervention of creditors, or purchasers."[55]

The most serious disagreement among the judges concerned the question whether every generation of slaves claiming freedom under the wills should be held to service until age thirty. Wythe would have required that service only of slaves born before 1782, a position defended and explained by Roane. Carrington and Pendleton, on the other hand, held that all children "born of mothers, not thirty years of age at the birth of the child," must themselves serve to age thirty, and so on through the generations.[56] In the final analysis, then, although the court was prepared to forgo strict legal technicalities in sustaining Wythe's jurisdiction and the Pleas-

[54] Ibid., p. 339.

[55] Ibid., pp. 351–52.

[56] Ibid., p. 348.

ants slaves' claim to freedom, its flexibility ultimately allowed it also to tolerate that "new species of property" of which John Wickham had warned.

After the case was remanded back to Chancery, Wythe ordered that inventories be made of all the slaves affected by the court's ruling.[57] The 215 slaves originally distributed by the will of John Pleasants in 1771 had now grown to 431 (not including, of course, those who had run away, died, or gained freedom between 1771 and 1799). Of these, the court found 185 to be immediately entitled to freedom, either because they were thirty or older or because they had been born after their mothers had attained that age. The remaining 246 were obliged to complete a term of servitude ranging from a few months to thirty years, and their offspring (born before their mothers were thirty) were doomed to the same fate.[58]

How many slaves in all gained their freedom under the wills of John and Jonathan Pleasants cannot now be determined with certainty. That any did so was the result of a convergence of two powerful ideological forces in late eighteenth-century Virginia. The first of these was religious. A devout Friend, Robert Pleasants was deeply moved by religious principles in his efforts to free the slaves. Although he proved adept at drawing as well on the principles of liberty at the core of the political ideology of the American Revolution, the ideals of Christian justice and brotherhood were fundamental to his antislavery actions.

If the religious and benevolent principles of the Friends made Robert Pleasants and his fellow Quakers consistent opponents of slavery, the political ideology of the American Revolution, with its dual commitment to the rights of liberty and the rights of property, left a more ambivalent legacy. The judges and lawyers involved in the manumission controversy might have given priority to one of those ideals at the expense

[57] *High Court of Chancery: Pleasants v. Logan*, pp. 6–7.

[58] The printed inventories are ibid., pp. 8–18. Partial manuscript inventories of the slaves held by Samuel Pleasants, Jr., and by the estate of Charles and Mary Logan—Mary having apparently died by the time the case was concluded—can be found in the Pleasants Family Papers, BR Box 13 (42) and (50).

of the other: the repertory of legal doctrines available to them would have made it possible to free all of the slaves born after 1782 or to invalidate the bequests of freedom altogether. Instead, the members of Virginia's highest court chose to pay obeisance to both liberty and property. Their decision in 1799 involved a manipulation of legal doctrine that was demonstrably *"in favorem libertatis"* but that also worked in fact to create "a new species of property, subject to rules unknown to the law."[59]

John Pleasants probably never intended to entail the burden of thirty years' servitude on his slaves' descendants in perpetuity. That, however, is essentially how the High Court of Appeals translated his intentions, and that is how succeeding courts in Virginia tried to enforce the decree down to the Civil War, despite continued efforts by some of the Pleasants heirs to deny freedom to their slaves. As for the blacks themselves—born free if their mothers were over thirty, but otherwise condemned to wait that span of years before tasting freedom—one can only suspect that many felt like "Fanny, a bright Mulatto girl, seventeen years old," who in 1809 ran away from Samuel Pleasants, Jr., her master. "She is one of those," proclaimed a runaway advertisement in the *Richmond Enquirer,* "entitled to liberty when she arrives at a certain age, under the will of the late John Pleasants of Henrico county; in consequence of which, many of them are very ungovernable, . . . [for] many of her connections enjoy their liberty, and live in the adjacent counties."[60]

[59] *Pleasants et al.* v. *Pleasants,* 2 Call 319, 328.

[60] *Richmond Enquirer,* Oct. 3, 1809.

ANDREW R. L. CAYTON

"When Shall We Cease to Have Judases?" The Blount Conspiracy and the Limits of the "Extended Republic"

ON MONDAY, JULY 3, 1797, President John Adams gave his private secretary, Samuel B. Malcom, a message and several papers to deliver to the Congress of the United States. As Malcom prepared to climb the steps leading into the Senate building, he unexpectedly encountered Senator William Blount of Tennessee, who had abandoned the tedious proceedings inside for the pleasure of a walk. The senator asked the secretary the nature of his business. Malcom refused to answer, pleading secrecy, and proceeded on his mission. Some time later, when Blount returned from his stroll, he found his colleagues in an uproar. He quickly discovered why. Among the papers sent by President Adams was a letter written by Blount that clearly revealed his participation in a plan to attack Spanish territory in Florida and Louisiana with the aid of Great Britain and Indians. Called upon for an explanation, the usually composed Blount stammered with embarrassment and asked for time to prepare his answer. The Senate granted him twenty-four hours, but a panic-stricken Blount, who came close to running away, failed to appear on Tuesday to answer questions. The following Saturday, July 8, a shocked and disgusted Senate voted twenty-five to one to expel Blount for "having been guilty of a high misdemeanor, entirely inconsistent with his public trust and duty."[1] An outraged Abigail Adams privately denounced the humiliated senator, wondering if the United States would ever be free of such "Judases."[2] All things considered, the week of the twenty-first anniversary of the founding of the republic had not been a good one for William Blount.

In many ways, the senator's predicament was hardly surprising, for he had long lived on the edge of impropriety. The consummate eighteenth-century land speculator, Blount had made a career out of lobbying various governments for huge tracts of land as well as help in developing them into valuable commodities. Indeed, it was the pursuit of personal profit that gave his life direction, that ordered the rest of his existence. Historians who search the voluminous correspondence of this member of the 1787 Constitutional Convention for treatises on the nature of republican government will look in vain. Whether as a partner in his family's business or as governor of the Southwest Territory from 1790 to 1796, William Blount's eyes were always on the bottom line. Little wonder that historians such as Thomas Perkins Abernethy have described him as a thoroughly immoral character. Even Blount's defenders are left to damn him with faint praise—he was, they point out, merely behaving like a "businessman."[3]

My purpose here is not to rescue William Blount, who was

[1] *Annals of Congress*, 5th Cong., 1st sess., pp. 34–46. The best account of the little-studied "Blount Conspiracy" is Thomas Perkins Abernethy, *The South in the New Nation, 1789–1819* (Baton Rouge, 1961), pp. 169–91. See also, William H. Masterson, *William Blount, Businessman* (Baton Rouge, 1954), pp. 315–23; and J. Wendell Knox, *Conspiracy in American Politics, 1787–1815* (New York, 1972), pp. 97–107. Abernethy believed Blount "unscrupulous" but contended that he was expelled from the Senate unjustly for writing "a letter which involved neither crimes nor any disloyalty to the government of the United States" (p. 191).

[2] Abigail Adams to Mary Smith Cranch, July 6, 1797, Stewart Mitchell, ed., *New Letters of Abigail Adams, 1788–1801* (Boston, 1947), p. 100.

[3] Thomas Perkins Abernethy, *From Frontier to Plantation in Tennessee: A Study in Frontier Democracy* (Chapel Hill, 1932), pp. 51–55; Masterson, *William Blount*. Abernethy's judgment was less harsh when he published *South in the New Nation* in 1961.

hardly an admirable man, from his critics, but to understand the circumstances that brought him to that remarkable day in the Senate. It is a story that takes us beyond the question of Blount's character into the contested areas of economic development, federal power, and emerging conceptions of regional identity that were at the heart of the politics of the early American republic. My argument is that historians have concentrated so much on what was wrong *personally* with Blount and other speculators, whose monstrous land grabs strike us as—at best—ethically dubious, that they have neglected to stress what was exceedingly problematic about the political environment in which these men operated.

When Abigail Adams compared Blount to Judas, she was simply interpreting human behavior in an eighteenth-century vocabulary that emphasized the importance of individual responsibility in the workings of history.[4] Enlightened, rational people such as Abigail and her husband were forever explaining events they did not like as the results of conspiracies among men of flawed character. Two centuries later, most historians tend to see human behavior as somewhat more complicated. Recent reconstructions of the worlds of artisans, women, Native Americans, and African-Americans have helped us to understand how human beings form distinctive cultural identities through constant interaction with other peoples as well as their environments. But our understanding of land speculators, who were almost exclusively prominent white males, remains surprisingly simplistic. It is true that Abigail Adams was essentially correct when it came to Blount's character. By almost anyone's standards, he was a reprehensible person, deceptive, dishonest, and unscrupulous to the very core of his being.

Still, land speculators like Blount were not lacking in principles or a coherent vision of the future. If, by and large, they were men committed to the somewhat novel idea of the unbridled pursuit of profit, they were also committed to the rapid commercial development of the transappalachian West.

---

[4] Gordon S. Wood, "Conspiracy and the Paranoid Style: Causality and Deceit in the Eighteenth Century," *William and Mary Quarterly*, 3d ser. 39 (1982):401–41.

Among the prerequisites for the attainment of this goal was the establishment of a powerful government—some form of unchallenged, legitimate authority—on the frontier. Men such as Blount did not necessarily care which government that might be, thus leaving themselves open to charges ranging from treason to hypocrisy. Nonetheless, they remained remarkably consistent in their quest for a stable political presence that would guarantee land titles, support internal improvements, and defend settlers (that is, customers) from all enemies.[5]

From the late 1780s, Blount was convinced that the government of the United States was the primary candidate for that position in the Old Southwest. When he turned to another source of authority in 1797, it was not from a desire to undermine the power of the United States. To the contrary, Blount contemplated a conspiracy with Great Britain because the United States government had demonstrated little more than impotence in the Old Southwest. Whether that failure was a result of a calculated policy he could not be certain, although he knew that the Washington administration had spent a great deal of money and resources in the Old Northwest. But clearly it was the weakness, not the strength, of the federal government south of the Ohio River that led Blount to those moments of crisis in the Senate in July 1797. Put another way, behavior Abigail Adams instantly identified as the result of a lapse of character might reasonably be understood today, at least in part, as the actions of a man who believed that the political structures created by the Constitution of 1787 had failed him. Blount's Conspiracy was a logical outcome of the inability of the Washington administration to establish the le-

[5] See Edward J. Cashin, "Georgia: Searching for Security," and Lance Banning, "Virginia: Sectionalism and the General Good," in Michael Allen Gillespie and Michael Lienesch, eds., *Ratifying the Constitution* (Lawrence, Kans., 1989), pp. 93–116, 261–99, for discussion of southern attitudes toward the proper role of the federal government in the expansion of the republic. See also Drew R. McCoy, "James Madison and Visions of American Nationality in the Confederation Period: A Regional Perspective," in Richard R. Beeman, Stephen Botein, and Edward C. Carter II, eds., *Beyond Confederation: Origins of the Constitution and American National Identity* (Chapel Hill, 1987), pp. 226–58.

gitimacy and the value of the national government in all of the several regions of the "extended republic."

THE REGIONAL CONTEXT OF THE CONSPIRACY

To the extent that it had any coherence at all, the Blount Conspiracy was of a piece with numerous other filibustering schemes that gave the Old Southwest in the early republic the political character of nineteenth- and twentieth-century Central America. An ill-advised, amorphous plot to seize the remnants of the decaying Spanish empire in the Southwest with the aid of the British government and American Indians, it apparently originated with John Chisholm, a former British soldier, Indian trader, and ally of Blount. His particular target was Spanish Florida. Chisholm, who had been held prisoner in Pensacola, detested the Spanish. In late 1796 he approached British minister Robert Liston seeking material assistance for a proposed assault on West Florida. While Liston refused to sanction the scheme, he did little to discourage the hotheaded Chisholm. In January 1797 Liston informed the British government that one thousand to fifteen hundred whites, "principally British Subjects, attached to their Country and Sovereign" were "ready to enter into a plan for the Recovery of the Floridas to Great Britain" in return for several ships, some supplies, and commissions.[6]

Chisholm told William Blount about his project in December 1796. Blount took the idea and ran with it. By early 1797, the senator was discussing the possibility of an attack with the land jobber and British citizen Dr. Nicholas Romayne and sounding out his friends on the idea. In the infamous letter that led to his expulsion from the Senate, Blount assured Indian agent James Carey in April 1797 that while he was "not quite sure," he believed that "the plan . . . will be attempted this fall," and "if the Indians act their part, I have no doubt

[6] Robert Liston to Lord Grenville, Jan. 25, 1797, Frederick Jackson Turner, ed., "Documents on the Blount Conspiracy, 1793–1797," *American Historical Review* 10 (1905):576–77. In *South in the New Nation* Abernethy argues that Liston was actually manipulating Chisholm (p. 174).

but it will succeed. A man of consequence has gone to England about the business; and if he makes arrangements, I shall myself have a hand in the business, and shall probably be at the head of the business on the part of the British."[7] While the conspiracy never reached fruition, Blount's plans were much grander than Chisholm's. Apparently there would be a three-pronged attack on the Spanish empire. The first would seize New Madrid and silver mines on the Red River; the second, led by Blount, would take New Orleans; and the third, under the command of Chisholm, would occupy Pensacola. The main body of troops in each expedition would consist of a combination of white frontiersmen and Indian allies. As for Great Britain, in return for providing stores and ships, it would receive Louisiana or Florida. His Majesty's government would then declare New Orleans a free port and open the Mississippi River to unrestricted use by both American and British citizens.[8]

And what of the benefits to William Blount and like-minded men? Historians have never had much trouble identifying them. In brief, land speculators in the Old Southwest were in serious financial troubles in 1796–97. Blount, in particular, was bankrupt. Only his position as a United States senator prevented local officials in his home state of North Carolina from arresting him. Meanwhile, he transferred his property—including his land and twenty-six slaves—to his half brother Willie to save it from repossession by his creditors.[9] Blount and others in Tennessee, moreover, were discontented under the Washington administration and depressed by the election of John Adams as president. The conspiracy, risky business that it was, nevertheless offered an opportunity to open vast amounts of land for commercial development by removing the Spanish presence and preventing any rumored transfer of the region to the militant and unreliable French. Blount and other speculators who claimed millions of acres in

[7] William Blount to James Carey, Apr. 21, 1797, *Annals of Congress,* 5th Cong., 1st sess., p. 42.

[8] Statement of John D. Chisholm to Rufus King, Dec. 9, 1797, Turner, ed., "Documents on the Blount Conspiracy," p. 307.

[9] Abernethy, *South in the New Nation,* p. 185.

what is now the states of Alabama, Mississippi, and Tennessee, would see the value of their holdings skyrocket. They would be able to pay off their debts and achieve a high degree of personal independence. Not that Blount's conspiracy involved secession or the creation of another country. To the contrary, according to Blount's biographer, the whole scheme was little more than a business proposition to him, something that should in no way interfere with his reelection to the Senate in 1799.[10] If historians have found the goals of the conspiracy murky, they have always found the motivation behind it crystal clear. In a word, it was individual profit.

Now all of this is perfectly reasonable as far as it goes and perhaps the wisest thing to do would be to leave it at that. But the Blount Conspiracy raises several questions about the extension of federal authority into the transappalachian West that historians have not directly considered. For example, why were there so many more conspiracies south of the Ohio River than north of it? And why were land speculators in the South so much more willing to challenge or bypass the authority of the United States government than their counterparts in the Old Northwest? To list the names of men who engaged in treasonable behavior, or at least contemplated it in the early republic, is to list the names of southerners—the founders of the state of Franklin, Blount, John Sevier, Andrew Jackson, James Wilkinson, George Rogers Clark. Aaron Burr would find far more encouragement for his vague plans in the valleys of the Tennessee and the Mississippi than in that of the Ohio. Indeed, the most remarkable thing about Blount's vague schemes was how very similar they were to those of dozens of other men in the Southwest.[11]

This is not to suggest that there was no antifederal feeling north of the Ohio, that crossing the river transformed people

[10] Masterson, *William Blount*, p. 40.

[11] The best studies of these episodes are the classic, authoritative works of Arthur Preston Whitaker: *The Spanish-American Frontier, 1783–1795: The Westward Movement and the Spanish Retreat in the Mississippi Valley* (Lincoln, Nebr., 1927), and idem, *The Mississippi Question, 1795–1803: A Study in Trade, Politics, and Diplomacy* (1934; reprint ed., Gloucester, Mass., 1962). These should be supplemented with Thomas Perkins Abernethy's *The Burr Conspiracy* (New York, 1954), and idem, *South in the New Nation*.

into law-abiding citizens of the United States. Clearly there was plenty of resistance to federal authority throughout the United States in the 1790s. On virtually every frontier some people refused to pay taxes, evaded the jurisdictions of courts, and, on occasion, simply rebelled.[12]

The peculiar characteristic of angry men south of the Ohio was that they were less interested in rebelling against national authority than they were in contemplating abandoning the government of the United States altogether. It was the relative absence of federal power, not the exercise of it, that nurtured conspiracy in the Old Southwest. In the middle ground of Kentucky, where national authority was established but not fully enforced, some prominent men waffled between ignoring federal laws such as the excise tax on whiskey and plotting alliances with the Spanish.[13] But in the Southwest Territory, the region that is now Tennessee, and the Mississippi Territory, local leaders were far less ambivalent about the United States. If the government created by the Constitution of 1787 could not serve their interests, they were prepared to desert it, partly because, unlike the citizens of the Northwest Territory, they had nothing to fear from it.

North of the Ohio, on the other hand, most great land speculators and other prominent figures worked within the political structures established by the United States. When some, mainly Virginians, disagreed with the ways in which the Northwest Territory was being run, they organized an opposi-

---

[12] See Peter S. Onuf, *The Origins of the Federal Republic: Jurisdictional Controversies in the United States, 1775–1787* (Philadelphia, 1983); Rachel N. Klein, *Unification of a Slave State: The Rise of the Planter Class in the South Carolina Backcountry, 1760–1808* (Chapel Hill, 1990), esp. pp. 9–77; Gregory H. Nobles, "Breaking into the Backcountry: New Approaches to the Early American Frontier, 1750–1800," *William and Mary Quarterly*, 3d ser. 46 (1989):641–70; Thomas P. Slaughter, *The Whiskey Rebellion: Frontier Epilogue to the American Revolution* (New York, 1986); and Alan Taylor, *Liberty Men and Great Proprietors: The Revolutionary Settlement on the Maine Frontier, 1760–1820* (Chapel Hill, 1990).

[13] Mary K. Bonsteel Tachau, *Federal Courts in the Early Republic: Kentucky, 1789–1816* (Princeton, 1978), esp. pp. 31–53, 95–126; and Patricia Watlington, *The Partisan Spirit: Kentucky Politics, 1779–1792* (New York, 1972).

tion and won power by creating a state government. Virtually no one suggested that they solve their problems by negotiating with other governments or by challenging the basic sovereignty of the United States over the territory.[14]

The most obvious reasons for this regional divergence in political behavior lie in demography and geography. Greater numbers of industrious New Englanders, New Yorkers, and Pennsylvanians settled in the Old Northwest, bringing with them a cultural predilection for social order as well as economic and social customs centered around a nascent commercial economy. Despite the fact that the Ordinance of 1787's prohibition of slavery north of the Ohio River was frequently violated, the Ordinance served as the constitutional capstone to the Old Northwest's character as a land of independent freehold farmers. In contrast, the greatest proportion of American settlers in the Old Southwest were southerners. They, too, were interested in commercial agriculture. But the existence of chattel slavery and the dominance of one staple crop produced a very different kind of society from what developed a few hundred miles to the north. The worlds of the Old Northwest and the Old Southwest, sketched so memorably (if schematically) by Stanley Elkins and Eric McKitrick a generation ago, were very different almost from the beginning. Indeed, one of the most striking things about the transappalachian West in the early republic was how quickly and thoroughly the Old Northwest was integrated, economically and politically, into the union while the Old Southwest remained somewhat peripheral to it.[15]

---

[14] Donald J. Ratcliffe, "The Experience of Revolution and the Beginnings of Party Politics in Ohio, 1776–1816," *Ohio History* 85 (1976):186–230; and Andrew R. L. Cayton, *The Frontier Republic: Ideology and Politics in the Ohio Country, 1780–1825* (Kent, Ohio, 1986).

[15] Stanley Elkins and Eric McKitrick, "A Meaning for Turner's Frontier," *Political Science Quarterly* 69 (1954):321–53, 565–602. See also Malcolm J. Rohrbough, *The Trans-Appalachian Frontier: People, Societies, Institutions, 1775–1850* (New York, 1978). On the Old Northwest, see Andrew R. L. Cayton and Peter S. Onuf, *The Midwest and the Nation: Rethinking the History of an American Region* (Bloomington, Ind., 1990), chaps. 2–3. On the Old Southwest, see Thomas D. Clark and John D. W. Guice, *Frontiers in Conflict: The Old Southwest, 1795–1830* (Albuquerque, 1989).

Historians anticipating the Civil War, however, have sometimes exaggerated the degree to which the two regions diverged demographically and economically in the first decades after the Revolution. Actually they had a great deal in common. Most of the important political leaders north of the Ohio River in the early republic were southerners, primarily Virginians. Many continued to own slaves or have indentured servants. As important as the influence of New Englanders was in the Old Northwest, they did not become a significant portion of the population until the 1820s and the 1830s. Demographically and politically, the Old Northwest was largely an extension of the South until after the War of 1812. Economically, too, the differences in crops and labor systems should not blind us to the fact that settlers in Ohio, Indiana, and Illinois were as interested in the opening of the Mississippi River as anyone in Tennessee.[16]

So, to return to the question, why were leading residents of the Old Southwest much more likely to engage in conspiring and filibustering than their counterparts in the Northwest? A more reasonable answer lies in the contrasting natures and behaviors of the major European and Native American powers on their respective frontiers.

To the south, the Spanish empire in the late eighteenth century was nearing the end of a long series of reforms that had revitalized its economy while undermining its political stability. Its strategically located settlements along the Gulf Coast and the Mississippi River—such as Pensacola, New Orleans, and Natchez—were well-established societies. The Spanish had come to America to stay; their presence along the northern rim of their ancient and profitable empire would not soon

[16] See John D. Barnhart, *Valley of Democracy: The Frontier versus the Plantation in the Ohio Valley, 1775–1818* (Bloomington, Ind., 1953); Andrew R. L. Cayton, "Land, Reputation, and Power: The Cultural Dimension of Politics in the Ohio Country," *William and Mary Quarterly*, 3d ser. 47 (1990):266–86; Paul Finkelman, "Evading the Ordinance: The Persistence of Bondage in Indiana and Illinois," *Journal of the Early Republic* 9 (1989):21–51; Richard Lyle Power, *Planting Corn Belt Culture: The Impress of the Upland Southerner and Yankee in the Old Northwest* (Indianapolis, 1953); and Douglass C. North, *The Economic Growth of the United States, 1790–1860* (Englewood Cliffs, N.J., 1961).

fade. In the 1790s, however, their imperial government was largely ineffective, suffering from the political miscalculations of Manuel de Godoy, the ideological pressures of the French Revolution, and the cumulative weakness of centuries of decline. The Spanish were a tempting target for ambitious Americans in the late eighteenth century; they were wealthy and historically impressive, but they lacked direction and efficiency. In the tradition of Francis Drake and Oliver Cromwell, men such as Blount found in the Spanish empire a distinguished opponent—and a vulnerable one.[17]

North of the Ohio River, settlers faced the British empire— an altogether different entity. The British interest in the Old Northwest was not a permanent one; it did not involve the protection of long-standing strategic and cultural centers. Canada was not Mexico; Detroit was not New Orleans. The British government's primary concerns were to protect their trade with the Indians in the region and to secure their presence in Canada. Their principal strategy was to aid Indians in military activities against the advancing Americans. Unlike the Spanish, they offered few incentives, either in the form of targets or money, to leading Americans to engage in plots north of the Ohio. Like the Spanish, the British government in the 1790s was far more preoccupied with issues in Europe—principally those raised by the French Revolution— than it was with problems in the North American backcountry.[18]

An even more critical reason for the divergence of the northern and southern frontiers lies in the natures of Native American societies. Here the tendency of historians has been to assume the existence of some uniformity in Indian behavior in the face of American aggression. Such a view obscures important regional differences. In the South, the major In-

[17]Stanley J. Stein and Barbara H. Stein, *The Colonial Heritage of Latin America: Essays on Economic Dependence in Perspective* (New York, 1970), pp. 86–119; John Lynch, *The Spanish-American Revolutions, 1808–1826* (New York, 1973), pp. 1–36; Whitaker, *Spanish-American Frontier;* and idem, *Mississippi Question.*

[18]Colin Calloway, *Crown and Calumet: British-Indian Relations, 1783–1815* (Norman, Okla., 1987).

dian groups—the Cherokees, Choctaws, Chickasaws, and Creeks—had been dealing with Europeans throughout the eighteenth century, particularly in the trade of deerskins and other goods for finished, especially British, products. Among the significant results of this economic exchange were a great many people of mixed blood, an increasing reliance on European technology, and the widespread practice of agriculture. On the southern frontier, many men—such as the Creek leader Alexander McGillivray—moved back and forth between Indian and European society quite easily. Englishmen such as William Panton and John Leslie, founders of the powerful trading firm in Spanish Florida, became familiar and powerful figures. The high levels of economic and cultural interaction in the South combined with the weakness of the Spanish to make the Indians in the region relatively powerful. Men such as McGillivray were eager to negotiate in the style of European diplomacy to protect their territorial integrity even as their cultural distinctiveness was dissipating.[19]

Gregory Evans Dowd has recently demonstrated that there was significant communication between the southern Indians and those living north of the Ohio River. In many ways, their situations were similar. French and British traders and officials had lived among the Miami, Shawnee, Delaware, and other Indians since the end of the seventeenth century, participating in the evolution of what Richard White has termed a "middle ground" of cultural misunderstanding. Still, eighteenth-century contact in the region between the Ohio River and the Great Lakes may have had a less decisive impact on Native Americans than south of Kentucky. Some scholars have suggested that there was less accommodation to European customs and methods in the northern region. R.

[19] Daniel H. Usner, *Indians, Settlers, and Slaves in a Frontier Exchange Economy: The Lower Mississippi Valley before 1783* (Chapel Hill, 1992); Michael D. Green, *The Politics of Indian Removal: Creek Government and Society in Crisis* (Lincoln, Nebr., 1982), pp. 1–43; James H. Merrell, *The Indians' New World: Catawbas and Their Neighbors from European Contact through the Era of Removal* (Chapel Hill, 1989); William G. McLoughlin, *Cherokee Renascence in the New Republic* (Princeton, 1986); John Walton Caughey, *McGillivray of the Creeks* (Norman, Okla., 1938); and J. Leitch Wright, Jr., *William Augustus Bowles, Director General of the Creek Nation* (Athens, Ga., 1967).

David Edmunds has written that, unlike the Chickasaws and the Choctaws, the Miami and the Shawnee had not "incorporated many of the white man's ways into their culture."[20]

It is possible that these differences created something of a regional variation in Native Americans' reactions to the expansion of the United States, which, in turn, affected the behavior of Anglo-Americans. If the northern Indians were in fact less "acculturated," they were also more thoroughly "nativist" in their hostility to white ways and more likely to engage in relatively united military resistance. The latter was most obviously the case in the early 1790s, when a coalition of Indians operating out of a string of villages on the Maumee River twice defeated sizeable American armies. Southerners such as William Blount may simply have felt more comfortable contemplating expeditions with Indian allies than their counterparts north of the Ohio River.

In any case, the most important reason for the greater rash of conspiracies in the Old Southwest was the inability—or unwillingness—of any European government to achieve anything approaching political hegemony in the area. As Frederick Jackson Turner wrote in 1905, "The real question at issue was whether the control of the entire Mississippi valley and the Gulf of Mexico should fall to France, England, or the United States."[21] In the 1790s none of these nations seemed particularly eager to assume responsibility for the Old Southwest. None wanted to commit the resources to achieve control of the area.

And such stability was crucial to the plans of men such as William Blount. They needed a powerful government that could defend their property interests from all potential enemies, that would ensure a kind of predictability and reliability

---

[20] R. David Edmunds, *Tecumseh and the Quest for Indian Leadership* (Boston, 1984), p. 152; idem, *The Shawnee Prophet* (Lincoln, Nebr., 1983). See also Gregory Evans Dowd, *A Spirited Resistance: The North American Indian Struggle for Unity, 1745–1815* (Baltimore, 1992), and Richard White, *The Middle Ground: Indians, Empires, and Republics in the Great Lakes Region, 1650–1815* (Cambridge, 1991).

[21] Frederick Jackson Turner, "The Policy of France toward the Mississippi Valley in the Period of Washington and Adams," *American Historical Review* 10 (1905):279.

in commercial transactions, and that would provide the military and diplomatic power necessary to achieve the peace that would bring settlers into the areas. If speculating was gambling, luck was on the side of those with the best connections and the best information. After all, men such as Blount rarely engaged in the actual business of selling land; they left that to agents, as tobacco planters left harvesting to slaves. Rather, as gentlemen-speculators, they lobbied, plotted, envisioned, and decided. They proved their skills, created an image for themselves as men of talent and influence, by succeeding in the adventure of speculation. To such men good relations with a powerful government were critical, not just because it had land to grant, but because it had the power to protect and defend the interests of those people who purchased land from it.[22]

In this sense, land speculators in the Old Northwest were much more fortunate than those in the Southwest, for in the North one government was eager to assert itself. Pushing aside squatters, Indians, and the British, the government of the United States established a high level of political stability north of the Ohio River in the 1790s. This achievement was much more than the creation of a colonial system and the appointment of territorial officials. It involved nothing less than becoming the most important power broker in the region. Under the Confederation, Congress eliminated all state rivals to its authority in the Northwest Territory by enticing them to surrender their claims to the region. Internationally, it voided Great Britain's pretensions through military victory and the terms of the Treaty of Paris in 1783. Then it provided for the regular survey and sale of public lands. The United States owned most of the Northwest Territory and it stood ready to enforce the procedures it had established there. When the New Jersey land speculator John Cleves Symmes, to whom Congress had sold hundreds of thousands of acres in the Great Miami Valley in 1787, tried to sell land beyond

[22] On land speculators in the late eighteenth century, see Marc Egnal, *A Mighty Empire: The Origins of the American Revolution* (Ithaca, N.Y., 1988); Peter S. Onuf, *Statehood and Union: A History of the Northwest Ordinance* (Bloomington, Ind., 1987), chaps. 1–2; and Taylor, *Liberty Men and Great Proprietors,* esp. pp. 31–59.

the limits of his purchase, the national government—in the person of territorial governor Arthur St. Clair—refused to let him get away with it. In so doing, St. Clair earned the eternal enmity of Symmes. But he also established his government as the arbiter of power and justice in the region. The federal government was the last court of appeal; it was sovereign in the Old Northwest.[23]

Just as crucial from the point of view of speculators and leading citizens in the Ohio country was the fact that the national government demonstrated its power through the use of the military. After the defeat of two expeditions in the early 1790s, the Washington administration dispatched the newly created Legion of the United States under the command of Anthony Wayne. In 1794 that well-organized and well-supported army defeated a coalition of Indians at Fallen Timbers and exposed the halfhearted nature of British policy in the region. The British were willing to aid and abet Indians in harassing the Americans, but they were not willing to fight for them. The subsequent Treaty of Greenville brought a sense of security to the upper Ohio Valley while Jay's Treaty ensured the completion of the British retreat from Detroit and other key posts. To be sure, the Indians and the British would remain powerful actors in the region for another two decades. But the federal government had nonetheless achieved the appearance of peace.[24]

By establishing the authority of the United States north of the Ohio River through military action and legal predictability, federal officials laid the foundations for the rapid commercial development of the Old Northwest in the early nineteenth century. Opposition to the actions of the national government there would be in Ohio, Indiana, and Illinois, but there was virtually no opposition to the government itself.

[23] Cayton, *Frontier Republic*, pp. 61–63.

[24] Calloway, *Crown and Calumet*, pp. 225–28; Wiley Sword, *President Washington's Indian War: The Struggle for the Old Northwest, 1790–1795* (Norman, Okla., 1985); Paul David Nelson, *Anthony Wayne: Soldier of the Early Republic* (Bloomington, Ind., 1985), pp. 228–83; and Francis Paul Prucha, *The Sword of the Republic: The United States Army on the Frontier, 1783–1846* (Bloomington, Ind., 1969), pp. 17–42.

The Old Northwest, the domain of the United States, was no proving ground for filibusters or conspirators because the federal government had decisively demonstrated not just its power, but its *value*.

The same could not be said in the Southwest Territory. Dorothy V. Jones has quite correctly suggested that until 1796 the United States government pursued "different policies" with regard to Native Americans that "corresponded to the strength and cohesion of the Indians" in the Southwest and the Northwest. But she exaggerates the strength of the federal government in the former and its weakness in the latter by 1796.[25] The confidence federal officials exhibited when dealing with the Old Northwest disappeared when the subject was the Southwest. While the Northwest Territory received an army in the 1790s, its counterpart in what is now Tennessee got only a few troops. Instead, territorial officials, led by Gov. William Blount, were left to their own devices. Improvisation was the name of the game on the Holston River. To be fair, the Washington administration had limited financial resources in the 1790s; it could not afford a two-front Indian war. But the cost of its success in securing the northern flank of the empire was the creation of ill-will and alienation in the Southwest; there was little incentive to support the United States government south of the Ohio River.[26]

THE POLITICAL CONTEXT OF THE CONSPIRACY

William Blount's progress from ardent supporter of the federal government in 1790 to implacable critic of it by 1796 was the most dramatic example of this price. Blount's political meanderings were not simply responses to frontier democracy or the actions of a chameleon. To the contrary, he was remarkably

---

[25] Dorothy V. Jones, *License for Empire: Colonialism by Treaty in Early America* (Chicago, 1982), pp. 169–73.

[26] On the discontent of Tennesseans with the government of the United States in the 1790s, see Masterson, *William Blount*, pp. 212–85; Craig Symonds, "The Failure of America's Indian Policy on the Southwestern Frontier, 1785–1793," *Tennessee Historical Quarterly* 35 (1976):291–315.

consistent. Blount had become a Federalist in the 1780s because he saw a powerful national government as the best way of bringing order to the frontier. Only something above the states, capable of dealing with Spain and England and supporting military operations against the Indians, would be able to provide the military and legal security to begin the development of the Old Southwest. It was for this reason that he supported the Constitution and sought appointment as territorial governor. He stopped supporting the Federalist government in the 1790s when he became convinced that it was not working out as a guarantor of stability in the region. While the Washington administration was succeeding admirably in that role in the Northwest, it had proved a dismal failure in the South. Blount abandoned the Federalists only when he became convinced that they had already abandoned him.[27]

Nothing was more revealing of the need for a strong, reliable government's presence than the incredible maze of land claims in the Southwest. Not only had the Spanish granted land to settlers in regions now claimed by the United States, the state of Georgia had also given away most of what is now Alabama and Mississippi—on more than one occasion. Unlike the states that claimed land north of the Ohio River, Georgia had refused to surrender its western claims to the United States in the 1780s. And by the end of the decade, its legislators were selling millions of acres at bargain prices. In 1789 the legislature sold over twenty-five million acres to three speculative companies for a total price of just under $200,000. The smallest of the three was the Tennessee Company, whose primary members were Zachariah Cox and John Sevier, which purchased title to what is now the northwestern corner of the state of Alabama, the Muscle Shoals area of the Tennessee River.[28]

---

[27] Abernethy, *From Frontier to Plantation*, p. 116. See also Cathy D. Matson and Peter S. Onuf, *A Union of Interests: Political and Economic Thought in Revolutionary America* (Lawrence, Kans., 1990). For a similar argument about Georgia and the ratification of the Constitution, see Cashin, "Georgia."

[28] Arthur Preston Whitaker, "The Muscle Shoals Speculation, 1783–1789," *Mississippi Valley Historical Review* 13 (1927):365–86.

William Blount had spent a great deal of time in the 1780s lobbying the legislature of Georgia for just such a purchase. Like most other grand speculators, he believed that Muscle Shoals was the key to economic control of the area south of Kentucky, east of the Mississippi River, west of the Carolina and Georgia lowcountry, and north of the Gulf of Mexico. Why? Because a short portage of a few dozen miles promised to connect the waters of the Tennessee with those of the Alabama and Tombigbee rivers, which in turn would lead people to Mobile Bay, the Caribbean, and the markets of the greater Atlantic world. Through the Muscle Shoals region would eventually pass the products of farmers throughout Tennessee (in which Blount had heavily invested) as well as the goods of northern Mississippi and Alabama. In the words of Tennessee governor John Sevier in November 1797, it would provide "an outlet to commerce equal if not superior to any in the United States."[29] No wonder Blount looked longingly at Muscle Shoals for two decades.

Still, he did not join in the 1789 speculation because he had placed his future in the hands of the national government. He simply did not believe that the state of Georgia was capable of protecting its sales. It could not guarantee them; the United States, on the other hand, might be able to do so. In the high-minded words of Blount's ally, North Carolina congressman and speculator Hugh Williamson, "The idea of buying Land to be jobbed away by Georgia Specks is not accordant with the feelings of the Nation."[30] And, after all, the national government had established the precedent of sales to groups of speculators with its 1787 grants to the Ohio Company of Associates. Thus it was that as governor of the Southwest Territory Blount warned Cox and others away from their abor-

[29] John Sevier to Andrew Jackson, Nov. 26, 1797, Sam B. Smith and Harriet Chappel Owsley, eds., *The Papers of Andrew Jackson*, 4 vols. to date (Knoxville, Tenn., 1980–), 1:155.

[30] Hugh Williamson to John Gray Blount, Aug. 15, 1790, Alice Barnwell Keith and William H. Masterson, eds., *The John Gray Blount Papers*, 3 vols., (Raleigh, N.C., 1953–65), 2:95.

tive settlement at Muscle Shoals in 1791.[31] Such activities would have to await the establishment of federal authority. Blount was willing to be patient; he was still a young man and the future of the republic in the Southwest looked bright.

If there were any power brokers in the Old Southwest in the late eighteenth century, however, they were the Creek Indian Alexander McGillivray and the trading house of Panton and Leslie in which McGillivray was a silent partner. McGillivray, like Blount, pursued a policy in the late 1780s designed to use the potential power of the new government under the Constitution as a guarantor of political stability and to render the aggressive, expansionist state of Georgia impotent. In the 1790 Treaty of New York, he got the federal government to promise to protect the Creeks and to recognize Indian negotiations with individual states (for example, Georgia). In consequence, the Creeks received the rights to their lands and the authority to deal with all white intruders on it.[32]

After McGillivray's death in 1793, the economic monopoly of Panton and Leslie, which the Creeks had helped to establish, gave it inordinate political power in the region. Operated by British subjects, Panton and Leslie was a firm based in St. Augustine that dominated the trade of present-day Florida, Alabama, and Mississippi. So influential with the Indians was Panton and Leslie that the ever-weakening Spanish government allowed it extensive trade concessions. With Indians owing it upwards of $200,000, the firm remained the dominant power in the Southwest even during the Anglo-Spanish War of 1798–1802.[33]

The point here is that the sovereign power of the United States was unable to displace its rivals in the Southwest. Indeed, it remained subordinate to them. It was McGillivray,

---

[31] William Blount to James Robertson, Sept. 3, 1791, Clarence E. Carter et al., comps. and eds., *The Territorial Papers of the United States*, 28 vols. (Washington, D.C., 1934–75), 4:79. See also Alexander McGillivray to baron de Carondelet, Apr. 10, 1792, in Caughey, *McGillivray*, p. 318.

[32] Michael D. Green, "Alexander McGillivray," in R. David Edmunds., ed., *American Indian Leaders: Studies in Diversity* (Lincoln, Nebr., 1980), pp. 54–56.

[33] Whitaker, *Mississippi Question*, p. 72.

after all, who sent the men who actually dispersed Cox's settlement at Muscle Shoals in 1793. And it was Panton and Leslie to which the Indians looked for trade. The United States government, in which Blount had put his faith and his investments, seemed more manipulated than in control. It had failed to secure control of the Southwest and left him in a vulnerable position economically and politically. Blount may have been the leading federal official south of the Ohio River, but he was less powerful than either McGillivray or Panton and Leslie.

Even the federal government's one great success in the Old Southwest—the 1795 signing of the Treaty of San Lorenzo with Spain—was less of a triumph than it first appeared. Negotiated by Thomas Pinckney, the treaty revealed the weakness of Spain internationally and its desire to reach some kind of accord with the United States in the face of mounting tensions in Europe. By the agreement, Spain agreed to establish its border with the Americans east of the Mississippi River at the thirty-first parallel. It also granted Americans the right to free navigation of the Mississippi and a three-year (renewable) right to deposit goods at New Orleans for shipment abroad without the payment of a duty. The Spanish also agreed to try to control the Indians. Immensely popular at the time of its ratification, Pinckney's Treaty seemed to resolve the pressing problems of the Southwest with the same finality as Wayne's victory at Fallen Timbers in the Northwest.[34]

To be sure, securing the right of navigation of the Mississippi was a major triumph for the Washington administration. But Pinckney's treaty did not accomplish as much as it appeared to. Not only did the Spanish delay in implementing the terms of the agreement, Americans interested in opening free trade routes other than the Mississippi still faced great difficulties. The boundary at the thirty-first parallel was an unworkable one, partly because it failed to take existing settlements into consideration. More important is the fact that the

---

[34] Samuel Flagg Bemis, *Pinckney's Treaty: A Study of America's Advantage from Europe's Distress, 1783–1800* (Baltimore, 1926); and Whitaker, *Mississippi Question,* pp. 51–78.

outlets into the Gulf of Mexico—especially Mobile Bay and Pensacola—remained in Spanish hands. While it would be impossible to overestimate the importance of New Orleans to the residents of the transappalachian West in the 1790s, it is easy to forget that many people envisioned other ports as potential rivals. At least in theory, Tennesseans could get crops to market faster by shipping them along the Tombigbee and Alabama rivers to Mobile and Pensacola than by sending them up the Tennessee to the Ohio and then back down the Mississippi. Pinckney's Treaty did not change that situation. Nor did it challenge in any way the economic and political power of Panton and Leslie. The United States appropriated $200,000 in 1795 and 1796 to purchase goods to initiate a rival trade, or factory system, with the Indians. But by 1801 it had spent only $90,000 of this and had failed to penetrate the Panton and Leslie empire in any significant way.[35] Thus Pinckney's Treaty was disappointing for men such as Blount, whose plans were less dependent on the opening of the Mississippi and New Orleans than they were on securing control of the region to the east of the Mississippi.

By the mid-1790s the disgruntled Blount was no longer as sanguine about the possibilities of national authority as he had been in 1787 or even 1792. In the Old Northwest the United States had embarrassed the British, defeated the Indians, secured land titles, and opened the region for settlement. In the Old Southwest the United States had achieved virtually nothing. The Spanish were still a powerful presence, the Creek Indians remained dangerous, land titles were up for grabs, and there was little prospect of economic development. The governor of Tennessee, John Sevier, continued to complain in 1797 about the failure of the "General Government" to draw an equitable boundary or to permit settlement at Muscle Shoals. "Instead of our state in its infancy being encouraged, fostered, and matured," Sevier told Andrew Jackson, "it appears that measures are calculating to check and destroy the happiness, if not its existence."[36]

[35] Whitaker, *Mississippi Question*, pp. 74–75.

[36] Sevier to Jackson, Smith and Owsley, eds., *Papers of Andrew Jackson*, 1:155.

When historians have not dismissed such sentiments out-
right, they have ascribed them to "western" resentment. But
Sevier's anger was less "western" than southwestern. To assume that the "West" meant everything beyond the Appalachians in the early republic is to fail to understand the
complexity of regional differences on the western side of the
mountains. Put simply, the Old Northwest had a huge head
start over the Old Southwest in laying the foundations of a
commercial society integrated into national networks.

If William Blount found John Chisholm's plans enticing in
late 1796 because of his troublesome financial situation, he
was also long since past waiting for the emergence of a government that would take charge of the situation on the frontier of the Old Southwest. For over a decade his plans had
lain dormant while he waited for the government of the
United States to assert its authority, bring military and legal
security to the region, and open channels to the Gulf of Mexico. In 1795 Blount happily participated in the reconstituted
Tennessee Company's purchase of the Muscle Shoals region
from a compliant and well-bribed Georgia legislature, and he
later looked favorably on Cox's abortive efforts to settle it.[37]
Clearly, Blount's attitude had changed. And why not? Certain
of what Thomas Perkins Abernethy described as "the apparent willingness of Congress to sacrifice the Southwest for the
sake of other interests," is it surprising that in 1797 he was
eager to pursue other possibilities?[38]

Blount's fear that the Spanish would turn over Louisiana
and Florida to the French was genuine, partly because the
United States was powerless to do anything about it. In a deposition prepared for Blount's impeachment, Nicholas Romayne reported that in February 1797 he and Blount agreed
that the unsettled state of affairs in the Southwest and the
prospect of control by "the sans-coulottes" would indefinitely
depress the land market in the region. Blount replied that he

[37] Abernethy, *South in the New Nation*, pp. 154–55. The purchase was part
of the notorious Yazoo land grab. See ibid., pp. 136–68; and C. Peter Ma-
grath, *Yazoo: Law and Politics in the New Republic. The Case of Fletcher v. Peck*
(New York, 1966).

[38] Abernethy, *From Frontier to Plantation*, p. 143.

"had taken great pains to settle" Tennessee "and to render it important." But "he had been treated very ill by the President, or some of the Executive officers of the United States." Blount supposedly "wept" at the thought. While Romayne was undoubtedly being overdramatic, the essence of Blount's complaint was true. The former governor had reason to indulge in some self-pity. Eventually, the two men speculated, the West might have to separate from the United States. Romayne compared the recent demand for land in the Genesee Valley of New York with that for land in Tennessee and observed that "it was a pity Louisiana also, as well as Canada, could not be in the hands of the English, as neighborhood to that Government added so much to the value in the sale of lands." Romayne might have added that there was greater security of title in western New York than in Tennessee. In any case, Blount concurred that the British were far preferable to the French.[39]

Blount and Romayne were eager to move quickly because they, like all speculators, were being hit hard by a financial panic in the spring of 1797. Paper fortunes disappeared almost overnight in what Blount's ally Hugh Williamson called "this breaking season."[40] The most famous of the victims of the economic contraction was Robert Morris who lost everything and ended up in debtors' prison. In New York City, Romayne complained bitterly that his debtors could not pay him, leaving him in arrears to his creditors.[41] "We are here much perplexed in money matters," he told Blount.[42]

Romayne blamed the financial panic on the prospect of an endless war in Europe between Great Britain and France, a conflict he believed must inevitably involve the United States. While a general European war provided a perfect time to at-

[39] Deposition of Nicholas Romayne, July 15–20, 1797, *Annals of Congress*, 5th Cong., 3d sess., p. 2358. See Liston to Grenville, May 10, 1797, Turner, ed., "Documents on the Blount Conspiracy," p. 589.

[40] Williamson to John Gray Blount, Feb. 2, 1797, Keith and Masterson, eds., *John Gray Blount Papers*, 3:131.

[41] Romayne to William Blount, Feb. 10, 1797, *Annals of Congress*, 5th Cong., 3d sess., p. 2340.

[42] Romayne to William Blount, Mar. 3, 1797, ibid., p. 2341.

tack Spanish possessions, it also threatened to disrupt all commerce for a long period of time. With Britain at war with France and Spain, there would be no peace, no stability, in the Old Southwest for years. Speculators needed some kind of predictability soon, or all would be lost.

Meanwhile, the current rumor that Spain intended to transfer Louisiana and the Floridas to France terrified men such as Blount because it promised to bring social as well as economic disorder to the region in which they had so much invested. Blount, after all, was a Federalist and no great admirer of the French Revolution. Pro-British in the European wars of the 1790s, he had been, in the words of Thomas Perkins Abernethy, "intensely hostile in his attitude toward" Citizen Genet; in June 1793 several Tennesseans had even offered a toast condemning "the murderers of Louis XVI."[43] Clearly revolutionary France was not the kind of government large land speculators wanted in charge of the Southwest. In this spirit, Romayne urged Blount in a March 1797 letter to "inflame" people in the West against the French. The propaganda involved more than the charge that they would close the Mississippi. With France in control, Romayne contended, "all properties in [Tennessee and Kentucky] will be of no value, as it will be in the neighborhood of a hostile and warlike people who will favor the liberation of all the slaves."[44] Blount replied that the French people "will oblige the Western people to come into all their measures and caprices, or they will shut up the navigation; they will sow discord among the people, and the value of lands and all property will be greatly reduced."[45] Thus French hegemony was to be dreaded for a combination of social and economic reasons. To be sure, it would devalue land, but largely because it would demand adherence to principles subversive of the social order.

If France was the epitome of chaos for Blount, Great Britain, which, not coincidentally, was at war with Spain in 1797,

[43] Abernethy, *From Frontier to Plantation,* p. 142.

[44] Romayne to William Blount, Mar. 15, 1797, *Annals of Congress,* 5th Cong., 3d sess., p. 2346.

[45] William Blount to [Romayne], Mar. 17, 1797, ibid.

epitomized the social and political stability critical to economic development. There, after all, was a truly powerful government, one that could be relied upon to support its allies in ways that the United States could not muster. Besides, Britain had ships and commercial contacts that would facilitate the development of the Old Southwest. Blount also knew that Britain had held Florida for two decades, from 1763 to 1783, and that emigration to the colony had flourished during the period.[46] An alliance with Britain would secure access to the Gulf and put the Floridas and Louisiana under the protection of a proven and reliable government. No longer would men such as Blount have to deal with the likes of a shaky Spain or the possibility of a Spanish transfer of its North American holdings to a militant and unstable France.

If the United States had exercised any real power in the Southwest, or indeed had shown any interest in doing so, the Blount Conspiracy might never have gotten beyond the fantasies of the blowhard Chisholm. Desperate to reverse their financial losses and achieve the political stability that was the prerequisite for the commercial development of the region, Blount and Romayne took matters into their own hands because they had no faith in the American government. As Romayne told Blount, "The prospects of things in the United States . . . will not be very flattering."[47] Alexander Hamilton and others did not want France in "our neighborhood," but they were not willing to do much about it.[48] President Adams did "not mean to give any tone to the Government, but to be led by the Senate and House of Representatives."[49] To be sure, Romayne warned Blount that if they proceeded with their plans, "with respect to the United States, we are to be pissed upon and degraded, or I am deceived."[50] But such a

---

[46] Bernard Bailyn, *Voyagers to the West: A Passage in the Peopling of America on the Eve of the Revolution* (New York, 1986), pp. 475–94.

[47] Romayne to William Blount, Mar. 11, 1797, *Annals of Congress,* 5th Cong., 3d sess., p. 2344.

[48] Romayne to William Blount, Mar. 15, 1797, ibid., p. 2345.

[49] Romayne to William Blount, Mar. 8, 1797, ibid., p. 2342.

[50] Romayne to William Blount, Mar. 17, 1797, ibid., p. 2346.

fate was not all that different from the one Blount had experienced as governor of the Southwest Territory. In 1797 Blount's goal was to bring stability to the Old Southwest in the absence of any discernible federal power in—or commitment to—that region. What was treason to a man whose national government seemed so indifferent to the needs of his region or so incapable of enforcing its will, as Blount's trial for impeachment would soon demonstrate so dramatically?

THE CONSPIRACY AND THE HONOR OF THE UNITED STATES

Back in Philadelphia in 1798, members of Congress, agitated by the prospects of war with France and a general lack of domestic tranquillity, were acutely aware of the fact that even a threat so underdeveloped and abortive as the Blount Conspiracy was an exposure of the weakness of their government. Historians have usually found little to interest them in the congressional debates over the Blount Conspiracy. The arguments centered on such procedural questions as whether the House could impeach Blount since he was no longer a member of the Senate and whether a senator was really an officer of the government and thus impeachable. There was no substantive discussion of Blount's motives or behavior since everyone assumed he was guilty. "All concur in giving him up," John Marshall told George Washington.[51] Without denying that political machinations lay behind much of the debates, it is also true that there was at least one constant theme running through them—the vulnerability of the federal government.

After his expulsion from the Senate, Blount returned to Tennessee, where he was elected to the state senate. Secure in his position locally, Blount flouted the authority of Congress by refusing to appear before it to answer the charges against him.[52] In so doing, he challenged the right of Congress to try him and succeeded in embarrassing the government of the

---

[51] John Marshall to George Washington, July 7, 1797, Herbert A. Johnson et al., eds., *The Papers of John Marshall*, 6 vols. to date (Chapel Hill, 1974–), 3:97.

[52] *Annals of Congress*, 5th Cong., 1st sess., p. 45, 3d sess., pp. 2457, 2469.

United States. Its inability to bring him to trial—the Senate eventually voted to dismiss the impeachment because he would not appear—was yet another example of its impotence in the Southwest. The Senate's sergeant-at-arms could not even get anyone in Knoxville to help him arrest Blount and had to return empty-handed to Philadelphia.[53] Blount successfully insulted the honor and dignity of the government whose authority he had tried to establish in Tennessee. But whose fault was the weakness of the federal government in the Southwest anyway? Was Blount, who had been lobbying for a strong national presence in the region for almost a decade, responsible? Or was his refusal to appear before Congress while he was elected to the state senate in Tennessee something of a symbolic representation of his opinion of a government that had deserted him? From Blount's perspective, the government of the United States had very little honor to protect.

Congressmen on all sides railed at being trapped by the former senator. No matter what they did, whether they proceeded with the impeachment or abandoned it, Blount's failure to appear for a trial before the Senate emasculated them. The great debate in the House was not over Blount's guilt but over the question of whether the dignity of the government required him to be present for his trial in the Senate. Federalists such as Samuel W. Dana of Connecticut demanded that the process proceed without Blount physically present. Impeachment, Dana contended, was neither a civil nor a criminal trial in the United States. Rather, "it is a political process, having in view the preservation of the Government of the Union." The legitimacy of the Constitution depended upon "the high authority of public opinion and of the high value of reputation to every man who is a candidate for public office." In this sense, impeachment destroyed Blount by removing his honor. This "punishment . . . is wholly a declaration of public opinion, not only that the person receiving it has proved himself unworthy of his present office, but that there is such a baseness attached to his character as to render him unfit for any office in future." Any other construction of the case, Dana

---

[53] Abernethy, *From Frontier to Plantation,* pp. 189–90.

concluded, would allow a person found guilty to "afterwards smile at the impotency of its vengeance."[54]

Others contended that to try Blount in abstentia was to admit defeat from the beginning. Congressman Robert Goodloe Harper of South Carolina (himself a Yazoo speculator) believed that the process had to be a criminal proceeding precisely because Blount's reputation—a man's "dearest possession"—was at stake. At stake, too, was the reputation of the United States. "Ought the public to be suffered to see the foolish spectacle of the House of Representatives going up to the Senate from day to day, to try a man who is laughing at them in the State of Tennessee, or the District of Maine?" The majority of the House disagreed, after much debate, and voted to proceed with the impeachment.[55]

In the Senate, while the specific issue was whether a senator was really an officer of the government, the same concern for federal authority appeared over and over again. The House manager, James A. Bayard of Delaware, emphasized that "impeachment . . . is not so much designed to punish an offender as to secure the State." Ultimately, the majority of the Senate decided not to pursue the impeachment, declaring that they lacked the jurisdiction to do so.[56] Years later, President Adams was still angry that because of delays and endless debate the guilty man "was finally suffered to escape with impunity."[57]

Thus William Blount evaded impeachment and won the right to laugh at the government of the United States. He continued to engage in numerous, often questionable, land transactions until his death in 1799. Completely transformed into a strong opponent of the government of the United States, the former territorial governor and senator began to write the kind of words that frontier historians influenced by

[54] Samuel W. Dana, in *Annals of Congress,* 5th Cong., 3d sess., p. 2475.

[55] Robert Goodloe Harper, ibid., p. 2475.

[56] James A. Bayard, ibid., p. 2251. The vote to dismiss the charges is ibid., pp. 2318–19.

[57] John Adams, "Review of the Propositions for Amending the Constitution Submitted by Mr. Hillhouse to the Senate of the United States, in 1808," in Charles Francis Adams, ed., *The Works of John Adams,* 10 vols., (Boston, 1850–56), 6:536–37.

Frederick Jackson Turner never tired of quoting. In May 1798 Blount saw no reason to fear the "Consequences" of a war with France "on this Side of the Mountain—This mountain once viewed as a great obstacle to the Settlement of this Country will prove a happy Line of Division between the eastern & western states and perhaps of *Empires* in less than 10,000 years."[58] No doubt the embittered Blount was serious. But this language is at odds with his actions before the spring of 1797. For more than a decade, Blount had demanded that the United States establish a stable, powerful presence in the Southwest.

THE CONSPIRACY AND THE LIMITS OF NATIONAL POWER

If the Blount Conspiracy was one of Blount's many efforts to stabilize the Southwest, it was also a melodramatic reminder of the consequences of the Federalists' inability to create equitable and workable structures of power in every region of the United States. The whole point of the Federalist programs in both the 1780s and the 1790s was to create a strong national government that would *impress* the citizens of the various states with its power and majesty. The Washington administration demonstrated its ability to enforce its decisions in a multitude of ways, ranging from Hamilton's economic program to the ratification of Jay's Treaty. But it was on the frontier that the federal government acted most directly and convincingly. The suppression of the Whiskey Rebellion and the defeat of the Indians in the Old Northwest were the most tangible manifestations of the power of the government of the United States.[59]

While the national government consolidated its position up the middle of its rising empire, however, throughout the 1790s it left its southwestern flank to its own devices. Given the Federalists' consistent neglect of the critical region south of the Ohio River, it is hardly surprising that the residents

[58] William Blount to Thomas Hart, May 18, 1798, Keith and Masterson, eds., *John Gray Blount Papers*, 3:229.

[59] Slaughter, *Whiskey Rebellion*.

of the Holston, Tennessee, and Mississippi valleys felt little inclined to respect the authority of the United States.

In fact it was not until two years after the exposure of the Blount Conspiracy that Alexander Hamilton got around to addressing directly the problem of federal authority west of the Appalachians. In the midst of preparing—and agitating—for war with France, Major General Hamilton asked Brig. Gen. James Wilkinson to prepare "a correct system for the management of our Western Affairs in their various relations." He was particularly interested in what to do about Louisiana and the Floridas.[60]

Wilkinson's lengthy report began, appropriately, with the Northwest, urging the abandonment or consolidation of "several useless Posts," a tribute to the government's success in that region. Then he turned to "the Mississippi and Southern Frontier." "The handful of Men now on that Station," he argued in a succinct statement of the United States government's weak position, "could make but feeble resistance, even against the enthusiastic yeomanry of Louisiana once put in motion. It appears rational and necessary, that we should determine either to Defend the Country, or to abandon it; in the first case, the means should be correspondent, and in the last case, the Troops now there should be withdrawn, for in the present State of Hands the Game on our part may soon become a desperate one." Wilkinson, of course, wanted the government to seize New Orleans; failing that, he urged a string of posts from Fort Adams along the national boundary manned by three regiments of infantry, three companies of artillery, two troops of cavalry, and two galleys.[61]

Hamilton was pleased with Wilkinson's report and wrote to

[60] Alexander Hamilton to James Wilkinson, Aug. 3, 1799, Harold C. Syrett et al., eds., *The Papers of Alexander Hamilton*, 27 vols. (New York, 1961–87), 23:303. In 1798, Hamilton had cautiously encouraged Francisco de Miranda to develop the idea of a combined British-American assault on the Spanish territory. Far shrewder than Blount, Hamilton said he "could personaley have no participation in it unless patronised by the Government of this Country." Still, if circumstances were favorable, he would "be happy in my official station to be an instrument of so good a work." See Hamilton to Miranda, Aug. 22, 1798, ibid., 22:155–56.

[61] Wilkinson to Hamilton, Sept. 6, 1799, ibid., 23: 378, 382–84.

President Adams, urging his promotion to major general.[62] In the end, however, his response demonstrated the continuing emphasis of Federalists on the Old Northwest. The region south of the Ohio River was simply too much trouble. Hamilton refused to contemplate a string of posts along the southern boundary of the United States because "the Indians must be first reconciled there" and he did not want to be accused of "an extreme frittering of our force." While Hamilton approved the maintenance of a strong unit at Fort Adams, he preferred to station the reserve corps near "the rapids of the *Ohio*" and not near Natchez, as Wilkinson had proposed. Why? "The stationing of a large body below would give jealousy to the Spaniards and lead to the measure of augmenting their regular force" while "stationing above" would excite "no jealousy. . . . For attack or defence the regular force can descend with the addition of the force of the Country." In sum, "in this situation, the force will look to various points; to the Northern Indians, to the disaffected of the neighbouring country &c &c."[63]

George Washington fully concurred with Hamilton's opinion. In fact the commanding general not only strongly opposed "placing a considerable force at the Natches," he wanted the greatest force at Fort Washington (Cincinnati). Troops from that established post could descend the rivers to the south quickly while remaining close enough to deal with Indians around the Great Lakes. More to the point, Washington thought that "in the case of Insurrections above or below, it [Fort Washington] is equally as well, if not better situated."[64]

In the end, Washington and Hamilton were more concerned with preserving federal authority in areas in which the United States had already demonstrated its power—the Ohio Country, Kentucky, and western Pennsylvania—than in areas it had not. Hamilton later observed to Secretary of War James McHenry that "our intire force, which . . . can be applied to the purposes of our Northern Western and Southern fron-

[62] Hamilton to John Adams, Sept. 7, 1799, ibid., p. 394.

[63] Hamilton to Washington, Sept. 9, 1799, ibid., pp. 406–7.

[64] Washington to Hamilton, Sept. 15, 1799, ibid., pp. 417–18.

tiers, is manifestly inadequate. All that can be done is to make such a distribution of it as will bear a proportion to the different objects."[65] Hamilton was, of course, correct. But the difficulty of the situation does not eliminate the fact that, as always, the security of the Southwest was not high on the list of those "objects."

To some extent, of course, the Jeffersonian Republicans compensated for the Federalist neglect of the Old Southwest. They purchased Louisiana from France, cooperated with the firm of Panton and Leslie (or John Forbes and Company after 1804) in getting Indians to concede land in return for the settlement of debts, resolved the chaotic land claims in the Mississippi Territory, and opened the public lands for sale. Still, the impact of the choices federal officials made with regard to the West in the 1790s was not ephemeral. For they had established a pattern—or what the Federalists would have called a "tone"—that was not easily reversed. National policy did not make the Old Southwest and the Old Northwest different. But it did encourage a strong divergence of opinion regarding the role and value of the federal government in the two regions. The *legitimacy* of the government of the United States was never established as firmly in the Southwest as it was in the Northwest.[66]

The War of 1812 confirmed the pattern of regional discrimination in American frontier policy established in the 1790s. Between 1812 and 1814 the national government concentrated its resources on ill-advised invasions of Canada from the Old Northwest. Even if the bumbling efforts of Michigan Territory governor William Hull ended in disaster and the victory of Indiana Territory governor William Henry Harrison at the Battle of the Thames was hardly a glorious one, the northwestern regions of the American empire at least received the full attention of federal officials in completing the

[65] Hamilton to James McHenry, Oct. 22, 1799, ibid., pp. 549–50.

[66] For elaboration of this point see Andrew R. L. Cayton, "'Separate Interests' and Nation-State: The Washington Administration and the Origins of Regionalism in the Trans-Mississippi West," *Journal of American History* 79 (1992): 39–67.

conquest of native peoples it had initiated in the 1790s. Peace and political predictability came to the Old Northwest under the banner, tattered though it surely was, of the national government.[67]

Meanwhile, much to President James Madison's dismay, the military campaigns in the Southwest were almost entirely local affairs. East of the Mississippi River, Andrew Jackson led the Tennessee militia in the destruction of the Creek nation in 1813 and 1814. The critical battle in the South, Horseshoe Bend, was a regional triumph, as was the improvised, anticlimatic victory over the British at New Orleans in January 1815. Neither national nor territorial officials played significant roles in either event. In 1818 Jackson, who as a good Tennessean had been much more interested in defending Pensacola and Mobile than New Orleans in 1814, summarily occupied West Florida without the approval of the national government. The general's illegal actions raised considerable controversy in Washington. They also, according to Samuel Flagg Bemis, "put just the right pressure on Spain at just the right time" to help Secretary of State John Quincy Adams conclude a treaty with Spain ceding Florida to the United States.[68]

By 1819, in short, Jackson had accomplished precisely what his patron William Blount had wanted twenty years earlier— the political stability that was the key prerequisite for the rapid commercial development of the lands east of the Mississippi. The thousands of people who poured into the region after the War of 1812 created the states of Alabama and Mississippi at roughly the same time Indiana and Illinois were admitted to the union. But the citizens of the Old Southwest had no reason to look at the federal government with either gratitude or respect. Unlike their counterparts to the north

---

[67] J. G. A. Stagg, *Mr. Madison's War: Politics, Diplomacy, and Warfare in the Early American Republic, 1783–1830* (Princeton, 1983).

[68] Samuel Flagg Bemis, *John Quincy Adams and the Foundations of American Foreign Policy* (New York, 1949), pp. 300–316, quotation p. 316. On the War of 1812 in the South, see Stagg, *Mr. Madison's War*, esp. pp. 358–59, 488–91. On Jackson and his role in these events, see Robert V. Remini, *Andrew Jackson and the Course of the American Empire, 1767–1821* (New York, 1977).

of the Ohio River, they had long since learned not to expect much from the United States. In the end they initiated and completed the conquest of the southern flank of the American republic largely on their own, not because they were intrinsically "democrats" or "localists," and certainly not because they were "Judases," but because they had no other choice. The residents of the American Southwest, like William Blount before them, did not reject national authority in some frenzy of frontier distinctiveness as much as they filled a vacuum left by the government of the United States.

BERNARD W. SHEEHAN

The Indian Problem
in the Northwest
From Conquest to
Philanthropy

IN ONE OF the more revealing episodes in Hugh Henry Brackenridge's *Modern Chivalry*, which began appearing in install-
ments in 1792 at the height of George Washington's Indian
war, Captain Farrago meets a frontier confidence man interested in employing his Irish servant Teague to impersonate
an Indian chief in an upcoming treaty negotiation. Teague
spoke Gaelic, which was easily passed off to Indian commissioners as a native tongue. The treaty concluded, Teague and
the confidence man could expect to abscond with the thousands in goods that were always distributed on such occasions.
Captain Farrago doubted that the commissioners could be so
gullible. "That is an easy matter," said the confidence man.
"Indian speeches are nearly all alike. You have only to talk of
burying hatchets under large trees, kindling fires, brightening chains; with a demand at the latter end, of blankets for
the backside, and rum to get drunk with." Besides, "the government is at a great distance. It knows no more of Indians
than a cow does of Greek."[1] Native treaty making was surely
a more consequential affair than Brackenridge allowed, but
he was not far from the mark when he wondered just how
much the government knew about Indians.

[1] Hugh Henry Brackenridge, *Modern Chivalry*, ed. Claude M. Newlin
(New York, 1962), pp. 55–57; Steven Watts, *The Republic Reborn: War and the
Making of Liberal America, 1790–1820* (Baltimore, 1987), pp. 50–51.

190

And yet at the close of the Revolution, American Indian policy was prompted by more than ignorance. Mingled with the pleasure Americans felt at the establishment of Independence was a profound sense of betrayal by the Indian tribes that had supported the British during the war. Thomas Jefferson revealed the depth of his own feeling in the Declaration of Independence and by refusing Henry Hamilton, who had been accused of promoting "savage" war, the courtesies of military captivity. The officers who led Gen. John Sullivan's expedition into the Iroquois country in 1779 made their own views known when they raised a toast to "Civilization or death to all American savages."[2] This loathing for the Indians and their ways, common among Americans at the time, drew on the long experience of colonization, but there can be little doubt that the ideological excitement of the Revolution together with the bitter struggle on the frontier intensified hatred. As a consequence, when the war ended, formulators of government policy toward the tribes flirted with the most draconian measures.

At the same time Americans remained ambivalent over the "problem" of the Indian. Superficially the native people commanded a great deal of attention, though seldom as permanent residents of the continent. Unless Indians could play a mythic part in the formulation of an American vision or engaged in actual conflict with white settlers over land, they could be conveniently ignored. And, as the frontier receded toward the north and west, that seemed increasingly the appropriate reaction. Indeed, during the War for Independence, despite the anger directed at the tribesmen, Washington had no trouble in concentrating his attention on the main arena of conflict. He knew that defeating the Indians would not bring Independence. It was not until two years after the frontier conflict in the north began that he dispatched Sullivan against the Iroquois. Unsurprisingly, therefore, the Peace of Paris made no mention of the native people. Neither side, apparently, thought that the Indian had any contribution to make to a settlement between Britain and America. And yet the Indian would not simply evanesce, ei-

[2] Quoted in William T. Hagan, *American Indians* (Chicago, 1961), p. 38.

ther figuratively or in reality. In the years after the Revolution few of the major issues that plagued the Confederation and the new nation did not in some way involve the native people. The American penetration beyond the mountains by midcentury had already brought on direct conflict between frontiersmen and warriors and exacerbated the imperial contest. With a switch in imperial personnel, those hostilities continued through the Revolution and into the later period. After the establishment of Independence, Spain on the southern border and Britain in the north manipulated the tribes to maintain their position on the continent. The success of the European powers in making their influence felt west of the mountains and the failure of the federal authorities to protect the frontier against the tribesmen provoked the rise of separatist movements in the newly settled regions. Tension between state and federal jurisdiction, acute over western lands in the 1780s, spilled into the question of authority over Indian affairs. Indeed few issues did not in some way touch the Indians. War with the tribes reawakened the historic dispute over a standing army and the taxation needed to support it. And, finally, the disdain for life on the border, so much a staple of political discourse in the East, invariably implicated the Indian either as a victim of the unruly frontiersmen or as an exemplar for their behavior.

Thus the American native who presented the new republic with some of its most vexing policy decisions between the Peace of Paris in 1783 and the Treaty of Greenville in 1795 was at once "savage," invisible, and ubiquitous, a perplexing creature indeed. Of course the root question concerned sovereignty over the land.[3] That European settlers would eventually (sooner or later, depending on the commentator) occupy the land encompassed by the Treaty of Paris few could doubt. But just how the Indian figured in the process had never been completely settled. In the past the process had

---

[3] See Wilcomb E. Washburn, *Red Man's Land / White Man's Law: A Study of the Past and Present Status of the American Indian* (New York, 1971); and John T. Juricek, "English Claims in North America to 1660: A Study in Legal and Constitutional History," Ph.D. diss., University of Chicago, 1970.

been gradual with the assumption that the tribes possessed some right to their lands, enough to require that certain procedures be followed in their acquisition, usually purchase, though conquest was also accepted. With the completion of the Revolution there was plainly an impulse among some Americans to settle the issue finally by rejecting native claims out of hand on the basis of conquest and establishing American sovereignty and ownership of the land. The implication followed that the western lands to the Mississippi should be free for immediate occupation by the white frontier population. Of course nothing of the sort occurred since the tribes had not been conquered, did in fact possess the land, and were determined to keep the whites at bay.

The tribes may not have been conquered in the sense of suffering defeat and suing for peace, but the Revolution had certainly been a traumatic experience for them. The Iroquois in New York and the polyglot tribal groupings in the Northwest came out of the conflict convinced that their long contest with the white man had reached a decisive stage. The political structure of the Iroquois, in decline since midcentury, collapsed at the close of the war. The council fire at Onondaga had been extinguished during the war and was not rekindled after the peace. Half of the confederacy moved to Canada, breaking irrevocably the bond that had united the Iroquois for centuries. Malaise settled on the longhouse. West of the Ohio the blow had been less severe but the crisis was no less acute. There was no place else to move. On what has come to be called the middle ground, whites and Indians carried on a complex relationship, which involved a degree of cultural accommodation between the two sides but at the same time set the scene for the disintegration and defeat of the native way of life. Many tribesmen found hope in nativism and the creation of pan-Indian alliances with other native peoples, but neither provided much help and might have been themselves symptoms of decline. The British Indian department promoted the formation of a western confederacy, but nothing, it seemed, could quite disguise the underlying social and political disarray. Under the circumstances conquest may have been an exaggerated description of American achievements in the war, but it was not an unrealistic prediction of what would soon occur.[4]

First peace had to be made with the tribes. Washington summarized the problem neatly in 1783: "The Settlement of the Western Country and making a Peace with the Indians," he wrote to James Duane, "are so analogous that there can be no definition of the one without involving considerations of the other."[5] This was precisely the problem taken up by a congressional committee headed by Duane in the fall of that year. The object was to lay the foundation for separate treaties with the northern and southern tribes. The committee report contained an interesting amalgam of ideas, more significant for what it suggested than for what it concluded. The Indians were to be informed that the British had relinquished their claim to all the lands south of the Great Lakes. Since the Indians had joined the British in the war, they also had been defeated and might be required to retire with their allies to the north. This was the famous "conquest theory," but its mere expression was about the limit of its use by the congressional policymakers. Having stated the abstract proposition, the committee proceeded to make it null. It was, said the committee, "just and necessary" that a boundary be established between the whites and Indians, thereby accepting, at least in fact, the legitimacy of native land possession. After waiving the right of conquest, the American case seemed then to rest more on necessity than right. The new government had agreed to grant bounty lands to its former soldiers and required new territory for immigrants who continued to arrive on its shores. Although it was without the means to purchase these lands, they were needed to serve as a fund for the security of the national debt. As practical and conventional as the report turned out, it had broached the idea of conquest, a

[4] For the Iroquois see Anthony F. C. Wallace, *The Death and Rebirth of the Seneca* (New York, 1969); for the midwestern tribes see Richard White, *The Middle Ground: Indians, Empires, and Republics in the Great Lakes Region, 1650–1815* (Cambridge, 1991); and Gregory Evans Dowd, *A Spirited Resistance: The North American Indian Struggle for Unity, 1745–1815* (Baltimore, 1992).

[5] George Washington to James Duane, Sept. 7, 1783, John C. Fitzpatrick, ed., *The Writings of George Washington*, 39 vols. (Washington, D.C., 1931–44), 27:139.

notion that would plague American Indian policy until the mid-1790s.[6]

Duane was more revealing in the advice he gave to George Clinton, governor of New York, on a prospective state treaty with the Iroquois. His principal concern seemed to be that the Iroquois should be under the jurisdiction of the state rather than the Confederation, but in the process he laid out a view of Indian relations entirely compatible with the conquest theory. It was an "indispensable Necessity," he wrote, that the Indians recognize that whatever territorial rights they may once have possessed, "these Tribes should be reconciled to the Idea of being Members of the State, dependant upon its government and resting upon its Protection." Above all, the native leaders must be relieved of the idea that they treat with the state commissioners on the basis of equality. Neither the state nor the Confederation should again adopt "the disgraceful system of pensioning, courting and flattering them as great and mighty nations." Duane thought this change in policy might easily be implemented by subtle changes in the mode of expression used with the native people. The phrases commonly employed—Six Nations, Council Fire at Onondaga, confederates—must be abandoned. Even the idea of a treaty, which conveyed the impression of dealings with an independent power, should be avoided. Enough that they should be reminded of their perfidious behavior during the Revolution and the kindness and forbearance that was now offered to them. They will once more "be restored . . . in their native Land," lands now *reserved* for their use by the state.[7]

Duane had practical reasons enough for recommending this switch in attitude toward the tribes. Land claims by enterprising New Yorkers, interstate rivalry, and competition between state and Confederation power justified a quick assumption of state jurisdiction over the Iroquois. But his motivation seemed to have deeper sources. The Revolution

---

[6] "Report of Congressional Committee on Treaty with the Indians," Oct. 15, 1783, Worthington Chauncey Ford et al., eds., *Journals of the Continental Congress, 1774–1789*, 34 vols. (Washington, D.C., 1904–37), 25:680–95.

[7] Hugh Hastings, ed., *Public Papers of George Clinton*, 10 vols. (Albany, 1899–1914), 8:328–32.

above all established the independence of the Americans from the power of the empire. Autonomous or even semi-independent tribes in the western portions of New York, and by implication between the Alleghenies and the Mississippi, constituted an affront to that independence. If the new authorities return to the practice of treating the Indians as if they were "great and mighty nations," wrote Duane, "this Revolution in my Eyes will have lost more than half its' Value."[8]

But Duane had not, any more than had his committee, recommended that the Indians should be immediately displaced. How tempting was such a suggestion was revealed by Peter Schuyler, the experienced Indian negotiator from Albany. In a letter to the president of Congress in the summer of 1783, he painstakingly outlined the arguments against the implementation of the conquest theory. In the end his analysis was also practical. His language assumed that the Indians' behavior in the war entirely justified their expulsion. To accomplish this end, however, would require more war and too much money. And even if the Indians could be driven out, the expulsion would likely prove temporary. In time the tribesmen would drift back across the border. If by some chance they stayed in Canada there would be few advantages for the struggling Confederation. The warriors would add to the strength of the British, would have a safe haven from which to harass the frontier, and would certainly close the fur trade to American commerce. If permitted to remain within the borders of the Confederation, the Indians presented no permanent obstacles to expansion. Schuyler had every confidence that treaties might be made with the Indians opening ample lands for settlement. In the long run native society would prove incapable of opposing the occupation of the western lands. As so many others believed at the time, he contended that the very presence of white settlements in the vicinity of the Indians would cause the decline of native life and

[8] Ibid., p. 329; see also J. David Lehman, "The End of the Iroquois Mystique: The Oneida Land Cession Treaties," *William and Mary Quarterly*, 3d ser. 47 (1990):523–47.

the inevitable transfer of their land. Under the circumstances overt conquest was hardly necessary.[9]

After reading Schuyler's letter, sent to him by Duane, Washington agreed to the justice but impracticality of the conquest theory. He had no doubt that Britain had ceded to the United States the "Sovereignty" of the country east of the Mississippi and that the behavior of the Indians during the war as allies of the British warranted their displacement. "But," he added, "we prefer Peace to a state of Warfare, as we consider them a deluded People; as we persuade ourselves that they are convinced, from experience, of their error in taking up the Hatchet against us, and that their true Interest and safety must now depend upon *our* friendship. As the Country is large enough to contain us all; and as we are disposed to be kind to them and to partake of their Trade, we will from these considerations and from motives of Comp[assio]n draw a veil over what is past and establish a boundary line between them and us beyond which we will *endeavor* to restrain our People from Hunting or Settling, and within which we will not come, but for the purposes of Trading, Treating, or other business unexceptionable in its nature." Washington seemed particularly taken with Schuyler's estimate of the long-term effects of the white man's world on the native people. But experience as a speculator in frontier lands led him to add another potential difficulty. Schuyler had been concerned that New York would preempt Confederation control of the West and precipitate Indian war. Washington was concerned that the lands should be controlled by Congress so that they might be distributed among the veterans of his much-abused army. He wanted to "People the Country progressively" so that "our Settlements would be compact, Government well established, and our Barrier formidable" against the British and the Indians. He feared that the lands would fall into the hands of jobbers and monopolizers or, worse, that the new nation would witness the "settling, or overspreading [of] the Western Country . . .

[9] Peter Schuyler to President of Congress [Elias Boudinot], July 29, 1783, Papers of the Continental Congress, Reel 173: 601–5, Record Group 360, National Archives, Washington, D.C.

by a parcel of Banditti, who will bid defiance to all Authority" and certainly cause the Indian to continue hostilities. The only practical way to get the lands into the hands of the deserving was to avoid war, which of course meant that the idea of conquest would have to be dropped.[10]

Thus in the summer and fall of 1783 Schuyler, Washington, Duane, and the responsible congressional committee had all toyed with the idea that the Indians were a conquered people who might be required to give up their lands. All agreed to the abstract justice of the proposition, but none thought it a practical basis upon which to do business with the tribesmen. Not so, apparently, the commissioners assigned in the 1780s to make treaties with the tribes north of the Ohio. They followed their instructions in seeking boundaries between the Indians and the frontier population but only after laying great stress on the American belief that the Indians were a conquered people and announcing that the new nation claimed sovereignty over all the lands east of the Mississippi. The Indians had no reason to be pleased with the boundaries established after the Revolution but, understandably, the point that lodged in the native mind was the claim of conquest. Whether without that claim the new nation could have avoided war with the northern tribes seems doubtful, but there can be little doubt that the assertion of the claim both exacerbated and prolonged the conflict.

The commissioners sent to Fort Stanwix in 1784 to make the first treaty with the northern tribes certainly showed no signs of the ambivalence apparent in the minds of the formulators of policy. Richard Butler, Arthur Lee, and Oliver Wolcott were determined to establish the sovereignty of the United States over the lands inhabited by the Indians at the same time that they insisted on the supremacy of the Confederation government over the states in Indian affairs. They shunned the New York delegation that had already met with the Iroquois contrary to congressional wishes. A delegation from Pennsylvania that planned to meet after the main negotiations and had announced its subordination to the congres-

[10] Washington to Duane, Sept. 7, 1783, Fitzpatrick, ed., *Writings of Washington*, 27:133–40.

sional commissioners received more amicable treatment. Not so the marquis de Lafayette, who turned up with an entourage before the main proceedings began with the intention of addressing the Indians. With a certain ill-grace the commissioners agreed to Lafayette's making the speech, but they made it understood that they did not like the competition. Having established their own position, the commissioners made a quite direct approach to the Iroquois representatives. They informed the Indians that they were a "subdued people," that the king of Great Britain had ceded his claims on the continent to the United States, and that the United States could by "right of conquest" claim the whole of the Indian territory. They went on to dictate a boundary that pushed the natives into the western corner of New York and took besides southern Ohio up to the Great Miami River. And they made no offer to pay for the land, the customary practice in such transfers.[11]

Curiously, the commissioners feared that their instructions would make the negotiations more difficult. The boundary had been fixed by the Congress, and the commissioners were given no authority to deviate from it, even if they saw the possibility of obtaining a more advantageous border. Moreover, they had not been commissioned to open trade with the Indians, a serious defect since they knew well enough that an enduring peace could only be established if the tribes were assured a ready supply of goods. These were pertinent objections to congressional policy, but the commissioners failed to see the consequences of their own employment of the conquest theory for the making of a solid peace. Perhaps Arthur Lee revealed the basis of their tactics. He had not been convinced, he wrote, that the Indians could be brought to submission until the last speech had been delivered and the articles of the treaty accepted. "But they are Animals," he continued, "that must be subdued and kept in awe or they will be mischievous, and fear alone will affect this submission."[12]

[11] Neville B. Craig, ed., *The Olden Time* 2 (reprint ed., Pittsburgh, 1876): 404–32.

[12] Richard Butler and Arthur Lee to Chairman of the Committee of the States, July 26, 1784, Papers of the Continental Congress, Reel 69:725–28;

The same attitudes and tactics persisted when two of the commissioners, Lee and Butler, went west in the winter of 1784–85 to meet representatives of the western tribes at Fort McIntosh, a post thirty miles down the Ohio from Pittsburgh where they were joined by George Rogers Clark. Only a small delegation of Delawares and Wyandots and some fugitive Ottawas and Chippewas appeared at McIntosh. The following year the commissioners confronted the Shawnees at Fort Finney, a small post at the mouth of the Miami River. In both instances the commissioners dictated the peace, established the Ohio boundary arbitrarily, and allotted the lands west of the border to native people on the supposition that all the lands to the Mississippi belonged to the United States. They went so far as to settle a land dispute within the Indian territory between the Delawares and the Wyandots. The commissioners believed that they had succeeded in making peace in eastern and southern Ohio not by the usual accommodations of Indian diplomacy but by more decisive methods. "A sense of superiority," they reported, "has infinitely more influence on an indian mind, than that of benefits bestowed, or faith engaged." [13]

In fact the commissioners had left chaos and hostility behind them in the West. The Iroquois delegation at Stanwix had been reasonably representative. Cornplanter, at least, had attended and signed the treaty, though Joseph Brant had left early. His absence represented a serious division among the Iroquois, which much diminished the effectiveness of that native grouping in future relations with the United States. Within a short time the Iroquois repudiated the treaty, Cornplanter pleading for a revision in a desperate attempt to bolster his own position among his people. [14] In the Northwest the agreements at McIn-

---

James Madison to Thomas Jefferson, Oct. 11, 1784, William T. Hutchinson et al., eds., *The Papers of James Madison*, 22 vols. to date (Chicago and Charlottesville, Va., 1962–), 8:117; Louis W. Potts, *Arthur Lee: A Virtuous Revolutionary* (Baton Rouge, 1981), p. 270.

[13] Randolph C. Downes, *Council Fires on the Upper Ohio* (Pittsburgh, 1940), pp. 292–98; Craig, ed., *Olden Time*, 2:522–25; Papers of the Continental Congress, Reel 37:271–75.

[14] Papers of the Continental Congress, Reel 69:407–9, 164–65.

tosh and Finney never gained acceptance. The British Indian department, supported by Brant, who shifted his field of activity to the West, urged resistance and the formation of an Indian confederacy. The congressional commissioners had pursued a policy that had yielded vast stretches of new territory but on the basis of a theory that would soon help provoke a war that the new government wished devoutly to avoid.

The Indians learned from the British that the American interpretation of the Treaty of Paris would not bear close scrutiny. Brant went to England and returned with royal assurance that the king had not given away the Indian lands, though he returned with little else.[15] As George Hammond later made clear to Alexander Hamilton, the treaty of peace "could unquestionably *transfer* no other rights of soil or of any other nature than such as his Majesty had actually *enjoyed.*" But there was the rub. One can doubt that the Indians quite caught the meaning of the phrase "rights of soil" used by Hammond and by John Johnson even before Stanwix in reassuring the tribesmen that the rumors they had heard about American claims could not be true.[16] The British had no trouble telling the native people that the Americans had obtained no right to put them off their lands, but they could not quite explain the full meaning of the Peace of Paris.

When Henry Knox took control of the war office in late 1785, it was apparent that the desired peace had not materialized. Nor had the finances needed to pursue a war policy appeared. These, after all, were dependent on the distribution of western lands, the very cause of native discontent in the West. The institutionalization of the expansion into the new territories in the ordinances of 1785 and 1787 only increased the tension.[17] Indeed the Northwest Ordinance could be

[15] Isabel Thompson Kelsay, *Joseph Brant, 1743–1807: Man of Two Worlds* (Syracuse, N.Y., 1984), pp. 381–92; Josiah Harmar to Henry Knox, July 16, 1785, Papers of the Continental Congress, Reel 164:71.

[16] "Conversation with George Hammond," Nov. 22, 1792, Harold C. Syrett et al., eds., *The Papers of Alexander Hamilton,* 27 vols. (New York, 1961–87), 13:213.

[17] Robert M. Taylor, Jr., ed., *The Northwest Ordinance: A Bicentennial Handbook* (Indianapolis, 1987), pp. 61–65.

taken both ways. It assumed the eventual displacement of the Indians, but it also asserted that Indian lands should not be taken from them without their consent, a provision hardly compatible with the idea of conquest. Knox had never favored the conquest theory, and he now pointedly abandoned it as even the tenuous basis for official policy. He resolved on a new treaty with the northwestern tribes that would return to the traditional policy of purchase. In an oblique recognition that the treaties of the early 1780s had been irregular, he instructed the commissioners to offer payment for the lands already acquired. The treaty negotiations were held at Fort Harmar in December-January, 1788–89. Once again the actual deliberations did not conform to the congressional instructions. Despite an explicit statement of policy at the national level, when the native delegation resisted his proposals, Arthur St. Clair had recourse to the principle of conquest. The Indians tried first negotiating for the Ohio River boundary that would have repealed McIntosh and Finney. When that met resistance, they tried Brant's proposal, the Muskingum. But St. Clair would accept nothing but a substantial ratification of the previous treaties, which drew the boundary at the Miami River. In the end the agreement was dictated, the Indians were divided but mostly opposed, and peace did not come to the Northwest.[18]

The failure of the Fort Harmar treaty led directly to war. The desultory attacks by the frontier populations launched from western Pennsylvania and Kentucky gave way to the formal expeditions of Josiah Harmar in 1790 and Arthur St. Clair in 1791 and the successful invasion of the Indian country by Anthony Wayne in 1793–94. Paradoxically it was during this period of open conflict that the Washington administration conceived a clearer idea of Indians' rights to the land that decisively abandoned the conquest theory and began the formulation of a philanthropic version of the Indians' future.

---

[18] Reginald Horsman, *Expansion and American Indian Policy, 1783–1812* ([East Lansing, Mich.], 1967), chap. 3; Ford et al., eds., *Journals of the Continental Congress*, 33:385–91; 34:124–26; *Military Journal of Major Ebenezer Denny* (Philadelphia, 1859), pp. 127–30.

Knox believed that the Fort Harmar treaty had established a new national policy toward the Indians. He informed Washington that Congress, by deciding in July 1788 to appropriate money to extinguish Indian title to lands that the United States already claimed, had formally abandoned the fiction that the Indians had been conquered. By instructing St. Clair to proceed at Fort Harmar on the basis of preemption and obtain "regular conveyances" of the lands up to the Great Miami, the Congress implicitly acknowledged that the treaties of McIntosh and Finney had been illegal. It could not be denied, asserted Knox, "that the Indians possess the natural rights of man, and . . . they ought not wantonly to be divested thereof." His meaning was clear enough. The Indians possessed a "right of the soil," the right to sell land or not to sell it as they wished. But they had no right to sell it other than to the United States. They did not hold political sovereignty in their territory, and they did not own the land in fee simple. Only the United States could claim "general sovereignty" over the Indian territories.[19]

In a variety of guises the issue came before the cabinet in the early 1790s. Jefferson took the lead in articulating policy. When the question of the Yazoo grants arose, he began by explaining the basis of the United States claims on the continent. On "thinly occupied" territory the right of the natives constituted an "exception" to the right of the newcomers, meaning that the newcomers had a right against other nations but not against the natives. This formulation gave the newcomers the exclusive right of acquiring the land, but it imposed no obligation on the natives to give it up. The native title could be obtained by either war or contract. Shortly after Jefferson expressed his view, Hamilton fell into one of his conversations with George Hammond over British influence in the north. Hamilton referred to Jefferson's position, asserting the right of preemption. He noted, however, that the "general sovereignty" of the United States over the tribes had

[19] Knox to Washington, June 15, 1789, William W. Abbot et al., eds., *The Papers of George Washington: Presidential Series*, 4 vols. to date (Charlottesville, Va., 1987–), 2:493; Knox to Washington, July 7, 1789, *American State Papers: Indian Affairs*, 1:53; Knox to Washington, Jan. 4, 1790, ibid., p. 61; Knox to Joseph Brant, June 27, 1792, ibid., p. 236.

yet to be precisely defined. Until then the United States had not gone further in regulating the internal affairs of the Indians than to forbid the presence among them of unlicensed traders. But Hammond took this to mean that the United States would interpret British efforts to create a barrier state in the Northwest as an infringement on American sovereignty.[20]

The question came up again in 1793 when Washington was contemplating instructions to the commissioners who were to be sent to Sandusky in a last effort to make peace before Wayne continued his march into the Indian country. The immediate issue concerned whether, as the price of peace, the commissioners should be allowed to cede back to the tribes some of the lands obtained in the treaties of the 1780s. Hamilton, Knox, and Edmund Randolph agreed that some lands might be relinquished for peace, so long as they were not lands already committed by the government. Jefferson argued that the commissioners might stipulate that the United States would not for the present settle some of those lands, but he was adamant that the government could not give up any of its territory. As Jefferson explained later in his autobiography, the right of preemption gave the United States no "dominion, or jurisd[ictio]n, or paramountship" over Indian lands while they possessed the right of soil. The Indians owned "the full, undivided & independent sovereignty as long as they chose to keep it." But once it was transferred to the United States, the sovereignty became absolute and permanent.[21] It does seem that Jefferson was slightly disingenuous here, since the right of preemption was itself scarcely compatible with his apparently broad conception of native sovereignty.

That preemption formed the bedrock of government pol-

---

[20] Julian P. Boyd et al., eds., *The Papers of Thomas Jefferson*, 28 vols. to date (Princeton, 1950-), 16:407; "Conversation with George Hammond," Syrett et al., eds., *Papers of Hamilton*, 13: 213.

[21] Boyd et al., eds., *Papers of Jefferson*, 22:285n; Thomas Jefferson, "The Anas," in Paul Leicester Ford, ed., *The Writings of Thomas Jefferson*, 10 vols. (New York, 1892–99), 1:218–20; Syrett et al., eds., *Papers of Hamilton*, 14:142–43.

icy toward the Indians had become clear by 1792 when Rufus
Putnam negotiated a treaty with the Illinois tribes that contained an article insufficiently explicit on the issue. Knox
questioned his Revolutionary colleague on its meaning before
submitting the treaty to the Senate. That body, after short de-
liberation, refused to ratify the treaty precisely because it
failed to affirm the principle of preemption.[22]

Thus in 1793 Benjamin Lincoln, Beverly Randolph, and
Timothy Pickering trekked west hoping to meet the tribes at
Sandusky and either to forestall the last and potentially blood-
iest act in the war or establish the moral justification for seeing
it through to the end. Finally in July they met with a delegation of western Indians at Matthew Elliott's farm south of Detroit. Here Lincoln described the current American position
with patience and clarity. He disowned the commissioners at
Stanwix and McIntosh. "We . . . frankly tell you that we think
that those commissioners put an erroneous construction on
that part of our treaty with the king." They had no right to
claim more than preemption. "Brothers we now concede this
great point. We by the express authority of the President of
the United States, acknowledge the property or right of soil
. . . to be in the Indian nations, so long as they desire to occupy the same." Preemption stemmed from an agreement
among the white nations concerning their claims on the continent. As a consequence of the American victory in the Revolution, the king agreed that the Americans possessed the
exclusive right to purchase the Indian lands between
the Ohio and the Mississippi. No matter the equivocation
in the phrase "property or right of soil," the Indians caught
the point this time and explicitly rejected it. They insisted
on the Ohio River border and denied that they were bound
by any agreement between the king and the Americans. The
Indians considered themselves free "to make any bargain or
cession of lands whenever and to whomsoever we please."
After Wayne settled the issue at Fallen Timbers, Pickering, by

[22] "Treaty between the United States and the Wabash and Illinois Indians," in Rowena Buell, ed., *The Memoirs of Rufus Putnam* (Boston, 1903), pp.
363n, 364–65; Rufus Putnam to Knox, Dec. 20, 1792, ibid., p. 374; *Journal
of the Executive Proceedings of the Senate*, 2d Cong., 2d sess., pp. 128, 134,
145, 146.

then secretary of war, still felt it necessary to instruct Wayne in detail. He thought the conquest principle had "probably been the main spring of the distressing war on our frontiers," and he went over the argument for preemption once again. By now the tribes could do little but grant the point.[23]

The conquest theory and the right of preemption did not stand in isolation. At the western negotiations in 1793 the more immediate issue was the location of the western border. American settlements had already crossed the Ohio and the treaties of the 1780s were in great measure designed to ratify that fact. But the western Indians had never really recognized the legitimacy of those settlements despite the acquiescence of some tribesmen at the treaties of McIntosh and Harmar. Conquest and preemption held major significance for the future of Indian-white relations, but in the immediate situation those principles were hostage to the desperation of the native people to keep the settlers east and south of the Ohio and the determination of the Washington administration to establish the legality of future white settlement.

To complicate matters, these wilderness concerns were played out in an international arena. The British retained their hold on the western posts and, at least for the present, were determined to maintain their influence with the western tribes. American efforts to tailor an Indian policy that maintained peace while allowing for frontier expansion ran directly counter to British interests. Whether without British interference the Americans would have been successful seems unlikely, but in fact whatever actions the Washington administration took in the 1790s had to account for the powerful influence of the British among western tribesmen.[24]

The intentions of John Graves Simcoe, the lieutenant-

[23] Benjamin Lincoln, "Journal of a Treaty Held in 1793 . . . ," *Collections of the Massachusetts Historical Society,* 3d ser. 5 (1836):148–50, 166; Timothy Pickering to Anthony Wayne, Apr. 8, 1795, Richard C. Knopf, ed., *Anthony Wayne, A Name in Arms . . .* (Pittsburgh, 1960), pp. 398–99.

[24] Samuel Flagg Bemis, *Jay's Treaty: A Study in Commerce and Diplomacy,* rev. ed. (New Haven, 1962), chaps. 6 and 8; Alfred L. Burt, *The United States, Great Britain, and British North America from the Revolution to the Establishment of Peace after the War of 1812* (1940; reprint ed., New York, 1961), chaps. 6 and 7.

governor of Upper Canada, were never as clear as they might have been. His aides in the British Indian department, Alexander McKee and Matthew Elliott, kept the Indians supplied with the instruments of war, while he pushed himself forward as a mediator between the United States and its Indian enemies, proposing at the same time that a substantial segment of the Northwest should be set aside as a neutral barrier state. The Washington administration accused the Indian department of fomenting the conflict in the Northwest, rejected any hint of mediation, and took the proposed barrier as a direct assault on the nation's sovereignty. Simcoe's overt aggressiveness, however, masked the weakness of the British position in the West. He feared war with the United States and hence designed his policy to compensate for his vulnerability. Although he could not be displeased with the success of the warriors against Harmar and St. Clair, he believed that further conflict would eventually alienate the Indians from Britain and diminish the fur trade. He wanted the Indians united and strong so they would remain a protective barrier between the new expanding nation and Canada.[25]

The responsible Americans, Washington, Knox, and the commissioners assigned to meet the Indians at Sandusky, missed the subtleties of Simcoe's problem. They wanted peace on the frontier and an advantageous boundary, and they were convinced that neither could be obtained if the British continued their machinations south of the Great Lakes. Thus in 1793 the border was the most pressing problem. American settlements then stretched along the Ohio to the Miami with outposts farther west at the falls of the Ohio and in the French settlements in Illinois. The contested treaties of the 1780s had set the boundary at the Miami-Cuyahoga line, and that is what the commissioners had been instructed to obtain once again in the proposed Sandusky meeting. For the withdrawal of Indian objections to McIntosh, Finney, and Harmar, the commissioners would disown the conquest theory and offer

---

[25] The best account of John Graves Simcoe's activities remains Burt, *United States and British North America*, pp. 120–40; see also Simcoe to George Hammond, Aug. 24, 1793, E. A. Cruikshank, ed., *The Correspondence of Lieut. Governor John Graves Simcoe*, 4 vols. (Toronto, 1923–26), 1:68–69.

substantial compensation. They could not give up any lands that had already been settled or sold. In the 1780s the western tribes had shown signs of a willingness to settle for a boundary at the Muskingum, but with the success of their arms and increasing unity under the stimulus of the British agents they stiffened their demands. At a conference at the Au Glaize on the Maumee in October 1792 the tribes had insisted that they could not take a single step back from the Ohio, the boundary established in 1768 at the first treaty of Fort Stanwix.[26] The Ohio line was out of the question for the Americans, but in truth they knew little of the Indian position. Knox had invited Joseph Brant to Philadelphia in June 1792 and had been convinced by the Iroquois leader that the tribesmen would settle for the Muskingum.[27] Knox seems to have thought this proposition worth talking about, though nothing he wrote to the commissioners indicates a willingness to agree to that line. Neither Knox, Brant, nor the commissioners had their way. The Sandusky meeting never took place because the tribesmen insisted on the Ohio as a basis for discussions, which the commissioners could not concede. The Indians could not be moved by the abandonment of the conquest theory, the offer of substantial compensation, or hints at a new philanthropic policy.[28]

The failed Sandusky meeting showed the western tribes at the highest point of their unity and power, though even in that situation their underlying weakness was apparent. The Iroquois, themselves divided, had long since made it clear that they could not support the continuation of the war. On their New York lands they were virtually surrounded by whites and could hardly risk opposition to white encroachment on their own territory, much less support the increasingly remote cause of the western tribes. Despite their recent success, the western Indians seemed to sense their own vul-

[26] Cruikshank, ed., *Correspondence of Simcoe*, p. 242; Reginald Horsman, *Matthew Elliott, British Indian Agent* (Detroit, 1964), p. 72.

[27] Kelsay, *Brant*, pp. 470–71.

[28] Frederick S. Allis, Jr., ed., Timothy Pickering Papers microfilm, Reel 60:164A-65, Massachusetts Historical Society, Boston; Commissioners to Simcoe, June 7, 1793, Cruikshank, ed., *Correspondence of Simcoe*, 1:350.

nerability. Without the prodding of the British agents, it seems likely that they would have met with the commissioners and followed Brant's lead in accepting a boundary west of the Ohio.[29] They were divided among themselves, the Iroquois and lake Indians in favor of concessions and the Shawnees, Wyandots, Delawares, and Miamis adamant for the Ohio.[30] In addition, leadership rivalry had developed between Little Turtle of the Miamis and the Shawnee chief Blue Jacket. Indeed, it is possible that Little Turtle, who had led the warriors against Harmar and St. Clair, actually favored concessions.[31] As it turned out, the British Indian department had its way, and the Indians lost at Fallen Timbers and were forced at Greenville to acquiesce in a far less advantageous border than would have been required of them at Sandusky. Along with the land went any serious Indian opposition to the United States government's exercise of the right of preemption.

The House of Representatives took up the issue of Indian land rights in 1796 in the deliberations over the Indian intercourse bill. The debate concerned a clause in the bill that required trespassers on lands assigned to the Indians at Greenville to forfeit any preemptive claim they may have had to those lands.[32] Many veterans who had been granted these future rights had wearied of waiting for the Indians to give up their title and had proceeded to mark off their lands and in some cases to settle them, provoking Indian retaliation. The provision was designed to establish a secure title for the Indians and at the same time to assert yet again the authority

---

[29] Whether the British influenced the Indians to insist on the Ohio boundary remains a complex issue. It seems likely that Alexander McKee and Matthew Elliott did so without orders from Simcoe (see Cruikshank, ed., *Correspondence of Simcoe*, 2:14–16, 34–35, 68–69, 85–86; Allis, ed., Pickering Papers, Reel 59:184). The best summary is in Horsman, *Elliott*, pp. 86–91.

[30] Brant to Simcoe, July 28, 1793, Cruikshank, ed., *Correspondence of Simcoe*, 1:402–3.

[31] Harvey Lewis Carter, *The Life and Times of Little Turtle: First Sagamore of the Wabash* (Urbana, Ill., 1987), pp. 120, 134.

[32] The debate can be followed in the *Annals of Congress*, 4th Cong., 1st sess., pp. 894–904.

of the federal government over the western territory and Indian affairs. On one side of the argument stood frontier and local interests that tended to favor any measure likely to loosen the native hold on the land. On the other were New Englanders determined to defend the authority of the new government on the frontier and expressing a vaguely philanthropic interest in the native people. The heart of the dispute turned on the nature of Indian land possession.

James Hillhouse of Connecticut and Theodore Sedgwick of Massachusetts delivered the major speeches on the Indian side. Hillhouse made the most uncompromising case for the Indians. He admitted that they were "men in uncivilized life" and differed in their "customs and habits" from the white man. Yet, he argued, "they were justly entitled to the lands which they possessed." Not only had the denial of this title caused great turmoil on the frontier, it was the principal cause of the Indian wars. More important, the title had been recognized by the United States in treaties. The "God of Nature" gave the Indians their land. He went on to ask: "Who were the proprietors of this country previous to its being known to civilized nations (as they were called)? Were not those people? And had they not always been in the peaceable enjoyment of it? Who gave us the right to call their title in question, or forcibly to thrust them out? They had," he added, "suffered enough from the fraud and violence of those who, since the discovery of America, had been seeking to dispossess them of their lands." Hillhouse did not say so, but the weight of his argument opposed the preemptive right of the government. Sedgwick took a similar tack though he came to a different conclusion on preemption. He began by denying that there was any difference in the kind of ownership of land exercised by Indians and white men. There was no justification, he asserted, for the argument that civilized men have greater right to land because they improve it. That was an idea identified with the age of cupidity and the policies of Spain. He could not believe that "at the close of the eighteenth century, and in this place, doctrines of this kind would have been held." The idea implied the rejection of the security of property. Under that principle no owner of unimproved acreage would be safe. He equated native possession of land with native right.

Indian "rights on their possessions were as sacred as the rights of civilized life." They could not be deprived of their rights simply "because they did not dress like us, were not equally religious, or did not understand the arts of civilized life." So long as the whites contended that the Indians were without rights they may "expect scenes of blood on their frontier." As for preemption, Sedgwick argued that it was a "good and reasonable" principle resting on a "natural foundation." But, because he saw the principle arising from relations between the European powers, he did not seem to notice that it seriously impaired native land rights. Preemption was designed to keep the discoverers from fighting among themselves, thus presenting the natives with the spectacle of "two nations, with all the arts of civilization and the cupidity of buccaneers" revealing their own "savage passions."

The argument for the frontier was opened by James Holland of North Carolina. He rejected the Hillhouse-Sedgwick position that the Indians possessed a "fee simple" ownership of their lands. On the contrary, he contended, the Indians had never owned those lands. In British law all titles resided originally in the king unless specifically granted. "The savages of these Provinces, when under the British Government, were considered a conquered people, and tenants at will." The proof of this condition was the inability of the Indians to convey a title without the permission of the Crown, and then what they did convey was merely a "right of occupancy." The king had never granted fee-simple ownership. Nor had the situation of the Indians changed as a consequence of Independence. They were still tenants at will incapable of any conveyance without the consent of government. James Madison echoed Holland's argument. All the European powers with possessions in America had long agreed that the Indians had only a qualified right to the land and thus could be prevented from selling the land to foreigners. Albert Gallatin spent most of his time defending the frontiersmen's right to their claims on Indian land, but he seemed most exercised by the insistence that these claims were the principal cause of frontier turmoil. There "was no idea more groundless," he contended, "than that the mischiefs committed by the Indians upon the frontiers were in general occasioned by previous injuries done to them." Since 1783 the warriors had been the aggressors. "Not a single acre of land had been taken from them but what had been fairly purchased." He did not say what exactly had been fairly purchased, but he made it clear that arguments over law became trivial on the frontier where actual land possession was crucial and the bitterness and brutality of life had been a reality for generations. Indian depredations could be halted only by changing the Indians, not by enforcing the law.

By a close vote, 33 to 28, the frontier position that had won in committee failed in the House.[33] The debate brought to the surface sectional differences over Indian policy that would become major disputes in later generations. For now, three positions had been defined. At the poles were the frontier argument that the natives simply had no claim to the land that needed to be considered and the largely New England view that Indian claims deserved all the recognition of fee-simple ownership. In the middle was the administration contention that the native people had only a qualified claim to the land that gave the United States the right of preemption. The New Englanders spoke from a deep sympathy for the native people that revealed how alienated they had become from the frontier enterprise. The administration was then faced with the task of satisfying the expansive intentions of the frontier population while maintaining a modicum of decency toward the tribes. It was a difficult line to walk.

And, of course, the effort failed. Despite the Washington administration's almost frantic exertions to avoid war, conflict had erupted in the Northwest in 1790. It was in this context that Henry Knox formulated his plan for doing good to the Indians. There is no reason to doubt his sincerity when he added "humanity and Justice" to "Policy" and "that respect which every nation sacredly owes to its own reputation" in explaining the basis for "a noble liberal and disinterested administration of indian affairs." No doubt Indians in the throes of transculturation would be less obstreperous neighbors, but Knox plainly had in mind a more altruistic endeavor. It was the "sensation of a philosophic mind" that led him to embark

[33] Ibid., pp. 904–5.

on a plan to impart "our Knowledge of cultivation, and the arts, to the aboriginals of the Country."[34]

The Knox plan for the native future seemed to clash with an observation that had long since become commonplace among white men as they contemplated the Indian. It was widely believed that the Indian had no future. Knox himself had made the point more than once. As the white settlements approached the native villages, the basis of the Indian economy would disappear and their society collapse. As Washington put it, "The gradual extension of our Settlements will . . . certainly cause the Savage as the Wolf to retire; both being beasts of prey tho' they differ in shape."[35] But of course, the object of the Knox plan was precisely the opposite. He hoped that the native adoption of the white man's way of life would allow the Indians to survive and thus relieve the white man's conscience of the burden of having destroyed them. Ironically, the only way to save the Indian was to arrange for him to cease to be an Indian. Knox apparently did not see the contradiction between his plan and the prediction of the Indians' future any more than he appreciated the irony.

Despite his Enlightenment confidence in the susceptibility of humanity to improvement, he recognized the practical obstacles to success. He had no doubt that, whatever the "stubborn habits" of human beings, they were capable of melioration and change. To suppose the opposite was "entirely contradicted by the progress of society from the barba-

[34] Knox to Washington, June 15, 1789, Abbot et al., eds., *Papers of Washington*, 2:490–94; Knox to Washington, July 7, 1789, ibid., 3:134–41. Washington may have been less eager than Knox. A few years before, when the countess of Huntington wrote to enlist his aid in a scheme to civilize the tribesmen, he responded politely, admitting the desirability of the plan, but apparently without conviction (see Washington to countess of Huntington, Feb. 27, 1785, Fitzpatrick, ed., *Writings of Washington*, 28:87; and Washington to countess of Huntington, June 30, 1785, ibid., 28:180–81).

[35] Washington to Duane, Sept. 7, 1783, Fitzpatrick, ed., *Writings of Washington*, 27:139–40; Schuyler to President of Congress [Boudinot], July 29, 1783, Papers of the Continental Congress, Reel 173:601–5; Alexander Hamilton to George Clinton, Oct. 3, 1783, Syrett et al., eds., *Papers of Hamilton*, 3:468; Knox to Washington, June 15, 1789, and Knox to Washington, July 7, 1789, Abbot et al., eds., *Papers of Washington*, 2:494, 3:138–39; Lincoln, "Journal of a Treaty," pp. 138–41.

rous ages to its present degree of perfection." And yet he could not deny that the conversion of the Indians would be "an operation of complicated difficulty." It would "require the highest knowledge of the human character, and a steady perseverence in a wise system for a series of years." And, he added, "it could not be effected in a short period." Knox envisioned nothing less than inducing "among the Indian tribes a love for exclusive property," but in truth his plans were modest. Central to his proposal were missionaries who would live among the Indians and would be "well supplied with all the implements of husbandry and the necessary stock for a farm. These men should be made the instruments to work on the indians—presents should commonly pass through their hands or by their recommendations—They should in no degree be concerned in trade, or the purchase of lands to rouse the Jealousy of the indians—They should be their friends and fathers." Other than introducing domestic animals among the natives, continuing the British practice of present giving, and supporting selected Indian boys in schools, Knox had little more to offer. He concluded by admitting that if this new policy did not "fully effect the civilization of the Indians," it would at least attach them to the interests of the United States, preserve the peace, and be a good deal less expensive than fighting a war.[36]

By far the most comprehensive and vigorous advocate in the 1790s of a philanthropic Indian policy was Timothy Pickering.[37] One of those Revolutionary veterans who had had difficulty making a success of civilian life, he had made it known in the late 1780s that he would accept public employment. Although he knew nothing of Indians, Washington sent him in 1790 to deal with the Iroquois at Tioga. With Harmar poised to move against the western tribes, the administration was eager to keep the Iroquois neutral. Pickering threw himself into his new assignment, learning what he could about

[36] Knox to Washington, July 7, 1789, Abbot et al., eds., *Papers of Washington*, 3:139–40; Knox to Iroquois Chiefs, Feb. 8, 1791, *American State Papers: Indian Affairs*, 1:145.

[37] David McLean, *Timothy Pickering and the Age of the American Revolution* (New York, 1982), pp. 318–19.

the procedures in such Indian negotiations and expressing a deep moral commitment to honest treatment of the tribes. His success at Tioga led Washington and Knox to use his services once again in 1791 on a similar errand. Pickering quickly became a major voice on Indian affairs. The administration solved his employment problem by making him postmaster general. He soon became directly responsible for Indian affairs when in 1794 he succeeded Knox as secretary of war.[38]

Pickering broached the question of civilizing the Indians in a letter to Washington soon after his return from Tioga. He began by noting the government's previous commitment to a philanthropic policy, particularly a provision in the Creek treaty of 1790 that required the administration to furnish the Indians with domestic animals and farming tools. Instructing the native people in the "most important of all arts, the art of husbandry" would "reclaim them from the savage to the civil state." But the efforts made thus far had failed, and "hence many, perhaps most people think the idea of civilizing the Indians perfectly Eutopian." He was particularly concerned about criticism of attempts to educate Indian boys. These promising students were sent to schools and colleges in the white man's world, but they soon returned to their own country where they again became "mere savages." This criticism, he argued, missed the mark. The problem was not education itself but the kind offered to the Indians. They were given learning suitable to the "children of men of fortune," which served them ill when they returned to their people. In this setting they could survive only by returning to hunting. "But being hunters, they soon became savages; and all their civil learning is lost upon them." At Tioga, Pickering thought he saw the solution. "Prevent the necessity of their becoming hunters, and they may be gradually civilized." They should be taught reading and writing and trained in farming. "In a word, bringing them up precisely in the manner in which our substantial farmers educate their own sons." At twenty-one they should be given a yoke of oxen, a plow, and the instru-

[38] See McLean, *Pickering,* chap. 9; and Gerard H. Clarfield, *Timothy Pickering and the American Republic* (Pittsburgh, 1980), chap. 10.

ments of husbandry. Land they have in abundance, "inviting the hand of Cultivation." He recommended the dispatch of an agent ("whose prudence equals his benevolence") to the tribes most disposed to change. The plan should be voluntary and experimental and thus should be continued only if it proved to be useful and agreeable to the Indians. A "discreet" schoolmaster was to teach reading, writing, and arithmetic, and two or three young men would offer instruction in farming. In this manner he hoped that the native people in time would "learn and practice the arts of civil life," for he could not "admit the idea that their minds are cast in a mould so different from that of the rest of their species as to be incapable of cultivation."[39]

If, concluded Pickering, the idea was "interesting to humanity: it is peculiarly interesting to the United States." He expected that the annual cost for the first two or three years would not exceed two thousand dollars. Afterwards the expense would depend on the cattle and equipment supplied to the Indians. But the cost was hardly a problem. It might be defrayed by the Indians themselves through periodic cessions of land. With the success of the program the natives would find their extensive hunting grounds useless and be more inclined to sell the land to buy domestic animals and equipment. Pickering later made it clear that he expected the government to engage the voluntary services of the churches in their philanthropic endeavors, which would control expenses.[40]

Washington ran hot and cold on civilization proposals, but he responded favorably to Pickering's plan. He particularly liked his suggestions for Indian education. He thought that past efforts had done little good for the Indians. "Reason might have shewn it, and experience clearly proves it to have been the case. It is perhaps productive of evil. Humanity and good policy must make it the wish of every good citizen of the United States that husbandry, and consequently civilization should be introduced among the Indians." He drew

[39] Pickering to Washington, Jan. 7, 1791, Allis, ed., Pickering Papers, Reel 61:164–65.

[40] Ibid., pp. 165–65A; Pickering to Israel Chapin, Apr. 29, 1792, ibid., Reel 62:26–26A.

the obvious inference from Pickering's letter and offered him the position as superintendent of northern Indians. Pickering turned the job down but let it be known that he was available for future work with the natives. Washington may have been particularly taken with Pickering's scheme because it was of modest proportions. Soon after, Cornplanter made a more ambitious proposal that Washington thought far too expensive. For the present Pickering had become the administration's man on Indians.[41]

Although Pickering's concern for Indians extended mainly to policy, the native people had apparently awakened in him not only a deep sympathy but an interest in the character of their world. When he journeyed to Newtown Point in the summer of 1792 to make a treaty with the Iroquois, he carried a memo from Benjamin Rush. The Philadelphia physician, reflecting the broader interests of the Enlightenment, sought answers to an array of questions—mostly medical but many touching on other aspects of native culture. He wanted information on the incidence of various diseases and their remedies, about birth and death, the nursing of babies, the menarche, aging, and the native psyche. Pickering responded with typical thoroughness, offering a good deal more information than Rush had requested. His source was an otherwise unidentified informant named Brooks. He listed a number of native diseases and their cures including, interestingly, bleeding. He reported that Indian women were more forward sexually than whites, that Indians slept more but dreamt less than their white neighbors, and were more prone to suicide. He seemed much affected by the question of suicide, for he took the trouble to describe a number of recent cases. In time his frequent dealings with the native people and his acquaintance with such Indian experts as the missionaries John Heckewelder and Samuel Kirkland made him something of a source on native ways.[42]

---

[41] Washington to Pickering, Jan. 20, 1791, Fitzpatrick, ed., *Writings of Washington*, 31:199–200; Clarfield, *Pickering*, pp. 121–23.

[42] The Benjamin Rush request is dated May 2, 1791. Pickering's response is undated (Allis, ed., Pickering Papers, Reel 61:184–86A. See also "Notes for Duponceau," [1796], ibid., Reel 62:259–63A).

Perhaps Pickering's principal contribution to Indian-white relations was his insistence on honesty. After returning from Tioga and his first encounter with the Iroquois, he assured Washington that the Indians were not difficult to please. "A man must be destitute of humanity, of honesty or common sense," he wrote, "who should send them away disgusted. He must want sensibility if he did not sympathise with them on their recital of injuries they have experienced from white men." Faced with a frontier population that settled Indian land illegally and land jobbers who preyed on the tribes in quest of grants, he sympathized with the natives. "Let the purchase of their land be explicitly declared when they are called to a treaty," he reminded himself. "They have generally been taken by surprise. They are invited to a treaty under pretense of making peace, and brightening the chain of friendship: while the main object for the most part is to strip them of their land."[43] Even if the administration had subscribed to such sentiments, no American politician in the age of expansion was likely to stick to them for long. Washington and Knox had both uttered some favorable words about Indians, but they were confronted with an Indian war that taxed their sympathies. While negotiating the Treaty of Newtown Point, Pickering had invited the Iroquois to come to Philadelphia to discuss the implementation of his civilization plan. After the Indian delegation reached the city, Washington and Knox pointedly shifted the object of the meeting, at the same time excluding Pickering from the discussions. They decided that gaining the Iroquois as mediators with the western tribes was at the moment more important than Pickering's plan. Pickering exploded. He wrote Washington a letter of singular intensity protesting the change and warning of dire consequences. "Indians have been so often deceived by white people," he concluded, "that *white man* is, among many of them, but another name for *liar*. Really, Sir, I am unwilling to be subjected to this infamy. I confess I am not indifferent to a good name, even among Indians. Besides they viewed, and expressly considered *me* as *your representative*, and my prom-

[43] Pickering to Washington, Dec. 31, 1790, ibid., Reel 61:119; Pickering to Iroquois Chiefs, July 4, 1791, ibid., pp. 80–82, Reel 62:96.

ises, as the promises of 'The Town Destroyer.' Sir, for your honor, and the honor and interests of the United States, I wish them to *know* that *there are some white men who are incapable of deceiving.*" It was vintage Pickering, aggrieved, self-righteous, eloquent, and quite right. The letter had its effect. Pickering was brought into the negotiations, and the administration reemphasized the civilization policy and avoided mention of mediation until the original purpose of the meeting had been achieved.[44]

Pickering sometimes found the tribesmen exasperating. He said at one point that he "was never more weary of Indian negotiations: more than the patience of Job is requisite, to endure their delays, their trifling and their drunkeness." Of the many Indian leaders he dealt with, he cited only three (Hendrick, Good Peter, and Cornplanter) who could be relied on to stay sober. But despite his frustrations he never resorted to the usual means of lubricating the rough places in Indian negotiations. He rejected overt bribery. He did think that the native leaders might profit from visits to the white man's world where they might "wonder and admire" the power and splendor they were shown. But direct bribery to a few chiefs he thought both "transient and uncertain." He went so far as to warn the Iroquois against becoming dependent on the white man's largesse. White men, he told them, do not take presents and they have abundance. He had in mind a sober, prosperous, and independent Indian who would be indistinguishable from his white neighbor.[45]

Speaking the truth did not much alter the message. Pickering hewed close to the philanthropic line. If the native people were to survive, they must change their lives. Pickering, however, stressed imitation. In a detailed and explicit way, he held up the white man's mode of life as an example for the Indians to follow. At Newtown Point in July 1791 he drew for the Iroquois a bleak contrast between their own wonted style of liv-

[44] Pickering to Washington, Mar. 21, 1792, ibid., Reel 62:11–12A; Clarfield, *Pickering*, pp. 131–36.

[45] Pickering to Iroquois Chiefs, July 5, 1791, Allis, ed., Pickering Papers, Reel 60:84–84A; Pickering to Knox, Aug. 10, 1791, ibid., p. 116; Pickering to Knox, Nov. 7, 1794, ibid., p. 208.

ing and what they could expect if they would follow the white man's lead.

> Why do the white people, your neighbors, multiply so fast? Because they cultivate the ground: because some are smiths to make plough-irons, hoes, axes, scythes, and all their iron tools: because some are carpenters who (besides building houses and barns) make ploughs casts and other things of wood, for the use of farmers: and thus supplied with the necessaries, the farmers raise abundance of cattle and corn wheat and other grain, to feed so many thousands of families, and after feeding their own families, they have still a great deal left; so that they are never in want. Why are the white people so well clothed? because the women spin and weave. Why are the white people so well furnished with all necessaries and conveniences, and with the ornaments of dress of which they as well as the Indians are so fond? Because they know and practice many trades or kinds of work, which I cannot describe because you have no names for them. Why have the white people more knowledge than the Indians? Because they read books. For these books have been written by wise men during many hundred years past. So that the white people have the advantage not only of the wisdom of the wisest men living, but of the wisdom of the wisest men who have lived during many hundreds of years past. For tho' now dead they still speak what they wrote in books and papers, a hundred or a thousand or two thousand years ago, being as well understood as when first written.

For the Indians the choice was stark. They must "become as knowing as the white people." "For if you persist in following all your ancient customes," he warned, "what can save you from the fate of the other Indian nations . . . ? Some of whom are reduced to a handful, while others have altogether perished, so that not one remains alive."[46]

On the return from Newtown Point, Pickering became an active propagandist for his plan. He laid out a detailed scheme for changing the Indian. A government-appointed superintendent should be responsible for choosing instructors for the Indians, characterized by "sobriety-honesty-good nature-and-industry." He expected that four philanthropic

[46] Speech to the Iroquois, July 4 and 5, 1791, ibid., pp. 78–88.

establishments would be created among the Iroquois. These bases of civilization would have a resident carpenter, blacksmith, and schoolmaster, all of whom should be farmers. The wives of these agents were to teach the Indian girls to spin, knit, and manage a dairy and a household. On hundred-acre farms near each establishment, the Indian boys would learn the art of agriculture with tools supplied by the government. Flax would be raised so the girls could spin and the children wear linen. On Sunday religious instruction should be offered but no revealed religion before the fifth year. He insisted that the schools teach only English. "The Indian language is the great obstacle to the civilization of the Indians. The sooner it is removed the better." But, he cautioned, "The government to which the Indians are accustomed is so gentle, everything bearing the semblance of *severity* must be carefully avoided. Not a blow should be struck—more even reproof given but with mildness—and in the form of *advice*." Finally, he insisted that Indians should not be made servants. They should not be required to engage in any activity that white men themselves did not perform.[47]

Pickering expected steady advancement and at a minimum price. At the first stage he recommended appropriate rewards for successful children: a blanket, a breechclout, or a petticoat. At the end of the first year the clothing allowance would cross the cultural divide: a linen shirt for the boys and a shift for the girls. After the second year boys who had made progress in reading, writing, and farming would receive a suit of clothes, overalls, and a hat. Girls who had done well would be given a short gown, a woolen waistcoat, a petticoat, and a wool hat. Then at age twenty married students would receive oxen, farming tools, and household implements.[48] Not until early in the next century would so detailed a plan be proposed to the government.

The new policy, no doubt, grew out of the Revolutionary experience. But, then, so did the principle of conquest. Aside from all the practical reasons impelling Americans to regard

<hr />

[47] Ibid., Reel 62:17–18; Pickering to Samuel Kirkland, Dec. 4, 1791, ibid., Reel 61:304–5A.

[48] Ibid., Reel 62:18A-20.

Indian lands as the spoils of war, many American policymakers did feel genuinely betrayed by the behavior of the Indians
in the conflict. They had arrayed themselves on the side of
tyranny and vice against liberty and virtue. The equation between savagery and tyranny was easily made. Still, it was not
long before putative victory over the warriors gave way to reality, just as the triumph of the Revolution itself began very
soon to seem a rather mixed blessing. The openness of the
frontier in the post-Revolutionary era turned out to be both
an opportunity and a hazard. It was an arena for the expansion of the virtuous republic and a setting where virtue was at
risk. The theme of self-assertion implicit in the enterprise of
frontier expansion conflated readily with the principle of conquest, but, as Knox noted, in the 1790s at least neither self-
assertion nor conquest were easily reconciled with virtue. Philanthropy, it would appear, offered the new republic an opportunity to save both the Indian and its virtue.[49]

[49] Watts, *Republic Reborn*, p. 14.

JOHN LAURITZ LARSON

"Wisdom Enough to Improve Them"
Government, Liberty, and Inland Waterways in the Rising American Empire

WHY CREATE THE American republic? For what purpose did the inhabitants of British North America—arguably the freest and wealthiest people on earth in the middle of the eighteenth century—throw off colonial rule and establish a union of independent states? Led by the rhetoric of the Founders into believing that the republic's goals were virtuous and its truths self-evident, Americans over the course of two centuries have argued (and continue to argue today) that the meaning of American liberty is transparent and that all subsequent history and practical politics can be judged by the light of the creators' original intentions. But such a reification of the founding experience badly distorts our understanding of how American republicanism took shape, how it evolved into American democracy, and how the purpose of government has changed within the framework of American constitutions. Professional historians writing about the American Revolution now place at the center of the story not a transparent mission but an experiment in republicanism. Of course, modern scholars disagree about the origins, character, and influence of American Revolutionary republicanism, but no serious work of history fails to acknowledge at least the widespread use of republican language in giving form to the hopes and dreams of the American founding generation.[1]

This pervasive use of the same words has encouraged explanations of the American Revolution that attribute to the whole body of Revolutionary actors the motives and reasons of an articulate few. The mistake is doubly easy to make because gentlemen of the eighteenth century presumed to speak for the lower orders while common people sometimes seized the rhetoric of republicanism as an invitation to speak for themselves. In reality, there were many different revolutions within the American Revolutionary movement, and this fact profoundly influenced politics in the post-Revolutionary era. Many Americans—especially propertyholders of elite or middling status—joined the experiment in republicanism in order to protect the liberty and happiness they already enjoyed. Others—journeymen, farmworkers, laborers, women, slaves, religious Dissenters—hoped through Revolutionary self-creation to pry open even further the structures of a society already fluid by European standards but still hierarchical in its expectations and in danger of growing more so. Still others of all ranks resisted the Revolutionary movement, fearing the chaos of experimentation or distrusting the integrity of local revolution-makers—whose character they sometimes knew too well![2]

[1] For orientation to this vast literature, see Peter S. Onuf, "Reflections on the Founding: Constitutional Historiography in Bicentennial Perspective," *William and Mary Quarterly*, 3d ser. 44 (1989):342–75; Gordon S. Wood, "The Fundamentalists and the Constitution," *New York Review of Books*, Feb. 18, 1988; Thomas L. Pangle, *The Spirit of Modern Republicanism: The Moral Vision of the American Founders and the Philosophy of Locke* (Chicago, 1988); Forrest McDonald, *Novus Ordo Seclorum: The Intellectual Origins of the Constitution* (Lawrence, Kans., 1985); Leonard W. Levy, *Original Intent and the Framers' Constitution* (New York, 1988); Michael Lienesch, *New Order for the Ages: Time, the Constitution, and the Making of Modern American Political Thought* (Princeton, 1988); and the forum "The Creation of the American Republic, 1776–1787: A Symposium of Views and Reviews," in *William and Mary Quarterly*, 3d ser. 44 (1987):550–640.

[2] For a sampling of different approaches see Gordon S. Wood, *The Creation of the American Republic, 1776–1787* (Chapel Hill, 1969); Gary B. Nash, *The Urban Crucible: Social Change, Political Consciousness, and the Origins of the American Revolution* (Cambridge, Mass., 1979); Edward Countryman, *The*

For all these citizens of the new United States, the Peace of Paris in 1783 officially marked the end of Revolutionary destruction and the beginning of national creation. The work of discrediting the old order, however incomplete, was over; the work of reconstruction and innovation lay ahead. If Revolutionary republicanism had projected one clear and universal meaning (as *Publius* strove to argue in *The Federalist*), this work of positive creation would have been difficult enough. But republicanism in fact sustained all kinds of visions, rooted in different classic texts, different intellectual justifications, different personal, regional, and class aspirations. Constitutional conventions first formally addressed this problem, reflecting the novel American assumption that written constitutions could radically reorganize the state, define the role of citizens in politics, and confer upon the whole extraordinary proceeding the blessing of perfect legitimacy. In practice, however, constitutional agreements proved fragile and elusive as local, class, and ideological differences emerged from under the consensus of wartime patriotism. Furthermore, for every advocate of systematic theory there were dozens of new citizens who would judge the virtue of republican government by the quality of life they enjoyed under its protection. Exercising over and over again the radical promise of self-creation that lay at the heart of republican theory, these expedient Revolutionaries would revise and reinvent their governments and society until the exercise itself became imbedded in the system.[3]

American Revolution (New York, 1985); Robert A. Gross, *The Minutemen and Their World* (New York, 1976); Pauline Maier, *The Old Revolutionaries: Political Lives in the Age of Samuel Adams* (New York, 1980); A. Roger Ekirch, "Whig Authority and Public Order in Backcountry North Carolina, 1776–1783," in Ronald Hoffman, Thad W. Tate, and Peter J. Albert, eds., *An Uncivil War: The Southern Backcountry during the American Revolution* (Charlottesville, Va., 1985); Paul A. Gilje, *The Road to Mobocracy: Popular Disorder in New York City, 1763–1834* (Chapel Hill, 1987); and Alfred F. Young, "George Robert Twelves Hewes (1742–1840): A Boston Shoemaker and the Memory of the American Revolution," *William and Mary Quarterly*, 3d ser. 38 (1981):561–623.

[3] For three contrasting interpretations of *The Federalist* see Pangle, *Spirit of Modern Republicanism;* Morton White, *Philosophy,* The Federalist, *and the*

LAUNCHING THE "EXTENDED REPUBLIC"

Nothing seemed more natural, at least for some American leaders, than to launch the new republic by taking vigorous government actions to promote the general welfare, but few objectives proved harder to define. "Internal improvement" was the rubric under which early Americans gathered up a variety of ambitions to make roads, bridges, and canals, to establish schools and universities, and to encourage science, invention, and exploration—all sorts of public programs likely to spread enlightenment and benefit the whole people. Never simply schools, canals, or highways, these public works represented the first tangible fruits of popular government. For many Americans the test of liberty would be the benefit (or injury) they received as a result of their new federal and state governments' internal improvement programs. Therefore they approached these early promotions with jealous eagerness, and in the process they often rekindled conflicts of interest that constitution-writers had smothered with delicate compromise language.

It is the burden of this essay to show how one man's design for internal improvement—George Washington's vision of inland navigation—grew out of the Revolutionary promise itself and helped shape his vision of a brave new future toward which the republican experiment progressed. Hardly a representative man, Washington was acclaimed by his peers to be the "first citizen" of his day. Perhaps more than anybody else in federal America, he cherished the subject of this symposium: the launching of the extended American republic. His dream of opening a Potomac route to the West played an im-

Constitution (New York, 1987); and Albert Furtwangler, *The Authority of Publius: A Reading of the Federalist Papers* (Ithaca, N.Y., 1984). See generally Cathy D. Matson and Peter S. Onuf, *A Union of Interests: Political and Economic Thought in Revolutionary America* (Lawrence, Kans., 1990); Willi Paul Adams, *The First American Constitutions: Republican Ideology and the Making of the State Constitutions in the Revolutionary Era* (Chapel Hill, 1980); Jack N. Rakove, *The Beginnings of National Politics* (Baltimore, 1979); Richard R. Beeman, Stephen Botein, and Edward C. Carter II, eds., *Beyond Confederation: Origins of the Constitution and American National Identity* (Chapel Hill, 1987); Michael Allen Gillespie and Michael Lienesch, eds., *Ratifying the Constitution* (Lawrence, Kans., 1989).

portant role in focusing both his understanding of popular government and his vision of a rising American empire.

GEORGE WASHINGTON'S DESIGN

October 1783 found George Washington in Princeton, cooling his heels, having "the enjoyment of peace, without the final declaration of it." Formalities bound him to the army but left him nothing useful to do. Inactivity depressed him, and for relief he recently had toured the waterways of upstate New York, dreaming of interior development. "Prompted by these actual observations," he wrote to the chevalier de Chastellux, "I could not help taking a more contemplative and extensive view of the vast inland navigation of these United States." Poring over available maps and information, the restless general marveled that Providence had "dealt her favors to us with so profuse a hand. Would to God," he concluded, "we may have wisdom enough to improve them."[4]

It is important that Washington used the term *wisdom* in this homely context. His prayer was not for money, or time, or technical expertise—it was for wisdom. Apparently he worried about the wisdom of his newly liberated countrymen; he questioned their ability or willingness to do the right thing. His Continental army had suffered scandalously at the hands of the people. Now Congress sat in exile in Princeton, driven out of Philadelphia by angry, unpaid soldiers. Great possibilities—or anarchy—lay ahead. Washington's phrase resonated with the urgency and apprehension that filled the atmosphere of the postwar republic.

Like all true revolutionaries, Washington cherished a vision of the rising new nation he had worked so hard to rescue from the British. His vision comprehended the existing Atlantic community, while his imagination leaped across the mountains to embrace seemingly limitless space in the continental interior. "I shall not rest contented," he promised Chastellux,

[4] George Washington to the chevalier de Chastellux, Oct. 12, 1783, John C. Fitzpatrick, ed., *The Writings of George Washington*, 39 vols. (Washington, D.C., 1931–44), 27:189–90.

"till I have explored the Western Country, and traversed those lines . . . which have given bounds to a New Empire."[5] True to his word (always!) Washington toured the western country the following September, gathering firsthand images and information from which he forged his own design for the enjoyment of American liberty. That design became the centerpiece of his ambition for the new nation, and it worried him always that people might lack wisdom enough to pursue it.

Western lands had fascinated Washington since his 1748 trip as a youthful surveyor into Lord Fairfax's western domain. For the next twenty years he bought up depreciated military warrants and pressed his claims to huge western tracts, the British Proclamation of 1763 notwithstanding. In the last years before the Revolution, Washington labored to pry open the western country and to interest provincial legislatures in the Potomac route to the West. "Immense advantages" awaited Virginia and Maryland, he argued in 1770, if they would make the Potomac a great "Channel of Commerce between Great Britain" and the interior.[6]

"Great Channel" here originally meant less than modern readers might expect, and for this reason Washington's early vision seemed all the more practicable. By clearing boulders and trash from the riverbeds and building portage roads between streams (or around unmovable obstructions), he hoped to facilitate the passage of canoes and flat-bottomed bateaux, especially during high-water seasons. The downstream movement of bulky furs and foodstuffs concerned him more than return transportation for manufactured goods, which could better stand the cost of land carriage. Such limited expectations render sensible the small sums often spent by individuals and local governments toward the improvement of these rivers. At the same time European engineering offered splendid encouragement for greater ambitions. The famous Lan-

[5] Ibid.

[6] Washington to Thomas Johnson, July 20, 1770, ibid., 3:19; see Charles H. Ambler, *George Washington and the West* (Chapel Hill, 1936), pp. 21–27, 136–74; and Corra Bacon-Foster, *Early Chapters in the Development of the Potomac Route to the West* (1912; reprint ed., New York, 1971), pp. 3–30.

guedoc Canal across the south of France (with over one hundred locks and fifty aqueducts) had been completed in 1681, and the duke of Bridgewater's very recent canal-building success in England convinced American dreamers such as Washington that technical solutions lay just ahead even for the Great Falls of the Potomac, an eighty-foot shelf of rock some twenty miles upstream from Washington's Mount Vernon.[7]

The Revolutionary War postponed improvement of the Potomac route, but Washington's interest in the project only increased with the winning of Independence. In early 1784 he reiterated to Thomas Jefferson the compelling advantages of the Potomac navigation, adding now his belief that the "Yorkers will delay no time to remove every obstacle in the way" of their own route to the Great Lakes. Most Virginians did not see the "truly wise policy of this measure," and they certainly resisted "drawing money from them for such a purpose."[8] Even so, Washington hoped as he went west in September to explore the Ohio country that men of "discernment and liberality" could be made to see the value of the project.

Firsthand knowledge only quickened Washington's convictions. He saw or heard how a short portage between the Miami and Sandusky rivers might link the entire Great Lakes system with the Ohio; how the Allegheny, the Monongahela, the Kanawhas, and their many branches might be connected with the Susquehanna, Potomac, and James to form passages from the Ohio waters to the Atlantic coast. Geographical features came so near to meeting in a network that it seemed to Washington as if nature were designed expressly for improvement by the new United States.[9]

As things stood in 1784, however, such improvements were

[7] Alvin F. Harlow, *Old Towpaths: The Story of the American Canal Era* (New York, 1926), p. 4; Thomas F. Hahn, *The Chesapeake and Ohio Canal: Pathway to the Nation's Capital* (Metuchen, N.J., 1984), p. 16.

[8] Washington to Thomas Jefferson, Mar. 29, 1784, in Julian P. Boyd et al., eds., *The Papers of Thomas Jefferson*, 28 vols. to date (Princeton, 1950–), 7:49–51.

[9] Donald Jackson and Dorothy Twohig, eds., *The Diaries of George Washington*, 6 vols. (Charlottesville, Va., 1976–79), 6:57–68.

not forthcoming. Western Pennsylvanians talked of opening the Susquehanna (which ran to Baltimore), but Philadelphia's merchants blocked their efforts. New York's near-level routes to the lakes were well known, but British troops still occupied the Great Lakes forts. The people of the West themselves had not the means to make improvements and, more distressing, no "excitements to industry." The "luxuriency of the Soil" gave too easy a living, while the impossibility of trade discouraged ambition. But open a good communication with these settlements, Washington insisted, and the exports to the East must increase "astonishingly." Even more important, the political allegiance of the pioneers undoubtedly would follow their commerce. "The Western Settlers," he observed, stood "as it were on a pivet—the touch of a feather would almost incline them any way." So long as Spain held the Mississippi and Britain the Great Lakes, the Atlantic states enjoyed a unique opportunity to "apply the cement of interest," binding all parts of the union with "one indissolvable band." [10]

The Potomac navigation activated Washington's whole vision of the rising American empire. The West held the key to America's future greatness. The "vacant" lands back of the Atlantic states promised safety and prosperity for generations to come. Agriculture, he assumed, would occupy the masses, but without markets farmers regressed toward a state of nature. Therefore commerce must propel the nation forward, and inland navigation would bind the wilderness communities to the union by chains of commercial interest. National character, prosperity, respect among nations, the security of the union (and by implication the liberty that flowed from Independence)—public issues at the center of Washington's concern— all depended on embracing westward emigration within the American national system. Inland navigation made the United States conceivable, and Washington's vision soared high above the diggings: "I wish to see the sons and daughters of the world in Peace and busily employed in the more agreeable amusement of fulfilling the first and great commandment, *Increase and Multiply:* as an encouragement to which we have opened the fertile plains of the Ohio to the poor, the needy and the op-

[10] Ibid., p. 66.

pressed of the Earth." Washington's America was nothing less than "the Land of promise, with milk and honey."[11]

Private interest, Virginia pride, and concern for the welfare of the union mingled in Washington's mind as he gazed west from the banks of his river. Nearly sixty thousand acres of his own western lands promised to rise in value with the opening of transmontane commerce.[12] His sense of urgency and his insistence that the Potomac was *by nature* the ideal route reflected a keen spirit of rivalry with other states that antedated the Revolution. Yet his persistent use of the language of national interest and political security rang true despite his obvious personal interests. For years he had cultivated national credibility; now he used it to promote his design for the river, Virginia, and the new United States.

THE QUESTION OF GOVERNMENT POWER

Washington pressed his vision on everyone he knew. Henry Knox, Richard Henry Lee, Benjamin Harrison, the marquis de Lafayette, Chastellux, James Madison, Jefferson, Charles Carroll of Carrollton, Robert Morris—all received long letters full of enthusiasm about inland navigation and the western country. In these same letters Washington often brooded over signs of chaos and disorder that seemed to be multiplying across America, reflecting the close connection in his mind between the question of government power and the opportunity to found an American empire. Petty visions competed everywhere. Interested parties worked against his navigation schemes in order to protect immediate or transient advantages. In the West, squatters seized Washington's unimproved lands and dared any man to dispossess them. Speculators engrossed huge tracts northwest of the Ohio, provoking Indian reprisals. It seemed as if nothing

[11] Washington to the marquis de Lafayette, July 25, 1785, Fitzpatrick, ed., *Writings of Washington*, 28:206. See Andrew R. L. Cayton, *The Frontier Republic: Ideology and Politics in the Ohio Country, 1780–1825* (Kent, Ohio, 1986), pp. 1–50; Peter S. Onuf, *Statehood and Union: A History of the Northwest Ordinance* (Bloomington, Ind., 1987), pp. 1–20.

[12] See Ambler, *Washington and the West*, p. 173.

could be done about these outrages. A "kind of fatality" attended "all our public measures," the general confided to his close friend Henry Knox, because the people in the states were "torn by internal disputes, or supinely negligent and inattentive to every thing which is not local and selfinteresting."[13]

In a seamless tapestry Washington saw his trouble with frontier squatters, the selfish localism of his Virginia neighbors, the indifference of the states toward the federal Congress, irresponsibility in public finance, and reckless assaults on the public domain all springing from the same malaise. "The want of energy in the Federal government," he concluded, "has brought our politics and credit to the brink of a precipice; a step or two farther must plunge us into a Sea of Troubles, perhaps anarchy and confusion." His prescription for national health? Instill vigor in the federal government, adopt an orderly plan for settling the West, and set to work immediately on inland navigation.[14]

Close to home, the same dynamics of conflict plagued Washington's efforts to launch the American empire by improving the Potomac navigation. Such engineers as could be found assured Washington and his friends that all technical problems could be solved. The objective was compelling, and the estimates by experts were encouraging; only human folly seemed to stand in the way. Because the Potomac formed the boundary between Maryland and Virginia, both states had to sanction improvements. But Baltimore merchants schemed to block the project in favor of a Susquehanna Canal chartered in Maryland in 1783, while Virginians outside the Potomac Valley showed a maddening indifference to the general's grand design. Finally, in late 1784, the two legislatures authorized a joint-stock company to improve the river and

[13] Washington to Henry Knox, Dec. 5, 1784, Fitzpatrick, ed., *Writings of Washington*, 28:4–5; see also Washington to Jacob Read, Nov. 3, 1784, ibid., 27:486.

[14] Washington to Johnson, Oct. 15, 1784, ibid., 27:481; Washington to George William Fairfax, June 30, 1785, ibid., 28:184; see vol. 28 generally for these themes.

collect tolls in perpetuity, according to fixed schedules. Commissioners were named to lay out and construct good roads (at public expense) from the head of navigation to the "most convenient" western waters, thereby completing communications with the frontier.[15]

The charter delighted Washington, yet his thoughts kept drifting back to the *public* and *political* urgency behind the project. He seemed disappointed that the two states "under their present pressure of debts" were so "incompetent to a work of this sort." The "objects in view" were "pregnant with great public utility," but would private parties really take hold? To Robert Morris, Washington explained that were he "disposed to encounter present inconvenience for a future income" he would "hazard all the money" he could raise on the Potomac navigation. But in fact he did not hazard all his money, and there lingered in his views a nagging concern that where his purse failed others would too. Friends of the measure were "sanguine," he wrote Lafayette, but "good wishes" were "more at command, than money." Because "extensive political consequences" depended on these projects, he was "pained by every doubt of obtaining the means" for their completion.[16]

In Washington's mind there was much more to inland navigation than clearing boulders from a riverbed and digging canals around the falls. He was building a nation, not a canal, and he preferred to think that men of vision would see the wisdom of his plan, seize it with the sovereign hands of government, and pursue it to the benefit of all. But Washington knew how investors behaved: as early as 1770, when Mary-

[15] See James W. Livingood, *The Philadelphia-Baltimore Trade Rivalry, 1780–1860* (Harrisburg, Pa., 1947), pp. 33–34; The General Assembly Session of October 1784: Editorial Note, William T. Hutchinson et al., eds., *The Papers of James Madison*, 22 vols. to date (Chicago and Charlottesville, Va., 1962–), 8:123; Bacon-Foster, *Early Chapters*, pp. 42–43 (see pp. 210–25 for the Potomac Company charter).

[16] Bacon-Foster, *Early Chapters*, pp. 44–46; Washington to Robert Morris, Feb. 1, 1785; Washington to Lafayette, Feb. 15, 1785; Washington to Jefferson, Feb. 25, 1785; all in Fitzpatrick, ed., *Writings of Washington*, 28:48–55, 71–81, quotations pp. 55, 73, 79.

land's Thomas Johnson tried to solicit subscriptions to open the Potomac, Washington explained that some were "actuated" by "public spirit," and some by the hope of "salutary effects." The latter *"must* naturally incline" toward support, but those who were "unconnected with the river" would not. Why not vest the enterprise by legislation with "a kind of property in the navigation"—that is, tolls—to gain support of a third class of men, "the monied gentry, who tempted by lucrative views would advance largely on account of high interest." The corporation thus became a useful instrument for hitching self-interest to the public good.[17]

The Potomac Company charter reflected these assumptions. Because local jealousies prevented him from getting "public money," Washington proposed "a happy medium," a charter that would not "vest too much power and profit in a private company" but still hold out "sufficient inducements to engage men to hazard their fortunes in an arduous undertaking." To "give vigor to the undertaking" he then convinced each state to subscribe for blocks of shares. Profit was bait to lure investors, not an end in itself, and the legislatures prescribed rates of tolls to protect their unextinguished public interest in the operations.[18]

Washington clearly understood the power of greed to stimulate people's ambitions, and he believed from an early day that government, even when it failed to act directly, still could harness that energy in the public interest. No modern economic liberal, he never imagined that government action in the economy inherently was wrong. Neither did he fantasize that in their untutored' pursuit of private gain, individuals would accomplish *automatically* what was best for all. Interest

[17] Washington to Johnson, July 20, 1770, Fitzpatrick, ed., *Writings of Washington,* 3:18.

[18] Washington to James Madison, Dec. 28, 1784, ibid., 28:19; Washington to Congress, Dec. 3, 1784, Hutchinson et al., eds., *Papers of Madison,* 12:478; Washington to Henry Knox, Jan. 5, 1785, Fitzpatrick, ed., *Writings of Washington,* 28:24. Madison used the word *bait* in a letter to Jefferson containing a thorough account of the Potomac and James River bills, Jan. 9, 1785, Hutchinson et al., eds., *Papers of Madison,* 8:224. See also Oscar Handlin and Mary Handlin, "Origins of the American Business Corporation," *Journal of Economic History* 5 (1945):1–23.

needed guidance from wisdom, and now that American governments were safely republican, their exercise of power to promote welfare was more appropriate than ever.

Washington's dream of improving the Potomac route stirred an important question facing this liberty-loving people: Could wisdom and greatness be pursued among a free people whose ambitions were narrow and private? Yes, Washington answered, if well-designed government and right policy gave shape to the people's freedoms. He explained for Jefferson the example of foreign trade: "Our Citizens *will not* be restrained" from commerce, so "it behooves us to place it in the most convenient channels, under proper regulations, freed *as much as possible* from those vices which luxury, the consequence of wealth and power, naturally introduce."[19] Interest was to be guided by wisdom. Right national policies alone could secure the new nation, its commerce, and its frontier domain. Otherwise the new United States would be torn apart from without or from within.

TOWARD A NEW CONSTITUTION

Making wise policies, especially on a national scale, proved almost impossible in the Confederation era. At every step men of narrow views seemed to prove that mere liberation, without energetic governance, led to chaos and certain destruction. Throughout 1785, as the Potomac Company set to work on his river, Washington watched national harmony dissolve. "It does not appear to me," he wrote in February, "that we have wisdom, or national policy enough to avert the evils which are impending. How should we, when contracted ideas, local pursuits, and absurd jealousy are continually leading us from those great and fundamental principles which are characteristic of wise and powerful Nations?"[20]

[19] Washington to Jefferson, Mar. 29, 1784, Boyd et al., eds., *Papers of Jefferson*, 7:51.

[20] Washington to Knox, Feb. 28, 1785, Fitzpatrick, ed., *Writings of Washington*, 28:93. See Peter S. Onuf, *Origins of the Federal Republic: Jurisdictional Controversies in the United States, 1775–1787* (Philadelphia, 1983); and Rakove, *Beginnings of National Politics*, esp. pp. 360–99.

Western lands produced much of the interstate squabbling that discouraged the nation's first hero. While Congress debated land policy Washington pressed for "compact and progressive seating" of western lands in order to "give strength to the Union; admit law and good government; and foederal aids at an early period." Restrict development of the interior to one or two states at a time, he argued. An unrestricted land policy would "be more advancive of private interest, than the public welfare." He worried that the "astonishingly great" emigration to the West included too many "people who are not very subordinate to the Laws and Constitutions of the States" from which they came. After May 1785, when Congress finally adopted a land ordinance without the restrictions Washington proposed, he thought they had surrendered "what little power they have, to the States individually which gave it to them."[21]

On the equally desperate matter of commercial regulation, Washington supported national protection and promotion. Fellow Virginians fretted that navigation acts would profit New England at the expense of southern consumers, but Washington rebuked them. In "every matter of general utility," he countered, some "States may be more benefited than others." But too jealous a regard for such particular interests undermined "national character" and made the United States look "ridiculous" in the eyes of the world. "We are either a united people under one head, and for federal purposes," thundered the general, "or we are thirteen independent sovereignties, eternally counteracting each other." Fix your fortunes on the national empire, Washington reasoned, then promote agriculture and commerce alike.[22]

By the autumn of 1785 Washington's frustration with Con-

[21] Washington to Hugh Williamson, Mar. 15, 1785; Washington to Richard Henry Lee, Mar. 15, 1785; Washington to Barbé Marbois, June 21, 1785; Washington to Lafayette, July 25, 1785; all in Fitzpatrick, ed., *Writings of Washington*, 28:108–9, 169, 208. See also Onuf, *Origins*, pp. 149–72; and Onuf, *Statehood and Union*, pp. 21–43.

[22] Washington to James McHenry, Aug. 22, 1785, Fitzpatrick, ed., *Writings of Washington*, 28:227–28, 230; see also Rakove, *Beginnings of National Politics*, pp. 334–51, 354–59.

gress was complete. "Illiberality, Jealousy, and local policy" had rendered it a "nugatory body." The truly extraordinary thing was "that we should confederate as a Nation, and yet be afraid to give the rulers of that nation, who are the creatures of our own making . . . sufficient powers to order and direct the affairs of the same." Still, disappointments mounted apace. A commercial depression undercut America's economic recovery. The 1786 Annapolis Convention on interstate commerce, born of Washington's own Mount Vernon conference the year before, collapsed in apathy. Shays's Rebellion in Massachusetts raised the specter of domestic insurrection, while a vote in Congress to "forbear" American claims to the Mississippi River produced an explosion of separatist fever in the West.[23]

During this "critical period" Washington's despair steadily deepened. The stubborn refusal of state leaders to empower the Congress with "ample" authority appeared to be the "very climax of popular absurdity and madness." Still the crisis would not pass. "I am mortified beyond expression," he wrote in 1786, afraid that Americans had proved mankind to be "unfit for their own Government."[24] About the only good news he received in these years was of the Potomac navigation, where by early reports difficulties seemed to "rather vanish than increase." The lack of a resident engineer left the directors uncertain at times precisely how to proceed, but by the summer of 1786 some two hundred men labored to good effect at several sites along the river. With hope perhaps intensified by the confusion rising around him, Washington reported to his foreign correspondents that the "seeds of population" were scattering "far into the wilderness," agriculture was "prosecuted with industry," and the "works of Peace,

[23] Washington to James Warren, Oct. 7, 1785, Fitzpatrick, ed., *Writings of Washington,* 28:290–91; see volumes 28 and 29 generally. For the importance in Virginia of the Mississippi River negotiations, see Lance Banning, "Virginia: Sectionalism and the General Good," in Gillespie and Lienesch, eds., *Ratifying the Constitution,* pp. 261–99.

[24] Washington to Henry Lee, Apr. 5, 1786; Washington to John Jay, May 18, 1786; Washington to Jay, Aug. 1, 1786; all in Fitzpatrick, ed., *Writings of Washington,* 28:402, 431, 501–3; Washington to Henry Lee, Oct. 31, 1786, ibid., 29:33–34.

such as opening rivers, building bridges, &c.," were "carried on with spirit."[25]

Washington invariably juxtaposed, in his correspondence, reports of progress on the Potomac navigation with gloomy accounts of the state of national affairs. The one advanced, the other endangered his objective of securing the extended American republic. As winter closed in on 1786, Washington entertained no doubts about the Potomac canal, but he wondered if the union would survive to enjoy it. "Public virtue" had deteriorated so rapidly that he thought only some "means of coercion" could "enforce Obedience to the Ordinances of the Gen'l. Government." Certain Virginians, led by Gov. Patrick Henry, promised to bolt the union rather than suffer any national tyranny. Others, led by Madison, plotted desperately to bring Virginia into just such a "proper federal System." Washington prudently stood apart from the scheming, agreeing only at the final hour to attend the Philadelphia Convention, where he inevitably was elected to preside.[26]

Gradually, during the long hot summer in Philadelphia, a suitable frame of government took shape. Very late in the Convention Benjamin Franklin, who shared Washington's vision of a rising empire in the West, moved to insert "a power to provide for cutting canals where deemed necessary." Roger Sherman of Connecticut objected to expenses that would benefit only "places where the canals may be cut." Such local jealousy always pained the general, who silently chaired the proceedings. Madison tried to substitute a broader power "to grant charters" for promoting internal improvements, and James Wilson explained that some power was necessary "to prevent a *State* from obstructing the *general* welfare." But local feeling and fear of monopolies prevailed. The nationalists fell

[25] Washington to Fairfax, Nov. 10, 1785, and Washington to Chastellux, Aug. 18, 1786, ibid., 28:312, 523; see Bacon-Foster, *Early Chapters*, pp. 57–84.

[26] Washington to Jay, Mar. 10, 1787, and Washington to Madison, Mar. 31, 1786, Fitzpatrick, ed., *Writings of Washington*, 29:176, 190–91; Madison to Washington, Dec. 7, 1786, and Madison to Jefferson, Mar. 19, 1787, Hutchinson et al., eds., *Papers of Madison*, 9:199–200, 318–20. See Douglas Southall Freeman, *Washington*, abr. Richard Harwell (New York, 1968), pp. 533–39.

back on what they had secured so far: a government resting on the people, empowered to raise revenues and enforce its laws, independent of state authorities, and competent to regulate trade, finance, and foreign policy. More than that they could not win.[27]

THE PROMISE OF THE NEW REGIME

Was Washington pleased with the Constitution? It might have been "more perfect," he explained to Patrick Henry, but it was "the best that could be obtained at this time." Men might give "*ostensible* reasons" against ratification, he confided to Bushrod Washington, but "the real ones" were dishonest, "concealed behind the Curtain." Washington could not imagine any danger from too much power in the new frame of government: "No man is a warmer advocate for proper restraints and wholesome checks in every department of government than I am; but I have never yet been able to discover the propriety of placing it absolutely out of the power of men to render essential Services, because a possibility remains of their doing ill."[28] In that spirit he anxiously watched the ratifications in the states. By the autumn of 1788 Washington's retirement at Mount Vernon seemed doomed once more by the universal assumption that he must serve as the first president of the new United States.

Would the new government yield wisdom and policy enough to "avert the evils" impending? At first, certainly not. The ratification contests were bitter, and Washington knew that the Constitution enjoyed fragile support, especially among politicians. Hardly endowed with the "general *controuling* power" Washington originally desired, the new regime would need nurturing before it could be used to accomplish

[27] Max Farrand, ed., *Records of the Federal Convention of 1787,* rev. ed., 4 vols. (1937; reprint ed., New Haven, 1966), 2:615–16, 620. For a new narrative about the convention, see Christopher Collier and James Lincoln Collier, *Decision at Philadelphia* (New York, 1987).

[28] Washington to Patrick Henry, Sept. 24, 1787, and Washington to Bushrod Washington, Nov. 10, 1787, Fitzpatrick, ed., *Writings of Washington,* 29:278, 312.

greater things.[29] The victory for national power was still tentative, and ironically the sensitivities of office forced the new president to quiet his personal advocacy of national authority and western canals in order to secure the Constitution itself.

Fragments of a 1789 address, probably intended for the opening of Congress but abandoned without explanation, reveal how much the new president *wished* to say as he took up his novel station. Ratification was but the beginning of the experiment, and much depended on the character of Americans and their actions in the decade ahead. "If the blessings of Heaven showered thick around us," Washington wrote, "should be spilled on the ground or converted to curses, through the fault of those for whom they were intended, it would not be the first instance of folly or perverseness in short-sighted mortals."[30] His confidence in the wisdom of a liberated people remained incomplete, so he poured his larger vision of improvement and positive government into his charge to the members of Congress:

> It belongs to you especially to take measures for promoting the general welfare. It belongs to you to make men honest in their dealings with each other, by regulating the coinage and currency of money upon equitable principles; as well as by establishing just weights and measures upon an uniform plan. Whenever an opportunity shall be furnished to you as public or as private men, I trust you will not fail to use your best endeavors to improve the education and manners of a people; to accelerate the progress of arts and Sciences; to patronize works of genius; to confer rewards for inventions of utility; and to cherish institutions favourable to humanity.

Such "employments," he concluded, "cannot fail of being acceptable in the sight of the Divinity."[31] This was energetic government, laid down in strong, active verbs. Good things were to be brought about, not just allowed to emerge by them-

---

[29] Washington to Fairfax, June 30, 1785, ibid., 28:184.

[30] Washington, "Proposed Address to Congress," ibid., 30:296–308, quotations p. 301.

[31] Ibid., pp. 307–8.

selves. Before Alexander Hamilton ever whispered in the president's ear, Washington had opened the window of "loose construction" through which enemies of the Federalist party one day would think they saw tyranny returning.

But Washington did not deliver these opinions. He said far less on January 8, 1790, when he finally addressed the federal Congress. Gone were his challenge to "short-sighted mortals" and his outline of the nation's business. This message invited Congress to consider the obvious issues, indulging only the briefest nod toward internal improvement and education. Unreconciled passions and conflicting interests burdened the first efforts of the new regime with extravagant and jealous expectations. At the center of it all, Washington trembled for fear that "public measures" would disappoint the people and their praises would turn to "censures."[32] Having been handed sovereign power, he found he could but delicately use it for fear of fracturing public confidence and unleashing once more the disintegrative forces of local jealousy, private greed, and a popular distrust of government.

DISAPPOINTMENTS IN THE FEDERALIST ERA

Washington's vision of a rising American empire derived from habits of thought that he shared with most politically conscious Americans. A self-educated tidewater planter, Washington imbibed political ideas not in the libraries but in conversations at dinner and gaming tables, at theaters or country tavern hearths. Like most of his peers, he reasoned inductively, drawing universal principles from personal experience. In support of his beliefs he offered "character," buttressing both logic and language with appeals to his own virtue and honest intentions. *The* national model of virtue and integrity, Washington was made the first president and guardian of the new Constitution; yet his most deeply held convictions about wisdom, power, and improvement in the new United States did not square with those of many of his coun-

[32] Washington, "First Annual Message to Congress"; and Washington to Edward Rutledge, May 5, 1789, ibid., 30:491–94, 309.

trymen. Taken at face value, Washington's views should have
bothered the American people at least as much as their behavior worried him.[33]

Washington had yearned for a national government because he presumed that a class of men much like himself
could use it to police the passionate masses. In practice, however, Americans recognized no such leadership class (even if
the rhetoric lingered). They distrusted the opinions of strang-
ers, and they entertained fantastic notions about the character
of their countrymen at a distance.[34] Washington believed that
power, once properly derived, should be wielded freely by legitimate authorities. But Americans had just escaped the grip
of power, and most of them would not "glide insensibly" (to
use John Adams's unfortunate phrase) into submission to new
authorities.[35] Washington dreamed of an American empire,
giving pause to those who thought that "empire" was the opposite of "liberty." Finally, Washington conceived improvement in terms of benevolence—a gift enhancing the receiver
according to the purpose of the benefactor—while many contemporaries thought more of innovation, the fruit of liberation and ambition, without moral or political design.

Not surprisingly, therefore, events in the 1790s disappointed Washington repeatedly. First, while he delicately
tended the frame of government, his friends and neighbors
practically abandoned the Potomac navigation. The want
of a skilled engineer and a shortage of funds crippled the
project before the locks at Great Falls were completed. True,
the minimal hopes for bateaux navigation might be met
without taming this difficult cataract; but the real promise of

[33] On Washington's character see James Thomas Flexner, *Washington, the
Indispensable Man* (Boston, 1969); and Garry Wills, *Cincinnatus: George Washington and the Enlightenment* (Garden City, N.Y., 1984).

[34] See, for example, Jefferson's lurid interpretation of New England soci-
ety at the time of Shays's Rebellion in Ronald L. Hatzenbuehler, "'Re-
freshing the Tree of Liberty with the Blood of Patriots and Tyrants':
Thomas Jefferson and the Origins of the U.S. Constitution," in David E.
Narrett and Joyce S. Goldberg, eds., *Essays on Liberty and Federalism: The
Shaping of the U.S. Constitution* (College Station, Tex., 1988), pp. 94–95.

[35] Quotations from Wood, *Creation of the American Republic*, p. 131.

improvement lay in uninterrupted travel up and down the whole river. A concentration of money urgently was needed, but people held back. Washington's neighbor, Henry Lee, one of the "monied gentry," put his money not in canal shares but in land speculation at the site of the Great Falls canal, where he shamelessly cheated the company that promised to increase his wealth. Other private investors, impatient for profits, defaulted on their subscriptions after two or three assessments. The state of Virginia, pressed by local interests, forced the company to spread its meager resources over minor upstream improvements even though the main locks had not been built. Deprived of vigorous support, the project never received a fair test. The Potomac needed national money and interstate cooperation to realize its considerable potential. But wisdom and design could not be mobilized behind Washington's most tangible national objective.[36]

Elsewhere competition for the trade of the West produced conflicts that challenged Washington's belief in the Potomac's natural superiority. Pennsylvania interests, led by the ubiquitous Robert Morris, launched a program of improvements designed to open the Susquehanna and divert its trade through the Schuylkill River to Philadelphia. Baltimore merchants struggled to direct the same Susquehanna traffic all the way to the Chesapeake Bay and their own fine harbor. Philip Schuyler and others in New York sponsored similar companies to open waterways to that state's northern and western frontiers. In these cases *state* pride and ambition, not integrated national welfare, energized the projects. The same jealous spirit blocked one of the more useful, achievable, and clearly national improvements discussed in that generation: a canal between the Delaware River and Chesapeake Bay. The First Congress's discussion of a permanent home for the new federal government turned into an unbelievable circus of manipulation, corruption, and intrigue (in which Washington himself and the Potomac promoters ironically displayed their

[36] Bacon-Foster, *Early Chapters*, pp. 85–99; Charles Royster, *Light-Horse Harry Lee and the Legacy of the American Revolution* (New York, 1981), pp. 55–113, 169–85. The Great Falls locks were finally opened in 1802, although the navigation at that time was still far from satisfactory (see Hahn, *Chesapeake and Ohio Canal*, pp. 16–17).

own egregious self-interests). In all, while a "spirit of improvement" swept the land, it lost all color of moral purpose or
unified design.[37]

The new federal government proved virtually helpless to
impose or even encourage such national objectives, especially
if they touched the ground. For no better reasons than the
promotion of commerce and the safety of seamen, Congress
did adopt lighthouses and navigation aids as part of their duty
to regulate commerce. Seaboard governments had always assumed this responsibility, but somehow lighthouses never
stood as a precedent for more domestic internal improvements. Secured by its place in the Constitution, the federal
post office might have laid down a spatial design. But the
power to locate post roads placed such useful patronage in
congressmen's hands that they refused to allow any general
system to limit their possible options. When wars and rumors
of war threatened the safety of American ports, congressmen
denounced comprehensive designs and bickered insanely
over which state, city, and harbor should receive the greatest
share of federal largesse. In 1796 Madison, the architect of
unified national power, introduced a modest proposal to survey a Maine-to-Georgia post road—a national trunkline route
for improving communications—yet even this application of
powers the Framers explicitly intended sparked a rousing
and suspicion-filled debate.[38]

Only the fiscal system, crafted by Treasury secretary Hamil-

[37] See [Robert Morris], *An Historical Account of the Rise, Progress, and Present
State of the Canal Navigation in Pennsylvania* (1791), in *American State Papers:
Miscellaneous*, 1:830–34; Nathan Miller, "Private Enterprise in Inland Navi-
gation: The Mohawk Route Prior to the Erie Canal," *New York History* 31
(1950):398–413; Ralph D. Gray, *The National Waterway: A History of the Chesa-
peake and Delaware Canal* (Urbana, Ill., 1967); Charlene Bangs Bickford and
Kenneth R. Bowling, *Birth of the Nation: The First Federal Congress, 1789–1791*
(New York, 1989), pp. 55–60; Kenneth R. Bowling and Helen E. Veit, eds.,
Documentary History of the First Federal Congress, vol. 9, *The Diary of William
Maclay and Other Notes on Senate Debates* (Baltimore, 1988), pp. 131–70.

[38] See John Lauritz Larson, "'Bind the Republic Together': The National
Union and the Struggle for a System of Internal Improvements," *Journal of
American History* 74 (1987):368–70. Lighthouse petitions, for example, can
be found in Records of the United States House of Representatives, Record
Group 233, Box HR 6A-F2.1, National Archives, Washington, D.C., and

ton and enacted by the first two Congresses, reflected the national scope, unified design, and orderly discipline Washington had wanted from a national government—and in the process of imposing this design the administration fractured its popular following. Assumption of state obligations and the funding of the whole public debt created millions in new federal bonds backed by the taxing power of the government. An English-style national bank then monetized the debt and established at a stroke a national market for money that could be controlled by banker elites. Hamilton's bank served regional interests and the speculator class, or so Madison said. With the help of Jefferson, Madison led an opposition in Congress that soon spilled out-of-doors, creating the first American party system. By the end of Washington's second administration his government stood as the bulwark of a party with an angry and popular opposition clamoring to topple the regime.[39]

DESIGN VERSUS LIBERATION

In Washington's lifetime, neither the moneyed gentry nor the common people rose to the standards of citizenship Washington had hoped to inspire. But what of Washington himself? For all the "disinterestedness" of his public posture, his Potomac canal was very much a local improvement, and he resented the designs of Pennsylvania and New York improvers as much as others resented his. Furthermore, the campaign to locate the capital near his hometown of Alexandria strained his disinterested guise. The suppression of the Pennsylvania "Whiskey Rebels" and the denunciation of "certain self-

---

are cited here by the gracious permission of Donnald K. Anderson, Clerk of the House.

[39] See Forrest McDonald, *Alexander Hamilton: A Biography* (New York, 1979), pp. 117–305; Janet A. Riesman, "Money, Credit, and Federalist Political Economy," in Beeman, Botein, and Carter, eds., *Beyond Confederation*, pp. 128–61; Noble E. Cunningham, *The Jeffersonian Republicans: The Formation of Party Organization, 1789–1801* (Chapel Hill, 1957); William Nisbet Chambers, *Political Parties in a New Nation: The American Experience, 1776–1809* (New York, 1963).

created societies" (the Democratic-Republican Clubs) drew violent attacks on his lieutenants and even on Washington himself. This is not to argue that Washington dissembled when he called for patriotic forbearance; rather, the culture that understood and sustained such disinterested poses was collapsing. Ambition and sharp dealing once had brought shame upon a person, but Americans were redefining ancient virtues. Already in July 1790, when the new regime was scarcely a year old, William Maclay boiled over with disgust at the venality of men in government: "The President has become in the hands of Hamilton The Dishclout of every dirty Speculation, as his name Goes to Wipe away blame and Silence all Murmuring."[40]

The Constitution survived, not as an instrument of grand design but as a framework for negotiating conflicts among diverse and ambitious new Americans. For that reason many Founders never felt secure in the achievement of their Revolutionary goals. Washington's 1796 "Farewell Address," which advised the people to "resist with care the spirit of innovation" in politics, must have sounded quaint against the backdrop of full-throated partisan hostilities that typified the preceding year. Philadelphia editor Benjamin Franklin Bache found the limits of opposition rhetoric with this 1795 attack: "If ever a nation was debauched by a man, the American nation has been debauched by Washington." Usually Washington escaped such personal derision because of his extraordinary reputation. But Hamilton was vilified regularly as a "bastard" and the "American Walpole," while John Adams, the second Federalist president, could not shake the appellation "avowed MONARCHIST."[41]

[40] Bowling and Veit, eds., *Diary of William Maclay*, p. 321. See Gordon S. Wood, "Interests and Disinterestedness in the Making of the Constitution," in Beeman, Botein, and Carter, eds., *Beyond Confederation*, pp. 69–109; Bickford and Bowling, *Birth of the Nation*, pp. 55–60; John L. Brooke, "Ancient Lodges and Self-Created Societies: Voluntary Association and the Public Sphere in the Early Republic," and Thomas P. Slaughter, "'The King of Crimes': Early American Treason Law, 1787–1860," in this volume.

[41] Washington, "Farewell Address," in Arthur M. Schlesinger, Jr., ed., *History of American Presidential Elections, 1789–1968*, 4 vols. (New York, 1971), 1:86–93, quotation p. 89; *Philadelphia Aurora*, quoted in Page Smith, "The

For all his genuine wisdom and delicate leadership, Washington's government could not destroy those fractious interests and local jealousies that composed the "impending evils" of 1786. Instead politics under the new Constitution domesticated these expressions of popular innovation, giving them permanent place in the life of the new republic. America's genteel Revolutionary leaders had never intended such a radical outcome. Most of them had felt at least some degree of sympathy with Adams's comparative assessment of the American and French revolutions: "Ours was resistance to innovation; theirs was innovation itself."[42] If men like Jefferson and Madison adjusted more willingly or more successfully to the new permanent state of liberation, even these Republican party leaders labored to perpetuate designs against the disintegrative forces of freedom. Liberty without design (called "license" by this generation) was an idea not yet appealing to Americans.

Far from shaping the promise of the federal regime, Washington's personal design for American development through inland navigation and western integration marked just one end of a spectrum on which Americans would paint many shades of meaning for the terms of modern republicanism. The new government had saved the experiment with liberty, precisely as Washington had hoped. But liberty itself, within the framework of the Constitution, produced an explosion of innovation and ambition that more resembled the chaos men such as Washington had tried to avert. The Potomac Canal, the settlement of the West, the integration of the states within the union—none of these objectives proceeded as he wished. Particularism and individualism refused to be channeled, as Washington had hoped, by right policies and national structures. Instead liberty increasingly meant freedom for Americans to exploit their continent and their neighbors with

---

Election of 1796," ibid., 1:64; Drew R. McCoy, *The Elusive Republic: Political Economy in Jeffersonian America* (Chapel Hill, 1980), p. 153; Chambers, *Political Parties in a New Nation,* pp. 113–69, quotation p. 116.

[42] Quoted in Keith Ian Polakoff, *Political Parties in American History* (New York, 1981), p. 37.

accelerating abandon. Washington had tried his best to secure order and energetic government, to impose design and close the window of revolution. But he could not stop the transformation of a culture that would always revere his name, his deeds, his very words, even while it destroyed the meaning of his vision and perverted his designs for national integration, wise legislation, and improved inland navigation.

GARY J. KORNBLITH

Artisan Federalism
New England Mechanics and
the Political Economy
of the 1790s

ON JANUARY 26, 1792, over twelve hundred Bostonians
crowded into Fanueil Hall to decide the fate of a plan for municipal reform. An ad hoc committee appointed by the town
meeting the month before had recommended the creation of
an elected town council to assume most of the legislative and
some of the executive functions of the town meeting. Supporters argued the plan would increase governmental efficiency and enhance law enforcement. Opponents charged it
would undermine the longstanding democratic right of direct
participation in public decisions and lead to the concentration
of power in a few hands. Bostonians as a whole were deeply
divided about the proposal. When it was put to a voice vote
on January 26, "the moderator . . . declared himself unable
to determine which side had prevailed."[1]

As was customary in such cases, the town meeting then
agreed to a procedure whereby special "tellers" nominated by
each side in a controversy, along with the town selectmen,
would count voters as they filed out of the hall, proponents
and opponents leaving separately. Those against the plan

For helpful comments on earlier versions of this essay, the author wishes to
thank Heather Hogan, Carol Lasser, Pauline Maier, and Sean Wilentz.

[1] *American Apollo*, Mar. 29, 1793, quoted in Joseph T. Buckingham, *Speci-
mens of Newspaper Literature*, 2 vols. (Boston, 1850), 2:60. See also *Boston Town
Records, 1784–1796*, Reports of the Record Commissioners of the City of
Boston, vol. 31 (Boston, 1903), pp. 272–76.

promptly chose state senator Benjamin Austin, Jr., to be their teller. Those in favor of reform duly selected Benjamin Russell, editor and publisher of the *Columbian Centinel*. Upon learning of Russell's selection, however, Austin announced that "he must decline serving; that he would cheerfully serve with Dr. Jarvis, Dr. Eustis, *or any other gentlemen,* but not with *such a fellow as Ben Russell.*"[2] After the choice of another teller, the town meeting rejected the proposal for reform by a comfortable margin.

The following day Russell tracked down Austin at the public exchange and demanded an explanation for his obnoxious conduct. Austin replied "that he would have nothing to do with Ben Russell; and afterwards added, that he did not choose to put himself upon a par with Ben Russell." Russell retaliated by spitting in Austin's face and denouncing "him with virulent and abusive language."[3] Although he suffered no lasting physical harm, Austin subsequently filed a civil suit against Russell, asking for £1,000 in damages. The case came to trial in March 1793. After hearing the relevant testimony, a jury sympathetic to Russell's cause but bound by the letter of the law in such matters awarded Austin the modest sum of £1. Neither Austin nor Russell ever publicly expressed remorse over their conduct.[4]

What makes this incident especially noteworthy is that Austin and Russell were both prominent spokesmen for, and energetic mobilizers of, Boston artisans during the Federalist era. Their quarrel had ramifications well beyond the contempt they felt for each other personally. They competed for political leadership within the artisan community, and they advocated conflicting partisan strategies for promoting the mechanic interest in the new republic. Both boasted sizable local followings throughout the 1790s.

Coproprietor (with his brother) of a ropewalk and a midscale mercantile concern, Benjamin Austin, Jr., helped to or-

---

[2] *American Apollo,* Mar. 29, 1793, quoted in Buckingham, *Specimens of Newspaper Literature,* 2:61.

[3] Ibid.

[4] Ibid., 2:61–63; *Columbian Centinel,* Mar. 27, 1793.

ganize the short-lived Association of Tradesmen and Manufacturers of the Town of Boston in 1785, and he subsequently
gained notoriety for a series of harsh attacks on the Massachusetts legal profession published under the pseudonym "Honestus." Like John Hancock and Samuel Adams, with whom he
was allied politically, Austin had reservations about the cen-
tralizing tendencies of the federal Constitution, but he
stopped short of publicly identifying himself as an Antifederalist during the struggle over ratification. In the 1790s he
played a major part in the rise of the Democratic-Republican
party in Boston. Over the course of the decade he wrote innu-
merable polemics for the *Independent Chronicle,* and in 1793
he helped to launch the Massachusetts Constitutional Society,
Boston's version of a Democratic-Republican society. He also
stood regularly for election to state and national offices. Although he was never elected to Congress, he served several
terms as a senator in the Massachusetts General Court.[5]

Benjamin Russell, by contrast, emerged as an important
figure in Federalist circles during the 1790s. Having appren-
ticed under Isaiah Thomas during the Revolution, he
founded the *Massachusetts Centinel* with a partner in 1784 and
soon took up the cause of strengthening the national government. In January 1788 he helped to organize the famous mass
meeting of Boston mechanics held at the Green Dragon tavern to demand approval of the federal Constitution by the
state's ratifying convention. In 1790 he reaffirmed his nationalist commitment by changing the title of his newspaper to
the *Columbian Centinel,* and under his editorial direction the
paper staunchly supported the policies of both the Washington and Adams administrations. At the same time he took
great pride in his craft identity. In 1795 he joined in founding
the Boston Mechanic Association (later restyled the Massa-

---

[5] For biographical accounts of Benjamin Austin, Jr., see Buckingham,
Specimens of Newspaper Literature, 1:268–80, and *Dictionary of American Biogra-
phy,* s.v. "Austin, Benjamin." A brief recollection of Austin by his nephew,
James Trecothick Austin, can be found in "Autobiography of James Treco-
thick Austin," James Trecothick Austin Papers, Massachusetts Historical So-
ciety, Boston. For an analysis of Austin's attacks on the legal profession, see
Sidney Kaplan, "'Honestus' and the Annihilation of the Lawyers," *South
Atlantic Quarterly* 48 (1949):401–11.

chusetts Charitable Mechanic Association), and for the next thirty years he served it faithfully as a member and an officer.[6]

Given their common concern to promote the collective interest of Boston's artisan community, the fact that Austin and Russell took opposing sides in the partisan struggles of the 1790s raises questions about recent scholarship on artisanal ideology and behavior in the Federalist era. Most notably, it suggests that historians may have exaggerated the extent of political consensus among urban tradesmen during this period and attributed to them—as a class—greater radicalism than many artisans actually displayed. Further elaboration of these related points requires a brief review of the relevant historiography.

In 1964 Alfred F. Young published a pathbreaking essay titled "The Mechanics and the Jeffersonians: New York, 1789–1801." According to Young, after overwhelmingly supporting ratification of the federal Constitution, New York City artisans gradually grew disenchanted with Federalist policies during the 1790s, and, by the close of the decade, most switched their allegiances to the Republican opposition. Young noted that not all New York artisans made this transition, and he specifically disclaimed any notion that the Republicans were "a labor party." Yet he argued that "Republican thought was unmistakably shaped by the party's mechanic constituency," and he suggested that artisans helped sharpen the egalitarian edge of Republicanism at the same time they blunted its supposed agrarian bias. Thus, by Young's account, New York artisans made a significant contribution to the development of the first party system, both in

[6] For biographical accounts of Benjamin Russell, see Buckingham, *Specimens of Newspaper Literature*, 2:1–45; Francis Baylies, *Eulogy on the Hon. Benjamin Russell, Delivered before the Grand Lodge of Free and Accepted Masons of the State of Massachusetts, March 10, 1845* (Boston, 1845); Benjamin Franklin V, ed., *Boston Printers, Publishers, and Booksellers, 1640–1800* (Boston, 1980), s.v. "Russell, Benjamin"; John Bixler Hench, "The Newspaper in a Republic: Boston's *Centinel* and *Chronicle*, 1784–1801," Ph.D. diss., Clark University, 1979, pp. 36–48. On Russell's experience as an apprentice to Isaiah Thomas, see W. J. Rorabaugh, *The Craft Apprentice: From Franklin to the Machine Age in America* (New York, 1986), pp. 17–20, 23.

terms of political practice and in terms of ideological principles.[7]

Subsequent scholarship on artisan behavior during the
Federalist era has tended to embed similar findings within the
general context of the so-called republican (small *r*) synthesis.
In his prize-winning book *Chants Democratic*, Sean Wilentz argues brilliantly that New York's mechanics developed a distinctive brand of republicanism—what he calls "artisan
republicanism"—that "hardened in the 1790s, as the craftsmen came to terms with what the Revolution meant to them."
This hardening occurred in tandem with the mechanics' shift
into the Democratic-Republican party. "By 1800," Wilentz
writes, "a clear mechanics' interest had developed, in league
with Republican politicians, fed by protariff sentiments in the
trades, and fully integrated as a pressure group in the city's
politics."[8]

Likewise, Charles G. Steffen explains that in Baltimore by
the mid-1790s artisans were prepared "to articulate their own
radical vision of republicanism, a distinctly mechanic republicanism." Battles for a more democratic city government and
against the ratification of the Jay Treaty combined to propel
Baltimore mechanics from Federalist to Republican ranks.
"Through the Mechanical Society and militia," Steffen writes,
"the workingmen built themselves into one of the best organized political blocs in Baltimore and the backbone of the
emerging Republican party."[9]

[7] Alfred F. Young, "The Mechanics and the Jeffersonians: New York,
1789–1801," *Labor History* 5 (1964):247–76, quotations pp. 270–71.

[8] Sean Wilentz, *Chants Democratic: New York City and the Rise of the American
Working Class, 1788–1850* (New York, 1984), pp. 61–103, quotations pp. 63,
71. See also Howard B. Rock, *Artisans of the New Republic: The Tradesmen of
New York City in the Age of Jefferson* (New York, 1979), pp. 23–27.

[9] Charles G. Steffen, *The Mechanics of Baltimore: Workers and Politics in the
Age of Revolution, 1763–1812* (Urbana, Ill., 1984), pp. 121–68, quotations
pp. 121, 143. Along somewhat similar lines, Ruth Bogin has interpreted
artisan ideology and behavior in post-Revolutionary America as part of a
"new moral economy" that mixed traditional notions of economic justice
with more radical egalitarian ideas. "Small farmers and artisans," she contends, "believed that the distribution of income and wealth had a moral

Dissenters from the "republican synthesis" also highlight the alienation of urban artisans from Federalism in the 1790s, though they interpret this defection from different perspectives. On the one hand, Ronald Schultz attributes the triumph of Democratic-Republicans in Philadelphia in 1800 to the "recreation of a radical-artisan political coalition" based on appeals to a small-producer tradition that had taken root long before the Revolution.[10] On the other hand, John R. Nelson, Jr., points to the growing disenchantment of mechanics and manufacturers as proof that Alexander Hamilton's economic program, notwithstanding the rhetoric of the *Report on Manufactures,* was heavily biased toward import merchants and speculators and against domestic producers. As good economic men, Nelson contends, artisans voted their private interests and joined the Jeffersonian coalition in promoting an attractive liberal alternative to Hamilton's wrongheaded mercantilist program.[11]

The purpose of this brief summary of historical scholarship is not to raise once more the question of whether Jeffersonianism is better understood as a radically democratic, classically republican, or modern liberal constellation of ideas. Instead, I want to suggest that the pattern of political evolution these scholars of artisanal behavior have identified and tried to explain was a regionally specific phenomenon. As shall be documented at length below, the mechanics of urban New England acted differently. While artisans in New York, Philadelphia, and Baltimore defected in droves to Republican party ranks in the 1790s, their counterparts in Boston, Provi-

---

dimension—an ethical component—and that a moral economy pointed in the direction of equality"—equality of condition, not just of opportunity (Ruth Bogin, "Petitioning and the New Moral Economy of Post-Revolutionary America," *William and Mary Quarterly,* 3d ser. 45 [1988]:391–425, quotation p. 423).

[10] Ronald Schultz, "The Small-Producer Tradition and the Moral Origins of Artisan Radicalism in Philadelphia, 1720–1810," *Past and Present,* no. 127 (1990):84–116, quotation p. 109.

[11] John R. Nelson, *Liberty and Property: Political Economy and Policymaking in the New Nation, 1789–1812* (Baltimore, 1987), pp. 80–90.

dence, and Salem proved markedly more loyal to the Federalist cause. To be sure, Benjamin Austin, Jr., won his share of
political battles in Boston. Yet the town's Federalists carried
the most critical contests of the decade, and they did so with
the active help of Benjamin Russell and other local artisans.
Furthermore, the Republican party held far less appeal for
mechanics in Providence and Salem than it did in Boston. In
urban New England, it seems, the main current of artisan republicanism (or, alternatively, artisan liberalism) in the 1790s
was artisan Federalism.

To understand why most urban New England artisans continued to support Federalist candidates and policies long after
the bulk of their Mid-Atlantic brethren had switched allegiances, one may begin with the structural differences between the two regions. Demographically, the Mid-Atlantic
region attracted a much higher proportion of immigrants and
grew at a much faster rate than did New England during the
eighteenth century.[12] The consequences for urban development were evident in the first federal census. Having been at
midcentury the largest city in British North America, Boston
in 1790 boasted a population less than half the size of Philadelphia's—approximately 18,000 inhabitants, compared to
over 42,000. Likewise, the population of Salem (New England's second largest city in 1790) was only one-quarter the
size of New York's—less than 8,000 inhabitants, compared to
roughly 32,000.[13] From the perspective of the burgeoning
metropolises of the Mid-Atlantic region, New England's leading cities near the end of the century remained relatively
modest, almost intimate, communities.

This difference in urban scale had implications for the organization of local crafts. As Richard S. Dunn has highlighted

[12] Jim Potter, "Demographic Development and Family Structure," in Jack
P. Greene and J. R. Pole, eds., *Colonial British America: Essays in the New His-
tory of the Early Modern Era* (Baltimore, 1984), pp. 139–44. See also Bernard
Bailyn, *Voyagers to the West: A Passage in the Peopling of America on the Eve of the
Revolution* (New York, 1986), pp. 205–18.

[13] Jacob M. Price, "Economic Function and the Growth of American Port
Towns in the Eighteenth Century," *Perspectives in American History* 8
(1974):176–77.

in his survey of labor systems in eighteenth-century America, production remained heavily family-based in New England long after Mid-Atlantic employers had turned to the extensive use of indentured servitude and then wage labor as alternatives.[14] As late as the mid-1790s, there were relatively few journeymen employed in Boston trades. According to data developed from local tax lists (which are unusual in explicitly distinguishing master craftsmen from journeymen), in 1796 master carpenters outnumbered journeymen carpenters by a ratio of six to one, master tailors outnumbered journeymen tailors by over five to one, master blacksmiths outnumbered journeymen blacksmiths by four to one, and master coopers outnumbered journeymen coopers by three to one.[15] One may reasonably infer from this data that production in Boston and other urban centers in New England was largely confined to small enterprises, often one-adult shops, and oriented mainly to the local market.[16]

Another factor that distinguished the artisan experience in urban New England was the sense of citizenship, of belonging to a corporate community. In her comparison of Boston and New York in the eighteenth century, Pauline Maier has pointed out that "politics moderated the distance between

[14] Richard S. Dunn, "Servants and Slaves: The Recruitment and Employment of Labor," in Greene and Pole, eds., *Colonial British America*, pp. 180–88. The distribution of occupations by economic sector was remarkably similar in late eighteenth-century Boston, New York, and Philadelphia, however. See Price, "Economic Function," pp. 128–37.

[15] Taking Books for 1796, Boston Tax Records, Boston Public Library. For an in-depth analysis of Boston carpenters during the 1790s, see Lisa Beth Lubow, "Artisans in Transition: Early Capitalist Development and the Carpenters of Boston, 1787–1837," Ph.D. diss., University of California, Los Angeles, 1987, pp. 190–224.

[16] For evidence on Providence, see Gary J. Kornblith, "'Cementing the Mechanic Interest': Origins of the Providence Association of Mechanics and Manufacturers," *Journal of the Early Republic* 8 (1988):364–72. For evidence on Salem, see Bernard Farber, *Guardians of Virtue: Salem Families in 1800* (New York, 1972), pp. 96–110; Margaret Burke Clunie, "Furniture Craftsmen of Salem, Massachusetts, in the Federal Period," *Essex Institute Historical Collections* 113 (1977):191–203.

rich and poor in Boston."[17] At the town meeting, men of wide-ranging occupations and strata assembled to debate public issues and make collective decisions. If patterns of deference prevailed in the selection of town officers, mechanics nonetheless enjoyed respect as fellow citizens whose views and votes counted on central matters confronting their community.[18]

Not surprisingly, given this political heritage, urban New Englanders were, on the whole, more firmly united in their support of the patriot cause than their Mid-Atlantic brethren. To be sure, there were tories and trimmers in urban New England. John W. Tyler has found that approximately one-third of Boston's merchants were openly loyalist.[19] Yet a greater proportion were patriot, and Samuel Adams and other radical leaders shaped a durable local coalition in favor of revolution. While craftsmen in Philadelphia and New York formed separate mechanics' committees in the early 1770s, artisans in Boston, Providence, and Salem felt no compulsion to organize on their own.[20] And notwithstanding occasional outbursts of anger and resentment, artisans in urban New

[17] Pauline Maier, "Boston and New York in the Eighteenth Century," *Proceedings of the American Antiquarian Society* 91 (1982):187.

[18] For a concise history of Boston's town meeting, see George B. Warden, "Town Meeting Politics in Colonial and Revolutionary Boston," in Ronald P. Formisano and Constance K. Burns, eds., *Boston 1700–1900: The Evolution of Urban Politics* (Westport, Conn., 1984), pp. 13–26. On the governance of Boston during the Confederation era, see Myron Floyd Wehtje, "A Town in the Confederation: Boston, 1783–1787," Ph.D. diss., University of Virginia, 1978, pp. 74–153.

[19] John W. Tyler, *Smugglers and Patriots: Boston Merchants and the Advent of the American Revolution* (Boston, 1986), pp. 241–42.

[20] For a comparison of Boston, New York, and Philadelphia on the eve of the Revolution, see Gary B. Nash, *The Urban Crucible: Social Change, Political Consciousness, and the Origins of the American Revolution* (Cambridge, Mass., 1979), pp. 339–84. Alfred F. Young makes a similar point about the relative absence of mechanic consciousness in pre-Revolutionary Boston in "George Robert Twelves Hewes (1742–1840): A Boston Shoemaker and the Memory of the American Revolution," *William and Mary Quarterly*, 3d ser. 38 (1981):599.

England continued to defer to the leadership of merchants and local authorities throughout the War for Independence.[21]

Only after the war did New England artisans begin to organize and affirm their autonomy as a distinctive social interest. In 1785 Boston artisans formed the Association of Tradesmen and Manufacturers to encourage growth of the national carrying trade and to discourage the rising tide of foreign imports.[22] In 1789 Providence artisans established the Providence Association of Mechanics and Manufacturers "for the promotion of Home Manufactures, [for] cementing the Mechanic Interest, and for raising a Fund to support the Distressed."[23] Yet in each instance the organizers were careful not to offend local merchants, who responded with polite professions of respect for artisans' concerns. Even as mechanic consciousness grew in urban New England, tensions between merchants and artisans were muted by rituals of mutual consultation and collaboration.

Probably most important in sustaining cordial relations between merchants and mechanics in postwar urban New England was shared hostility to an increasingly assertive agrarian interest. In Rhode Island, the self-styled "Country"

[21] On wartime Boston, see Esther Forbes, *Paul Revere and the World He Lived In* (Boston, 1942), pp. 251–367; Dirk Hoerder, *Crowd Action in Revolutionary Massachusetts, 1763–1780* (New York, 1977), pp. 313–89; and Barbara Clark Smith, "The Politics of Price Control in Revolutionary Massachusetts, 1774–1780," Ph.D. diss., Yale University, 1983, pp. 354–510. On wartime Providence, see Nancy Fisher Chudacoff, "The Revolution and the Town: Providence, 1775–1783," *Rhode Island History* 35 (1976):71–90; Lynne Withey, *Urban Growth in Colonial Rhode Island: Newport and Providence in the Eighteenth Century* (Albany, 1984), pp. 77–89. On wartime Salem, see James Duncan Phillips, *Salem in the Eighteenth Century* (Boston, 1937), pp. 361–442; Ronald N. Tagney, *The World Turned Upside Down: Essex County during America's Turbulent Years, 1763–1790* (West Newbury, Mass., 1989).

[22] Gary J. Kornblith, "From Artisans to Businessmen: Master Mechanics in New England, 1789–1850," Ph.D. diss., 2 vols., Princeton University, 1983, 1:56–71; Mary Roys Baker, "Anglo-Massachusetts Trade Union Roots, 1130–1790," *Labor History* 14 (1973):389–90.

[23] Association Minute Book 1, Feb. 27, 1789, Records of the Providence Association of Mechanics and Manufacturers, Manuscript Collection, Rhode Island Historical Society Library, Providence.

party won control of the General Assembly in 1786, and, over the objections of urban creditors, the state quickly began issuing paper currency as legal tender. Unsympathetic to rural debtors, Providence artisans joined with local merchants in shutting their shops to avoid accepting paper bills on par with specie. Providence artisans also sided with local merchants— and against farmers—in supporting ratification of the federal Constitution. Indeed, in May 1790, with Rhode Island still standing outside the newly refashioned union, the Providence town meeting threatened to secede from the state if approval of the federal Constitution was further delayed.[24]

The political situation was more complicated in postwar Boston, where the partisan division between followers of John Hancock and followers of James Bowdoin cut across occupational lines.[25] Yet Bostonians came together in the fall of 1786 to oppose the rural Regulation that culminated in Shays's Rebellion. Merchants and mechanics alike regarded the application of force to obstruct judicial proceedings as a treacherous attack on the principles of republican government. Whatever the merits of the Regulators' complaints, they argued, the proper mode for redressing grievances was the election and instruction of representatives to the General Court. By an overwhelming vote, the Boston town meeting endorsed Samuel Adams's angry declaration that "a State of *Anarchy* is to be dreaded Above all other *Calamities.* . . . To say, *the majority shall not govern*, is saying either that we will reduce ourselves to a state of nature, or reject the ideas of civil liberty, establish a despotism, and be subject to the sovereign pleasure of one man."[26]

Even Benjamin Austin, Jr., whose previous attacks on lawyers and the Massachusetts legal system had made him ap-

---

[24] Kornblith, "'Cementing the Mechanic Interest,'" pp. 358–60, 373–76.

[25] On the John Hancock-James Bowdoin rivalry, see Anson Ely Morse, *The Federalist Party in Massachusetts to the Year 1800* (Princeton, 1909), pp. 19–33; Van Beck Hall, *Politics without Parties: Massachusetts, 1780–1791* (Pittsburgh, 1972), pp. 131–38.

[26] *Massachusetts Centinel*, Sept. 13, 1786. On Adams's position, see William Pencak, "Samuel Adams and Shays's Rebellion," *New England Quarterly* 62 (1989):63–74.

pear supportive of the Regulators' cause, publicly denounced Shays's Rebellion in harsh and uncompromising terms. Austin disavowed any tie to the insurgency and charged rebel leaders with plotting "an entire revolution in government, and a levelling of all property." "None but the profligate, unprincipled, and wicked, can wish their success," he wrote under the pseudonym (once again) of "Honestus."[27]

After the rebellion was crushed by military force, Boston artisans divided on whether to reelect a vengeful Bowdoin to the governorship or to replace him with the more conciliatory Hancock.[28] Many artisans felt further punishment of the rebels would be counterproductive. But local mechanics never displayed any concerted desire to forge a social alliance with disgruntled farmers against Boston's merchant elite in the late 1780s. On the contrary, when it appeared likely that rural opposition would block ratification of the federal Constitution in Massachusetts, Boston craftsmen rallied en masse to the Federalist cause.

In the resolutions adopted at the Green Dragon tavern on January 7, 1788, Boston artisans framed their arguments for the Constitution in explicitly economic terms. "It is our opinion," they explained, "that if said constitution should be adopted by the United States of America, trade and navigation will revive and increase, employ and subsistence will be afforded to many of our townsmen, who are now suffering from want of necessities of life." Should the Constitution be rejected, however, "the small remains of commerce yet left us, will be annihilated, the various trades and handicrafts dependent thereon must decay; our poor will be increased, and many of our worthy and skilful mechanicks compelled to seek employ and subsistence in strange lands."[29] Significantly, they made no reference to the potential for a national protective tariff under the Constitution. They highlighted instead the

[27] *Independent Chronicle*, Jan. 11, 1787.

[28] For a contemporary estimate of how Boston tradesmen split their votes in this election, see *Massachusetts Centinel*, Apr. 4, 1787.

[29] Ibid., Jan. 9, 1788. On this meeting, see also Merrill Jensen, John P. Kaminski, and Gaspare J. Saladino, eds., *Documentary History of the Ratification of the Constitution*, 10 vols. to date (Madison, Wis., 1976-), 15:290–95.

benefits that would accrue to local artisans from mercantile expansion: more employment, greater material security, and a higher standard of living. Tradition holds that their arguments helped to persuade Samuel Adams to drop his opposition to the Constitution and thereby paved the way for ratification in Massachusetts.

For most urban New England artisans, the advent of the new national government brought the prosperity they so urgently sought. Shortly after the Congress got underway in New York in the spring of 1789, Boston artisans sent a petition asking for greater protection of local manufactures.[30] In 1790 Providence artisans tried to mobilize mechanics nationwide on behalf of higher tariffs.[31] Yet protectionist sentiment within the trades receded as the region's commercial economy improved. In May 1792, while New Yorkers reeled from the impact of William Duer's financial collapse, a correspondent in Providence celebrated the atmosphere of "general Enterprise" supposedly sweeping the nation as men of all occupations were "very busily engaged, in devising and executing new Ways and Means of acquiring Wealth and Honour." "In this Town," he observed, "the Motto is 'Every one to his Trade, and to his Merchandise.'"[32] A Boston correspondent in December 1792 estimated that Boston's output of boots, shoes, and slippers had doubled since 1788, while cabinetmaking, papermaking, printing, and a host of other trades were also flourishing.[33] Two years later, another Boston observer estimated that "not less than four hundred and fifty sail of ships, brigs, schooners, sloops, and small craft, are now in this port." "The prospect is pleasing," he added, "as it af-

[30] "Shipbuilding and Manufactures," *American State Papers: Finance*, 1:10–11.

[31] Kornblith, "'Cementing the Mechanic Interest,'" pp. 377–79.

[32] *United States Chronicle*, May 10, 1792. On the impact of William Duer's failure on New York artisans, see Young, "Mechanics and the Jeffersonians," p. 254. For a discussion of artisanal discontent in Connecticut in the spring of 1792, see James P. Walsh, "'Mechanics and Citizens': The Connecticut Artisan Protest of 1792," *William and Mary Quarterly*, 3d ser. 42 (1985):66–89.

[33] *Columbian Centinel*, Dec. 5, 1792.

fords the expectation of employment for the industrious mechanick and labourer, who may not now, we think, be idle,
unless they choose it."[34]

Within the context of this economic upswing, the Federalist
coalition continued strong in urban New England. In Salem,
which emerged as a major center for East Asian trade during
the Federalist era, political harmony reigned until leading
merchants divided sharply over family issues and foreign policy in 1798–99.[35] The only hint of deep-seated artisanal discontent to surface publicly before 1800 concerned the state
militia law. In May 1795 Salemites instructed their state representatives to seek reform: "The poor Mechanick has been
drafted and held to march (if ordered) under a severe penalty, to protect the Life and Property of his rich and most
Honorable exempted neighbour. . . . God Deliver us from
such Vassalage!"[36] This complaint did not develop into a partisan issue, however, and even after Salem's mercantile elite
split into two camps at the end of the decade, few artisans or
other townspeople identified themselves as Jeffersonian Republicans.[37] Antifederalist candidate Jacob Crowninshield
won a majority of Salem's votes for congressman in 1800, but

[34] [Thomas Pemberton], "A Topographical and Historical Description of
Boston, 1794," *Massachusetts Historical Society Collections,* 1st ser. 3 (1794; reprint ed., 1810):287. On Boston's economic recovery, see also John D.
Forbes, "The Port of Boston, 1783–1815," Ph.D. diss., Harvard University, 1936.

[35] William T. Whitney, Jr., "The Crowninshields of Salem, 1800–1818: A
Study in the Politics of Commercial Growth," *Essex Institute Historical Collec-
tions* 94 (1958):1–13. See also James Duncan Phillips, *Salem and the Indies:
The Story of the Great Commercial Era of the City* (Boston, 1947), pp. 101–47;
Samuel Eliot Morison, *The Maritime History of Massachusetts, 1783–1860*
(1921; reprint ed., Boston, 1979), pp. 79–95; Philip Chadwick Foster
Smith, "William Bentley on Trade and the Marine Artificers," *Essex Institute
Historical Collections* 113 (1977):204–15.

[36] *Salem Gazette,* May 19, 1795.

[37] Elections in Salem before 1800 seem to have focused mainly on questions of personality, not political program or ideology. In his diary, however,
William Bentley suggests that underlying tensions between rich and poor
influenced voters' choices. See *The Diary of William Bentley, Pastor of the East
Church, Salem, Massachusetts,* 4 vols. (Salem, Mass., 1905–14), 2:13, 176.

he supported John Adams for reelection as president, as did Salemites as a whole.[38]

Even more than Salem, Providence was a Federalist stronghold until after the turn of the century. Results from the election of 1800 are especially revealing. Rhode Island was one of the few states that year to provide for direct popular choice of presidential electors, and Providence voters made their preference overwhelmingly clear. They cast 512 ballots for the Federalist slate and only 56 for the Republican—a margin sufficiently lopsided to carry the state as a whole for the incumbent president.[39]

Only in Boston did Republicans raise a serious challenge to Federalist dominance from the early 1790s forward. Yet no wholesale shift in allegiances took place among Boston's tradesmen. Although Benjamin Austin, Jr., gave Fisher Ames a close race for his congressional seat in 1792, and in 1793, in a special congressional election, he actually carried Boston (but not the entire electoral district), Ames defeated Dr. Charles Jarvis handily in 1794.[40] Equally important, Federalists won the most important local debates over federal policy in the middle years of the decade.

In early 1794 Austin and other leading Democratic-Republicans asked the Boston town meeting to endorse officially James Madison's proposal for commercial discrimination against Great Britain. Resentment of British interference with American commerce was widespread, and the measure won the town meeting's provisional approval on February 13, 1794. Federalists fought back, however, with arguments that Madison's proposal, if adopted by the federal government, would inevitably lead to war. Many Bostonians were persuaded. On February 25 the town meeting reversed itself by voting to postpone further consideration of the matter in-

[38] Whitney, "Crowninshields of Salem," pp. 10–13.

[39] *Providence Gazette,* Nov. 29, 1800. A poll list is included in Providence Town Meeting Minutes, April 1800-August 1808, Nov. 19, 1800, Providence Town Papers, vol. 178, Man. Coll., R. I. Hist. Soc. Libr.

[40] *Columbian Centinel,* Nov. 3, 1792; Jan. 19, 1793; Apr. 3, 1793; Nov. 5, 1794; Winfred E. A. Bernhard, *Fisher Ames: Federalist and Statesman, 1758–1808* (Chapel Hill, 1965), pp. 204–7, 238–40.

definitely.[41] Reporting this outcome with evident satisfaction, Benjamin Russell's *Columbian Centinel* commented confidently "that when the mercantile and mechanic professions have time to deliberate, they see their best interests, and pursue them."[42]

Boston Federalists had more difficulty defusing public outrage over the Jay Treaty. A town meeting on July 13, 1795, voted unanimously that the treaty, "if Ratified, will be highly Injurious to the commercial interest of the United States, derogatory to their National Honour, and Independence, and may be dangerous to the Peace & Happiness of their Citizens."[43] Yet less than a month later, the local chamber of commerce publicly endorsed ratification of the treaty, and Federalists circulated a petition dissenting from the official town position.[44] By the spring of 1796 the weight of public opinion in Boston had clearly shifted. In mid-April, Federalists circulated a new petition calling on the House of Representatives to implement the treaty without delay.[45] Although Democratic-Republicans angrily charged their opponents with using intimidation to swell the subscription list, on April 25 a heavily attended town meeting voted formally to endorse "the object and sentiments contained in the memorial . . . by a very great majority."[46]

Over the next three years, Boston grew increasingly Feder-

[41] *Boston Town Records, 1784–1796,* pp. 347–48; Bernhard, *Fisher Ames,* pp. 221–26.

[42] *Columbian Centinel,* Feb. 26, 1794.

[43] *Boston Town Records, 1784–1796,* p. 407.

[44] *Columbian Centinel,* Aug. 15, 1795; Aug. 19, 1795.

[45] William Bruce Wheeler, "Urban Politics in Nature's Republic: The Development of Political Parties in the Seaport Cities in the Federalist Era," Ph.D. diss., University of Virginia, 1967, pp. 367–75. Wheeler includes photocopies of the petition and another protreaty circular between pp. 375 and 376.

[46] *Boston Town Records, 1784–1796,* pp. 428–29. According to Austin, the treaty's supporters "increased their subscription-paper, not by the deliberate determination of the inhabitants but by that *personal influence* which their preeminent situation gave them over the judgement of those to whom they applied" (Benjamin Austin, Jr., *Constitutional Republicanism, in Opposi-*

alist. In 1798 a petition praising President John Adams's policy toward France attracted more than eighteen hundred signatures, including—observed the *Centinel*—"MERCHANTS, TRADERS, AND RESPECTABLE MECHANICS of every description."[47] The same year Federalist Harrison Gray Otis defeated his Republican challenger for Congress by a margin in Boston of better than three to two. But internal divisions eventually weakened the Federalist cause. In 1800, while many prominent Boston Federalists worked not-so-covertly against Adams's reelection, local Republicans staged a comeback. Elbridge Gerry narrowly carried Boston in the gubernatorial contest in the spring, and in the fall congressional election Federalist Josiah Quincy won the city by only a very slim margin.[48] Still, in 1800, Federalist candidates enjoyed more extensive support in Boston than in New York, Baltimore, or Philadelphia. It appears that Boston artisans were divided in their political allegiances throughout the Federalist era, but most of them rallied most of the time to the Federalist, rather than to the Democratic-Republican, party banner.

This is not to say that New England artisans who voted for Federalist candidates necessarily embraced the same principles as genteel Federalist statesmen and polemicists. James M. Banner, Jr., has identified "harmony, unity, order, solidarity" as "the basic motifs of Massachusetts Federalist thought."[49] He has further suggested that "Massachusetts Federalism was . . . a protest against the gathering forces of unfettered middle-class capitalism"—an assessment that meshes nicely with Joyce Appleby's analysis of Jeffersonian-

tion to Fallacious Federalism; As Published in the Independent Chronicle, under the Signature of Old-South [Boston, 1803], p. 12).

[47] *Columbian Centinel*, May 5, 1798.

[48] Wheeler, "Urban Politics in Nature's Republic," pp. 376–98; Samuel Eliot Morison, *The Life and Letters of Harrison Gray Otis, Federalist, 1765–1848*, 2 vols. (Boston, 1913), 1:176–98.

[49] James M. Banner, Jr., *To the Hartford Convention: The Federalists and the Origins of Party Politics in Massachusetts, 1789–1815* (New York, 1970), p. 53.

ism as a celebration of such forces.[50] Yet the Federalism of New England artisans does not fit neatly into Banner's paradigm, nor does it correspond to other scholars' descriptions of Federalist ideology as essentially elitist and conservative.[51] Artisan Federalism, it seems, was a distinctive brand of Federalism.

While artisan Federalists valued "harmony, unity, order, solidarity," they cared more deeply about promoting equitable economic development. They had little use for classical models of republicanism, and they looked to the future with optimism and enthusiasm, not vexation or regret. As believers in both progress and equal rights, they regarded balanced economic growth as virtually a panacea for current problems of social injustice and political conflict. From their perspective, modern prosperity promised to knit citizens more closely together than the ancient virtues of austerity and self-sacrifice. In short, by means of balanced economic growth, they hoped simultaneously to enhance public wealth, to promote private gain, and to distribute economic rewards fairly among the major classes of society—understood to be the agricultural, mercantile, and mechanic interests.

Not surprisingly, artisan Federalists placed special emphasis on the social and economic benefits wrought by the mechanic arts. In the preamble to their original constitution, adopted in 1795, the founders of the Federalist-dominated Boston Mechanic Association boldly asserted that "the combination of the Mechanic Powers hath proved the source of those use-

[50] Ibid., p. 70; Joyce Appleby, *Capitalism and a New Social Order: The Republican Vision of the 1790s* (New York, 1984).

[51] See, for example, David Hackett Fischer, *The Revolution of American Conservatism: The Federalist Party in the Era of Jeffersonian Democracy* (New York, 1965), pp. 1–28; Linda K. Kerber, *Federalists in Dissent: Imagery and Ideology in Jeffersonian America* (1970; reprint ed., Ithaca, N.Y., 1980), pp. 173–215; Richard Buel, Jr., *Securing the Revolution: Ideology in American Politics, 1789–1815* (Ithaca, N.Y., 1972), pp. 91–112. For an analysis that emphasizes differences among Federalists in the 1790s, see Manning J. Dauer, *The Adams Federalists* (1953; reprint ed., Westport, Conn., 1984). For an analysis that emphasizes Massachusetts Federalism's centrist tendencies, see Ronald P. Formisano, *The Transformation of Political Culture: Massachusetts, 1790s-1840s* (New York, 1983), pp. 57–170.

ful Arts and Sciences, which have ameliorated the condition of Man and given to Society its wealth and respectability."[52] Underlying this assertion was a belief in the relatively high productivity, as well as the more evident social utility, of artisanal labor.

In a lecture presented before the Providence Association of Mechanics and Manufacturers in 1798, member Isaac Greenwood (a Federalist) provided an intriguing analysis of how the mechanic arts contributed to the public welfare. "In a country without manufactures," he explained, "where the inhabitants depend on the culture of the earth for their support, they may, in their individual capacities, be in some degree independent; but, with their utmost exertions, they can scarcely do more than subsist themselves; and viewed aggregately, as a nation, they cannot possibly become rich." Greenwood reasoned that agricultural labor was in practice (if not in principle) less productive than mechanical labor. The value of a farmer's products was essentially limited by "the intrinsic worth" of the raw materials involved, including land, he said. By contrast, "the manufacturer may, from a very small stock, receive emoluments proportioned to the quality of his workmanship, without much regard to the intrinsic value of the material."[53]

In a subsequent lecture to the Providence Association, member John Howland, also a Federalist, took Greenwood's argument one step further. Turning the logic of Thomas Jefferson's well-known response to Query 19 in the *Notes on the State of Virginia* on its head, Howland contended that a nation's "riches, its power, its commerce, its literature, and in most cases, its liberties, have generally accompanied its manufactures and its arts." Howland took aim at Jefferson by name. Charging that "most of the people in Virginia and North Carolina, who *can* read, and who have any influence in govern-

[52] *Constitution of the Associated Mechanics of the Town of Boston* (Boston, [1795]), p. 3.

[53] "Mr. Greenwood's Lecture," in Edwin M. Stone, *Mechanics' Festival* (Providence, 1860), appendix pp. 6–7. Isaac Greenwood voted for the Federalist slate of presidential electors in 1800 (Providence Town Meeting Minutes, Nov. 19, 1800).

ment ... look up to him with as much veneration as the idolatrous Jews did to the golden calf," Howland derided Jefferson's views on political economy—particularly his "wish that our workshops may remain in Europe"—as but "groveling opinions." "Yet there are more than two millions of people in this country who think him to be a great and wise man!" Howland lamented in disgust.[54]

For Howland the recent history of revolutionary France vividly illustrated the dangers posed by a too powerful agricultural interest. Analyzing the causes of the Terror, he minimized the importance of the Jacobins' heretical religious views and their sharply antiaristocratic politics. Instead, he emphasized the role of longstanding agrarian hostility toward urban society, merchants and mechanics included. "The country interest only was represented [in the convention]," he explained, "and the world has witnessed the result, which was written in the towns, in the characters of blood."[55]

If Federalist artisans feared the effects of an oversized agricultural sector, they heralded the extensive opportunities wrought by commerce. Declared Greenwood, "It is commerce (the *primum mobile* of which is manufactures and agriculture), that draws gold and silver, the mainsprings of action, into any State,—a truth illustrated in the present condition of Spain, the mines of Mexico being scarcely sufficient to pay for the merchandise and commodities imported from other European nations."[56] A nation without merchants and without a healthy commercial sector was bound to stagnate. By putting commodities and money in motion, both internal trade and

[54] "Mr. Howland's Lecture," in Stone, *Mechanics' Festival*, appendix p. 15.

[55] Ibid., appendix p. 14. In sending a published copy of this talk to Paul Revere, John Howland commented, "I cannot vouch for the popularity of some of the paragraphs but the sentiments are such as have some how or other got into my head and if they should afford yourself or any of the family part [of] an Evenings Amusement they will at least gratify one wish of my Heart which is never to give any of my Friends thirty minutes pain" (Howland to Revere, Feb. 25, 1799, *Microfilm Edition of the Revere Family Papers, 1746–1964* [Boston, 1979], Reel 1).

[56] "Mr. Greenwood's Lecture," in Stone, *Mechanics' Festival*, appendix p. 4.

foreign commerce provided incentives for farmers and mechanics to increase production and generate new wealth.
From this perspective, the social interdependence encouraged by an expanding market economy was clearly preferable
to the Spartan independence associated with agrarian self-
sufficiency.[57] By Greenwood's account, the key to success in
political economy was not autarky but a favorable balance of
trade.

Yet in advocating commercial growth as well as the encouragement of manufactures, Federalist artisans recognized the
potential for conflict between merchants and mechanics over
governmental policy. The membership certificate adopted by
the Boston Mechanic Association in 1800 expressed graphi-
cally the artisanal concern that the interests of merchants and
mechanics be given equal weight. Above an eagle representing "the Government of the United States—under whose fostering care *Commerce* and the *Mechanic Arts* have flourished"—
was situated a scale-beam with bales symbolizing commerce
suspended from one side and craftsmen's tools hanging from
the other. This careful arrangement conveyed "the truth of
the maxim contained in the *motto* of the Association, that,
equally balanced, the Merchant and Mechanic in being '*Just*,'
may '*Fear Not*.'"[58]

It would be a mistake to regard Federalist artisans as poor
deluded victims of paternalistic manipulation or some other
hegemonic device. They had their own ideas about what sort
of political economy would advance their prosperity and promote the rise of a strong and stable republic, and they acted
rationally and deliberately on the basis of their beliefs. A few
weeks before voting overwhelmingly for John Adams for
president in 1800, for example, members of the Providence

[57] On the commercial alternative to the Spartan ideal in republican
thought, see Drew R. McCoy, *The Elusive Republic: Political Economy in Jeffersonian America* (1980; reprint ed., New York, 1982), pp. 48–104; Cathy D.
Matson and Peter S. Onuf, *A Union of Interests: Political and Economic Thought
in Revolutionary America* (Lawrence, Kans., 1990), pp. 11–30; and Gordon
S. Wood, *The Radicalism of the American Revolution* (New York, 1992), pp.
215–18.

[58] Joseph T. Buckingham, *Annals of the Massachusetts Charitable Mechanic
Association* (Boston, 1853), p. 71.

Association of Mechanics and Manufacturers sent a memorial to Congress "praying that additional Duties be Levied on Articles imported."[59] They were not echoing mercantile opinion on this point; they were speaking for themselves.

What, then, distinguished artisan Federalism from artisan Republicanism? An analysis of Benjamin Austin, Jr.'s, writings during the 1790s reveals a commitment to commercial growth, domestic manufacturing, and balanced economic development not unlike that of his Federalist antagonists. No less than they, he envisioned a mutually beneficial alliance between mechanics and merchants. Yet whereas artisan Federalists feared that an unduly powerful agrarian interest might unbalance the nation's political economy, Austin worried instead about the threat to stability allegedly posed by stockjobbers and speculators—to his mind, an unscrupulous, nonproductive class whose interests contradicted those of merchants, mechanics, and farmers alike. "Every man who reflects justly, knows that the Constitution was originally established for the happiness and prosperity of *the whole people,* and not for the emolument and grandeur of a few individuals," he wrote under the pseudonym "A Republican" in the fall of 1792.[60] "It is not *necessary* that money should be taken from the industrious, to pamper the indolent. . . . Neither is it *necessary,* that the duties paid by the Merchant should be deposited in the several Branch Banks [of the Bank of the United States], for the *use* and *profit* of a few Speculators, and Monopolizers."[61]

Besides this emerging internal danger, Austin fixed his attention on an enduring external threat to the republic's survival: Great Britain. Although he questioned the fairness and wisdom of the imposts levied by Federalist Congresses, he

[59] Memorial to the House of Representatives of the United States, Association Minute Book 2, Oct. 17, 1800, Records of the Providence Assn.

[60] "The Crisis No. II," *Independent Chronicle,* Sept. 27, 1792. For evidence that Austin wrote this essay, see ibid., Apr. 4, 1793.

[61] "The Crisis No. IV," ibid., Oct. 25, 1792. For an analysis of Austin's political thought in relation to that of other Boston Republicans, see Paul Goodman, *The Democratic-Republicans of Massachusetts: Politics in a Young Republic* (Cambridge, Mass., 1964), p. 101.

embraced Madison's plan for commercial discrimination with ardor. Austin repeatedly denounced Great Britain for restricting American access to the West Indies, interfering with the American carrying trade, and fostering a costly Indian war on the nation's western frontier. Likewise, he characterized British imports as luxuries that endangered the moral character as well as the material well-being of American citizens. On one occasion he went so far as to argue that "it would be for the real interest of this country, if no vessels, arrived among us, unless loaded with *raw materials* for our own manufacturers, or the necessary articles for carrying out agriculture, navigation, and fisheries."[62] Yet Austin was not consistent in his support for protectionism. A self-professed advocate of the mercantile as well as the mechanic interest, he wished to redirect American trade away from Britain (and toward France) for the purpose of increasing—not reducing—American involvement in world markets. In New England, at least, neither artisan Federalists nor artisan Republicans advocated a tariff barrier that would seriously hamper commercial growth.

In light of the ideological affinities between artisan Federalism and artisan Republicanism, the fierceness of partisan antagonism within Boston trades during the Federalist era remains hard to fathom. This essay began with a confrontation between Benjamin Austin, Jr., and Benjamin Russell that took place in January 1792—before the sharp polarization over policy toward Britain and France, before the Whiskey Rebellion, before the uproar over the Jay Treaty, before the XYZ Affair, and before the Alien and Sedition Acts. The occasion was a debate over the structure of local government, but evidently the hatred between Austin and Russell had been mounting for quite some time. Unfortunately, the genesis of their personal rivalry is a mystery. Joseph T. Buckingham, himself a veteran of Boston's newspaper wars, confessed in his *Specimens of Newspaper Literature*, published in 1850, "I could never discover the origin of the almost deadly feud, which existed between Benjamin Austin, jun., and Benjamin Russell; and it may be questioned whether any one can refer

[62] *Independent Chronicle*, Feb. 24, 1794.

to any specific act or word, as the cause of it."[63] Yet the very intensity of their quarrel is significant. It serves as a salutary reminder that in the early years of the republic, the personal was political and the political was personal—not only in the genteel circles of the cabinet and the Congress but also in the more plebian arenas of the town meetings, streets, and work-shops of urban New England.[64]

[63] Buckingham, *Specimens of Newspaper Literature*, 2:351.

[64] On the interrelationship between personal and political conflict in the upper echelons of American government in the 1790s, see Stanley Elkins and Eric McKitrick, *The Age of Federalism: The Early American Republic, 1788–1800* (New York, 1993).

JOHN L. BROOKE

Ancient Lodges and Self-Created Societies

Voluntary Association and the Public Sphere in the Early Republic

ON THE MORNING of September 18, 1793, an elaborate procession moved through the woods and open fields of the newly established District of Columbia, the city of Washington. Batteries of volunteer artillery fired salutes as the brothers of Lodge 22 of Alexandria, in full regalia and led by their past master, General and President George Washington, paraded from the banks of the Potomac River to the site of Lafayette Park. Here joined by the brethren of two Maryland lodges, the officers of the Grand Lodge of Maryland, and assorted surveyors, commissioners, stonecutters, and mechanics, the procession marched up the track marking Pennsylvania Avenue to Capitol Hill. To the thunder of continuing volleys of artillery fire and surrounded by a wide circle of assembled Masons, President Washington, with the Maryland grand master and three lodge masters, climbed down into a builder's trench and laid a silver plate on the

I would like to thank Maurice Bric, Steven Bullock, Ronald Formisano, Lou Masur, Michael Schudson, Sean Wilentz, and Robert W. Williams who, in commentary or conversation, sharpened my understanding of the problems discussed in this essay. I would very much like to thank Philip Lampi for sharing his township election data, and the staff at the Van Gordon-Williams Library at the Museum of Our National Heritage in Lexington, Massachusetts, where much of the research for this paper was done.

273

cornerstone of the Capitol. After offerings of corn, wine, and oil (Masonic emblems of nourishment, joy, and refreshment), prayers, Masonic chants, and fifteen final cannonades, the company "retired to an extensive booth" for a fine picnic. That afternoon Washington presided over an auction of town lots in the newly surveyed city.[1]

This highly orchestrated ceremony placed Freemasonry at the privileged center of public culture in the new United States. The Masons convening under George Washington that September morning stood at the apex of a network of association and fraternity that stretched from Wiscasset, Maine, to Lexington, Kentucky, to Augusta, Georgia. Including in 1793 roughly two hundred local lodges organized under nine state grand lodges, by 1800 Freemasonry would number over five hundred lodges with perhaps 25,000 members. These men comprised about 3 percent of the adult white male population enumerated in the United States census of 1800 and significantly more of those at least minimally propertied—and thus enfranchised—who could afford the assessments and fees of the order.[2] Its aura of secrecy and even mysticism, its elaborate regalia and formal processions, gave Freemasonry a cultural intensity unequaled in the early republic. And Freemasonry was to be an antidote to partisan strife. Regularly gathering in lodge meetings, Masons were bound together by

[1] Joseph B. Varnum, *The Seat of Government of the United States* (Washington, D.C., 1854), pp. 31–32; James Sterling Young, *The Washington Community, 1800–1828* (New York, 1966), p. 19; Edward T. Schultz, *History of Freemasonry in Maryland . . .*, 4 vols. (Baltimore, 1884–88), 1:191–94.

[2] These figures are based upon an analysis of lodges listed in Thomas S. Webb, *The Freemason's Monitor, or, Illustrations of Masonry: In Two Parts* (New York, 1802), pp. 277–87; idem, *The Freemason's Monitor, or, Illustrations of Freemasonry: In Two Parts*, new ed. (Providence, 1805), pp. 297–317; and in the records and histories of the various grand lodges. My figure of 547 lodges in 1800–1805 (list dates differ by state) is significantly higher than that of 347 lodges with 16,000 members cited in William P. Vaughn, *The Antimasonic Party in the United States, 1826–1843* (Lexington, Ky., 1983), p. 11. I have used his multiplier of forty-six members per lodge to arrive at my estimate of 25,000 members. There were 694,075 white males over the age of twenty-four in 1800 (Bureau of the Census, *Historical Statistics of the United States: Colonial Times to 1970*, 2 vols. [Washington, D.C., 1975], 1:16). See Appendix, table 2.

an endless sequence of initiation rituals that inculcated the principles of disinterested virtue and brotherly love. As the Rev. George Buist reminded the Grand Lodge of South Carolina on St. John's Day in 1793, three months after the ceremonies on Capitol Hill, Freemasonry united "men of all ranks and conditions, of all parties and sects, of all nations and religions"; it demanded "rectitude and moderation of conduct"; it excluded "all strife and debate, all riot and intemperance." Freemasonry rested on the authority of a tradition of biblical origins, literally running back to Adam in the Garden of Eden. Where history had seen the rise and fall of empires and republics, Freemasonry "alone [had] preserved its original purity"; lodges of such ancient origins could provide a backbone of cultural stability for the new nation.[3]

These ideals of ancient authority, virtue, and ritual hierarchy were eminently well designed for the purposes of forging what Robert H. Wiebe has called the "politics of character," symmetrical, balanced, and unanimous, in a new republic emerging from the furnace of revolutionary creation.[4] Freemasonry itself was only the best organized (and documented) of a vast array of voluntary societies deployed in the self-conscious construction of public culture in the young republic. Actors of all persuasions were convinced that the survival of this republic required the creation of mediating institutions—and printed means of communication and persuasion—that would mold and direct what contemporaries already called the "public mind."[5] The 1790s saw a ferocious conflict between Federalists and Republicans over the control and definition of this mediating public culture. As national governmental routines were established, the absence of an accepted and defined role for political opposition and debate

[3] George Buist, *A Sermon, Preached in the Presbyterian Church, of Charleston, before the Incorporated Grand Lodge of Masons of South-Carolina, Ancient York Masons . . . December 27th, 1793* (Charleston, S.C., 1794), pp. 24–25.

[4] Robert H. Wiebe, *The Opening of American Society: From the Adoption of the Constitution to the Eve of Disunion* (New York, 1984), pp. 35–66.

[5] Josiah Bartlett, in grand lodge address to John Adams, quoted in Vernon Stauffer, *New England and the Bavarian Illuminati* (New York, 1918), p. 325.

and the republican imperative of a virtuous people fueled insatiable efforts to control and direct public opinion. This competition for the public mind was grounded in the terms of the constitutional settlement of the Revolution. Sovereignty rested in the people, not the government, and those aspiring to influence and leadership had to win constituencies by argument and organization, while at the same time avoiding the appearance of partisanship. The vehicle of this competition was a fusion of voluntary associations and partisan press, creating embryonic and diffuse cultural affinities and political interests—it mobilized publics, but by no means created political parties.

With the press, voluntary societies stood at the epicenter of efforts to define and redefine the public arena in the new nation; all through the 1790s they provided both vehicle and issue for partisan strife. Their members marched in public ceremonies for the celebration of the Constitution, the presidential inauguration, and the grand tours of Washington's first administration, the laying of cornerstones and the public mourning of Washington's death. Voluntary societies saluted Citizen Genet in 1793 and were condemned by George Washington in 1794. They emerged in combination with a competitive press, and with that press they were attacked by the Federalists in 1798—the partisan press in the Sedition Act and the secular societies in Jedediah Morse's crusade against the Illuminati.[6]

This dimension of the political struggles of the 1790s comprised the self-conscious and contested construction of what scholars of the eighteenth century are calling the "public

[6] John R. Howe, "Republican Thought and the Political Violence of the 1790s," *American Quarterly* 19 (1967):147–65; Gordon S. Wood, "Conspiracy and the Paranoid Style: Causality and Deceit in the Eighteenth Century," *William and Mary Quarterly*, 3d ser. 39 (1982):401–41; Richard Hofstadter, *The Idea of a Party System: The Rise of Legitimate Opposition in the United States, 1780–1840* (Berkeley, Calif., 1969); Seymour M. Lipset, *The First New Nation: The United States in Historical and Comparative Perspective* (New York, 1966), pp. 17–111; Wiebe, *Opening of American Society*, pp. 1–125; Joyce Appleby, *Capitalism and a New Social Order: The Republican Vision of the 1790s* (New York, 1984); Stanley Elkins and Eric McKitrick, *The Age of Federalism: The Early American Republic, 1788–1800* (New York, 1993), pp. 451–55.

sphere of civil society." Building on a seminal work written three decades ago by the German philosopher Jürgen Habermas, a recently burgeoning body of theoretical and historical analysis has developed a precise definition of "the public sphere" as the institutions of civil association and literate discourse intervening between state and society, specifically the private spheres of the market and the family, as the middle class took shape over the eighteenth century. As most commonly described, the public sphere emerged in the circulation of people and ideas in the clubs, coffeehouses, and literary journals of late Stuart and Hanoverian England, rapidly expanding in eighteenth-century Britain, France, and Holland with the establishment of regular newspapers, critical discourses and literatures, and dense networks of reading clubs, salons, and Masonic lodges. Participation in this consensual "classical public sphere" was to be limited to the "political nation" of literate property holders, fusing the tastes, manners, and inclinations of the landed aristocracy with the rising urban middle class; its language was the cool, rational discourse of what Henry F. May has defined as the "moderate Enlightenment."[7] More precise than "public culture" or "political culture," the concept of a "public sphere of civil society" is particularly useful in the context of the early republic, suggesting new ways we can link perspectives on society, culture, and politics.

The evolving literature on the public sphere has a series of important faultlines, dividing theorists who stress opposition or consensus, openness or closure, in its eighteenth-century manifestations. As formulated by Habermas, the public sphere consisted essentially of critical thought crystalized in print—in journals and newspapers—that both fed and fed upon the growth of an opposition to the unfettered domain of absolutist power. In his account, the public sphere was an open and universal arena of rational discourse. Central to this

[7] Jürgen Habermas, *The Structural Transformation of the Public Sphere: An Inquiry into a Category of Bourgeois Society,* trans. Thomas Burger (Cambridge, Mass., 1989), pp. 14–67; idem, "The Public Sphere: An Encyclopedia Article," with an introduction by Peter Hohendahl, *New German Critique* 3 (1974):45–55; Henry F. May, *The Enlightenment in America* (New York, 1976), pp. 3–101.

analysis of the public sphere is a contest with the state, the carving out of an autonomous arena of public opinion, that would eventually undermine and destroy absolutist authority.

Habermas's depiction of a open and unitary public sphere is challenged from two competing yet ultimately reconcilable perspectives. One important strand of thinking about the eighteenth-century public sphere emphasizes consensus, hegemony, and power. Running from Reinhart Koselleck's depiction of French Freemasonry as less an opposition to the absolutist state than a privatistic extension of it, filled with the functionaries of the service elite, this perspective paints a less obviously teleological picture, or suggests a teleology running to totalitarianism, as François Furet suggests, rather than to liberalism. Here the institutions of a public sphere are the private, even secret, contexts, in which common understandings can be shaped, understandings that in France reinforced and then transmuted, rather than directly challenged, the assumptions underlying absolutism.[8] And even if one sets aside Koselleck's and Furet's pessimistic teleology, Freemasonry can certainly be interpreted as an exemplar of a consensual impulse, meeting in secret, banning political discussion, binding the fraternity in fictive rituals and fictive hierarchies. And important tendencies within the eighteenth-century public sphere, whether intellectual or associational, mimicked the closure of Freemasonry, claiming a role "as the filtering agent for a purified public consensus," a virtual representation of the whole of civil society, rather than a ground for the framing of a broad-based public opinion.[9]

[8] Reinhart Koselleck, *Critique and Crisis: Enlightenment and the Pathogenesis of Modern Society* (1959; English trans., Cambridge, Mass., 1988); François Furet, *Interpreting the French Revolution*, trans. Elborg Forster (New York, 1981); Anthony J. La Vopa, "Conceiving a Public: Ideas and Society in Eighteenth-Century Europe," *Journal of Modern History* 64 (1992):89–98.

[9] La Vopa, "Conceiving a Public," pp. 111–12. For a few important approaches in a vast literature on the public sphere in eighteenth-century France, see Robert Darnton, *The Literary Underground of the Old Regime* (Cambridge, Mass., 1982); Lynn Hunt, *Politics, Culture, and Class in the French Revolution* (Berkeley, Calif., 1984); Roger Chartier, *The Cultural Origins of the French Revolution*, trans. Lydia G. Cockrane (Durham, N.C., 1991); Margaret C. Jacob, *Living the Enlightenment: Freemasonry and Politics in Eighteenth-*

If this consensual model of the public sphere has focused on late Ancien Régime France, a version of this model has been applied to the British scene as well. Peter Hohendahl and Terry Eagleton suggest that the commonality of intellectual discourse in Hanoverian Britain, establishing the boundaries of polite and rational culture, was in itself a form of hegemonic political action, erasing the passionate divisions of the seventeenth century and providing a basis for the consensus underlying the Whig establishment. Margaret C. Jacob has argued similarly that the origins of the English grand lodge in 1717 must be seen in terms of a broader campaign for stability and legitimacy that encompassed Newtonian science, Whig political culture, and Masonic fraternity.[10]

Another group of scholars carries the critique of Habermas in another direction, emphasizing those excluded from the institutions of the bourgeois public sphere. The exclusion of women and laboring people from the societies and lodges that made up the structural core of the social Enlightenment certainly compromises Habermas's depiction of an open and accessible public sphere. Thus a powerful, gender-based reinterpretation of the public sphere has developed, as has the outline of an analysis of plebeian and radical voices in a public sphere, emerging to challenge the political and cultural hegemony embodied in bourgeois discourse and institutions. All of these perspectives suggest, as Geoff Eley puts it, that we think of the eighteenth-century public sphere as "fractured and contested" rather than unitary and consensual.[11]

Century Europe (New York, 1991); and Dena Goodman, "Public Sphere and Private Life: Toward a Synthesis of Current Historiographical Approaches to the Old Regime," *History and Theory* 31 (1992):1–20.

[10] Terry Eagleton, *The Function of Criticism* (London, 1984), pp. 9–43; Peter Hohendahl, *The Institution of Criticism* (Ithaca, N.Y., 1982), pp. 52–54; Margaret C. Jacob, *The Radical Enlightenment: Pantheists, Freemasons, and Republicans* (London, 1981), 142–55.

[11] Joan Landes, *Women and the Public Sphere in the Age of the French Revolution* (Ithaca, N.Y., 1988); Nancy Fraser, "Rethinking the Public Sphere: A Contribution to the Critique of Actually Existing Democracy," in Craig Calhoun, ed., *Habermas and the Public Sphere* (Cambridge, Mass., 1992), pp. 109–43; Mary P. Ryan, "Gender and Public Access: Women's Politics in

There is no need for a tidy resolution of our account of the eighteenth-century public sphere as oppositional or consensual, fractured or unitary, open or closed. Rather, it is best that we pay close attention to context and possibility, to hegemony and opposition, to intention and reality. In the wider Anglo-American context, we can suggest that unity and hegemony in the public sphere gave way to fracture and challenge. The public sphere framed around the moderate Enlightenment, with its language of reason, hierarchy, and balanced order, was effectively hegemonic in Georgian England and provided a compelling model for the gentry elites of the eighteenth-century colonies and early republic. But increasingly, in both Britain and the colonies, there were alternatives and challenges flowing from the priorities of locality and province, from "radical Whiggery" and from the "revolutionary Enlightenment," to again use Henry May's convenient labels.[12] Conversely, we should also be aware of the potential for hegemonic impulses to be reasserted, and new forms of consensus to be established, often in the name of the nation.[13]

The competing theorists of the public sphere provide a very useful set of perspectives for approaching the public culture of the 1790s in the United States. Rather than being ex-

---

Nineteenth-Century America," ibid., pp. 259–88; Geoff Eley, "Nations, Public, and Political Cultures: Placing Habermas in the Nineteenth Century," ibid., pp. 289–339, quotation p. 326; La Vopa, "Conceiving a Public," pp. 98–115.

[12] May, *The Enlightenment in America*. Here it might be noted that the broader literature on republican thought presupposes the existence of a contested public sphere. See Caroline Robbins, *The Eighteenth-Century Commonwealthman* (Cambridge, Mass., 1961); Bernard Bailyn, *The Ideological Origins of the American Revolution* (Cambridge, Mass., 1967); Gordon S. Wood, *The Creation of the American Republic, 1776–1787* (Chapel Hill, 1969); J. G. A. Pocock, "The Varieties of Whiggism from Exclusion to Reform: A History of Ideology and Discourse," in *Virtue, Commerce, and History* (New York, 1985), pp. 215–310; and John Brewer, *Party Ideology and Popular Politics at the Accession of George III* (New York, 1976).

[13] Here I am thinking of Linda Colley's challenge to E. P. Thompson in *Britons: Forging the Nation, 1707–1837* (New Haven, 1992).

amined on its own terms, public life in the early republic has most often been dissected with the purpose of pinpointing the emergence of modern political party structures. Such analyses have often, though not invariably, assumed a decisive differentiation between the contest for power and the creation of culture. The conception of the public sphere offers us a new means of exploring this public life on its own terms, and to explore the complex relationships between cultural and political domains, which clearly saw a complex and fertile fusion in the 1790s. Prescriptions of political order flowed easily into prescriptions of social and cultural life. Benjamin Rush wanted to use education "to convert men into republican machines," and Federalists and Republicans had radically different ideas about what sort of machine they wanted to emerge from a new American education. The very material and aesthetic fabric of life was imbued with political implication at the height of the partisan controversies of the 1790s. Literary culture served the rhetorical purposes of defining and redefining republican virtue, as Cathy N. Davidson and Michael Warner have argued. Even the invention of bridge designs and labor-saving machinery contributed to the construction of the "imagined community" that Benedict Anderson suggests lies at the heart of modern nationalism. This problem of the cultural grounding of revolutionary politics and nation-building has been a central theme in new interpretations of the French Revolution. In the United States of the 1790s it is best to see this emerging construct as plural rather than singular, with Federalists struggling with Republicans to assert competing images of nationality.[14]

[14] On the contested construction of culture in the early republic, see among others, David Hackett Fischer, *The Revolution of American Conservatism: The Federalist Party in the Era of Jeffersonian Democracy* (New York, 1965); Donald H. Stewart, *The Opposition Press in the Federalist Period* (Albany, 1969); Joseph J. Ellis, *After the Revolution: Profile in American Culture* (New York, 1979), pp. 73–110; Carl F. Kaestle, *Pillars of the Republic: Common Schools and American Society, 1780–1860* (New York, 1983), p. 7; Cathy N. Davidson, *Revolution and the Word: The Rise of the Novel in America* (New York, 1986), pp. 151–211; Michael Warner, *The Letters of the Republic: Publication and the Public Sphere in Eighteenth-Century America* (Cambridge, Mass., 1990). On Thomas Paine, Joel Barlow, and Robert Fulton as inventors and entrepreneurs, see

The absence of political party organizations, the suspicion of party and faction, and the driving imperatives to define American republicanism and to shape collective opinion meant that public life in the 1790s was articulated in a manner quite different than it was even in the first decades of the nineteenth century and certainly in the 1830s. The various interpretations of the public sphere provide useful models for assessing this contest for the "hearts and minds" of the citizens of the early republic. Here, though I will touch on the thriving analysis of politics and print culture,[15] I will focus on the sociological fabric of the public sphere, the voluntary societies, and especially upon the place and role of Freemasonry.

Appleby, *Capitalism and a New Social Order*, pp. 89–90; see Brooke Hindle, *Emulation and Invention* (New York, 1981), on the fluid relationship between intellect and invention in the early republic. The theoretical literature informing this essay includes, in addition to the literature on the public sphere noted above, Clifford Geertz, *Negara: The Theater State in Nineteenth-Century Bali* (Princeton, 1980); Victor Turner, *Dramas, Fields, and Metaphors: Symbolic Action in Human Society* (Ithaca, N.Y., 1974); Sally F. Moore and Barbara G. Myerhoff, eds., *Secular Ritual* (Assen, Netherlands, 1977); Joseph J. Femia, *Gramsci's Political Thought: Hegemony, Consciousness, and the Revolutionary Process* (Oxford, 1981); Benedict Anderson, *Imagined Communities: Reflections on the Origins and Spread of Nationalism* (London, 1983); Sean Wilentz, ed., *Rites of Power: Symbolism, Ritual, and Politics since the Middle Ages* (Philadelphia, 1985); T. J. Jackson Lears, "The Concept of Cultural Hegemony: Problems and Possibilities," *American Historical Review* 90 (1985): 567–93; and Lynn Hunt, ed., *The New Cultural History* (Berkeley, Calif., 1989).

[15] William L. Joyce et al., eds., *Printing and Society in Early America* (Worcester, Mass., 1983); David D. Hall and John B. Hench, eds., *Needs and Opportunities in the History of the Book: America, 1639–1876* (Worcester, Mass., 1987); Davidson, *The Revolution and the Word;* David Lundberg and Henry F. May, "The Enlightened Reader in America," *American Quarterly* 28 (1976):262–93; David Lundberg, "New England Society Libraries and the Common Reader of the 1790s" (Paper delivered at the Seventy-eighth Annual Meeting of the Organization of American Historians, Minneapolis, April 1985); Robert A. Gross, *Books and Libraries in Thoreau's Concord* (Worcester, Mass., 1988); Lawrence Buell, *New England Literary Culture: From Revolution through Renaissance* (New York, 1986), pp. 24–41, 84–102, esp. p. 32; Richard D. Brown, *Knowledge Is Power: The Diffusion of Knowledge in Early America, 1700–1865* (New York, 1989), pp. 197–217; and Charles E. Clark, *The Public Prints: The Newspaper in Anglo-American Culture, 1665–1840* (New York, 1994).

The formative role of the voluntary societies in the public arena lay in their nonpartisan appearance: in a variety of ways the societies were private entities acting more and less explicitly to advance the public good. The societies were one of the key points of intersection between the cultural forging of "national imaginations" and the political struggle for national power. They instructed in science and the arts through discourse and debate, they inculcated lessons of virtue and order in rituals and ceremony, they healed the wounds of civil strife through conviviality and fraternity, and at times they served as de facto engines of political mobilization. But in a time when the organized pursuit of power was highly suspect, the voluntary associations usually acted indirectly, to influence through the construction of culture rather than to control through the pursuit of power. In this role the societies were more national in their reach than print culture itself, the leading component of the public sphere. While the South was traditionally lacking in presses and newspapers, it made up this deficit in its greater number of Masonic lodges, relative to the white population.[16]

The construction of a public sphere had significantly different textures in the different regions of the early republic, and this construction would also take on very different textures over time. In overview—for my patient readers—this essay explores a dialectical contest between classical and oppositional public spheres running from the 1750s through 1800. In sequence, a weakly articulated colonial Hanoverian public sphere espousing the ideal of the "moderate Enlightenment" was challenged by provincial imperatives and destroyed by "radical Whiggery"—organized in either public conventions or self-created voluntary societies. While these two manifestations of "radical Whiggery" continued to shape the Revolutionary arena, nationalists began to reconstruct a consensual "classical public sphere" giving primacy to the moderate Enlightenment—most successfully in the Masonic order. Successfully diffusing radical Whiggery by the early 1790s, this new synthesis was challenged by the construction of an oppositional public sphere, first manifested in 1793 and 1794 in the press

[16] See Appendix, table 2.

and in the self-created societies of the revolutionary Enlightenment. In their reaction, the Federalists abandoned the moderate Enlightenment in a move toward Calvinist and statist
reaction: in doing so they effectively forfeited Freemasonry to
the Republican opposition. It is here that I make my most substantive contribution, describing in some detail the growing
Republican influence in Freemasonry, which explains, I suggest, both Jedediah Morse's campaign against the Illuminati
and one of the means by which the Jeffersonians were able to
capture the center of American political culture in 1800.

COMPETING PUBLIC SPHERES IN THE
COLONIAL WORLD

The political implications of voluntary association in the early
republic had a long and tangled history, running back well
over a century. It is increasingly apparent that the culture of
clubs and societies was fundamental to the structure and dynamic of eighteenth-century colonial politics, especially in the
seaport towns, but to some degree also in the staple-
producing plantation districts. In effect, the politics of voluntary association of the 1790s was the final fluorescence of a
long tradition, soon to be replaced by the party process.

Male social life on both sides of the eighteenth-century British Atlantic was progressively shaped by a convivial world of
association revolving around the public taverns and inns. By
the 1740s the American seaport towns of Boston, New York,
Philadelphia, and Charleston were developing a tangle of tavern cliques, mug clubs, merchants' and artisans' societies, ethnic mutual aid societies, and various more and less formal
gatherings for political debate and literary exchange.[17] J. A.

---

[17] Carl Bridenbaugh, *Cities in the Wilderness: The First Century of Urban Life
in America, 1625–1742* (New York, 1938), pp. 436–42; idem, *Cities in Revolt:
Urban Life in America, 1743–1776* (New York, 1955), pp. 162–63, 363–64;
Carl Bridenbaugh and Jessica Bridenbaugh, *Rebels and Gentlemen: Philadelphia in the Age of Franklin* (New York, 1942), pp. 22–26; John Money, *Experience and Identity: Birmingham and the West Midlands, 1760–1800* (Montreal,
1977), pp. 121–49; John Brewer, "Commercialization and Politics," in Neil
McKendrick, John Brewer, and J. H. Plumb, *The Birth of a Consumer Society:
The Commercialization of Eighteenth-Century England* (Bloomington, Ind.,

Leo Lemay, Elaine G. Breslaw, and David S. Shields have demonstrated that these clubs were the focal point of early eighteenth-century public life, where satirical verses and play-lets were read and circulated in manuscript, in an era when newspaper publication was subject to censorship. Political sat-ire could have many uses, puncturing the governor's preten-sions, as in the play "Belcher's Apostate," read in Boston's taverns and societies in 1731, or diffusing partisan differ-ences, as in the ribald verses exchanged at the meetings of the Tuesday Club at Annapolis.[18] And for artisans and laboring people of the seaport towns, the culture of tavern and club extended from convivial drinking to the outdoor exertions of fire company, militia, and the mob: the neighborhood crowd mobilized for public purposes. In Boston the two sides of this club culture were effectively united in the influence of the Caucus, the political club managed by Elisha Cooke in the popular interest against that of the royal governor. In a bril-liant new study, David W. Conroy has argued that in 1719 Cooke initiated a change in Massachusetts license laws that made taverns the focal points in an emerging public sphere of secular discourse—both spoken and printed—shaping popular politics first in Boston and then throughout rural Massachusetts before the Revolution.[19]

1982), pp. 197–262; Peter Clark, *The English Alehouse: A Social History, 1200–1830* (London, 1983), pp. 1, 9, 234–35, 258; idem, review of *The History of the Ancient and Honorable Tuesday Club, William and Mary Quarterly*, 3d ser. 49 (1992):153–57; Eley, "Nations, Public, and Political Cultures," pp. 294–306, 325–31.

[18] J. A. Leo Lemay, "Richard Lewis and Augustan American Poetry," *PMLA* 83 (1968):80–101; Elaine G. Breslaw, "Wit, Whimsy, and Politics: The Uses of Satire by the Tuesday Club of Annapolis, 1744 to 1756," *William and Mary Quarterly*, 3d ser. 32 (1975):295–306; David S. Shields, *Oracles of Empire: Poetry, Politics, and Commerce in British America, 1690–1750* (Chicago, 1990), pp. 6–8, 95–172.

[19] Bridenbaugh, *Cities in Revolt*, pp. 293–96, 364; George B. Warden, "The Caucus and Democracy in Colonial Boston," *New England Quarterly* 43 (1970):19–45; Gary B. Nash, *The Urban Crucible: Social Change, Political Consciousness, and the Origins of the American Revolution* (Cambridge, Mass., 1979); David W. Conroy, *In Public Houses: Drink and the Revolution of Authority in Colonial Massachusetts* (Chapel Hill, 1995), esp. pp. 157–240.

In the American colonies, then, the public sphere fermenting in clubs and societies was more often one of opposition than of classical Hanoverian consensus.[20] The construction of such a consensus behind the governor's interest, however, might be attempted through the means of that same club culture. Here, it seems, lies the formal origin of Freemasonry in America, with the establishment of St. John's Lodge in Boston in July 1733, on the same day that the St. John's Grand Lodge was organized under a warrant issued by the London Grand Lodge. Formed at the height of Boston's market-regulation crisis, the lodge seems to have been part of an effort to undermine the influence of Cooke's Caucus. Gov. Jonathan Belcher's son Andrew was elected to offices in both lodges, and the governor himself (made a Mason in London in 1704), met regularly with the fraternity. In sharp contrast to the public service of the men of the Caucus, among the seven men sworn into office in St. John's Lodge in the summer of 1733, only two ever served in any public office in Boston, each serving a term as constable. Instead, the connections of Boston's earliest Masons were to the Anglican church, naval contracts, and the customs service. Accused of advocating "cheap grace" and mocked for their "pompous order," these Freemasons stood isolated in the governor's camp in Boston of the 1730s.[21]

Freemasonry in Europe could have connotations of enlightened opposition, and on occasion those connotations reverberated in the colonies. Thus a group of disaffected planters in Georgia in the 1730s banded together as a Masonic "Scotch

[20] See Warner's analysis of publication in *Letters of the Republic*, pp. 1–72; and Bernard Bailyn's discussions of the politics and culture of provincialism in *The Origins of American Politics* (New York, 1967) and *The Peopling of British North America* (New York, 1986).

[21] Harvey N. Shephard, comp., *History of Saint John's Lodge of Boston* . . . (Boston, 1917), pp. 4–12; Robert F. Seybolt, *The Town Officials of Colonial Boston, 1634–1775* (Cambridge, Mass., 1939), pp. 171, 201; Nash, *The Urban Crucible*, pp. 167, 294; David S. Shields, "Clio Mocks the Masons: Joseph Green's Anti-Masonic Satires," in J. A. Leo Lemay, ed., *Deism, Masonry, and the Enlightenment: Essays Honoring Alfred Owen Aldridge* (Newark, Del., 1987), pp. 109–26.

Club," writing satires of James Oglethorpe's utopia.[22] And, as Steven C. Bullock has demonstrated, the diffusion of insurgent Ancient Rite Freemasonry to the colonies in the 1750s brought a popularizing of the order, with Masonry spreading to urban artisans and small shopkeepers and into the rural districts.[23] But, on balance, with its deference to the metropolitan authority of the English grand lodges and its elaborate ritual and hierarchy, Masonry—especially that of the so-called Modern Rite—was more often the cultural milieu of more conservative forces in colonial society, including many who would be loyalists during the Revolution. In New York province, Sir William Johnson, the royal authority in the Mohawk valley, was a leading Freemason. In South Carolina leading Masons included William Bull II, who rose from Speaker of the House to the Governor's Council to acting governor between the 1740s and the 1770s, and Sir Egerton Leigh, the master of the grand lodge and variously the king's attorney general and surveyor general and governor's councilor. In North Carolina, Freemasonry was organized under the sponsorship of a Joseph Montfort, an English immigrant who served as clerk of courts in Halifax County and as the powerful treasurer for the province's Northern District. And in Virginia, Lord Botetourt, a highly popular governor briefly serving from 1768 to his death in 1770, as a sponsor of high culture presented an elaborate master's chair to the Williamsburg Lodge.[24]

[22] Shields, *Oracles of Empire,* p. 53.

[23] Steven C. Bullock, "The Revolutionary Transformation of American Freemasonry, 1752–1792," *William and Mary Quarterly,* 3d ser. 47 (1990):347–69.

[24] Albert G. Mackey, *The History of Freemasonry in South Carolina . . .* (1861; reprint ed., Charleston, S.C., 1936), pp. 44–52; Bridenbaugh, *Cities in Revolt,* p. 363; Thomas C. Parramore, *Launching the Craft: The First Half-Century of Freemasonry in North Carolina* (Raleigh, N.C., 1975), pp. 21–42; Rhys Isaac, *The Transformation of Virginia, 1740–1790* (Chapel Hill, 1982), pp. 213–16, 229; William M. Brown, *Freemasonry in Virginia (1733–1936)* (Richmond, 1936), p. 32; in general, see Steven C. Bullock, "The Ancient and Honorable Society: Freemasonry in America, 1730–1830," Ph.D. diss., Brown University, 1986, pp. 7–101, 103–43.

Such patronage was emblematic of the position of colonial Freemasonry. In the broader network of club culture, Freemasons alone literally drew authority from the transatlantic relationship and could claim a special legitimacy in this connection. In the last decades of the colonial era the Masonic order, followed by a gradient of genteel clubs and societies, was beginning to serve the function of a colonial extension of the unitary and consensual Hanoverian public sphere. They mobilized the moderate Enlightenment in cultural reinforcement of both local elites and royal establishments over these tumultuous provinces. Intended to stabilize the status quo, this cultural mobilization would have the opposite effect. The accelerating colonial attraction to this Hanoverian "public sphere," inextricably bound up in consumption of the whole range of British goods from teaware to country ideology, was driving colonial Americans toward dependency—and revolution.[25]

SELF-CREATED SOCIETIES, RADICAL WHIGGERY, AND THE REVOLUTION, 1765–87

Radical Whiggery, with its pessimistic assessment of human motivations and fear of corrupting imbalance, both derived and diverged from the moderate Enlightenment, running as an underground current beneath the intellectual and political establishment to explode in revolution. Rejecting the patronage and dependency epitomized by the colonial adoption of English Masonic warrants, the American Revolution would be literally an enormous project in self-creation, the assertion of popular sovereignty.[26] Freemasonry, recently emerging in the

[25] John Clive and Bernard Bailyn, "England's Cultural Provinces: Scotland and America," *William and Mary Quarterly*, 3d ser. 11 (1954):200–213; Jack P. Greene, "Search for Identity: An Interpretation of the Meaning of Selected Patterns of Social Response in Eighteenth-Century America," *Journal of Social History* 3 (1970):189–224; Timothy Breen, "'Baubles of Britain': The American and Consumer Revolutions of the Eighteenth Centuries," *Past and Present*, no. 119 (1988):73–104; Gordon S. Wood, *The Radicalism of the American Revolution* (New York, 1992), pp. 11–92.

[26] Appleby, *Capitalism and a New Social Order*, pp. 79–105.

colonies and destined to mushroom across the landscape of the early republic, played little or no role in the Revolutionary process. Revolutionary legitimacy would lie in popular consent, not ancient authority. The specific instruments of the Revolutionary project would be popular societies, in effect private voluntary associations, whose legitimacy rested in their acceptance and transformation into public governments. This was not a simple process.

From 1765 through 1776 the agents of resistance, rebellion, and revolution were organized in extralegal bodies of voluntarily associated men claiming to act in the common public interest. All of these Revolutionary associations fell somewhere on a continuum between private club and public agency. On the one hand, committees, conventions, and associations often acted with de facto governmental powers, conveyed by the authority of town meetings and constituted and provisional legislatures. On the other hand, many of these associations were literally "self-created societies," to use Washington's language of the 1790s, bodies of men organized and acting on their own authority to advance the Revolutionary cause. The Sons of Liberty were of this self-created variety, rooted in agreements drawn up by groups of merchants and artisans in the major port towns. In Boston and Charleston, the Sons of Liberty were shaped by existing social and political clubs, the Boston Caucus and Loyal Nine, the Charleston Fire Company and the Charleston Fellowship Society. There was thus a broad connection between the Sons of Liberty and the radical, oppositional side of eighteenth-century British club culture.[27] Conversely, the mainstream of the genteel club culture of the merchants and gentry stood aloof from the mechanic-based Sons of Liberty. Other than the tradition that Joseph Warren's St. Andrew's Lodge played a role in the Boston Tea Party, there was little involvement of Masonry in the Revolutionary crisis, and a large body of the colonial Masons eventually became loyalists, especially but not exclusively the

[27] Richard Walsh, *Charleston's Sons of Liberty: A Study of the Artisans* (Columbia, S.C., 1959), pp. 29–30, 38; Pauline Maier, *From Resistance to Revolution: Colonial Radicals and the Development of American Opposition to Britain, 1765–1776* (New York, 1972), pp. 85–86.

colonial elites who followed the Modern Masonic ritual sanctioned by the London Grand Lodge.[28]

In some circumstances the self-created Sons of Liberty acted with legitimacy conferred by public institutions. In Connecticut their actions were ratified by town meeting resolves, and during the Townshend Act crisis the assemblies in Connecticut, New York, and New Jersey all passed votes endorsing the nonimportation associators. In Virginia and North Carolina, a more tenuous legitimacy was conferred by meetings that included sitting representatives.[29] But the most important fusing of Revolutionary action with public authority came in the crisis years of 1774 to 1776 and most clearly in provinces where a broad unanimity of support for the whig cause could be mustered. In Massachusetts, Samuel Adams used the Boston town meeting to establish the legitimacy of a provincial network of committees of correspondence, building on the colony's experience with an extralegal convention of towns in 1768, itself modeled on the convention of 1689 during the rebellion against Gov. Edmund Andros. With the royal assumption of judicial salaries, the occupation of Boston, and the alteration of the charter in the summer of 1774, a shadow government emerged rapidly, encompassing town committees, county conventions, and a provincial congress. The language of a "Solemn League and Covenant" and the "body of the People" invoked in Boston in 1774 expressed a very self-conscious effort to tie Massachusetts's rebellion to corporate traditions running deep into the seventeenth century.[30] In Virginia in 1774 the election of representatives by

[28] Edith Steblecki, *Paul Revere and Freemasonry* (Boston, 1985), p. 27; Bernard Fäy, *Revolution and Freemasonry, 1680–1800* (Boston, 1985), pp. 238–40; Bullock, "Ancient and Honorable Society," pp. 156–60; Philip Davidson, *Propaganda and the American Revolution, 1763–1783* (Chapel Hill, 1943), pp. 100–101.

[29] Maier, *From Resistance to Revolution*, pp. 115–17.

[30] Richard D. Brown, *Revolutionary Politics in Massachusetts: The Boston Committee of Correspondence and the Towns, 1772–1774* (Cambridge, Mass., 1970); idem, "The Massachusetts Convention of Towns, 1768" *William and Mary Quarterly*, 3d ser. 26 (1969):94–104; Richard C. Simmons, "The Massachusetts Revolution of 1689: Three Early American Broadsides," *Journal of American Studies* 2 (1968):1–12; Nash, *Urban Crucible*, pp. 356–62.

county constituencies conveyed legitimacy upon a provincial convention, which in turn authorized a network of county committees of correspondence and safety. The county courthouses, long the focus of civil ritual in Virginia, were the site of elaborate public rituals in which the gentry brought the Revolution to the people of Virginia. In both New England and in Virginia, popular consensus and provincial traditions meant that Revolutionary institutions rapidly assumed de facto governmental powers. In reality extralegal and "private," these institutions claimed and received allegiance as legitimate public bodies.[31]

The Revolutionary process was not so smooth where the whig cause was vigorously contested by loyalist forces or undermined by neutralism; in these places the Revolutionary institutions retained the character of self-created societies struggling in a very contested arena. In New York, the Revolutionary committees began in mass meetings and crowd actions held in New York City in response to the Coercive Acts, the Continental Association, and the fighting at Lexington and Concord, but it was not until the summer of 1775 that a public convention would be formed. Rooted in the constituencies of the Sons of Liberty, the committees continued to struggle for power with both loyalism and the new state assembly.[32] In Pennsylvania the struggle was even more pronounced. Given the refusal of the proprietary legislature to sanction resistance into 1776, the committee movement was literally self-created, based upon the votes of meetings of interested activists rather than even a fiction of the population as a whole. The voluntary organization of the Revolution in Pennsylvania was realized in the Associators, who constituted

[31] John E. Selby, *The Revolution in Virginia, 1775–1783* (Williamsburg, 1988), pp. 8–10; Isaac, *Transformation of Virginia*, pp. 310–11; idem, "Dramatizing the Ideology of Revolution: Popular Mobilization in Virginia," *William and Mary Quarterly*, 3d ser. 33 (1976):357–85; Jack P. Greene, "'Virtus et Libertas': Political Culture, Social Change, and the Origins of the American Revolution in Virginia, 1763–1766," in Jeffery J. Crow and Larry E. Tise, eds., *The Southern Experience in the American Revolution* (Chapel Hill, 1978), pp. 55–108.

[32] Edward Countryman, *A People in Revolution: The American Revolution and Political Society in New York, 1760–1790* (Baltimore, 1981), pp. 123–30, 135–54, 169–90; Nash, *Urban Crucible*, pp. 369–74.

themselves a militia without any public sanction, on the model of voluntary subscription established by the Benjamin Franklin's Associator militia in 1748. This indeterminate voluntarism also was manifested in the constitutional convention of 1776, called on the initiative of the Philadelphia committee and producing a constitution whose legitimacy was contested until it was totally revised in 1790.[33] Farther south, key Revolutionary associations grew out of the voluntary action required to administer urban places that had little in the way of public services. The Sons of Liberty in Maryland were directly rooted in a group of artisans and merchants known as the Baltimore Mechanical Company, formed in 1763 to police the streets and fight fires. In Charleston the Sons of Liberty were constituted as the Charleston Fire Company, which, with the membership of groups like the Fellowship Society and the Wilkes Society, shaped the origins of a "General Meeting of Inhabitants . . . at the Liberty Tree" Tavern, which served as a focus of extralegal organization through the 1770s.[34]

John Shy has argued that all Revolutionary institutions were in fact private and voluntary, whether or not they claimed public authority. What mattered was the conferral of a de facto legitimacy from a united people, as in Massachusetts or Virginia, as against struggle as self-created societies in a conflicted polity, as in Pennsylvania and New York. This distinction would have important implications for the contest over association and a public sphere in the 1790s.[35]

---

[33] Nash, *Urban Crucible,* pp. 231–32, 377–79; Richard A. Ryerson, *The Revolution Is Now Begun: The Radical Committees of Philadelphia, 1765–1776* (Philadelphia, 1978), pp. 25–64, 89–115, 202–6, 241; Steven Rosswurm, *Arms, Country, and Class: The Philadelphia Militia and the "Lower Sort" during the American Revolution, 1775–1783* (New Brunswick, N.J., 1987), pp. 49–53; Wood, *Creation of the American Republic,* pp. 335–36.

[34] Ronald Hoffman, *A Spirit of Dissension: Economics, Politics, and the Revolution in Maryland* (Baltimore, 1973), pp. 38–41; Maier, *Resistance to Revolution,* p. 85; idem, "The Charleston Mob and the Evolution of Popular Politics in Revolutionary South Carolina, 1765–1784," *Perspectives in American History* 4 (1970):183.

[35] John Shy, *A People Numerous and Armed: Reflections on the Military Struggle for American Independence* (New York, 1976), pp. 174–76.

Both publicly sanctioned and self-created Revolutionary institutions continued to act into the late 1770s and 1780s, and increasingly both became the focus of concern of conservative forces seeking to restore order and to defend property. In parts of Massachusetts county conventions claimed public authority, first in the absence of a popularly ratified constitution and then as ongoing meetings of county communities, gathered under the protection of the state bill of rights to confer and to instruct and petition the legislature. From 1776 until 1780 the Berkshire Constitutionalists used conventions to oppose the restoration of civil courts until a new state constitution was written and ratified. After 1781 county conventions met throughout the state both to discuss growing problems of the economic depression and to criticize the structure of government under the new constitution, particularly the courts. During Eli's and Shays's rebellions the conventions and the bodies of Regulators associated with them claimed popular sanction for their petitions and crowd actions, claims often rooted in votes taken in town meetings. As elsewhere in the new states, their opponents questioned the right of the conventions to act in the public interest: they were "smaller bodies of men in the form and semblance of representative bodies" that had no place under the constitution. After Shays's Rebellion the conventions' claims to public authority were abandoned, and it would be another decade before the possibility of organizing such interests into political parties would begin to be explored.[36]

[36] Robert J. Taylor, *Western Massachusetts in the Revolution* (Providence, 1954), pp. 75–143; J. R. Pole, *Political Representation in England and the Origins of the American Republic* (New York, 1966), pp. 235–39; Van Beck Hall, *Politics without Parties: Massachusetts, 1780–1791* (Pittsburgh, 1972), pp. 178–84; David Szatmary, *Shays' Rebellion: The Making of an Agrarian Insurrection* (Amherst, Mass., 1980), pp. 38–40; John L. Brooke, "'To the Quiet of the People': Revolutionary Settlements and Civil Unrest in Western Massachusetts, 1774–1789," *William and Mary Quarterly*, 3d ser. 46 (1989):425–62. A significant number of the delegates to these conventions—and the local leaders of Shays's Rebellion—were tavernkeepers. See Szatmary, *Shays' Rebellion*, p. 64; Conroy, *In Public Houses*, p. 311; John L. Brooke, *The Heart of the Commonwealth: Society and Political Culture in Worcester County, Massachusetts, 1713–1861* (Cambridge, 1989), pp. 205, 218.

Conventions of the people would meet in New Hampshire and Vermont in 1786, but elsewhere in the Confederation radical politics was carried on by voluntary association. In New York the conflict between the popular committees and the state assembly persisted through the 1770s, and in Boston, Philadelphia, Baltimore, and Charleston private societies, rooted in the constituencies of the Sons of Liberty, formed to act against loyalists. In Baltimore the militant Whig Club was condemned by Maryland's Provisional Council of Safety for its violent actions against loyalists and nonassociators alike.[37] In Philadelphia a Whig Society formed in 1777 to act against loyalists after the British occupation evolved into the Constitutional Society, associated with the Committee of Privates and dedicated to defending Pennsylvania's radical constitution; they were opposed by a similarly organized Republican Society, which was linked with the First City Troop, Light Horse, which, in turn, was rooted in social hunting clubs among the gentry. In Georgia's factional politics of the 1770s, the radicals of St. John's Parish and their backcountry allies were organized as the Liberty Society, labeled the Nocturnal Club by their conservative antagonists.[38] In Charleston during the 1780s the Anti-Britannic Marine Society, mobilizing a "democratic faction" of artisans, lesser tradesmen, and sailors hard hit by the postwar depression, was rooted in a fabric of social, political, and benevolent societies stretching back to the 1760s: the Fellowship, John Wilkes, Palmetto, and Carpenters' societies, and wider circle of Liberty Tree men. And in localities throughout the country, the economic crisis of 1785–86 spawned not only public conventions and Regulator companies who acted for a redress of public grievances but a proliferation of private debtor's societies like the Reformation Men of Gloucester, Rhode Is-

[37] Countryman, *A People in Revolution;* Hoffman, *Spirit of Dissension,* pp. 164–65, 184, 188; Eugene Perry Link, *Democratic-Republican Societies, 1790–1800* (New York, 1942), pp. 26–27.

[38] Link, *Democratic-Republican Societies,* pp. 27–28; Rosswurm, *Arms, Country, and Class,* pp. 66–72, 176–77, 224–25; Harvey J. Jackson, "The Rise of the Western Members: Revolutionary Politics and the Georgia Backcountry," in Ronald Hoffman, Thad W. Tate, and Peter J. Albert, eds., *An Uncivil War: The Southern Backcountry during the American Revolution* (Charlottesville, Va., 1985), p. 299.

land, and surrounding towns who stood pledged to defend their fellow members' property from sheriff's sale.[39]

The nationalist initiatives to revise the Articles of Confederation and ultimately to replace it with the federal Constitution brought the emergence of yet another set of societies. In the summer of 1784 a group of prominent Virginians formed a society to protect the Confederation "from the innovations of ambition, and the designs of faction . . . by giving free and frequent information to the mass of the people." Many of the subscribers, including John Blair and James Madison, would in fact support constitutional "innovations" three years later, and one of the fundamental problems of the Antifederalist cause was their lack of institutional or rhetorical access to the public sphere. A Society for Political Enquiries, formed in Philadelphia in February 1787, had a profile quite similar to the Virginia group. Dedicated to understanding the "arduous and complicated science of government," this society had a bipartisan membership, but the leading roles of Benjamin Franklin and George Clymer suggest that it probably threw its influence on the side of the Constitution. Societies such as the Political Club of Danville, Kentucky, and the Whig Society, of Wytheville, Virginia, provided a focus for Antifederalism in a few localities. In New York City Gen. John Lamb, once of the Sons of Liberty, established a Federal Republican Committee and proposed to leading Antifederalists in other states the establishment of a network of societies to coordinate efforts to stop the Constitution. When the rush of state ratification overtook their planning, Republican societies in Virginia, New York, and Pennsylvania formed to demand the adoption of a Bill of Rights. The New York society urged groups in other states, and in the various New York counties, to establish societies and to work for amendments. Their support of George Clinton for vice-president was ratified by a similar group in Pennsylvania.[40]

[39] Walsh, *Charleston's Sons of Liberty*, pp. 115–16; Maier, "Charleston Mob"; Brooke, *Heart of the Commonwealth*, pp. 201–5; Szatmary, *Shays' Rebellion*, pp. 124–26.

[40] J. G. R. Hamilton, "A Society for Preservation of Liberty, 1784," *American Historical Review* 32 (1927):550–52; Isaac Leake, *Memoir of the Life and*

Of these Revolutionary institutions continuing to act into the 1780s, the county convention movement was doomed to disappear. The purest form of the Commonwealth whig tradition, the county conventions had acted as representations of the people, a continuing manifestation of direct democracy. If the public conventions flourished briefly in corporate New England, voluntary societies were more in evidence in the conflicted Mid-Atlantic and South. Often they had antecedents in the tavern culture of the colonial seaports; their failure to forge effective links with each other and with the world of print culture contributed in great measure to their failure to capture a critical margin of public opinion in 1787–88. Out of the orbit of these societies would emerge the institutional manifestation of the revolutionary Enlightenment—the Democratic-Republican societies of 1793–95.[41] But before this reemergence of organized radicalism, and in great measure explaining its defeat in the 1780s, another, much more powerful force in cultural politics had emerged, working to reshape the public mind.

NATIONALISTS AND A CONSENSUAL PUBLIC SPHERE, 1776–93

Revolutionary politics was carried forward by radical Whig associationalism, but the Revolution was consolidated by men who reasserted the classical public sphere and the moderate Enlightenment. They would claim more ancient authority than either public conventions or self-created societies of the people.

While civilian Masonic institutions from Massachusetts to South Carolina divided and then virtually collapsed with the onset of war, Freemasonry reemerged on a very different foot-

---

Times of General John Lamb (Albany, 1857), pp. 304–41; Link, *Democratic-Republican Societies*, pp. 17, 31–34; Robert A. Rutland, *The Birth of the Bill of Rights, 1776–1791* (1955; reprint ed., Boston, 1983), pp. 157, 160, 188; *Rules and Regulations for the Society for Political Enquiries* (Philadelphia, 1787); Harry M. Tinkcom, *Republicans and Federalists in Pennsylvania, 1790–1801* (Harrisburg, Pa., 1959), pp. 81–83.

[41] Link, *Democratic-Republican Societies*, pp. 19–70.

ing among the officers of the Continental army. Numbering ten lodges by the end of the war, military Freemasonry provided intellectual identity and social fraternity for American officers, just as it did in the British army. Briefly superseded by the Society of the Cincinnati, the Masonic lodges established by former Continental officers became a critical bulwark for nationalist and Federalist efforts to reshape policy and political culture in the Confederation era. Explicitly espousing moderation, order, and virtue, and claiming to transcend political divisions, Freemasonry provided a rich body of symbol and ritual and a cadre of like-minded men to reinforce Federalist efforts to establish a unitary, consensual public sphere in the young republic. And Freemasonry in the young republic, military or civilian, would claim a legitimacy distinct from other contemporary associations and that of colonial Freemasonry. Before the Revolution warrants granted by the English grand lodges, almost like charters of colonial government, gave American Freemasonry a special authority and a sense of distinction over other societies. Now, with the break with England, American Freemasonry would declare its own independence from Britain, but it also continued its claim to a special legitimacy.[42] This legitimacy came from the

[42] When white Freemasons declared their independence from England, they did not include their black brethren, with the result that African-American Freemasonry to this day derives its Masonic authority from an English lodge warrant. Prince Hall, a free black from the West Indies, was made a Mason by a British military lodge in Boston in March 1775. In 1784, after his African Lodge was denied a warrant by the Massachusetts grand lodge, Hall petitioned the Modern Grand Lodge in London for a charter, which was received in 1787 and enlarged into a grand lodge warrant in 1791. From Boston, Prince Hall's Masonic authority by 1797 spread to Newport and Philadelphia, where Richard Allen, James Forten, and Absalom Jones were early Masonic leaders, and by 1812 to New York City. The English authority for Prince Hall's grand lodge Freemasonry fit into a broader pattern of African-American political culture in the early republic. Since the Somerset decision of 1772, Britain stood as the center of abolitionist aspirations, especially in the increasingly explicit racist climate in the United States. Such as they were, American blacks' white allies were Federalists, and in Boston blacks inclined toward Federalism, Prince Hall volunteering the services of the lodge against the Shaysite rebels in 1786, and Boston blacks voting Federalist in the 1790s. Out of this uneasy connection among English emancipationism, Federalist philanthropy, and the

claims of Masonic history to ancient origins, running back to Solomon and even to Adam. An ancient institution, surviving the trials of the entire span of human history, Masonry would provide a beacon of stability and virtue for the new republic.[43]

The development of Continental Masonry began among the officers of the Connecticut Line, stationed in Dorchester, Massachusetts, during the siege of Boston. Chartered by the St. John's Grand Lodge in February 1776, the organization of the American Union Lodge was delayed until the winter encampment of 1778–79 at Redding, Connecticut, where officers and locals mingled in Masonic fraternity. The following June the American Union Lodge celebrated the festival of St. John the Baptist at West Point with General Washington, and by the following December Freemasonry had spread so widely that a St. John's Day ceremony at the Morristown encampment was attended by 104 officers, again led by Washington. Out of this day of ritual emerged a plan to form a national grand lodge, and in February 1780 a convention of delegates from military lodges proposed such a plan with George Washington to sit as grand master.[44]

Steven Bullock's recent study of Freemasonry provides a

---

black communities of the northern cities would emerge a central strand of American abolitionism. William H. Grimshaw, *Official History of Freemasonry among the Colored People in North America* (1903; reprint ed., New York, 1969), pp. 67–95, 108–12, 124–27; Sidney Kaplan and Emma N. Kaplan, *The Black Presence in the Era of the American Revolution*, rev. ed. (Amherst, Mass., 1989), pp. 202–14; Gary B. Nash, *Forging Freedom: The Formation of Philadelphia's Black Community, 1720–1840* (Cambridge, Mass., 1988), pp. 218–19; Linda K. Kerber, *Federalists in Dissent: Imagery and Ideology in Jeffersonian America* (Ithaca, N.Y., 1970), pp. 23–66; David Grimsted, "Anglo-American Racism and Phillis Wheatley's 'Sable Veil,' 'Length'ned Chain,' and 'Knitted Heart,'" in Ronald Hoffman and Peter J. Albert, eds., *Women in the Age of the American Revolution* (Charlottesville, Va., 1989), pp. 383–94, 440–41; Samuel Eliot Morison, *Harrison Gray Otis, 1765–1848: The Urbane Federalist* (Boston, 1969), p. 155.

[43] See discussions of post-Revolutionary Masonic independence and biblicism in Bullock, "Ancient and Honorable Society," pp. 160–65, 273–82.

[44] Ibid., pp. 148–49, 166–84; Dorothy Ann Lipson, *Freemasonry in Federalist Connecticut, 1789–1815* (Princeton, 1977), pp. 60–61; Ronald E. Heaton, *Masonic Membership of the Founding Fathers* (Silver Spring, Md., 1974), p. 74.

powerful explanation of its attraction for the Continental officers. The war posed critical problems of personal and social identity for men rising to ranks of command, often of relatively ordinary backgrounds. As Bullock argues, "For men uncertain of their honor and fearful of their reputation among their peers, their subordinates, and their superiors, Freemasonry provided the public honor they craved." The order associated them with Washington, who had set the standard of a gentleman officer corps in the first place, and with a pantheon of fallen Masonic heroes.[45]

If these officers saw a national grand lodge as a further avenue to honor and distinction, they were to be disappointed. The Pennsylvania Grand Lodge enthusiastically ratified the plan for a national grand lodge, but one of two competing grand lodges in Massachusetts was opposed, concerned about the differences between Modern and Ancient rituals observed in various parts of the Confederation.[46] Army officers soon turned their attention to forming a national society that no civilian could control. As its most recent historian has put it, the Society of the Cincinnati "began as a mutiny moderated into an organization." In May 1783, following the abortive conspiracy against the Confederation government, Continental officers met in their newly constructed "temple of virtue" in the Newburgh cantonment to establish a fraternity of brother officers. Their purposes were mutual charity, continuing affiliation, and political advocacy—in the interest of obtaining their back pay. As Bullock emphasizes, the Cincinnati offered the same rewards of status, honor, and distinction as did Freemasonry: exclusive membership in a society with branches in states and counties throughout the Confederation, an ornate badge that replaced the insignia of rank when the officers demobilized and lost their uniforms, and the promise of a hereditary transfer to generations to come.[47]

---

[45] Bullock, "Ancient and Honorable Society," pp. 183–84; see also Charles Royster, *A Revolutionary People at War: The Continental Army and American Character, 1775–1783* (Chapel Hill, 1979), pp. 88–96, 206–10.

[46] Bullock, "Ancient and Honorable Society," pp. 149–52.

[47] Minor Myers, *Liberty without Anarchy: A History of the Society of the Cincinnati* (Charlottesville, Va., 1983), pp. 1, 11, 13–14; Bullock, "Ancient and

While the Cincinnati became an important focus for nationalist sentiment, hostile to the popular politics pursued by both state legislatures and the radical Whig associations, Freemasonry did not disappear. In fact, as the Cincinnati came under attack from a variety of directions as an exclusive society that sought to impose its own interest upon the government, Freemasonry rapidly reemerged as a key vehicle of nationalist affiliation. The height of the political assault on the Cincinnati dated to 1783–85, and perhaps not coincidentally the reorganization of grand lodges in the states began in earnest in 1786. One grand lodge, that of Virginia, was formed in 1778, seven others in 1786 and 1787, and another five (all in New England) between 1789 and 1794. The constituencies of the Cincinnati and Freemasonry were very similar—more than a third of the original Cincinnati members in Connecticut and Pennsylvania were also Masons—and they responded to similar symbolic appeals. Joel Barlow, who joined the lodge in Hartford in 1788, could invoke before the Connecticut Cincinnati in 1787 the same pantheon of Revolutionary martyrs—Joseph Warren, David Wooster, and Richard Montgomery—as were repeatedly acclaimed by Masonic orators. Masonry would provide the rock upon which public culture—perhaps a unitary public sphere—in a new national republic might be constructed.[48]

Both the Cincinnati and Freemasons proved to be loyal soldiers in the struggle for a national constitution. Not bound by strictures against political agitation, orators addressing the Cincinnati societies in the summer of 1787 made passionate appeals for support for the Federalist cause. This was not to

Honorable Society," pp. 184–86; Richard H. Kohn, *Eagle and Sword: The Federalists and the Creation of the Military Establishment in America, 1783–1802* (New York, 1975), pp. 17–39; Merrill Jensen, *The New Nation: A History of the United States during the Confederation, 1781–1789* (New York, 1950), pp. 261–65.

[48] Bullock, "Ancient and Honorable Society," pp. 184–91; Myers, *Liberty without Anarchy*, p. 136; Webb, *Freemason's Monitor* (1805), pp. 297, 299–300, 302–3, 305, 307–10, 313–14, 316; Joel Barlow, *An Oration, Delivered at the North Church in Hartford, at the Meeting of the Connecticut Society of the Cincinnati, July 4th 1787 . . .* (Hartford, 1787), pp. 8–9.

be interpreted as partisanship; members who advocated the Constitution were "slaves to no party, but servants of the whole," Joel Barlow told the Connecticut Cincinnati. Reviling "the tumult and confusion of unwieldy popular assemblies," Robert R. Livingston urged the New York Cincinnati "to reject the trammels of party and call every man to his post, his abilities and virtues entitle him to occupy." The Cincinnati were associated under "benevolent principles" and, given their experience and station, were obliged to act as a catalyst for political change while the Revolution was "still unfinished." "It becomes the strongest duty of the social connexion," Barlow urged, "to enlighten and harmonize the minds of our fellow citizens." Their influence was to be as much by example as by argument: "Those possessed of abilities or information in any degree" were "to diffuse a spirit of candour and rational enquiry." [49]

Such rhetoric clashed with Washington's growing concerns about the society. Responding to Thomas Jefferson's warnings that he might lose popular credibility if he did not distance himself from the Cincinnati's apparent plan to found a national aristocracy—and perhaps a monarchy—he demanded that the society be reformed, telling its national meeting in Philadelphia in May 1787 to abandon the hereditary plan, to halt all national conventions, to stop wearing the society's badge, and to eliminate any part of their constitution "which has a political tendency." [50] Even if Washington had asked that they withdraw from politics, the Cincinnati were very much in evidence at the Philadelphia Constitutional Convention, numbering twenty-one among the fifty-five delegates. Though they were not united in their proposals in the convention, they were the target of Antifederalist hostility. Echoing Jefferson's advice to Washington, Elbridge Gerry of

[49] Barlow, *An Oration*, pp. 13–14; Robert R. Livingston, *An Oration, Delivered before the Society of the Cincinnati of the State of New-York . . . the Fourth Day of July* (New York, 1787), pp. 5, 7, 18.

[50] Myers, *Liberty without Anarchy*, pp. 94–97; James Thomas Flexner, *George Washington and the New Nation (1783–1793)* (Boston, 1969), pp. 63–68; Garry Wills, *Cincinnatus: George Washington and the Enlightenment* (Garden City, N.Y., 1984), pp. 138–48.

Massachusetts feared the overriding influence of national societies.

> The ignorance of the people would put it in the power of some one set of men dispersed throughout the Union & acting in concert to delude them in any appointment. He observed that such a Society existed in the Order of the Cincinnati. They are respectable, United, and influential. They will in fact elect the chief Magistrate in every instance, if the election is referred to the people. His respect for the characters composing this Society could not blind him to the danger & impropriety of throwing such a power into their hands.[51]

Gerry's concern was borne out in the state ratifying conventions, where both Cincinnati and Masons were solidly—if not unanimously—ranked behind the Constitution. According to Minor Myers, among perhaps ninety Cincinnati members sitting as delegates in the state conventions, only nineteen voted against ratification, including eleven in Virginia, four in North Carolina, and two each in South Carolina and New York.[52]

Two weeks after Pennsylvania ratified the Constitution, Masonic orator Charles Smith exhorted the Friendship Lodge in the frontier town of Sunbury to "anticipate, with joy, the happy period, when influenced by an efficient FEDERAL GOVERNMENT, even the remote wilds around us will become the habitations of a virtuous people." In a preface to his printed speech, Smith offered an apology of sorts for having strayed from "the ordinary method of *masonic* orations," and he seems to have been one of the very few to do so.[53] But if Masons publicly avoided the nationalist discourse that emerged from

[51] Myers, *Liberty without Anarchy*, pp. 98–102; Gerry quotation p. 99.

[52] Ibid., pp. 103–6. Myers simply states that all Cincinnati delegates in Pennsylvania, Delaware, Maryland, and New Hampshire voted to ratify, without providing any figures. Otherwise the Cincinnati delegates split 50–19 for the Constitution. Jackson Turner Main, *The Antifederalists: Critics of the Constitution, 1781–1788* (Chapel Hill, 1961), p. 191, notes ten Federalist Cincinnati delegates in Pennsylvania.

[53] Charles Smith, *Oration, Delivered in the Town of Sunbury . . .* (Philadelphia, 1788), p. 28.

the meetings of the Cincinnati, they certainly supported the Constitution. In eight states, among the eighty-three towns, districts, or counties where Masonic lodges were located, the delegates from sixty-four voted to ratify while those from eighteen were opposed.[54] Equally important, leading Masons in the grand lodges of all of the states except Massachusetts and Pennsylvania were Federalist partisans in 1787 and 1788. These included John Sullivan in New Hampshire, Pierpont Edwards in Connecticut, Jabez Bowen in Rhode Island, Robert R. Livingston in New York, David Brearley in New Jersey, John Blair, Edmund Randolph, and John Marshall in Virginia, Samuel Johnson and William R. Davie in North Carolina, John F. Grimké of South Carolina, and James Jackson of Georgia, all grand masters between 1787 and 1789 or within a very few years.[55]

[54] The states in this count are New Hampshire, Massachusetts, Connecticut, New York, Pennsylvania, Maryland, Virginia, and South Carolina. The Federalist towns, counties, and districts had 107 lodges, and the Antifederalist localities had 23. Two other towns with lodges in Massachusetts and Connecticut, and one Pennsylvania county, were divided evenly on the Constitution. Given the unanimous votes in Delaware, New Jersey, and Georgia, the late vote in Rhode Island, and the wide swings in the vote in North Carolina, these states were not included. Ratification votes from Orin G. Libby, *The Geographic Distribution of the Vote of the Thirteen States on the Federal Constitution, 1787–1788* (Madison, Wis., 1894), pp. 110–16. Lodges from: *Proceedings in Masonry . . . 1733–92* (Boston, 1895), pp. 482–86 (includes New Hampshire lodges until 1789); James R. Case, *Historical Sketch of the Grand Lodge of Connecticut, Organized July 8, 1789* (Hartford, 1963), pp. 1–5; *Transactions of the Grand Lodge of Free and Accepted Masons of the State of New York, 1816–1827* (New York, 1880), pp. 120–29; *The Grand Lodge of . . . Free and Accepted Masons . . . in Pennsylvania . . .* (Philadelphia, 1877), appendix pp. 1–9; Schultz, *Freemasonry in Maryland,* 1:149–50; Brown, *Freemasonry in Virginia,* pp. 73–74; Mackey, *Freemasonry in South Carolina,* pp. 63–68, 73, 533–79.

[55] Grand officers from: Harry M. Cheney, *Symbolic Freemasonry in New Hampshire* (Concord, N.H., 1934), p. 273; Henry W. Rugg, *History of Freemasonry in Rhode Island* (Providence, 1895), p. 748; Case, *Historical Sketch,* p. 22; Ossian Lang, *History of Freemasonry in the State of New York* (New York, 1922), p. 210; R. W. David McGregor, *History of Freemasonry in New Jersey* (N.p., 1937), p. 144; Brown, *Freemasonry in Virginia,* p. 167; Earley W. Bridges, *The Masonic Governors of North Carolina* (Greensboro, N.C., 1937), pp. 20–39, 89–124; William H. Rosier and Frederick L. Pearson, Jr., *The Grand*

On April 30, 1789, on a small balcony on the second floor of Federal Hall in New York City, George Washington was sworn in as the first president of the United States. The oath was administered by Robert R. Livingston, chancellor of the state of New York, grand master of the New York Grand Lodge, and an honorary member of the Society of the Cincinnati. As if to seal Freemasonry to this formative event, Livingston used a great bible hastily borrowed from the city's St. John's Lodge No. 1. For the next four to five years Masonry would continue to play a central role in Federalist efforts to shape a seamless unity of culture and polity in the young republic.[56]

Some Masons and Cincinnati members benefited from the ratification process quite directly, as the Confederation Congress granted the petition of the Ohio Company to take up land in the West. The settlements at Marietta, led by Rufus Putnam, would be dominated by Cincinnati members, and the old American Union Lodge, once of the Continental Line, was transferred to the Ohio settlements, becoming a focus of

---

Lodge of Georgia, Free and Accepted Masons, 1786–1980 (Macon, Ga., 1983), pp. 244–45; Mackey, *Freemasonry in South Carolina*, pp. 77–82; William R. Denslow, ed., *Ten Thousand Famous Masons*, 4 vols. (Trenton, Mo., 1961), 1:102, 108; 3:94–95; 4:10, 207. Federal offices from Linda Grant DePauw, ed., *Senate Executive Journal and Related Documents*, Documentary History of the First Federal Congress of the United States of America, March 4, 1789–March 3, 1791, vol. 2 (Baltimore, 1974), pp. 484, 539, 552; Delbert H. Gilpatrick, *Jeffersonian Democracy in North Carolina, 1789–1816* (New York, 1931), p. 32; Forrest McDonald, *We the People: The Economic Origins of the Constitution* (Chicago, 1958), p. 219.

[56] Flexner, *Washington and the New Nation*, p. 187; Denslow, ed., *Ten Thousand Famous Masons*, 3:94; George Dangerfield, *Chancellor Robert R. Livingston of New York, 1746–1813* (New York, 1960), p. 242; Rufus W. Griswold, *The Republican Court, or, American Society in the Days of Washington* (New York, 1855), pp. 138–42. For discussions of the role of Freemasonry in the construction of patriot loyalism in late eighteenth–century Britain, see John Money, "Freemasonry and the Fabric of Loyalism in Hanoverian England," in Eckhart Hellmuth, ed., *The Transformation of Political Culture: England and Germany in the Late Eighteenth Century* (Oxford, 1990), pp. 235–71; John Money, "The Masonic Moment, or, Ritual, Replica, and Credit: John Wilkes, the Macaroni Parson, and the Making of the Middle–Class Mind," *Journal of British Studies* 32 (1993): 358–95; and Colley, *Britons*, p. 227.

elite affiliation in this first midwestern society.[57] More importantly, Masons and Cincinnati members also functioned as a pool of trusted men in the appointments made by the first administration. These societies provided a social equivalent of the constitutional "filter" that Federalists felt would select the natural elite for national service. As Lisle A. Rose has summarized in his study of southern Federalism, "In large measure it was the membership of the Cincinnati Society, responding to appeals and favors of both Washington and Alexander Hamilton, that initially fulfilled Hamilton's desire to build nationwide partisan interests that would defend and protect a national administration and its policies."[58] Similarly, leading Freemasons who had supported the Constitution were also rewarded with federal appointments as judges, district attorneys, and commissioners of loans and distilled spirits, including—of those already mentioned—Sullivan, Edwards, Bowen, Brearley, Blair, Marshall, Randolph, and Davie, as well as Noah Smith of Vermont, Gunning Bedford of Delaware, and William Drayton of South Carolina.[59]

In tandem with filling executive posts in the new federal government, Washington and the Federalists turned their attention to another dimension of the public sphere: the self-conscious creation of a ritual and aesthetic environment—a veritable civic theater in a "republican court"—that would visually and socially reinforce the new government's authority and legitimacy. Here again the national societies played a critical role, of which the Masonic cornerstone ceremony on Capitol Hill was probably the most elaborated. Federalist aesthetics were fundamentally influenced by one man, Pierre Charles L'Enfant, a French volunteer officer in the Revolution who designed ceremonial pavilions and the badge for the Society of the Cincinnati before redesigning New York's Federal

---

[57] Myers, *Liberty without Anarchy*, pp. 107–14; *History of the American Union Lodge No. 1, Free and Accepted Masons of Ohio, 1776–1933* (Marietta, Ohio, 1933).

[58] Lisle A. Rose, *Prologue to Democracy: The Federalists in the South, 1789–1800* (Lexington, Ky., 1968), pp. 19–20.

[59] DePauw, ed., *Senate Executive Journal*, pp. 484, 489, 517–18, 523, 527, 529, 539, 543, 547–48, 552–53.

Hall and laying out the original plan for the District of Columbia. L'Enfant's badge was certainly in evidence at July
Fourth festivities and at Washington's levees and labored
birthday celebrations, even if Washington refused to wear it
after 1787. And both the Cincinnati and the Freemasons were
in constant attendance when Washington made his northern
and southern tours in 1789, 1790, and 1791, virtual royal
progresses through a relatively calm and peaceful new republic. On a single day in Boston in October 1789, he formally
received the Congregational clergy, the Society of the Cincinnati, and the representatives of the House and governor. In
Newport, the following August he received in series the
mayor, the clergy, and the local Freemasons; later that month,
leaving New York City for the South, he was escorted by a
procession including the Cincinnati. Entering Charleston in
May 1791 on a flotilla of ceremonial barges, Washington was
greeted by civil officials, the Cincinnati, and the York Grand
Lodge; a week later he was welcomed to Savannah by Gen.
James Jackson, past grand master of the Georgia Grand
Lodge, and dined with the Cincinnati several nights later.[60]

Washington's role in the cornerstone ceremony on Capitol
Hill two years later thus drew upon an established symbiosis
of presidential tours and the rituals of national societies. But
here Freemasonry had a particularly prominent role, given
its symbolic traditions of architectural construction. The September 1793 ceremony was only the most elaborate of many
such occasions. Masons marched and officiated at cornerstone
ceremonies for state houses from Massachusetts to Virginia.
In Washington the ceremony at Capitol Hill was the third
such event in two years, though the first to feature Washington in a presiding role. Masonic lodges had turned out for the
laying of the cornerstone of the District itself in April 1791
and the cornerstone of the White House in October 1792.[61]
In the receptions and celebrations of 1789 through 1793, the

[60] Flexner, *Washington and the New Nation*, pp. 172–79, 182–85, 228–31,
269, 286–91, 325–26; Griswold, *Republican Court*, pp. 177–78, 190–91, 227–
29, 277–83; Mackey, *Freemasonry in South Carolina*, pp. 83–85.

[61] Varnum, *Seat of Government*, pp. 29–30; Wilhelmus Bogart Bryan, *History of the National Capital from Its Foundation through the Period of the Adoption*

memory of common Continental service charismatically bound the national hero to local cadres of gentry, each reinforcing the legitimacy of the other. As Robert Wiebe puts it, wherever Washington "stood, the greatest revolutionary authority came to rest." The national societies were the institutional vehicle for perpetuating this charismatic memory and for associating it with points of authority on the republic's landscape. Extending Wiebe's analysis, the societies articulated in ritual form a unitary hierarchy of "first characters" running from the hero Washington to state, county, and local notables. This hierarchy of legitimating character and virtue comprised the social core of the Federalist public sphere.[62]

The Federalist construction of a consensual and unitary public sphere went far beyond the compass of the national societies and their framing ceremonies. As Richard D. Brown has demonstrated for Massachusetts, the 1790s saw an explosive proliferation of secular voluntary societies.[63] While many of these were Masonic lodges, and growth in the number of lodges was a national pattern, a large—and ultimately indeterminate—number were local debating societies and social libraries that often served as nodes in the broader Federalist public sphere. It was in these societies that little knots of gentry met in the late 1780s and 1790s to discuss literature, write essays, recite classical plays, and to debate public issues.

The Minervaean Society of Brookfield, Massachusetts, was an archetype of Federalist associationalism. The society was formed in the summer of 1787 by a group of gentry who recently had opposed the rising of Regulator insurgents in

---

of the Organic Act (New York, 1914), p. 204; Schultz, *Freemasonry in Maryland,* 1:414; Gerald W. Mullin, *Flight and Rebellion: Slave Resistance in Eighteenth-Century Virginia* (New York, 1972), p. 138; Steblecki, *Paul Revere and Freemasonry,* pp. 55–56.

[62] Wiebe, *Opening of American Society,* pp. 35–66, esp. pp. 43–44.

[63] Richard D. Brown's data on voluntary association in eighteenth-century Massachusetts indicates that lodges were an important part of the expansion of voluntary societies in the 1790s (Brown, "The Emergence of Urban Society in Rural Massachusetts, 1760–1820," *Journal of American History* 61 [1974]:40–41; see Appendix, table 2).

Shays's Rebellion. Assembling under the Congregational minister Nathan Fiske, society members wrote essays for the "Worcester Speculator" in Isaiah Thomas's *Massachusetts Spy,* presented "declamations" from classical plays and speeches, and engaged in "forensics" and "extempore disputes" on moral and public issues, the questions then put to a vote of the membership. Thus on January 1, 1790, after a four-way debate, the society voted that there should be no "discrimination among public creditors" between original noteholders and speculators. In subsequent meetings the society voted in favor of similarly conservative measures—that the state legislature had no right to instruct federal representatives, that imprisonment for debt was just, and that the loyalists ought to be naturalized. This group thus created a local public sphere of criticism and consensus on the model of the clubs of early Georgian England; appropriately, their president, Nathan Fiske, was compared with Addison. In these same years dozens of other societies and social libraries emerged with similar shared inclinations toward a deferential, enlightened, and nationalist public culture. It was in such settings that the Federalist literary aesthetics described by Lawrence Buell and Kathy Davidson were both created and internalized by a generation of post-Revolutionary gentry, fused with hierarchical assumptions about civic order. If Freemasonry inculcated the symbolic forms of the moderate Enlightenment, the Federalist literary societies were very much immersed in its content. In this regard they picked up the intellectual tradition that had been articulated in the urban colonial clubs and disrupted by the Revolution. Their proceedings were a vital part of the Federalists' efforts to command the public sphere in the early 1790s.[64]

The debating societies were dangerous though: even in the Minervaean Society their debates did not always favor the na-

[64] Brookfield, Mass., Minervaean Society Records, 1789–94, pp. 4–5, 18–19, 25, 67, American Antiquarian Society, Worcester, Mass.; Brooke, *Heart of the Commonwealth,* pp. 241–43; Alfred F. Young, *The Democratic-Republicans of New York, 1763–1797* (Chapel Hill, 1967), p. 400; Fischer, *Revolution of American Conservatism,* pp. 209–10; Robert A. Gross, *The Minutemen and Their World* (New York, 1976), p. 174; Gross, *Books and Libraries;* Buell, *New England Literary Culture,* pp. 24–41, 85–90; Davidson, *Revolution and the Word,* pp. 153–63, 196–200; May, *Enlightenment in America,* p. 355.

tional administration, and in its records one can sense the coming of partisan disagreement in a growing division in the votes and the withdrawal of future Jeffersonians. Here, then, were the benefits of Masonic prohibition on political debate. In his December 1793 address to the York Rite Masons in Charleston, George Buist noted that other "societies instituted for the laudable purpose of promoting knowledge and literature, had forsak[en] the peaceful walks of science, have become the tools of party."[65] Buist may well have been referring to established literary societies, but associational life in Charleston had been jolted four months previously by the establishment of the first political society since the Anti-Britannic Marine Society. That August the Republican Society of South Carolina had been formed, part of a new wave of partisan associationalism sweeping the republic. It was in this context that William Wyche warned New York's Horanian Literary Society the following May of the "pernicious spirit of party," arguing that if only the truth were observed there would be "but one opinion formed of all."[66]

Federalist intentions for shaping a unitary public sphere had been modeled on that of Augustan England. But under the impact of the French Revolution that public sphere of consensus and common discourse was collapsing in England, and under similar circumstances the United States was too diverse and democratic to conform to such a limited field and arena of discourse. An oppositional public sphere, articulated not in ancient lodges but self-created societies and bearing with it the revolutionary Enlightenment, was emerging in the summer of 1793.

THE REPUBLICAN OPPOSITIONAL PUBLIC SPHERE, 1793–95

Federalist ambitions to "have but one opinion formed of all" in a monolithic and hegemonic public sphere were never real-

[65] Buist, *Sermon*, p. 26.

[66] William Wyche, *Party Spirit: An Oration Delivered to the Horanian Literary Society at Their First Anniversary Meeting, on the 10th of May, 1794, at Tammany Hall* (New York, 1794), p. 10.

ized. From the onset of Washington's administration skeptics had lampooned the efforts to reinforce the dignity of the presidency with titles and levees, and as soon as Alexander Hamilton's fiscal plans became apparent in 1790 and 1791, serious political opposition began to take shape. The year 1793 brought the final blow to Washington's hopes for a harmonious, peaceable, deferential republic, as an increasingly radical French Revolution threatened to spread across the Atlantic. With these events an oppositional public sphere emerged, challenging hierarchy, moderation, and balance with a revolutionary Enlightenment.

The first building block of this oppositional public sphere was the press. In 1789 Hamilton had set up John Fenno as publisher of the *Gazette of the United States,* an organ that would "endear the General Government to the people." Two years later Thomas Jefferson, still working within the restrictions of a "court politics," began publishing attacks on Hamilton in Benjamin Franklin Bache's *General Advertiser* and then installed poet Philip Freneau in a State Department sinecure to publish the opposition *National Gazette* in his spare time. Over the next decade newspapers would be a central vehicle of a ferocious conflict between Federalists and Republicans over the control and definition of the public culture mediating among a leadership class, the electorate, and the people at large.[67]

The second critical vehicle in this conflict was the popular association. Political societies, such as they were, had disappeared since the constitutional debates of 1788, but in the summer of 1793—inspired by French example but driven by Hamiltonian policy—they suddenly reemerged. Between April 1793 and the end of the year eleven Democratic or Republican societies were formed from Charleston to Boston, followed by another twenty-four in 1794. In Washington's view, they were "the most diabolical attempts to destroy the best fabric of government, that has ever been presented for the acceptance of mankind." "Self-created," they violated the "fabric" of a federal republican consensus; they challenged

[67] John C. Miller, *The Federalist Era, 1789–1801* (New York, 1960), pp. 89–90; Stewart, *Opposition Press,* pp. 5–10.

the judgment and legitimacy of Washington's hierarchy of "first characters."[68]

One model for a Republican society was detailed in a manuscript written by one of Elbridge Gerry's constituents, William Manning of Billerica, Massachusetts. In his "Key of Libberty," Manning announced that the ruin of republics would come by the "combinations of the few, & the ignorance of the many." The combinations that he suspected were the bastions of Federalist culture: the Cincinnati, medical societies, chambers of commerce, academies, colleges, ministerial associations, and the lawyers' "Bar Meetings . . . [which had] become the most formidable & influential ordir of any in the Government."[69] This array of organized interests and elites was ranged against the people, who had at their command only their vote, which could only be prudently exercised with timely and appropriate political knowledge. "But this kind of knowledge," Manning argued, had been "almost ruened of late by the doings of the few"; the constitutionally guaranteed freedom of the press was undermined by the crushing economic and political pressures placed upon "Republican printers." Manning's solution was a paradigm for the creation of public culture in the 1790s; men should organize to share formative knowledge. His "Remidy" was a "Sociaty of frinds by name of the Labouring Society," modeled upon the Cincinnati, to be organized throughout the republic. Once associated in class, town, county, state, and continental meetings, the members would subscribe a magazine "in ordir to establish as cheep, easy & sure conveyance of knowledge & larning necessary for a free man." This flow of knowledge would bring about republican unanimity—"a similarity of sentiments & manners, Industry and Economy"—on the terms of the "Farmers, Mechanics, and Labourer in Amarica" rather

[68] Link, *Democratic-Republican Societies*, pp. 13–15; Washington quotation from Wiebe, *Opening of American Society*, p. 73.

[69] Samuel Eliot Morison, ed., "William Manning's *The Key of Libberty*," *William and Mary Quarterly*, 3d ser. 13 (1956):213, 224–30. For a thorough analysis of Manning, see Michael Merrill and Sean Wilentz, "William Manning and the Invention of American Politics," in Michael Merrill and Sean Wilentz, eds., *The Key of Liberty: The Life and Democratic Writings of William Manning, "A Laborer," 1747–1814* (Cambridge, Mass., 1993), pp. 3–86.

than the terms of those "orders of men who live without Labour." And the society could take an explicitly governmental
role, in Manning's stipulation in the third article of its constitution that it "examine all complantes against Juditial & Executive Officers for breaches of the Laws & Constitutions, &
when nesecary to make presentments, prosecutions, & manage impeachments."[70]

Powerful as it was, Manning's plan was never even published, and seems to have been a unique product of his particular circumstance. Manning's vision of an inclusive society of
political information and action was rooted in the world of
Massachusetts popular politics of the 1780s. Manning had
served as a selectman of Billerica in 1785 and 1786, a bastion
of the popular opposition before the Revolution and Antifederalist in 1788. There are strong echoes of the political culture
of the county conventions of the 1780s in Manning's plan,
especially in its proposal for oversight of the executive and
the judiciary, and there seems to be good reason for seeing
a link between the popular politics of the 1780s and strong
Republican voting in Middlesex County. But by the late 1790s
most of Shaysite Massachusetts to the west had turned to the
Federalist fold, in what John M. Murrin has termed a "stun-
ning" shift in political allegiances. Other than Manning's
plan, there were few connections between the county convention movement—and the Regulators—and the societies of
the 1790s.[71]

The Republican societies did have continuities running

---

[70] Morison, ed., "Manning's *Key of Libberty*," pp. 247–53.

[71] John M. Murrin, "The Great Inversion, or, Court versus Country: A
Comparison of the Revolution Settlements in England (1688–1721) and
America (1776–1816)," in J. G. A. Pocock, ed., *Three British Revolutions:
1641, 1688, 1776* (Princeton, 1980), p. 404; Brooke, *Heart of the Common-
wealth*, pp. 251–59. On Manning, see Ruth Bogin, "'Measures So Glareingly
Unjust': A Response to Hamilton's Funding Plan by William Manning,"
William and Mary Quarterly, 3d ser. 46 (1989):315–31; Stephen E. Patterson,
Political Parties in Revolutionary Massachusetts (Madison, Wis., 1973), p. 262;
Henry A. Hazen, *History of Billerica, Massachusetts . . .* (Boston, 1883), p. 306.
On Middlesex County, see Paul Goodman, *The Democratic-Republicans of
Massachusetts: Politics in a Young Republic* (Cambridge, Mass., 1964), pp.
82–85.

back to the radical Whiggery of the 1770s but these continuities were with a voluntary—even liberal—wing of the Revolutionary movement. The conventions had gathered and acted
on corporate assumptions as public entities; the self-created
societies of 1793 were rooted in the traditions and circles of
the voluntary societies of the 1770s and 1780s. Among the
members of the Democratic Society of Pennsylvania, David
Rittenhouse, Benjamin Rush, Charles Willson Peale, and Jonathan Bayard Smith had all been involved in the Whig Society
of 1776 or the Associators. In New York, David Gelston and
Melancton Smith linked the Republican Society of 1788 and
the Democratic Society of 1793; John Lamb, the president of
the earlier society and once a Son of Liberty, led the Jeffersonian New York Humane Society with Gelston, Smith, and
the two Clintons. In Boston's Constitutional Society, Benjamin Edes and William Cooper had once been Sons of Liberty
and members of the 1778 "Free and Independent Whig Society of Observation." In Baltimore, Archibald Buchanan, once
a member of the Mechanics Society, the Sons of Liberty, and
the 1774 Committee of Observation, served as secretary of
the Republican Society in 1794 and addressed the group that
Fourth of July. Beyond these perhaps symbolic continuities in
personnel there were continuities in practice: voluntary association, mutual visitation, and continuing correspondence.[72]

The voluntarism of the Republican societies, rooted in radical Whiggery and the more fluid dimensions of eighteenth-
century political clubbery, was reinforced by new intellectual
currents. These led to the revolutionary Enlightenment. As
Joyce Appleby has argued, the new departure in the "republican vision of the 1790s" was a fervent belief in individual capacities for self-improvement and perfection, a belief in
future possibilities, rather than Calvinist—and classical republican—certainties of innate depravity. Some of the impe-
tus for this newly libertarian ethic was rooted in indigenous

[72] May, *Enlightenment in America*, pp. 200–213; Philip S. Foner, ed., *The Democratic-Republican Societies, 1790–1800: A Documentary Sourcebook of Constitutions, Declarations, Addresses, Resolutions, and Toasts* (Westport, Conn., 1976), pp. 433, 439–41; Link, *Democratic-Republican Societies*, pp. 22, 27, 32; Young, *Democratic-Republicans of New York*, pp. 47, 393–94, 401; Leake, *Memoir of General John Lamb*, pp. 347–48; Hoffman, *Spirit of Dissension*, p. 40.

sources—the dissenters' awakenings, the promise of economic advancement, Jefferson's Declaration—but much of it came from revolutionary Europe, as Michael Durey and Richard J. Twomey have demonstrated. The emergence of popular associations in 1793 was part of a cycle of revolutionary influence moving around the north Atlantic. Inspired by American Independence and republicanism, the French Revolution in turn encouraged the emergence of radical politics in Great Britain, an oppositional public sphere challenging the Augustan consensus. Vigorously suppressed in England, Scotland, and Ireland, British radical émigrés carried their Paineite liberalism to America, and turned it against the Federalists. As much as Genet may have been a catalyst, the influence of the French Jacobin clubs on the American societies was in great part indirect, filtered through the radical Paineite societies in Britain—the Society for Constitutional Information, the London Corresponding Society, the Society of United Irishmen—from whence came Matthew Carey, James Callendar, Thomas Cooper, and William Duane. And there were, of course, home-grown Paineites and deists: John Fitch, Philadelphia inventor and sponsor of the Universal Society, Elihu Palmer, the blind deist of Newburgh, and Ethan Allen, the Green Mountain philosopher.[73]

In its full form, then, the revolutionary Enlightenment

[73] Appleby, *Capitalism and a New Social Order*, pp. 79–105; Michael Durey, "Thomas Paine's Apostles: Radical Emigrés and the Triumph of Jeffersonian Republicanism," *William and Mary Quarterly*, 3d ser. 44 (1987):661–88; Richard J. Twomey, "Jacobins and Jeffersonians: Anglo-American Radical Ideology, 1790–1810," in Margaret C. Jacob and James Jacob, eds., *The Origins of Anglo-American Radicalism* (London, 1984), pp. 284–99; Link, *Democratic-Republican Societies*, pp. 100–124; May, *Enlightenment in America*, pp. 202–22; Darline Shapiro, "Ethan Allen: Philosopher-Theologian to a Generation of American Revolutionaries," *William and Mary Quarterly*, 3d ser. 21 (1964):236–55; G. Adolf Koch, *Republican Religion: The American Revolution and the Cult of Reason* (New York, 1933), pp. 28–73; David F. Hawke, *Paine* (New York, 1974), pp. 373, 348, 382, 387–89. On the English situation, see E. P. Thompson, *The Making of the English Working Class* (New York, 1963), pp. 17–185; and, most recently, Iain McCalman, *Radical Underworld: Prophets, Revolutionaries, and Pornographers in London, 1795–1840* (New York, 1988), pp. 7–94.

meant the adoption of the tenets of Thomas Paine's *Rights of Man*, a radical equalitarianism and anticlericalism, an almost mystical fusion of democratic and scientific principles. Traditional restrictions on individual aspirations were to be swept aside, as were their social and material underpinnings. The societies were the focus of the emergence of a broad-based counterritualism, attacking Federalist culture in all its manifestations. French revolutionary slogans and songs, styles of personal address, month- and year-naming, and the imagery of the tricolor cockade and the liberty caps spread through the societies, and over the following decade French pantaloons and "directory" gowns chased older British clothing styles off the streets. Beyond—and often more permanent than—the Democratic societies, Republican associationalism spread to include urban artisan societies and fraternal groups such as the Tammany Society and a host of immigrant benevolent societies. Republicans were also able to dominate influential literary and scientific societies, such as New York's Friendly Society and Philadelphia's American Philosophical Society, led after 1791 by David Rittenhouse, undermining Federalist command of high culture. Kathy Davidson has argued that a Republican literary form of the picaresque emerged in these years, most obviously manifested in Hugh Henry Brackenridge's *Modern Chivalry.* With the growing tide of an opposition press, filled with direct and coded satirical attacks on the government, the Federalist unitary public sphere lay in ruins, shattered by the emergence of an opposition equally intent upon capturing the public mind and molding it into a new form.[74] And this contest could be played out at the local level, as illustrated by Stephen Burroughs's account of his efforts in the early 1790s to establish a lending

---

[74] May, *Enlightenment in America*, pp. 213, 219, 228; David Hackett Fischer, *Growing Old in America*, expanded ed. (New York, 1987), pp. 87–90; idem, *Revolution of American Conservatism*, pp. 183–87; Howe, "Republican Thought," pp. 147–51; Young, *Democratic-Republicans of New York*, pp. 201, 392–412; Sean Wilentz, *Chants Democratic: New York City and the Rise of the American Working Class, 1788–1850* (New York, 1984), pp. 68–70, 153–55; Davidson, *Revolution and the Word*, pp. 173–78.

library in a conservative Congregationalist parish on Long Island.[75]

The political purposes of the Democratic societies were to make government responsive to the people. Republicans rejected the Federalist assumption that a people might speak only to elect their representatives: Government was not to be at the discretion of a remote gentry, but a direct expression of popular will. Issues and policies, rather than character and virtue, should decide elections. As the Massachusetts Constitutional Society announced in a circular letter to the other societies, it was "the duty of the people, to watch the conduct of those to whom they have entrusted the administration of their government: being agents for this important business, they are accountable to their constituents for their measures and whenever they deviate from the great objects of their appointment, the people ought to be assiduous in exercising their constitutional authority to remove them from office." The societies had been formed as a "great bulwark" against the "artful designs" of those conspiring to destroy "liberty and equality"; they were to "harmonize the public mind, by becoming sources of authentic information." Here, then, lay the essential political function of the societies. They were not party organizations, advancing candidates for public office, but were conduits of "political knowledge," fabricators of an alternative political culture, a counterpublic sphere. But as the societies took hold, opposition candidates began to emerge and to win elections—and open rebellion broke out in western Pennsylvania. Federalists saw the collapse of the republic.[76]

FEDERALIST COUNTER-REVOLUTION, 1793–1800

From the summer of 1793 the Federalists were confronted with a powerful, widely ramified challenge to their control of

[75] Stephen Burroughs, *Memoirs of Stephen Burroughs* (1811, 1924; reprint ed., Boston, 1988), pp. 279–300.

[76] Appleby, *Capitalism and a New Social Order*, p. 56; Foner, ed., *Democratic-Republican Societies*, p. 259. On the debate over Democratic societies as polit-

public culture in the young republic, to their efforts to reassert a unitary public sphere. For the rest of the decade they would continue to assert a prerogative of defining the rhetorical and institutional arena mediating between national government and a widely scattered electorate. The high points of their campaign came in 1794 and 1798, when the Federalists twice attempted to smother a web of voluntary societies by rhetorical means, and once attempted to silence a burgeoning opposition print culture by statute law. In the process, they moved away from their cultural base in the moderate Enlightenment toward Calvinist counterrevolution, with disastrous result.[77]

"The self-created societies which have spread themselves over this country," George Washington wrote to John Jay on November 1, 1794, "have been labouring incessantly to sow the seeds of distrust, jealousy, and of course discontent, thereby hoping to effect some revolution in the government." There was "no doubt" in his mind that the Democratic societies were the "fomenters of the western disturbances." Two weeks later Washington publicly blamed them for the outbreak of the Whiskey Rebellion. In his review of the opposition to the excise, Washington found that "associations of men began to denounce threats against the officers employed. From a belief that, by a more formal concert, their operations might be defeated, certain assumed the tone of condemna-

---

ical organizations, see Fischer, *Revolution of American Conservatism*, pp. 109–12; John C. Miller, "First Fruits of Republican Organization: Political Aspects of the Congressional Election of 1794," *Pennsylvania Magazine of History and Biography* 63 (1939):118–43; and Nobel E. Cunningham, *The Jeffersonian Republicans: The Formation of Party Organization, 1789–1801* (Chapel Hill, 1957), pp. 62–66.

[77] The classical texts here are Howe, "Republican Thought"; Hofstadter, *Idea of a Party System*; James M. Smith, *Freedom's Fetters: The Alien and Sedition Laws and American Civil Liberties* (Ithaca, N.Y., 1956); Stauffer, *New England and the Bavarian Illuminati*; Link, *Democratic-Republican Societies*, pp. 175–209; May, *Enlightenment in America*, pp. 252–77; Gary B. Nash, "The American Clergy and the French Revolution," *William and Mary Quarterly*, 3d ser. 22 (1965):392–412; Wood, "Conspiracy and the Paranoid Style."

tion." "Riot and violence" had been caused "by the artifice of men who labored for the ascendancy over the will of others by the guidance of their passions."[78]

These sentiments applied as much to the societies as a whole; throughout the republic the societies had "assumed the tone of condemnation." Washington's critique was picked up by Federalists everywhere, but it was the New England clergy who most assiduously labored to discredit the broader public culture of Republicanism.

In April 1793, the Rev. David Tappan issued the first of these attacks in a sermon preached at Cambridge and Charlestown, Massachusetts, condemning the newly radical-ized French Revolution and warning that "a species of atheis-tic philosophy, which has of late reared its head in Europe . . . seems in danger of infecting" young minds in America. Eighteen months later, and five days after Washington's ad-dress to Congress, the Rev. David Osgood of nearby Medford in a Thanksgiving sermon specifically attacked the Demo-cratic societies as agents of French power. Read with delight by Federalist leaders throughout the northern states, Os-good's sermon rapidly went through six editions, and his ideas were repeated by a chorus of Congregational and Presbyterian ministers.[79]

In these Federalist attacks on the opposition societies and culture there were more than echoes of British suppression of the radical underground in the 1790s: American Federal-ists were not unaware of the more vigorous exertions of an-other government seemingly threatened by Jacobin subversion. The parallels between American and English con-servative defenses of the status quo were more explicit in 1798, in the midst of the XYZ controversy. That May, William Cobbett, alias Peter Porkupine, published an attack on the

[78] Henry P. Johnston, ed., *The Correspondence and Public Papers of John Jay, 1763–1826,* 4 vols. (1890–93; reprint ed., New York, 1971), 4:130; James Thomas Flexner, *George Washington: Anguish and Farewell (1793–1799)* (Bos-ton, 1969), pp. 183–84; Stauffer, *New England and the Bavarian Illuminati,* p. 109.

[79] Stauffer, *New England and the Bavarian Illuminati,* pp. 88–102, 111–16; Link, *Democratic-Republican Societies,* pp. 197–200; Nash, "American Clergy," pp. 397–99; May, *Enlightenment in America,* pp. 202–20.

American branch of the United Irishmen—formed to attain Irish independence from British rule—as agents of the "Parisian propogande," part of a conspiracy to aid the French in undermining the American government. Such opinions contributed to the passage of the Alien Laws that summer, severely restricting the rights of the immigrants who had gravitated to the republican cause. And the Alien Laws, with the Sedition Act, aimed at the Republican press, also introduced the coercive statist methods of political control that were deployed so effectively in Britain throughout the Napoleonic period.[80]

Cobbett's diatribe against the United Irishmen was connected to another link in the transatlantic attack on the influence of French Jacobinism. Cobbett was particularly incensed by the oaths to secrecy taken by the United Irishmen; he was also very interested in the thesis of the Abbé Baruel that a secret Masonic order called the Bavarian Illuminati had caused the French Revolution and was conspiring to undermine government and religion throughout Europe. This theory was popularized in a tract titled *Proofs of a Conspiracy against All the Religions and Governments of Europe, Carried On in the Secret Meetings of Free Masons, Illuminati, and Reading Societies* written by Dr. John Robison of Edinburgh. After editions came out in London, Edinburgh, and Dublin, William Cobbett sponsored its publication in New York in 1798. Robison's work was intended to defend English Freemasonry from the charge of Illuminism by focusing on the wildly elaborated and often very mystical masonry practiced in France and Germany, but the result in the United States was to cast a dark shadow of suspicion over the growing network of American lodges.[81]

[80] Smith, *Freedom's Fetters;* [William Cobbett], *Detection of a Conspiracy Formed by the United Irishmen, with the Evident Intention of Aiding the Tyrants of France in Subverting the Government of the United States of America* (Philadelphia, 1798), p. 3.

[81] Stauffer, *New England and the Bavarian Illuminati,* pp. 271–72n, 284; John M. Roberts, *The Mythology of the Secret Societies* (New York, 1972), pp. 207–10; McCalman, *Radical Underworld,* pp. 1, 50. I am indebted to Morris Bric for pointing out Cobbett's interest in the Illuminati. Umberto Eco's *Foucault's Pendulum* is the latest manifestation of a European fascination with secret societies.

The Baruel-Robison thesis was popularized most forcibly by the Rev. Jedediah Morse, the Congregational minister of Charlestown, Massachusetts, in three sermons delivered in May and November of 1798 and April 1799. Where Cobbett argued that the United Irishmen and the other clubs and societies of the revolutionary Enlightenment were part of an Illuminist plot, Morse implied that the bastion of the moderate Enlightenment, American Freemasonry, harbored the conspiracy. His first sermon, delivered in Boston and Charlestown on a Fast Day on May 9, warned his audiences of the threat of French governmental plans against the United States and introduced the Baruel-Robison thesis of an international Masonic conspiracy. Not mentioned in his spoken sermon was the question of whether American Freemasonry was "corrupted" by the Illuminati. In a series of footnotes to the printed version he assured his readers that, while the Illuminati were spreading through Masonic circles in Europe, he was sure that there were no Illuminist influences in American lodges, at least not in the "Eastern States." Six months later his Thanksgiving sermon warned generally of "foreign intrigue" of "wicked and artful men," while in footnotes and an appendix he argued variously that the Dorrilites (an ephemeral millenarian sect on the Vermont border), the Democratic societies, and the United Irishmen were all agents of the Illuminati. Finally, in April 1799, in his sermon *Exhibiting the Present Dangers*, Morse directly accused a lodge of being part of the Illuminati. A group of French Haitian exiles in Portsmouth, Virginia, had established in 1795 a lodge affiliated with the French Order of the Grand Orient, and Oliver Wolcott provided Morse with a lodge summons and roster of French and American members printed in 1798. From this material, Morse argued that there were seventeen Illuminated lodges in the United States, with roughly seventeen hundred members, all linked to France through charters and correspondence with the Grand Orient and amplified with stories about a French plot to incite slave rebellions.[82]

---

[82] Stauffer, *New England and the Bavarian Illuminati*, pp. 230–35, 264–72, 290–301; Link, *Democratic-Republican Societies*, pp. 198–99. For the continuing influences of Morse's antimasonry, see Paul Goodman, *Toward a Christian*

Morse's accusations set off a deluge of newspaper controversy, which, in the end, satisfied the public that the charges were spurious and undermined Federalist credibility on the eve of the election of 1800.[83] In the interval Morse was echoed by ministers throughout New England, including David Tappan and Timothy Dwight, and corresponded with an eager William Cobbett in Philadelphia, who filled his *Porkupine's Gazette* with supporting material. Attacks on the influence of the Illuminati rapidly became a central element of Federalist rhetoric, as they simultaneously moved to suppress the Republican press in an effort to destroy the underpinnings of their political opposition.

From the perspective of voluntary association, the most interesting sermon in the Illuminati crusade was delivered by the Rev. Joseph Lathrop of West Springfield, from whom Morse had borrowed his reference to the Dorrilites. Lathrop carried his attack against the very sinews of the public sphere, the reading societies and social libraries that were springing up throughout the country. Echoing a common theme in the rhetoric of Calvinist Federalism, Lathrop suggested that education was hydra-headed, opening a door "to literary and moral improvements, or for a corruption of sentiments and manners." The Illuminati had spread in Europe through reading societies as well as Masonic lodges, and so the education provided by local social libraries was suspect. His condemnation was inescapable. "If we, any where, see library companies industrious to collect and circulate deistical and other licentious books—any where—see men openly and boldly opposing the religion of the gospel, and these standing foremost among the candidates for public office . . . see attempts made to change our happy constitution . . . we may conclude, that, if not the members, yet, at least, the principles of these societies [the Illuminati] are deeply at work." One

Republic: Antimasonry and the Great Transition in New England, 1826–1835 (New York, 1988), pp. 54–79.

[83]Alan V. Briceland, "The *Philadelphia Aurora*, the New England Illuminati, and the Election of 1800," *Pennsylvania Magazine of History and Biography* 100 (1976):3–36; Stewart, *Opposition Press*, pp. 327–29, 410–17.

wonders if Stephen Burroughs's account of the library controversy on Long Island was colored by such Federalist attacks.[84]

THE REPUBLICANS ADOPT THE CONSENSUAL PUBLIC SPHERE OF THE MODERATE ENLIGHTENMENT, 1795–1800

We thus confront a series of paradoxes. The first involves the events of 1794, the second involves those of 1798. In 1794, while voluntary institutions, and Freemasonry in particular, were central to the Federalist construction of a unitary national public sphere, Washington felt free to attack them when they were deployed by an opposition. Only fourteen months separated the September 1793 cornerstone ceremony on Capitol Hill, when Washington presided over an elaborate Masonic ritual, and November 1794, when he publicly condemned the self-created societies. Similarly, John Marshall was serving as master of the Virginia Grand Lodge when he too condemned the Democratic societies as "pernicious" and "detached clubs."[85]

Republicans were quick to seize upon the inconsistency, though their focus was upon the Cincinnati. In December 1794 Thomas Jefferson, in a letter to James Madison, voiced an opinion that was echoed in Republican newspapers throughout the country and incorporated into William Manning's notes on the "Key of Libberty."

> The denunciation of the democratic societies is one of the extraordinary acts of boldness of which we have seen so many from

[84]Stauffer, *New England and the Bavarian Illuminati*, pp. 244, 246–52, 284–86; Joseph Lathrop, *A Sermon, on the Dangers of the Times, from Infidelity and Immorality, and Especially from a Lately Discovered Conspiracy against Religion and Government, Delivered at West-Springfield and Afterward at Springfield* (Springfield, Mass., 1798), pp. 12, 16–17, 22.

[85]John Marshall quotation in Wiebe, *Opening of American Society*, p. 74; Albert J. Beveridge, *The Life of John Marshall*, 4 vols. (Boston, 1929), 2:38–41; John Dove, comp., *Proceedings of the M. W. Grand Lodge of Ancient York Masons of the State of Virginia, from Its Organization, in 1778, to 1822 . . .* (Richmond, 1874), pp. 113–37.

the fraction of monocrats. It is wonderful, indeed, that the President should have permitted himself to be the organ of such an attack on the freedom of discussion, the freedom of writing, printing & publishing. It must be a matter of rare curiosity to get at the modifications of these rights proposed by them, and to see what line their ingenuity would draw between democratical societies, whose avowed object is the nourishment of the republican principles of our constitution, and the society of Cincinnati, *a self created* one, carving out for itself hereditary distinctions.[86]

Washington's thinking resolves this puzzle. He opposed self-creation, not association; he opposed political purposes, not public symbolism. Groups that formed of their own to influence public policy were suspect, even the Cincinnati, about which he had second thoughts after 1786, at Jefferson's recommendation. Similarly, he had advised Bushrod Washington not to form a Federalist Patriotic Society to instruct constitutional delegates in 1788. "May not a few members of this society, more sagacious and designing than the rest," he asked his nephew, "direct the measures of it to private views of their own?" Federalist or Republican, no society should presume to instruct "able and honest representatives" on "national questions." "Self-created societies" were simply the vehicles of individual ambition and violated the unitary fabric of the republic. Based in the simple will of a few men, they had no legitimacy in the public arena. But Freemasonry stood apart from politics, and was of ancient origin, claiming a history reaching back to biblical times. Freemasonry's antiquity put the lodges beyond the charge of self-creation.[87]

In the wake of Washington's public attack, Republicans made valiant efforts to defend their societies. "Are not all private associations established on the foundation of their own authority," asked one writer in New York's *Independent Gazette*, "an authority sanctioned by the direct principles of social life and guarenteed by the spirit of the laws?" Here associations

[86] Paul Leicester Ford, *The Writings of Thomas Jefferson*, 10 vols. (New York, 1892–99), 6:516–17; Link, *Democratic-Republican Societies*, pp. 193, 195.

[87] Myers, *Liberty without Anarchy*, pp. 93–98; Flexner, *Washington and the New Nation*, p. 119.

were defended as a natural right, while another writer in the *Gazette* pointed to the voluntary dimension of the Revolution itself. "Whatever the United States might have been previous to the American revolution, it is pretty evident that since their emancipation from British rapacity, they are a great self-created society . . . had the British succeeded in impressing our minds with a firm belief in the infamy of self creation, we should never have been free and independent to all eternity." Tunis Wortman and many other Republican orators spoke of the positive influence of free institutions on the "plastic nature" of the human character, and the roots of depravity in coercive governments, challenging the Calvinist thesis of innate qualities.[88] But, despite such brave words, the Republicans did abandon the political societies in the year following Washington's attack. The New York society survived into 1799, and those in Boston and Baltimore were meeting in 1796 and 1797, but these were the exceptions. Even as partisan divisions over the Jay Treaty divided Congress into increasingly consistent blocs, the vehicles that might have organized a popular constituency faded away.[89]

In effect, the emergent Republican opposition abandoned the institutional structures of a revolutionary Enlightenment in the interval between 1794 and 1798. Certainly oppositional energies were not totally blunted; the Republican press grew in quantity and audacity. But, after three decades of sporadic action, self-created political societies disappeared from the public arena in the mid-1790s, and though they reemerged in 1798 and the years following, they would never again provide a critical center of gravity. Explicit party organization would emerge among the Republicans with the 1800 election,

[88] *Independent Gazette*, Jan. 21, 28, 1795, quoted in Appleby, *Capitalism and a New Social Order*, pp. 68–69; Tunis Wortman, *An Oration on the Influence of Social Institutions upon Human Morals and Happiness . . . before the Tammany Society, May 12, 1796* (New York, 1796), pp. 1–13; see also Appleby, *Capitalism and a New Social Order*, pp. 78–105; and Brooke, *Heart of the Commonwealth*, pp. 264–68.

[89] Link, *Democratic-Republican Societies*, pp. 200–203. (Link tries to argue that the societies did not fade away, but his evidence suggests otherwise.) Young, *Democratic-Republicans of New York*, p. 576; Cunningham, *Jeffersonian Republicans*, pp. 65–66.

and decentralized, voluntary, political societies would occupy a secondary position. But, important to our story here, between 1795 and 1799 *neither* political societies *nor* political parties existed to structure a popular opposition.[90]

Our second paradox lies in the events of 1798: If Washington accepted Freemasonry and the moderate Enlightenment as the ethical and philosophical center of a Federalist public sphere, why was Jedediah Morse free to imply that American Freemasonry was corrupted—or on the verge of being corrupted—by the Bavarian Illuminati? Morse's campaign was an embarrassment to Masonic Federalists everywhere, including Washington himself, who had to answer at least two letters inquiring about Jacobinism, the Illuminati, and Freemasonry in the fall of 1798.[91] Certainly, Freemasonry was a threat to Morse's orthodoxy, but it is less clear what emboldened Morse to suggest that a seeming bastion of Federalist influence had been infiltrated by Jacobin Illuminists bent on the destruction of the republic. The answer may well be that Morse's concerns about a Masonic conspiracy may not have been as irrational as they have been portrayed.[92]

In something of a departure from historiographical tradition, I would like to suggest that Morse was reacting to a new reality in the American public arena: Freemasonry by 1798 was no longer an exclusive domain of the Federalists. What had once been a Federalist front, rooted in the Continental Line, a replacement for the Cincinnati, and staunchly behind

[90] Fischer, *Revolution of American Conservatism*, pp. 111–12, stresses the reemergence of societies after 1798, but most of these were well after 1800. See also Link, *Democratic-Republican Societies*, pp. 200–209; Edmund B. Thomas, Jr., "Politics in the Land of Steady Habits: Connecticut's First Political Party System, 1789–1820," Ph.D. diss., Clark University, 1972, p. 84.

[91] Reverend Snyder letters to George Washington, in Schultz, *Freemasonry in Maryland*, 1:260–63; James M. Banner, Jr., *To the Hartford Convention: The Federalists and the Origins of Party Politics in Massachusetts, 1789–1815* (New York, 1970), pp. 155–56; Stauffer, *New England and the Bavarian Illuminati*, pp. 229–87.

[92] For the traditional interpretation of Jedediah Morse, see Richard Hofstadter, *The Paranoid Style in American Politics and Other Essays* (New York, 1965), pp. 10–15; see discussion in Wood, "Conspiracy and the Paranoid Style," pp. 433–44.

the federal Constitution, had been quietly infiltrated, not by the Illuminati, but by American Republicans. Freemasonry's open membership—unlike the Cincinnati—and the movement of some nationalists into the Jeffersonian orbit, meant that in the years following the collapse of the self-created societies Republicans could begin to move into this popular institution, wrapping themselves in the legitimacy of ancient tradition and ordered ritual, claiming the ceremonial center of the moderate Enlightenment.[93]

In the pages that follow I present the evidence state by state

[93] It can be argued that Morse's theory of a radical Masonic conspiracy was grounded in important developments within Masonry as well. For an orthodox Calvinist, ordinary Craft Masonry posed the alternative of a deistic secular humanism, sidestepping the issues of Original Sin. The higher "sublime" degrees of Masonry, rooted as they were in a hermetic perfectionism, were even more heretical, for buried deep in their rituals was the prospect of a return to the prelapsarian state of the primal Adam. As Dorothy Lipson and more recent scholars have noted, Masonry in all its forms comprised a real ideological alternative to Calvinism. Similarly, the mystical, hermetic higher degrees were beginning to spread during the 1790s, most pervasively with the formation of Royal Arch chapters, but also through the French lodges established by Haitian exiles. The Grand Orient lodges were not alone in this regard: French lodges working higher degrees were established in many of the seaboard cities. The most elite of these was the Rite of Perfection (now known as the Scottish Rite), which was begun in France in 1758, spread to the West Indies, and was first established in Albany in 1767, followed by Lodges of Perfection in Boston, New York, Philadelphia, and Charleston. If deistic, these groups were not revolutionary; Federalist Stephen Van Rensselaer was a leading figure in the Albany Lodge. It is interesting to note that Charles Holt argued in the *New London Bee* that the Illuminati were a benevolent order founded in America in 1768. And in Europe, Masonry was indeed a subversive force. Margaret C. Jacob has argued that Masonry was fundamental to the Enlightenment culture that ultimately shaped the French Revolution, and Eric Hobsbawm has pointed out the roots of the culture of nineteenth-century radicalism and anarchism in eighteenth-century Masonic forms and traditions. Samuel H. Baynard, Jr., *History of the Supreme Council, 33, Ancient and Accepted Scottish Rite of Freemasonry, Northern Jurisdiction* ... (Boston, 1938); Albany Grand Lodge of Perfection, Transcribed Minute Book, 1767–74, 1821–25, and 1841–45, in the Van Gordon-Williams Library at the Museum of Our National Heritage, Lexington, Mass.; Link, *Democratic-Republican Societies*, p. 199n; Eric Hobsbawm, *Primitive Rebels: Studies in Archaic Forms of Social Movements in the 19th and 20th Centuries* (New York, 1959), pp. 162–65; Jacob, *Radical Enlightenment*, pp. 29–62, 215–49; and Roberts, *Mythology of the Secret*

for the Republican movement into Masonry in perhaps too-elaborate detail. The implications of this movement should be spelled out here briefly. The conservative reaction of Federalists to the rise of a Republican opposition shifted the entire intellectual framework of American political culture to the right. By 1798 the Federalists, increasingly a northern faction, had begun to move decisively away from the moderate Enlightenment toward Calvinist counterrevolution. At the same time Republicans abandoned the organizational manifestations of the revolutionary Enlightenment and moved into Freemasonry, the organizational and symbolic bastion of the moderate Enlightenment. This opened the way for orthodox Calvinists to condemn Masonry, an opportunity previously obscured by its association with Washington and its central role in the Federalist public sphere. But it also placed strategic Republican elites at the center of the intellectual spectrum, leaving them in control of central institutions and symbols of Revolutionary charisma, institutions and symbols that would maintain their authority until the death of William Morgan in 1826. This position of cultural authority did not hinder the Republican electoral victory in 1800.

The political mobilization of Freemasonry was shaped in great part by an enduring regional distinction. Historically lacking in public print, the white populations of the southern-most states of Virginia, the Carolinas, and Georgia were relatively well supplied with Masonic lodges during the late eighteenth century.[94] Already apparent in 1775, this pattern was even more exaggerated by the end of the 1780s, when the number of lodges had doubled in Virginia and North Carolina and more than tripled in South Carolina and Georgia.

Societies, pp. 90–202. On French Lodge in Baltimore, see Schultz, *Freemasonry in Maryland,* 1:345–49, 273.

[94] See Appendix, table 2. Given the strong persistence of Federalism in Maryland and Delaware, and the fact that the colonial lodges in these states were warranted by the Grand Lodge of Pennsylvania, I have included these slave states in a broader Mid-Atlantic region between the Potomac and the Hudson, and defined a Deep South as those states south of the Potomac. The senators and governors from Kentucky and Tennessee are included in this south of the Potomac group.

In effect, south of the Potomac, the late eighteenth-century public sphere was more likely to be shaped by the private and exclusive associationalism of the Masonic lodge and, north of the Potomac, by the public press. A distinction between a closed oral ritual and an open, printed disclosure is suggested by the publications of the Freemasons themselves. Masons across the North, and especially in New England, published a range of orations and sermons, defining and defending their order before the public. In sharp contrast, Masonic publications south of the Potomac focused almost entirely on internal matters, the proceedings of the grand lodges and books of ritual.[95]

After the rapid spread of lodges in the North in the 1790s, especially in Massachusetts, Vermont, Rhode Island, New York, and Pennsylvania, Freemasonry assumed a more national distribution. But it continued to occupy a central place in public life south of the Potomac. From 1797 to 1801, the years of increasingly intense partisanship following the Jay Treaty, roughly a quarter of the leading political figures in all of the states—sitting state governors and United States senators—were active Freemasons, and perhaps another tenth had prior but apparently lapsed Masonic affiliations.[96] The pattern was decidedly different from the late 1780s and early 1790s, when Freemasonry was strongly associated with Federalism: now the Republicans were most likely to be Freemasons. Republicans from south of the Potomac led in Masonic affiliation, with almost 40 percent being active in the lodges. They were followed by Republican governors and senators from the Mid-Atlantic between Maryland and New York and by southern Federalists. Republican governors and senators from below the Potomac were three times more likely to be active Masons than were Federalists from north of the Poto-

[95] See Appendix, table 4.

[96] See Appendix, table 1. Denslow, ed., *Ten Thousand Famous Masons,* includes all governors and federal senators who were Freemasons, but not federal or state representatives. Governors from J. E. Kallenbach and J. S. Kallenbach, eds., *American State Governors, 1776–1976,* 3 vols. (Dobbs Ferry, N.Y., 1977–82); senators from John F. Hoadley, *Origins of American Political Parties, 1789–1803* (Lexington, Ky., 1986), pp. 217–19.

mac. A subtext running through this connection of southern politics and Freemasonry was grounded in the constitutional authority of many legislatures, mostly southern, to elect the governor. Among these states, most prominently New Jersey, Virginia, the Carolinas, and Georgia, more than half of the governors elected between 1797 and 1801 had prior or active Masonic affiliation; less than a quarter of the governors elected by popular vote, mostly in northern states, had such Masonic affiliations. In a tradition with deep colonial roots, Freemasonry clearly provided a fraternal vehicle for the closed circle of elite southern politics in the 1790s.

Equally clearly, Freemasonry increasingly came to be connected with Jeffersonian Republicanism, a fundamental change from the circumstances of the previous decade. The dynamics of this transition can be assessed in number of ways. First, as we have already seen, the affiliations of political elites suggest something of the shift from Federalist to Republican in the Masonic center of gravity. Similarly, one can track the shifting political milieu of local lodge life in the changing correlation of lodge locations with voting patterns. But changes in the leadership of the grand lodges provide the most precise approach, as different political figures in the states found it useful—or problematic—to connect their names with a growing institution of national charisma.

The sheer growth of Freemasonry goes a long way toward explaining its changing political complexion. Exclusive, Freemasonry could not be exclusionary, and as its doors opened wider in the 1790s, the original Federalist cadre was bound to be diluted by men of differing opinions. In a majority of states this broadening membership appears to have driven the transformation of Freemasonry, with literal insurgencies occurring during the mid to late 1790s bringing Republicans to Masonic preeminence. But in a number of states, including Georgia, where Masonry had grown very rapidly in the 1780s, and New York and Pennsylvania, where it grew rapidly in the next decade, this transition occurred much earlier, simply because Masonic leadership shifted from Federalist nationalism to the opposition in the early 1790s.

In Georgia, New York, and Pennsylvania, Masonic leadership was in the hands of prominent political figures who during the early 1790s moved rapidly from nationalism into the opposition. In the wake of Georgia's exceptionally violent and faction-ridden Revolutionary experience, the establishment of a grand lodge in 1786 provided a means for the restabilizing of public life on conservative terms. The grand lodge leadership was dominated by figures of the old Savannah–Christ Church conservative faction, Samuel Elbert, James Jackson, George Houstoun, James Habersham, and by 1790 ten Georgia lodges united Masons from Savannah to the Augusta backcountry. A leader in the Georgia legislature throughout the 1780s and an honorary member of the Cincinnati, Gen. James Jackson was elected in 1789 both as grand master and to Congress as a Federalist. Once in Congress, however, Jackson moved rapidly into the opposition in reaction to Hamilton's fiscal initiatives and later to the struggle over the Yazoo lands. Jackson and fellow Republican and Mason Josiah Tatnall would both serve in the Senate and as governor at the end of the 1790s. From 1793 through 1814 the master of the grand lodge would also be a Republican, Justice William Stephens, appointed to the federal bench by Jefferson at Jackson's request in 1801.[97] Reflecting Freemasonry's conservative origins, the twenty-one lodges warranted by 1801 were concentrated in the more densely settled counties along the Savannah River encompassing the towns of Savannah, Augusta, and Washington, counties where Republican majorities were challenged by strong minorities of Federalists.[98]

Freemasonry in New York was similarly rooted in factional strife, and in a conservative element of the emerging Republican coalition. New York's post-Revolutionary Masonic history began in February 1784, when Robert R. Livingston of Cler-

[97] William B. Stevens, *A History of Georgia* . . . (1859; reprint ed., Savannah, 1972), p. 383; Kenneth Coleman, *The American Revolution in Georgia, 1763–1789* (Athens, Ga., 1958), pp. 194, 269–71; Jackson, "Rise of the Western Members," pp. 318–20; William W. Abbot, "The Structure of Politics in Georgia, 1782–1789," *William and Mary Quarterly*, 3d ser. 14 (1951):59, 61; Rose, *Prologue to Democracy*, pp. 59–62; James H. Broussard, *The Southern Federalists, 1800–1816* (Baton Rouge, 1978), pp. 252–53; Rosier and Pearson, *Grand Lodge*, pp. 25–29, 244–48; *Dictionary of American Biography*, s.v. "Jackson, James."

[98] See Appendix, table 15.

mont, a leading Mason before the war, reorganized the grand lodge and assumed the grand mastership. Having been allied to George Clinton during the Revolutionary struggles in New York, in the summer of 1784 Livingston moved in the nationalist camp of Alexander Hamilton and the Schuylers, marked by his election to honorary membership in the Society of the Cincinnati that July. The grand lodge, which numbered fifteen lodges by June 1788, was presumably a dimension of Livingston's efforts to build a nationalist interest in New York, though his appeal was probably more subtle than it was to the Cincinnati in July 1787, when he stridently urged the membership to take action to correct "the many evils that result from the want of a federal government."[99]

The intersection of Freemasonry and Federalist political environments was manifested in the June 1789 election for governor, in which all four counties with two or more lodges voted for the Federalist candidate, Robert Yates, while the state elected Antifederalist George Clinton. But Livingston cooled to the Federalists by the early fall, not having been offered a major post in Washington's cabinet. By 1791 he had returned to his wartime alliance with George Clinton and for the next decade controlled the right flank of New York's emerging Republican coalition. Livingston's grand lodge warranted a number of lodges in counties that tended to vote Republican, to the effect that the Federalist Masonic advantage (in counties with two or more lodges) disappeared in 1792 and 1795 and was reversed in 1798, when Livingston himself ran for governor, and in 1801, when Clinton won in a landslide. In both of these years roughly 60 percent of the Republican counties had two or more lodges, as against 45 percent for the Federalist counties.[100]

This shift toward the Clinton camp could be conflicted, as in New York's Holland Lodge, where, in December 1794, De Witt Clinton was elected master after a struggle between

[99] Lang, *Freemasonry in the State of New York*, pp. 79–80; Dangerfield, *Chancellor Robert R. Livingston*, pp. 209–33; Linda Grant DePauw, *The Eleventh Pillar: New York State and the Federal Constitution* (Ithaca, N.Y., 1966), pp. 46, 190–93; Livingston, *Oration*, p. 16.

[100] See Appendix, table 6.

"anti-Federalists" and "monarchists." A number of New York City societies, nominally nonpartisan, took on a Republican cast in these years, as suggested by Republican Samuel Miller's speaking schedule in the summer of 1795, when he addressed the grand lodge on June 24, and the assembled Mechanics, Tammany, and Democratic societies, and militia officers, on July 4.[101] This constellation of associations certainly played a role in the election of Robert Livingston's younger brother Edward to Congress in December 1794. Edward Livingston was a member of the Holland Lodge in 1788 and deputy grand master from 1801 to 1803, as well as a member of the Democratic and Tammany societies. Similarly, George Clinton himself was elected master of New York's Warren Lodge at its formation in 1800.[102]

There was, then, a Masonic connection among the key players among the Clinton-Livingston coalition. Except for the Van Rensselaers of Albany County, this connection did not extend to the leading players of the opposing factions in New York's complex politics. No record of Masonic membership survives for Alexander Hamilton, John Jay, Gouverneur Morris, or any of the Schuylers, among the leading Federalists. Neither Morris, Jay, nor any of four other Federalists serving as senator or governor between 1797 and 1801 were ever Masons, while all four Republicans (George Clinton, De Witt Clinton, John Armstrong, and James Watson) had active or prior connections with the Masons.[103] Similarly, centrist ad-

---

[101] Young, *Democratic-Republicans of New York,* pp. 398–400; Peter Paulson, "The Tammany Society and the Jeffersonian Movement in New York City, 1795–1800," *New York History* 34 (1953):72–84; Samuel Miller, *A Discourse Delivered in the New Presbyterian Church, New York, before the Grand Lodge of the State of New York . . . June 24, 1795* (New York, 1795); idem, *A Sermon, Delivered in the New Presbyterian Church, New York, July Fourth, 1795, at the Request of, and before, the Mechanic, Tammany, and Democratic Societies, and the Military Officers* (New York, 1795).

[102] Denslow, ed., *Ten Thousand Famous Masons,* 1:227, 3:93; William B. Hatcher, *Edward Livingston: Jeffersonian Republican and Jacksonian Democrat* (Baton Rouge, 1940), pp. 28–34; Young, *Democratic-Republicans of New York,* p. 400.

[103] Statement on Federalist leadership based on an examination of the biographies in Denslow, ed., *Ten Thousand Famous Masons,* and Heaton, *Ma-*

venturer Aaron Burr was not a Mason. When he and his following were shut out of patronage in 1801 by De Witt Clinton's control of the council of appointment, a Burrite scribbler produced a pamphlet entitled *A Full Exposition of the Clintonian Faction; and the Society of Columbian Illuminati . . .* , attacking Clinton's supposed connections to Elihu Palmer's *Temple of Reason* and "Theistic Church" in language drawn directly from Jedediah Morse's attack on Freemasonry and the Bavarian Illuminati in 1798.[104]

The Pennsylvania Grand Lodge, which still revered its founding "sublime philosopher" and nationalist Benjamin Franklin, also moved equally quickly into Republican ranks. Notwithstanding Masonic orator Charles Smith's Federalist rhetoric at Sunbury, there were no grand officers among Pennsylvania delegates ratifying the Constitution. Jonathan Bayard Smith, an old Associator who in 1793 served briefly as Thomas Mifflin's attorney general, was elected successively senior grand warden, deputy grand master, and grand master in 1786, 1787, and 1789. If he was part of Mifflin's Revolutionary center in Pennsylvania, Smith clearly stood at the Republican end of the spectrum. He was a member of a group of societies in the wider Republican circle: the American Philosophical Society, the Sons of St. Tammany, and the Democratic Society of Pennsylvania. Stepping down as grand master in 1794, Smith was reelected by the grand lodge from 1798 through 1802. Other grand officers who were members of the Democratic Society included Edward Fox, serving as grand secretary and junior grand warden in 1793 and 1794,

---

sonic Membership. Federalist Rufus King was a member of a lodge in Newburyport before moving to New York in 1788, but he apparently did not affiliate with any New York lodges (Heaton, *Masonic Membership,* pp. 33–34).

[104] Jabez Delano Hammond, *The History of Political Parties in the State of New York, from the Ratification of the Federal Constitution to December 1840,* 3 vols. (Albany, 1842–48), 1:153–55, 173–80; John Wood, *A Full Exposition of the Clintonian Faction, and the Society of Columbian Illuminati, with an Account of the Writer of the Narrative, and the Characters of His Certificate Men, as Also Remarks on Warren's Pamphlet* (Newark, N.J., 1802); Dixon Ryan Fox, *The Decline of Aristocracy in the Politics of New York* (New York, 1919), p. 58; Herbert Morais, *Deism in Eighteenth-Century America* (New York, 1934), pp. 120–38.

and Israel Israel, elected deputy grand master in 1799 after he lost a seat in the state senate the previous year in a highly controversial contested election. He would succeed Smith as grand master in 1803. Hugh Henry Brackenridge, Michael Leib, John Peter Gabriel Muhlenberg, and Thomas McKean had various Masonic affiliations, suggesting something of the dimensions of the Masonic connection among Pennsylvania's Republican leadership, but so too did Federalist James Ross.[105]

In Connecticut, Freemasonry was also led by men who moved from nationalism in the 1780s toward the Republican opposition in the 1790s. Connecticut Masonry was rooted in the southwest, often in towns with Anglican churches, and it was closely linked with the Masonry of the Continental Line. At least 40 percent of the Connecticut Cincinnati were also Masons, and the early meetings in 1783 leading to the formation of the grand lodge coincided with a popular convention movement that condemned the Cincinnati and opposed pensions for the former Continental officers, another suggestion that the new lodges were a refuge for men of Federal inclinations. Masonry was certainly one organizational node for Connecticut advocates of a stronger national government: seventeen of nineteen lodges chartered by 1788 were located in towns voting to ratify. Pierpont Edwards, the first grand master, was a Federalist delegate in the ratifying convention in February 1788, and Joel Barlow, who had urged the virtues of "permanent national government" upon the Connecticut Cincinnati in July 1787, joined the St. John's Lodge in Hartford the following January.[106]

But Edwards and Barlow, with the second grand master, William Judd, and Ephraim Kirby, another Masonic leader,

---

[105] Tinkcom, *Republicans and Federalists*, pp. 176–79; Foner, ed., *Democratic-Republican Societies*, p. 441; *Dictionary of American Biography*, s.v. "Smith, Jonathan Bayard"; Huss, *Master Builders*, p. 283; Denslow, ed., *Ten Thousand Famous Masons*, 1:121; 3:72, 174, 244–45; 4:71. There was no county-level correlation in Pennsylvania between voting pattern and lodge location in 1800.

[106] Case, *Historical Sketch*, pp. 1–7; Lipson, *Freemasonry in Federalist Connecticut*, pp. 62–72; Myers, *Liberty without Anarchy*, p. 136; Main, *Antifederalists*, pp. 107–9; Denslow, ed., *Ten Thousand Famous Masons*, 1:58; votes from McDonald, *We the People*, pp. 136–47.

soon became the nucleus of a slowly forming opposition in Connecticut. Dorothy Ann Lipson has described the Masons in Connecticut as a counterweight to the Congregational establishment, a secular institution that attracted those alienated from the Calvinism and authority of the orthodox ministers. Connecticut Masonry was at the root of at least one especially effective Republican attack on religious establishments. In 1799 John C. Ogden published a series of virulent essays in the *Philadelphia Aurora,* accusing the Federalist authorities in Connecticut of destroying an innocent widow in taking the collectorship of the port of New Haven away from her family. Ogden's father-in-law, Gen. David Wooster, the founder of Connecticut Freemasonry, had served as collector of the port until he joined the American forces in 1775, and after his death his widow endured financial ruin that might have been alleviated if the state had granted the collectorship to her son. (The New Haven collectorship would be given to Republican Abraham Bishop in 1801, who in 1800 had joined the attack on the Federalist clergy as the real Illuminati.)[107] The link between Masonry and Republican-sponsored disestablishment was firmly tied in 1818 when Oliver Wolcott, Jr., just elected governor as a Tolerationist, was elected master of the grand lodge.[108]

In the short run, however, important though it may have been for a strategic element of its leadership, Masonry had no decisive impact on the electoral fortunes of Connecticut's Republican opposition, scattered and unorganized before 1800. Republican activists in 1803 were roughly twice as likely as Federalist activists to have attended the grand lodge meetings in 1797, 1800, and 1803, but in the face of the orthodox attacks in 1798 the grand lodge elected Stephen Titus Hosmer, a moderate Federalist, to be grand master, in the

[107] For Connecticut politics, see Thomas, "Politics in the Land of Steady Habits"; Richard J. Purcell, *Connecticut in Transition, 1775–1818* (Middletown, Conn., 1963); Briceland, *"Philadelphia Aurora,"* pp. 9–10; Stauffer, *New England and the Bavarian Illuminati,* pp. 354–60; and *Dictionary of American Biography,* s.v. "Bishop, Abraham."

[108] Case, *Historical Sketch,* p. 7; Lipson, *Freemasonry in Federalist Connecticut,* pp. 114–15.

place of Republican William Judd. The distribution of Masonic lodges did not have a bearing on the distribution of Republican town majorities in the first decades of the nineteenth century, when voting returns for Connecticut become available. Connecticut Freemasonry provided a liberal haven for a number of nationalists turned Republicans, but Baptist and Separate societies were much more important in shaping the rank-and-file of the state's emerging opposition.[109]

Thus in Georgia, New York, Pennsylvania, and Connecticut, the Masonic leadership rapidly abandoned Federalist nationalism for various points along an emerging gradient in the Republican opposition. We might include in this category the southern frontier states of Kentucky and Tennessee, where Federalism never gained a foothold, and where prominent Republicans like Archibald Roane, Andrew Jackson, and John Brown were active Freemasons.[110] With Kentucky and Tennessee, something of a regional pattern begins to emerge. For the most part, it was in new southern frontier states and the large pluralistic states of the Mid-Atlantic that Freemasonry moved the most rapidly into the Republican orbit, orchestrated by powerful elites who apparently saw the lodge room as a useful extension of the political arena. In older and less pluralistic states—including most of New England, the smaller Mid-Atlantic states, and the large states south of the Potomac—the Federalist associations of Freemasonry would persist longer and its transition to Republicanism would be less orchestrated and more contested.

In three of the smallest northern states this transition did not take place until after 1800. In Delaware, when the state grand lodge was formed in 1806 from lodges warranted by

[109] Of the Republican leadership of 1803 identified by Thomas, 23.7 percent (14/59) attended the grand lodge meetings in 1797, 1800, and 1803, as against 12 percent (11/91) of the Federalist leadership (Thomas, "Politics in the Land of Steady Habits," pp. 304–6; and E. G. Storer, *The Records of Freemasonry in the State of Connecticut* . . . [New Haven, 1859], pp. 84–91, 122–29, 153–60). Voting analysis was based on locations of lodges listed in 1800 compared with town voting maps for 1803–13 and 1818 (Thomas, "Politics in the Land of Steady Habits," p. 218; and Purcell, *Connecticut in Transition*, p. 260).

[110] Denslow, ed., *Ten Thousand Famous Masons*, 1:140, 2:283–84, 4:44.

Pennsylvania and Maryland, the two leading grand officers, Gunning Bedford and Jesse Green, were both Federalists.[111] Similarly, the Masons in Vermont were dominated by Federalists through the 1790s. Judge Noah Smith, the grand master from 1794 to 1798, had accepted an appointment as federal supervisor of distilled spirits in 1791, and John Chipman, grand master from 1798 to 1814, was the uncle of Nathaniel and Daniel Chipman, leading Vermont Federalists. Nathaniel Chipman and Isaac Tichenor, both Masons, served as Federalists in the U.S. Senate successively from 1796 to 1803, Tichnor resigning to serve as governor from 1797 to 1806. The Masonic hegemony of this Federalist clique was disturbed by a small coterie of Republican Masons in Bennington, which included printer Anthony Haswell, convicted of sedition in 1800. But the popular base of Vermont Freemasonry seems to have been as Federalist as its leadership; of nineteen lodges formed by 1800, eleven were located in towns voting consistently Federalist, while only four were in consistently Republican towns.[112] In New Hampshire, Masons were led by Gen. John Sullivan, president of the state Society of the Cincinnati and New Hampshire's leading nationalist in the 1780s, to his death in 1790. While the succeeding officers of the grand lodge were less obvious partisans, ten of the state's thirteen lodges in existence in 1802 were located in towns voting Federalist in 1800. The pattern would begin to shift in the next decade, with an "ardent Republican" elected deputy grand master in 1801 and grand master in 1808.[113]

[111] Charles E. Green, *History of the M. W. Grand Lodge of Ancient, Free and Accepted Masons of Delaware* (Wilmington, Del., 1956), pp. 9–13; *Biographical Directory of the American Congress, 1774–1949* (Washington, D.C., 1950), s.v. "Bedford, Gunning, Jr."; *Mirror of the Times* (Wilmington), Oct. 18, 1800 (supplied by Philip Lampi).

[112] *Records of the Grand Lodge of Free and Accepted Masons of the State of Vermont, from 1794 to 1846 Inclusive* (Burlington, Vt., 1879), pp. 38–40, 418; *Biographical Directory of the American Congress,* s.v. "Chipman, Nathaniel," and "Tichenor, Isaac"; Denslow, ed., *Ten Thousand Famous Masons,* 1:207, 4:241. Smith, *Freedom's Fetters,* pp. 359–73; Fischer, *Revolution of American Conservatism,* pp. 240–41; Vermont voting data provided by Robert Shalhope.

[113] Lynn W. Turner, *The Ninth State: New Hampshire's Formative Years* (Chapel Hill, 1983), pp. 60–62, 270, 384–87; DePauw, ed., *Senate Executive*

In New Jersey and Rhode Island the transition to Republican leadership came late in the 1790s, in the midst of the partisan strife over the Sedition Act and the emergence of Republican organization. New Jersey's Freemasonry was not particularly dynamic in the 1790s, with relatively few lodges and dominated by men of Federalist inclinations. But in 1799 the grand lodge elected Joseph Bloomfield to be grand master. Originally a Federalist, Bloomfield had shifted to the Republican opposition in 1796 in reaction to the Jay Treaty; in 1800 he campaigned vigorously for the Republican ticket and presided over the party's state convention in Princeton that September. The Republicans failed to carry the state in 1800, but the three counties that they did carry had six lodges among them, as against four lodges scattered across six strong Federalist counties. Bloomfield was rewarded for his efforts when Republican assemblymen elected him governor in 1801—when he stepped down from the grand mastership—and reelected him to the governorship for the better part of the following decade. Later a congressman, Bloomfield's election as grand master in 1799 seems to have been a critical step toward leadership in the New Jersey Republican party.[114] The Republican emergence in Rhode Island seems to have begun a year earlier, in 1798. The first two grand masters, Christopher Champlin and Jabez Bowen, were both Federalists. But Bowen retired in 1798, to be followed by a series of other figures, including Christopher Olney in 1800 and Moses Seixas in 1802. Olney was a prominent manufacturer in Johnston, long an Antifederalist and Republican stronghold. Seixas had been elected in 1799 deputy grand high priest of the Royal Arch Freemasons in Rhode Island, following Republican Seth Wheaton, who had been elected in 1798. A

Journal, p. 517; Denslow, ed., *Ten Thousand Famous Masons,* 4:207; lodges from Webb, *Freemason's Monitor* (1802), p. 278.

[114] Carl E. Prince, *New Jersey's Republicans: The Genesis of an Early Party Machine, 1789–1817* (Chapel Hill, 1964), pp. 23, 36–37, 41–42, 53, 59–66, 70, 107, 142; McGregor, *Freemasonry in New Jersey,* pp. 82, 88, 93, 144; Denslow, ed., *Ten Thousand Famous Masons,* 1:108. Among the four New Jersey counties defined as having narrow Federalist majorities there were five lodges (Prince, *New Jersey's Republicans,* p. 66).

leading member of the Newport Jewish community, Seixas was the cashier of the Rhode Island Bank, an institution apparently dominated by Federalists. But his brother was Gershom Seixas, the hazan of a New York synagogue that was an important nexus in a connection of Jews up and down the Atlantic Coast who were drawn to the liberal promise of Jeffersonian Republicanism. When President John Adams called a Fast Day in 1798 as war seemed to be imminent, Gershom Seixas was one of three religious leaders in New York to deliver a sermon calling for peace with France.[115]

South of the Potomac, the Georgia Grand Lodge had moved early in Washington's administration into the Republican opposition, but in the three older and larger states the process was not so smooth. In North Carolina, Masonry was intimately interwoven with Federalism throughout the 1790s, connecting it with the political culture of the pre-Revolutionary tidewater elite. The grand lodge was led by men playing key roles in the nationalism of the 1780s and Federalism of the 1790s, among them Samuel Johnson, William Caswell, William R. Davie, Archibald McLaine, William Hooper, and John Steele. The Society of the Cincinnati collapsed in North Carolina by 1792, and thus the Masonic Lodges seem to have served as a particularly important vehicle of association for North Carolina Federalists while they were out of power between 1793 and 1798. Grand master between 1792 and 1798, though he had never been master of a lodge, William R. Davie organized the circulation of Federalist literature in the 1798 campaign and stepped down from grand lodge leadership on being elected governor that De-

---

[115] Rugg, *Freemasonry in Rhode Island*, pp. 274–76, 748, 750, 824; Richard M. Baylies, ed., *History of Providence County, Rhode Island* (New York, 1891), p. 792; Irwin H. Polishook, *Rhode Island and the Union, 1775–1795* (Evanston, Ill., 1969), pp. 111, 128n, 147–48, 229, 237–38; Patrick T. Conley, *Democracy in Decline: Rhode Island's Constitutional Development, 1776–1841* (Providence, 1977), p. 179; DePauw, ed., *Senate Executive Journal*, p. 539; Fischer, *Revolution of American Conservatism*, pp. 164–65, 225; Morris U. Schappes, "Anti-Semitism and Reaction, 1795–1800," *Publications of the American Jewish Historical Society* 38 (1948):109–37; Jacob R. Marcus, *United States Jewry, 1776–1985*, 4 vols. (Detroit, 1989–93), 1:179, 240, 442, 526–29, 579–80, 596.

cember. Throughout the 1790s Federalist congressmen from
North Carolina, led by five-term William Barry Grove of Fay-
etteville, were far more likely to be Freemasons, and the counties voting consistently Federalist in the next decade were
twice as likely to have Masonic lodges as the stronger Republican counties. Freemasonry was deeply rooted in an enduring
culture of the provincial tidewater elite in North Carolina and
during the 1790s did not admit—or attract—the popularly
elected Republican leadership based in constituencies dominated by small farmers in a backcountry already feeling the
influence of Baptist and Methodist revivalism.[116] But legislatively elected Republicans were quite different. Three of the
four Republican senators representing North Carolina from
1795 would have Masonic membership by 1798, and when
Republican Benjamin Williams was elected governor in 1799,
serving for the next three years, he too was a Mason. In North
Carolina, Republican governors and senators were increasingly comfortable with the Masonic understandings shaping
elite political culture in the tidewater, and for the next several
decades would maintain this Masonic connection.[117]

In Virginia the Republican influence in the ranks of Freemasonry rose and fell in the mid-1790s. In 1788 Freemasonry
was clearly linked with the nationalist cause, both in the persons of John Blair, Edmund Randolph, and John Marshall,
and in the location of Masonic lodges in older eastern counties whose delegates voted overwhelmingly to ratify the Federal Constitution, votes that determined the fate of the
Constitution in Virginia.[118]

[116] Gilpatrick, *Jeffersonian Democracy in North Carolina*, pp. 82–126; Rose,
Prologue to Democracy, pp. 77–80, 243; Curtis C. Davis, *Revolution's Godchild:
The Birth, Death, and Regeneration of the Society of the Cincinnati in North Carolina*
(Chapel Hill, 1976), pp. 53, 217. See Appendix, tables 10 and 11.

[117] Governors from Kallenbach and Kallenbach, eds., *American State Governors*, 1:440; senators from Hoadley, *Origins of American Political Parties*, pp.
215–19; Masonic affiliations from Denslow, ed., *Ten Thousand Famous Masons*, 1:107, 2:73–74, 3:142; Bridges, *Masonic Governors of North Carolina*,
pp. 125–93.

[118] See Appendix, table 7.

But over the next several years Virginia Masonry began to move toward the opposition, more in step with what would become the state's central tendencies. Between 1789 and 1795 lodges were formed in a number of counties in the center of the state—from Culpeper on the upper Rappahanock to Pittsylvania in the Southside—that had voted against the Constitution in 1788. These counties with new lodges also led the state in November 1795 in voting to condemn the Jay Treaty, while the eastern counties with older lodges split on the issue. Given that Democratic societies were formed in only three Virginia counties, it may well have been that new Masonic affiliations played some role in shaping a Republican coalition in the mid-1790s.[119]

At the same time, Masons were central players in a pivotal partisan conflict, as national divisions entered into the state arena for the first time. Henry (Light-Horse Harry) Lee, a member of Hiram Lodge in Westmoreland and governor since 1791, was a Federalist, though his distaste for Hamilton's fiscal policies led him to help Madison organize subscriptions for the *Aurora* in 1791. But when Lee accepted a Federal appointment as commander of forces marching against the Whiskey rebels, he was unseated by the House of Delegates at their November 1794 session. In his place the House elected another Mason, Robert Brooke, a staunch Republican partisan since 1791, later to be attorney general of the state between 1798 and 1800. Brooke's very partisan election was—in the assessment of both Richard R. Beeman and Norman K. Risjord—"a giant step toward the evolution of parties" in Virginia.[120] It was also bound up in a change in Masonic leadership. Brooke had been appointed deputy grand master by Grand Master John Marshall in October 1793; in November

---

[119] See Appendix, table 8.

[120] Norman K. Risjord, *Chesapeake Politics, 1781–1800* (New York, 1978), pp. 447–48; Richard R. Beeman, *The Old Dominion and the New Nation, 1788–1801* (Lexington, Ky., 1966), pp. 135–37; Cunningham, *Jeffersonian Republicans*, pp. 16–17; Charles Royster, *Light-Horse Harry Lee and the Legacy of the American Revolution* (New York, 1981), pp. 104–9, 130–37; Denslow, ed., *Ten Thousand Famous Masons*, 3:68.

1795 Marshall resigned his post of honor, and the grand lodge elected Governor Brooke in his place.[121] Beyond Brooke, Masonic affiliations, active or lapsed, encompassed a wide circle of Republican leaders, including Edmund Pendleton, Francis Preston, Philip N. Nicholas of the Richmond Junto, Senators Henry Tazewell, Wilson Cary Nicholas, and James Monroe, elected governor in 1799.[122]

The spread of Masonic lodges and affiliations was one of the underlying dimensions of the emergence of Virginia's Republican opposition in the mid-1790s. But in the years following, Masonry did not play a notable role in the Republican orbit. As in Connecticut, the order seems to have retreated from a partisan link with the Republicans with the Illuminati campaign of 1798. William Austin, a marginal Federalist figure who ran for governor in 1800, was chosen deputy grand master in December 1798 and grand master in December 1800.[123] Similarly, the location of lodges showed no particular relationship with the Virginia House of Delegates vote on the Virginia Resolutions in 1798.[124] In sum, Freemasonry was an important vehicle for nationalist affiliation in Virginia in the 1780s, spread into Republican counties in the context of the Whiskey Rebellion and the Jay Treaty, and became significant for at least some in the inner circles of Republican leadership. After 1796 formal party structures, manifested most obviously in the Republican county committees, became the focus of partisan organization, and Masonry reverted to its former role as a dimension of broader gentry connections.[125]

[121] Dove, comp., *Proceedings*, 1:113, 121, 135–38; Denslow, ed., *Ten Thousand Famous Masons*, 1:134.

[122] Henry Clay, the leading Whig Mason of the 1830s, studied law in Robert Brooke's office. Denslow, ed., *Ten Thousand Famous Masons*, 3:216, 266, 325, 365; 4:224.

[123] Dove, comp., *Proceedings*, 1:181, 219.

[124] See Appendix, table 9.

[125] Five Republican committeemen appointed in January 1800 attended the grand lodge meeting in December 1799. Dove, comp., *Proceedings*, 1:199–200; William P. Palmer et al., eds., *Calendar of Virginia State Papers and Other Manuscripts, from January 1, 1799 to December 31, 1807 . . .*, 11 vols. (Richmond, 1875–93), 9:77–81.

South Carolina had a long tradition of Freemasonry stretching back to the 1730s, a dimension of the dense associational life in Charleston in particular, where charitable organizations filled the void left by the lack of formal city government.[126] Beginning with the establishment of an insurgent grand lodge of "Ancient York Masons" in Charleston in 1787, Freemasonry began to spread rapidly in the city and into the upcountry districts. Coming in the midst of what David Ramsay termed "eight years of disorganization" following "eight years of war," this Masonic expansion seems to have played a part in South Carolina's Revolutionary settlement, coming in the wake of the reform of the courts in 1785 and just as the constitutional convention of 1790 began to meet backcountry demands by moving the capital from Charleston to Columbia.[127] By the turn of the century there was one lodge for every 5,000 whites in the state, and one for every 450 whites in Charleston, the highest concentration of Masonic institutions anywhere in the republic.[128]

As of 1788, South Carolina Freemasonry was firmly Federalist. The two competing Masonic bodies, the older Modern Grand Lodge and the new Ancient York Grand Lodge, were generally controlled by lowcountry Federalist partisans from the 1780s to the close of the 1790s. John F. Grimké, a Federalist delegate to the ratifying convention, was grand master of the Modern Grand Lodge from 1787 through 1800. The leadership of the Ancient York Grand Lodge was somewhat

[126] Walsh, *Charleston's Sons of Liberty*, pp. 29–31, 42, 65; William H. Pease and Jane H. Pease, *Web of Progress: Private Values and Public Styles in Boston and Charleston, 1828–1843* (New York, 1985), pp. 90–103, 142–50.

[127] Rachel N. Klein, *Unification of a Slave State: The Rise of the Planter Class in the South Carolina Backcountry, 1760–1808* (Chapel Hill, 1990), pp. 78–202, esp. pp. 142–48, quotation p. 109; Robert M. Weir, "'The Violent Spirit,' the Reestablishment of Order, and the Continuity of Leadership in Post-Revolutionary South Carolina," in Hoffman, Tate, and Albert, eds., *Uncivil War*, pp. 70–98; Mackey, *Freemasonry in South Carolina*, pp. 64–81.

[128] Mackey, *Freemasonry in South Carolina*, pp. 60–83; *General Rules and Regulations of the Grand Lodge . . . of South Carolina (Ancient York Masons)* (Charleston, S.C., 1795), pp. 17–18 (list of lodges in 1795); Webb, *Freemason's Monitor* (1805), pp. 314–16.

more varied, but in the end was dominated by Federalists through most of the 1790s. William Drayton, the first grand master from 1787 to 1789, accepted a federal judgeship in 1789. Between 1793 and 1798 the York Grand Lodge elected William Loughton Smith, Federalist congressman from the Charleston district from 1789 to 1797 and staunch ally of Alexander Hamilton, to serve as grand master. But before 1793 men of other persuasions also ranked among the York Grand Lodge leadership. In each year between 1787 and 1792 there was at least one future member of the Republican Society of South Carolina in the York Masonic leadership, culminating in the election of Thomas B. Bowen as grand master in 1792. But with the eruption of partisanship and the emergence of the Republican Society, these men were swept from the leadership of the York Grand Lodge, never to serve again.[129] The distribution of lodges in 1788 suggests the likelihood of a Federalist inclination among the Masonic rank and file. Eleven lodges, both Modern and Ancient, were located in Federalist Charleston, with four in coastal and middlecountry districts voting to ratify the Constitution, and two in Antifederal counties, one each in the middle country and the upcountry.[130] Over the next decade, however, the traditional coastal bias of Masonry would disappear. By 1795, and even more so in 1805, lodges were well established in the interior, especially in the upcountry districts, with surprisingly few lodges in the middle country. Laurens, Union, Chester, and Newberry districts alone accounted for ten lodges. All of these new upcoun-

---

[129] Grand Lodge officers from Mackey, *Freemasonry in South Carolina*, pp. 77–82; DePauw, ed., *Senate Executive Journal*, p. 543; Denslow, ed., *Ten Thousand Famous Masons*, 1:118, 4:163–64; Federalist affiliations from George C. Rogers, *The Evolution of a Federalist: William Loughton Smith of Charleston (1758–1812)* (Columbia, S.C., 1962); Fischer, *Revolution of American Conservatism*, p. 402; *Dictionary of American Biography*, s.v. "Smith, William Loughton"; Republican Society membership from subscribers' signatures to "Declaration of the Friends of Liberty and National Justice, July 13, 1793," Mss 1436, no. 10/11, Boston Public Library (signatures transcribed Apr. 14, 1794). Besides Thomas B. Bowen, Edward Weyman and Guilliam Aertson were both grand lodge officers before 1793 and then members of the Republican Society.

[130] See Appendix, table 12.

try lodges were affiliated with the newer Ancient York Grand Lodge, while the Modern Lodge remained isolated in Charleston.[131]

The leadership of the Ancient York Grand Lodge also changed drastically in the late 1790s. Federalist William L. Smith retained his grand mastership through 1798, but in 1799 the Rev. Henry Purcell was elected grand master, followed in 1800 by Gov. John Drayton. Elected lieutenant-governor in 1798, Drayton had become governor in January 1800 with the death of Edward Rutledge. The son of a powerful Charleston family and once a Federalist himself, John Drayton was by 1800 a staunch Republican. He and Purcell had served in the grand lodge briefly before 1794, as had Col. John Mitchell, the new deputy grand master, and they brought a number of new figures into the grand lodge leadership. One was Seth Paine, a Republican printer, and another was Benjamin Cudworth, a veteran of opposition politics in Charleston in the 1780s. Conspicuously absent among the grand lodge leaders in 1800 were British merchant Laurance Campbell, grand treasurer since 1792, and Presbyterian George Buist, chaplain under William L. Smith between 1794 and 1798, who in 1793 had congratulated the grand lodge for not having "become the tools of party."[132]

The grand lodge over which Drayton presided in 1800 was truly a state-wide organization, linking lodges in Charleston,

---

[131] Mackey, *Freemasonry in South Carolina*, pp. 65–73; Webb, *Freemason's Monitor* (1805), pp. 314–16.

[132] Rogers, *Evolution of a Federalist*, pp. 100, 158; Marvin R. Zahniser, *Charles Cotesworth Pinckney: Founding Father* (Chapel Hill, 1967), pp. 224, 238; Klein, *Unification of a Slave State*, p. 131; Jerome J. Nadelhaft, *The Disorders of War: The Revolution in South Carolina* (Orono, Maine, 1981), pp. 119–21; Buist, *Sermon*, p. 26. John Mitchell and Bowen were both leading figures in the Charleston Lodge of Perfection, formed in 1785 (Denslow, ed., *Ten Thousand Famous Masons*, 1:118, 3:211). Henry Purcell was something of a dissident within the Episcopal Church, publishing a tract protesting episcopal authority, *Strictures on the Love of Power in the Prelacy* . . . (Charleston, S.C., 1795). Paine was a partner to Peter Freneau in publishing the *City Gazette* and the *Carolina Gazette* between 1795 and 1802 (Clarence S. Brigham, ed., *History and Bibliography of American Newspapers, 1690–1820*, 2 vols. [Worcester, Mass., 1947], 2:1024–26).

the lowcountry, and the far upcountry. As governor, Drayton devoted considerable attention to cultivating such ties throughout the state. He was the first governor to tour the upcountry, reviewing the militia in the various districts, and in 1801 he urged that the state's "political union [would] be much advanced" if the South Carolina College should be established at Columbia rather than Charleston.[133] The Ancient York Rite lodges may well have served to advance this "political union" and the cause of the Republicans across the state, presumably creating circles of affiliation and patronage for rising upcountry elites. Little is known of these early upcountry lodges except their names and locations; one such lodge in Scuffletown in Abbeville district was later remembered as having initiated "a great many of the first men of Abbeville, Laurens, Greenville, and Pendleton." Certainly they were located in districts voting with the Republicans. After the turn of the century almost two-thirds of the leading Republican districts had local lodges, as against roughly a third of the leading Federalist districts.[134]

The connection between the Ancient York Grand Lodge with the emergence of Republican preeminence in South Carolina had an important epilogue in 1808. On June 28, 1808, the South Carolina legislature voted 101–2 to equalize representation between the lowcountry and the upcountry, long a critical point of contention between the regions. The following September, William L. Smith—recently converted to Republicanism following the *Chesapeake* affair—acted with John F. Grimké to engineer a union of the Modern and Ancient Grand Lodges. Just as the upcountry—in one observer's view—had "assimilated so nearly to the privileged districts below" to allow equal representation, two grand lodges were no longer necessary in a newly united state. Or so it seemed, until the following January, when twelve upcountry lodges in Republican districts (including York, Chester, Fairfield, Laurens, Newberry, and Edgefield), allied with three lodges from the lowcountry, seceded from the new Union Grand

---

[133] *Dictionary of American Biography*, s.v. "Drayton, John"; Klein, *Unification of a Slave State*, p. 241.

[134] See Appendix, tables 13 and 14.

Lodge. This upcountry secession, subsequently known as the Ancient York revival, was led by Judge William Smith of Pinckneyville and Yorkville, a staunch Old Republican and state rights advocate. Clearly, upcountry hostility to lowcountry control was undiminished by the new representation law, just as it seems quite evident that Grimké and William L. Smith had been attempting to claim the Masonic network for their brand of moderate Republicanism. The two Grand Lodges would again unite in 1817, but one wonders whether the Masonic fundamentalism of the Ancient York revival anticipated the political fundamentalism of the upcountry in the ensuing decades, as Judge William Smith's Old Republicanism became a ground upon which Calhounite nullification developed in South Carolina.[135]

The emergence of a Republican predominance in Maryland Masonry followed a path not unlike that in South Carolina, culminating in a literal struggle for control of the grand lodge. Maryland's grand lodge was formed in 1783 from lodges chartered in Pennsylvania and located in the Federalist counties of the Eastern Shore. In particular, the grand lodge was controlled between 1787 and 1796 by a cluster of Federalists from the town of Easton in Talbot County: Dr. John Coats, lawyer Nicholas Hammond, and Judge David Kerr. Seven of the eight lodges chartered by 1788 were located in counties voting to ratify the Federal Constitution.[136]

Over the 1790s Masonic lodges formed rapidly in the grow-

[135] Mackey, *Freemasonry in South Carolina*, pp. 89–123; Klein, *Unification of a Slave State*, pp. 257–68; Rogers, *Evolution of a Federalist*, pp. 373–74; on William Smith of Yorkville see *Dictionary of American Biography*, s.v. "Smith, William (c. 1762–1840)"; Denslow, ed., *Ten Thousand Famous Masons*, 3:163; William Freehling, *Prelude to Civil War: The Nullification Controversy in South Carolina, 1816–1836* (New York, 1965), pp. 97–103; Lacey K. Ford, Jr., *Origins of Southern Radicalism: The South Carolina Upcountry, 1800–1860* (New York, 1988), pp. 114–19; on the earlier unification of lowcountry Regular Baptists and upcountry Separate Baptists, see Klein, *Unification of a Slave State*, pp. 276–84. None of the fifteen lodges seceding in 1808 were located in counties voting against nullification in 1832.

[136] Schultz, *Freemasonry in Maryland*, 1:149–50, 377, 399–400, 409–11; Whitman H. Ridgway, *Community Leadership in Maryland, 1790–1840: A Comparative Study of Power in Society* (Chapel Hill, 1979), pp. 322, 325; ratification votes in Libby, *Geographic Distribution*, p. 114.

ing city of Baltimore, but less so in rural counties, so that by 1800 six of the fourteen working lodges were located in Baltimore, as against only one out of eight in 1788. Similarly, the leadership of the grand lodge began to be centered on Baltimore, beginning in 1794 with the election of Henry Wilmans, a recent German immigrant, as grand master. And, determined in great part by Baltimore's conversion to Republicanism, new lodges formed between 1788 and 1800 were overwhelmingly located in Republican areas: Where seven of eight lodges working in 1788 were located in Federalist counties, eight out of twelve lodges working in 1800 were in counties voting that year for the Republicans.[137]

Republican predominance in the grand lodge came in a partisan confrontation in the midst of the Quasi War with France and the Illuminati campaign. The central figure in this drama was a Baltimore Federalist named William Belton, who was elected deputy grand master in 1797 and grand master in 1798. Acting on his authority as deputy grand master in November 1797, Belton signed a public notice urging Masons to join a new Masonic militia company, recently formed to demonstrate Masonic loyalties to the federal government. Calls to join the company were repeated over the following year, and after his election as grand master Belton called a special meeting to compose a letter of loyalty and support to President Adams, as the Provisional army began to mobilize under George Washington. Belton also sent addresses to Washington as he passed through Baltimore in July and to his headquarters at Elkton. He ran afoul of Masonic regulations when he chartered a lodge on his own authority and then attempted to have the grand lodge issue a warrant to this "Patriotic or first Military Lodge." There had been rumblings of opposition in July, when his request that the grand lodge march in Masonic procession to deliver Washington's address was denied. In October charges were brought that he had both "constitute[d] an illegal Lodge of Masons" and

---

[137] L. Marx Renzulli, *Maryland: The Federalist Years* (Rutherford, N.J., 1972), pp. 217–18; Schultz, *Freemasonry in Maryland*, 1:149–50, 187, 204, 228, 238–39, 243–44, 252, 276, 287; 2:9. Two of the four lodges operating in Federalist counties were led by Republicans. See discussion of the Leonardtown and Frederick lodges below.

called a special meeting "and voted an address to the President of the United States on political subjects contrary to his obligations and charges." Countercharges were brought against his accuser, George Keating, who, it was claimed, had broken down a door and held a lodge meeting "with a number of men dressed in regimentals and armed with bayonets." Clearly partisan rage broke down the walls of harmony and love among Baltimore Freemasons in the crisis year of 1798.[138]

The resolution of the Belton affair would take months of meetings and the intervention of the grand lodge of Virginia. By the time that Maryland Masons sat down to listen to an address on their "voluntary contract of the most solemn nature to maintain Brotherly Love" in July 1799, the grand lodge had new and Republican leadership. Their new grand master was Maj. William Thomas, a planter and Republican leader in St. Mary's County, soon to be elected to the first of thirteen consecutive terms as president of the Maryland state senate. In August 1798, Thomas had organized a petition of Masons requesting to be released from a lodge in Port Tobacco to form a new lodge in Leonardtown. Their petition was granted on June 22, 1799, the same day as that of a lodge in Frederick, which also had a number of Republican members. The very next day William Thomas was elected grand master, to be reelected in 1800, apparently on the strength of a growing preponderance of Republican votes in the grand lodge. Maryland Republicans broke the predominance of Federalism in 1800 but failed to gain more than a narrow edge in the assembly elections; their majority would grow in the ensuing years. In a trajectory very similar to that of Joseph Bloomfield in New Jersey, William Thomas stepped down as grand master in 1801, the year of his election as president of the state senate. And not unlike the case in South Carolina, Masonry served as a bridge between city and countryside as Republicans began to gain control of state government.[139]

[138] Schultz, *Freemasonry in Maryland*, 1:263–74.

[139] Ibid., 276–85, 290–96, 306, 414–16; Ridgway, *Community Leadership*, p. 310; Renzulli, *Maryland: The Federalist Years*, pp. 217–18. See Ridgway,

In the midst of the Masonic controversies in Baltimore, the Reverend Snyder of the German Reformed Church in Frederick wrote to George Washington regarding John Robison's *Proofs of a Conspiracy*. As were many others, he was concerned "that some of the lodges in the United States might have caught the infection, and might co-operate with the Illuminati, or the Jacobin clubs in France." Washington assured the minister that none of the American lodges, derived from English Masonry, were "contaminated" by any secret order.[140] Passionate debate about secret conspiracies against the American republic swirled through this year of militant posturing against France. The question of the Bavarian Illuminati leads us finally to Massachusetts, where the Rev. Jedediah Morse first sounded the alarm of secret foreign plots. Here too we find Masonry taken over—if only briefly—by Republicans, and in a context that provides a very new perspective upon Morse's crusade.

Jedediah Morse of Charlestown and William Bentley of Salem, both ministers of established churches, stood at the opposing poles of ideological conflict in Massachusetts in the late 1790s. Where Morse led the forces of orthodox Calvinism in defense of the religious establishment and the primacy of the Federalist cause, Bentley led the theological liberals, staunchly supported the Republican opposition—and was a leading Mason. A month after Morse began his attack on the Illuminati in his May 1798 sermon at the New North Church in Boston, Bentley, addressing the Morning Star Lodge in Worcester, hinted that "the American geographer" might be driven to insanity in his "mad zeal" to uncover a conspiracy of Illuminati. That August, Bentley noted in his diary that Morse had "insinuated that I might be one of the Illuminati."

Community Leadership, pp. 77, 279, 360n, on the Republican Masons in Frederick and other voluntary associations and politics. Roger Nelson, Republican leader in Frederick County, was appointed junior grand warden under William Thomas. On the informal nature of Republican organization in Baltimore before 1801, see Frank A. Cassell, "The Structure of Baltimore's Politics in the Age of Jefferson, 1795–1812," in Aubrey C. Land, Lois Green Carr, and Edward C. Papenfuse, eds., *Law, Society, and Politics in Early Maryland* (Baltimore, 1977), pp. 279–86.

[140] Schultz, *Freemasonry in Maryland*, 1:259–63.

As if in defiance of Morse's accusation, in October Bentley accepted induction into the Royal Arch chapter recently chartered at Newburyport. Their conflict soon fell to the level of dirty tricks. In October 1799 the *Worcester Spy* printed a letter from a German authority, Dr. Christopher Ebeling, disputing the validity of Robison's *Proofs,* a letter that the public assumed had been addressed to Morse. Over a year later it became known that it actually had been sent to Bentley, who had sent it on to the *Spy,* where it was published by his good friend and fellow Mason Isaiah Thomas.[141]

Situated between Morse and Bentley stood another obscure but important figure. Dr. Josiah Bartlett served as grand master of the Massachusetts Grand Lodge from December 1797 through December 1799, during the height of the Morse controversy. In this capacity he worked to blunt the impact of Morse's attack, while avoiding the extremes to which Bentley was given. On June 25, 1798, the same day that Bentley was addressing the Morning Star Lodge in Worcester, Bartlett invited Morse to address the grand lodge, meeting in Concord to open a new lodge. In this forum Morse meekly avoided any reference to the Illuminati. But in June, Bartlett also sent an address to President Adams, complaining that "the illiberal attacks of a foreign Enthusiast, aided by the unfounded prejudices of his followers, are tending to embarrass the public mind, with respect to the real views of our society." After a published outcry from Morse, Bartlett published a series of letters in the *Massachusetts Mercury,* offering to disband Masonry in Massachusetts if charges of Illuminist corruption could be proven.[142]

---

[141] Stauffer, *New England and the Bavarian Illuminati,* pp. 317–18; William Bentley, *A Charge Delivered before the Morning Star Lodge, in Worcester, Massachusetts . . . June 25, 1798* (Worcester, Mass., 1798), pp. 26–27, 31; *The Diary of William Bentley, D.D., Pastor of the East Church, Salem, Massachusetts,* 4 vols. (Gloucester, Mass., 1962), 2:279, 320; William B. Sprague, *The Life of Jedediah Morse, D.D.* (New York, 1874), pp. 238–40.

[142] Stauffer, *New England and the Bavarian Illuminati,* pp. 325, 328–31; Jedediah Morse, *A Sermon Delivered before the Grand Lodge of Free and Accepted Masons of the Commonwealth of Massachusetts, at a Public Installation of Officers of Corinthian Lodge, at Concord . . . June 25, 1798* (Leominster, Mass., 1798); Bartlett's letter to Adams is in the *Proceedings of the . . . Grand Lodge . . . of Massachusetts . . . 1792–1815* (Cambridge, Mass., 1905), p. 131.

Bartlett might seem an insignificant player in this drama. But he was a leading notable—physician, justice of the peace from 1789, notary public from 1798, kin to the Gorham family, and founding member and former master of King Solomon's Lodge—in Charlestown, where Jedediah Morse was the only settled minister throughout the 1790s. As such, Morse and Bartlett were the two intellectual leaders in this turbulent seaport town, and a town that, with few exceptions, voted for Antifederalist and Republican candidates from the 1780s through the 1820s. In 1800 Republican Elbridge Gerry won 244 of 344 votes cast in Charlestown. And Morse's views aroused great hostility in this Republican stronghold. In 1795, when he attempted to quell a demonstration against the Jay Treaty, he was hit on the head with a thrown brick. In April 1799, when he presented his argument that there were seventeen Illuminated lodges in America, Nathaniel Ames reported that "half the people left the meeting, one telling the minister Morse there was no truth in what he said." Conversely, Bartlett was a popular man in Charlestown. In 1794 he headed a Masonic committee appointed "to erect a Monument in Mr. Russell's pasture," the forerunner of the present Bunker Hill Monument. In April, Bartlett had been elected moderator of the Charlestown town meeting, a post he would hold every year but one through 1800. In 1799, while still serving as grand master, he was elected representative to the General Court, and in 1798 and 1799 he was favored by the town for a seat in the senate to represent Middlesex County, which he won in 1800 with 320 votes from Charlestown voters.[143]

If Josiah Bartlett cut a more moderate figure than William Bentley and if (until 1800) he annually invited Jedediah Morse

[143] *Fleet's Pocket Almanack for . . . 1790 . . . to Which Is Appended the Massachusetts Register* (Boston, 1790), p. 126; *Fleet's Register, and Pocket Almanack for . . . 1799 . . .* (Boston, 1799), p. 42; *One Hundred and Fifty Years of King Solomon's Lodge, A. F. & A. M., 1783–1933* (N.p., 1933), pp. 21–23; Thomas B. Wyman, *The Genealogies and Estates of Charlestown, Massachusetts, 1629–1818* (1879; reprint ed., Boston, 1982), pp. 64–65, 424; Charles Warren, *Jacobin and Junto, or, Early American Politics as Viewed through the Diary of Dr. Nathaniel Ames, 1758–1822* (Cambridge, Mass., 1931), p. 122, quoting from Nathaniel Ames's diary, Apr. 10, 1799; Stauffer, *New England and the Bavarian Illuminati,* pp. 287–304; manuscript votes for governor, 1780–1840, Massachu-

to pray at the Charlestown town meeting, he was clearly the key ideological antagonist for his fellow townsman.[144] Given both the broader pattern of growing Republican influence in Free-masonry throughout the country and the specifics of cultural politics in Charlestown, one is tempted to suggest that Morse's campaign against the Illuminati was less paranoiac than a cal-culated attack upon the institutional base of the political oppo-sition. Such indeed was the tone of John Jay's comment to Morse in January 1799, written from a state where the Clinton-Livingston interest was very much interwoven with Freema-sonry. "Much ill-use has been and will yet be made of secret so-cieties," Jay wrote; "I think with you that they should not be encouraged, and that the most virtuous of them would do well to concur in suspending them for a while."[145] Did Josiah Bart-lett make "ill-use" of the Massachusetts Grand Lodge? Cer-tainly some Federalists thought so. Bartlett's election as grand master comprised an insurgency of sorts, as he had served in no posts under the previous grand master—Federalist Paul Revere—as was customary. In September 1798 the grand lodge was accused in the press of having "installed two Right Worshipful *Democrats*" when it opened the Meridian Lodge in Watertown.[146] This may have been only one of a number of po-litical lodge charters granted by Bartlett's grand lodge. Of the eight lodges opened during Bartlett's grand mastership, seven were in towns—including Watertown—which voted Republi-can in 1800, in contrast to the Federalism of the lodge towns in

setts Archives at Columbia Point; Timothy T. Sawyer, *Old Charlestown* (Boston, 1902), p. 263; James F. Hunnewell, *A Century of Town Life: A History of Charles-town, Massachusetts, 1775–1887* (Boston, 1888), pp. 30–31; "Charlestown, Mass., Town Records, vol. 9, 1779–1804," pp. 350, 374, 380, 392, 411, 427, 430, 440, 455, 461, Boston Pub. Libr. On Bartlett's role in setting up the Bun-ker Hill monument to Joseph Warren in 1794, see George H. Marden and George P. Kettell, eds., *By-Laws of King Solomon's Lodge, Charlestown . . . To-gether with Brief Extracts from the Records* (Boston, 1867), pp. 54–57; *One Hun-dred and Fifty Years of King Solomon's Lodge*, pp. 29–31.

[144] "Charlestown, Mass., Town Records," pp. 350, 374, 392, 411, 427, 430.

[145] Johnston, ed., *Correspondence and Public Papers of John Jay*, 2:252.

[146] *Diary of William Bentley*, 2:282.

1788, and of the towns where lodges were chartered in the years before 1798.[147]

In Massachusetts, as in at least nine states throughout the young republic, Freemasonry fell into the hands of the Republican opposition in the closing years of the 1790s. This development can be seen as a strategic retreat; in the face of Washington's condemnation of self-created societies, Republicans virtually abandoned the Democratic societies of 1793 and 1794, associations forged for purposes of political discussion, debate, and coordination, and directly modeled on the voluntary groups of the Revolutionary decades. The assumption of public, governmental roles by the Revolutionary societies in 1775 and 1776 stood at the center of Washington's fears when the Democratic societies began to act in the political arena in 1793 and 1794. The closing years of the 1790s saw the emergence of the structures of a party organization among the Republicans, but during these years Republicans in many states also were able to come to dominate Freemasonry, the central institution of the moderate Enlightenment and once the centerpiece of the consensual public sphere forged by the nationalists and the Federalists to stabilize the young republic. By associating with Masonry, however, the Republicans played into the hands of their most conservative opponents. Their own affinities with France, orthodox suspicions that French Masonry had played a key role in the French Revolution, the diffusion of mystical French degrees into the United States, the shared anticlericalism and deism of American Republicans and French revolutionaries, as well as the increasing disassociation of Federalism and Freemasonry all opened the door to the flamboyant charges of Illuminist conspiracy brought by Jedediah Morse.

WASHINGTON'S DEATH, REGIME STABILITY, AND THE THEATER STATE

The fortunes of Republican Freemasonry would be reversed suddenly and permanently in the final days of the eighteenth century. Hunkering down, if not staggering, under the blows

[147] See Appendix, table 5.

of Federalist Calvinism, Masonic Republicans nonetheless were poised to capture and redefine the core of the nation's public culture when—fortuitously—George Washington died at Mount Vernon on December 14, 1799. The outcome of a national rite of mourning would be to shift the balance of symbolic legitimacy from Federalists toward the Republicans, in the midst of the rage against the Alien and Sedition Acts and just as the 1800 election season got under way.

George Washington had been a Mason since 1752, when he entered the lodge at Fredericksburg, Virginia, and Masonry had an "uncontested claim to the right to be first among those who mourned his burial."[148] In a dramatic reversal of cultural priorities, commemorative rituals and funeral services throughout the country would be orchestrated according to Masonic custom, not Protestant liturgy. In these circumstances, Republican Masons were able to quietly break the Federalist monopoly over the cult of Washington.

In Massachusetts, Josiah Bartlett had just handed over the grand mastership to Samuel Dunn when Washington's death was announced in Boston. Though Dunn seems to have had Federalist inclinations—the only lodge chartered in 1800 was in Federalist Hardwick—Republicans were able to play conspicuous roles in the Masonic ceremonies for Washington acted out in Boston on February 11, 1800. With Dunn presiding over a procession of 1,600 uniformed Masons marching from the Old State House to the Old South Meeting House, Josiah Bartlett and another prominent Republican, Perez Morton, marched among six pallbearers carrying an urn, containing a lock of Washington's hair, mounted upon a pedestal covered with the emblems of "Faith, Hope, and Charity" and a weeping "Genius of Masonry." At the Old South, Federalist Timothy Bigelow delivered the eulogy after which— irony of ironies—arch-Republican William Bentley performed the funeral service. That night Bentley dined with Paul Revere, a Mr. Reynolds—who had built the urn and pedestal—and his friend Isaiah Thomas, the publisher of the *Spy*. Four days later Thomas, six years master of Worcester's

---

[148] Stauffer, *New England and the Bavarian Illuminati*, pp. 341–44; Lipson, *Freemasonry in Federalist Connecticut*, pp. 110–11.

Morning Star Lodge, presided over the military and Masonic ceremonies commemorating Washington at the federal encampment in Oxford, Massachusetts.[149]

Similar clusters of Republicans were centrally involved in the funeral rituals for Washington throughout the country. In Bennington, Vermont, the Masons of the Temple Lodge quickly organized a ceremony on the Masonic Fast Day of St. John the Baptist, regularly observed on December 27. This event had the character of a political rally for Anthony Haswell, a printer in Bennington who had been indicted the previous October for violating the Sedition Act and who would be convicted the next May. After a procession of militia, citizens, and Masons, Haswell delivered the oration taking the opportunity to fuse Republican and Masonic rhetoric, telling his audience that "the genuine sentiment of philanthropy prevailing, sanctions the republican idea, that '*Man is man, and who is more.*'" The committee requesting that he print his own address was comprised of two Bennington Masons, Andrew Seldon, a prominent Republican, and David Fay, Haswell's attorney in the Sedition case.[150] Down the Hoosic Valley in Troy, New York, the Apollo Lodge, under their master, Republican John Woodworth, led a procession of militia and citizens assembled on January 11 to hear a funeral sermon for Washington. In Baltimore the Masons on December 23 marched from Fell's Point to the Presbyterian Church, where they were ad-

[149] Brown, *Knowledge Is Power,* pp. 253–57; *Proceedings, 1792–1815,* pp. 156–64; Goodman, *Democratic-Republicans of Massachusetts,* pp. 100, 169, 184; *Diary of William Bentley,* 2:329; Esther Forbes, *Paul Revere and the World He Lived In* (Boston, 1942), pp. 395–97; Steblecki, *Paul Revere and Freemasonry,* pp. 60–63; Edward S. Nason, *A Centennial History of the Morning Star Lodge, 1793–1893* (Worcester, Mass., 1984), p. 169. For the cooperation of Bartlett and Morse in the ceremonies in Charlestown, see Marden and Kettell, eds., *Bylaws,* p. 59. See Bullock, "Ancient and Honorable Society," pp. 231–70, on the new emphasis on drama and ritual in American Freemasonry which developed around 1800.

[150] Anthony Haswell, *An Oration, Delivered at the Request of Temple Lodge in Bennington, Vermont, December 27th, 1799* (Bennington, Vt., 1800), p. 10, appendix; *Records of the Grand Lodge of . . . Vermont,* pp. 38–40; Smith, *Freedom's Fetters,* pp. 359–73. I am obliged to Robert Shalhope for pointing out Haswell's oration and circumstances.

dressed by Dr. John Crawford, recently named to his first term as deputy grand master with Republican William Thomas. In Frederick there were two Masonic celebrations, one on December 27, addressed by Republican Dr. John Tyler, and a second on February 22, the congressionally appointed Fast Day, addressed by the Federalist governor Thomas Johnson. On this same day the members of Friendship Lodge of Ancient York Masons in Charleston hosted the grand lodge officers in a ritual mourning for Washington. Meeting in a lodge room decorated with black crepe and death's heads, centering on a column-supported dome topped with a gilt urn and covering an emblematic coffin, they were asked by their orator Seth Paine, a Republican printer, "who will presume to say that Washington would have gloried in associating with a dangerous or vicious society of men?" Certainly not their new grand master, Republican Gov. John Drayton, who sat as the lodge's most honored guest.[151]

Exposed to the attacks regarding the Illuminati, the Masons restored their legitimacy by commanding the rhetorical and symbolic field in mourning for Washington. Throughout the country Republicans as Masons were strategically situated at the center of a defining national rite of mourning, and in some small measure the outcome of the election of 1800 rested upon the reconfiguration of the public sphere. As one Connecticut Federalist complained, Republican rhetoric about Federalist taxation, armies, and British affinities was supplemented in the summer and fall of 1800 with slogans about "Washington's grave stones."[152] Surviving Morse's on-

[151] Jesse B. Anthony, *History of King Solomon's Primitive Lodge No. 91, Free and Accepted Masons, Troy, N.Y. ...* (Troy, 1982), pp. 6–7; Jonas Coe, *A Sermon, Delivered before the Military Officers, Apollo Lodge, and a Large and Respectable Number of the Citizens of Troy, January 11, 1800 ...* (Troy, N.Y., 1800); Schultz, *Freemasonry in Maryland,* 1:278–79, 297–99; Ridgway, *Community Leadership,* pp. 53, 281; Renzulli, *Maryland: The Federalist Years,* p. 147; Mackey, *Freemasonry in South Carolina,* pp. 87–88; Seth Paine, *An Eulogy on General George Washington Pronounced in the Friendship Lodge #9, Ancient York Masons, in the Presence of the Grand Lodge of South Carolina ...* (Charleston, S.C., 1800), p. 20.

[152] Cunningham, *Jeffersonian Republicans,* p. 217.

slaught, Republican Masons were able to wrap themselves in Washington's Masonic honors, abandoned by Federalism as it moved to the right, toward orthodox Calvinism.

Ironically, Republican victory in 1800 may have hinged as much on the Illuminati as on the Alien and Sedition Acts. In the hands of John C. Ogden, Abraham Bishop, and other Republican publicists influenced by the *Aurora*, the label of the Illuminati was turned back upon the Federalist establishments in New England and extended to their counterparts in the Delaware Valley and the upper Chesapeake. Republicans were able to argue that the Federalist coterie of Congregational and Anglican ministers comprised the real Illuminati, conspiring against the interests and rights of the people. Donald H. Stewart and Alan V. Briceland both argue that these attacks were critical in this pivotal region, helping to swing the vote here toward the Republicans.[153]

But as much wild stories about the Illuminati, the ground for public culture in the new century was shaped by the Republicans' claim to the heritage of the moderate Enlightenment, recently abandoned by the Federalists. The result of the repositioning of the late 1790s left the Republicans with a strong claim to the center of the young republic's public sphere. With a claim to Masonic honors and institutions, they were situated between the extremes of the self-created societies of the revolutionary Enlightenment and the churches of the Calvinist counterrevolution. Without necessarily mobilizing Freemasonry in a conspicuous manner, the Republicans could enter the new decade assuming that the order was not arrayed against them, but rather included many men of influence well disposed to their interests, quite the opposite circumstance to the beginning of the 1790s.

This paper has moved from a broad consideration of associations in the public arena to a rather specific focus upon Republicans and Freemasonry. Neglected in this story are other major strands of development—the emergence of political party structure in the late 1790s, the persistence of local Republican clubs and reading societies, and the rising tide of

---

[153] Briceland, *"Philadelphia Aurora,"* pp. 33–35; Stewart, *Opposition Press,* p. 415; Stauffer, *New England and the Bavarian Illuminati,* pp. 345–60.

Baptist and Methodist evangelical Dissent, all of which shaped Republican fortunes at the turn of the century. These themes are critical to an understanding of Jeffersonian Republicanism as the rise of organized popular democracy, as well as to a complete understanding of the role of associations in the public sphere.[154]

But a somewhat different picture emerges from our focus on Freemasonry. Despite the core rhetoric of inclusion and democratic opportunity informing the general movement, Jeffersonian Republicanism would perpetuate rule by a benevolent gentry for another quarter century. In capturing Masonry, the Republicans had forged one of the bulwarks of the hegemony of their emerging regime. They had planted an anchor to windward in the institutional framework of the moderate Enlightenment, tempering if not abandoning the revolutionary Enlightenment of their origins. A fraternity of accepted and fee-paying equals, Masons were inculcated with virtue as they moved through an elaborate, fictive hierarchy in an endless sequence of initiations. Freemasonry proved as useful to the leading Republican gentry as it had seemed to the Federalists, more useful, in fact, because they were willing to open up the political process to a somewhat wider constituency than the Federalists. Masonry provided one framework of order and association for the men of moderate property who had been excluded from power by the Federalists and who comprised the electorate before the state constitutional revisions of the early 1820s. It connected them with men of prominence within the state and the nation, and it connected them with the symbols of nation-building charisma. It would continue to be a pillar of the new moderate Republican establishment until new forces were unleashed in the 1820s.

[154] Also ignored here is the way Freemasonry and fraternal organizations were already reshaping the contours of gender relations. See Goodman, *Toward a Christian Republic*, pp. 80–102; Mark C. Carnes, *Secret Ritual and Manhood in Victorian America* (New Haven, 1989); and Mary Ann Clawson, *Constructing Brotherhood: Class, Gender, and Fraternalism* (Princeton, 1989).

APPENDIX

Table 1. Masonic affiliations of governors and U.S. senators, 1797–1801

	Not Masons	Other Masonic affilia.	Active Free-masons	%	Total
All governors and U.S. senators, 1797–1801					
New England	23	1	4	14	28
New York to Maryland	25	9	5	13	39
South of the Potomac	20	5	15	37	40
Total	68	15	24	(22%)	107
Federalist governors and U.S. senators, 1797–1801					
New England	19	1	4	17	24
New York to Maryland	21	4	2	7	27
South of the Potomac	3	2	2	28	7
Total	43	7	8	(14%)	58
Republican governors and U.S. senators, 1797–1801					
New England	4	0	0		4
New York to Maryland	4	5	3	25	12
South of the Potomac	17	3	13	39	33
Total	25	8	16	(33%)	49
All governors, 1797–1801					
Elected by popular vote	13	1	3	18	17
Elected by legislature	8	3	6	35	17

SOURCES: William R. Denslow, ed., *Ten Thousand Famous Masons,* 4 vols. (Trenton, Mo., 1961); J. E. Kallenbach and J. S. Kallenbach, eds., *American State Governors, 1776–1976,* 3 vols. (Dobbs Ferry, N.Y., 1977–82), vol. 1; John F. Hoadley, *Origins of American Political Parties, 1789–1803* (Lexington, Ky., 1986), pp. 217–19.

Table 2. Lodges and newspapers in America, 1775–1800

	White pop.*	Masonic lodges	White pop./ lodge	Newspapers	White pop./ paper
			1775		
New England	670	21	31.9	15	44.7
New York–Maryland	817	22	37.1	13	62.8
Virginia–Georgia	624	29	21.5	9	69.3
Total	2,111	72	(29.3)	37	(57.1)
			1790		
New England	994	40	24.8	29	34.3
New York–Maryland	1,163	46	25.3	37	31.4
Virginia–Georgia	923	77	12.0	17	54.3
Kentucky	61			1	61.0
Total	3,139	163	(19.3)	84	(37.4)
			1800		
New England	1,216	171	7.1	70	17.4
New York–Maryland	1,602	208	7.7	100	16.0
Virginia–Georgia	1,154	157	7.4	46	25.1
Frontier states	322	11	29.3	11	29.3
Total	4,294	547	(7.8)	227	(18.9)

Sources: *Population:* 1775, estimated from Richard C. Simmons, *The American Colonies: From Settlement to Independence* (New York, 1976), pp. 175–77; 1790 and 1800, Bureau of the Census, *Historical Statistics of the United States: Colonial Times to 1970,* 2 vols. (Washington, D.C., 1976), 1:25–26, 28–29, 31–36.

Masonic lodges: Grand Lodge proceedings and histories; Thomas S. Webb, *The Freemason's Monitor, or, Illustrations of Masonry: In Two Parts* (New York, 1802), pp. 277–87; idem, *The Freemason's Monitor, or, Illustrations of Masonry: In Two Parts,* new ed. (Providence, 1805), 297–317.

Newspapers: 1775, 1790, Lester J. Cappon et al., eds., *Atlas of Early American History: The Revolutionary Era, 1760–1790* (Princeton, 1976), pp. 34, 68; David Hackett Fischer, *The Revolution of American Conservatism: The Federalist Party in the Era of Jeffersonian Democracy* (New York, 1965), pp. 413–29; Donald H. Stewart, *The Opposition Press in the Federalist Period* (Albany, 1969), pp. 869–93.

*Population in thousands.

Table 3. Masonic lodges per white population, by state, 1775, 1790, and 1800

	White pop. in 1775*	No. Masonic lodges 1775	Ratio	White pop. in 1790*	No. Masonic lodges 1790	Ratio	White pop. in 1800*	No. Masonic lodges 1805	Ratio
Maine	50	1	50	96	1	96	151	10	15
New Hampshire	80	1	80	142	5	28	184	16	11
Vermont				85	3	28	154	20	8
Massachusetts	294	6	49	373	14	27	417	70	6
Connecticut	192	11	17	233	15	15	245	46	5
Rhode Island	54	2	27	65	2	32	65	9	7
Total	670	21	(31.9)	994	40	(24.8)	1,216	171	(7.1)
New York	177	4	44	314	11	28	556	90	6
New Jersey	112	6	19	170	8	21	194	15	13
Pennsylvania	299	5	60	424	15	28	586	71	8
Delaware	30	2	15	46	3	15	50	6	8
Maryland	199	5	40	209	9	23	216	26	8
Total	817	22	(37.1)	1,163	46	(25.3)	1,602	208	(7.7)
Virginia	328	12	27	442	26	17	518	55	9
North Carolina	180	9	20	288	18	16	338	30	11
South Carolina	95	7	13	140	23	6	196	51	4
Georgia	21	1	21	53	10	5	102	21	5
Total	624	29	(21.5)	923	77	(12.0)	1,154	157	(7.4)

	White pop. in 1775*	No. Masonic lodges 1775	Ratio	White pop. in 1790*	No. Masonic lodges 1790	Ratio	White pop. in 1800*	No. Masonic lodges 1805	Ratio
Ohio							45	3	15
Tennessee							92	3	31
Mississippi							5	1	5
Kentucky				61			180	4	45
Total							322	11	(29.3)
Total	2,111	72	(29.3)	3,141	163	(19.3)	4,294	547	(7.8)

SOURCES: *Population:* 1775, estimated from Richard C. Simmons, *The American Colonies: From Settlement to Independence* (New York, 1976), pp. 175–77; 1790 and 1800, Bureau of the Census, *Historical Statistics of the United States: Colonial Times to 1970*, 2 vols. (Washington, D.C., 1976), 1: 25–26, 28–29, 31–36.

Masonic lodges: Grand Lodge proceedings and histories; Thomas S. Webb, *The Freemason's Monitor; or, Illustrations of Masonry: In Two Parts* (New York, 1802), pp. 277–87; idem, *The Freemason's Monitor; or, Illustrations of Masonry: In Two Parts*, new ed. (Providence, 1805), 297–317.

Newspapers: 1775, 1790, Lester J. Cappon et al., eds., *Atlas of Early American History: The Revolutionary Era, 1760–1790* (Princeton, 1976), pp. 34, 68; David Hackett Fischer, *The Revolution of American Conservatism: The Federalist Party in the Era of Jeffersonian Democracy* (New York, 1965), pp. 413–29; Donald H. Stewart, *The Opposition Press in the Federalist Period* (Albany, 1969), pp. 869–93.

*Population in thousands.

Table 4. Masonic publications by region, 1790–1800

| | Lodges in 1800 | Publications | | | |
| | | Sermons and orations (etc.) | | Proceedings (etc.) | |
	No.	No.	Ratio*	No.	Ratio*
New England	171	103	.60	35	.20
New York–Maryland	208	25	.12	36	.17
Virginia–Georgia	157	3	.02	45	.26
Total	536	131	(.24)	116	(.22)

SOURCES: Survey of publications listed in Charles Evans and Clifford K. Shipton, eds., *American Bibliography*, 13 vols. (Chicago and Worcester, Mass., 1903–55).

*Number of publications per lodge.

Table 5.   Freemasonry and votes for governor, by town, Massachusetts, 1800

	Towns with lodges formed by				
	1791	1792–94	1795–97*	1798–99#	1800
Federalist	8	3	6	1	1
Republican (%)	5 (38)	3 (42)	11 (55)	7 (87)	0
No vote	0	1	3	0	0
Total	13	7	20	8	1
High Republican† (%)	3 (23)	3 (42)	5 (25)	5 (62)	0

SOURCES: *Proceedings of the . . . Grand Lodge . . . of Massachusetts . . . 1792–1815* (Cambridge, Mass., 1905), pp. 245–47; manuscript votes for governor, 1800.

NOTE: Of the seventeen towns with lodges formed in or by 1788, twelve voted to ratify the constitution, one opposed, one was divided, and three did not vote (*Proceedings in Masonry . . . 1733–92* [Boston, 1895], pp. 482–86; *Proceedings, 1792–1815*, p. 245; ratification votes from Orin G. Libby, *The Geographic Distribution of the Vote of the Thirteen States on the Federal Constitution, 1787–1788* [Madison, Wis., 1894], pp. 111–12). The sole Antifederalist town was Danvers, where the United States Lodge, formed in 1778, collapsed before 1792 (*Proceedings, 1733–92*, p. 382).

*Revere's term.

#Bartlett's term.

†Town vote for Gerry 5 percent higher than county vote.

Table 6. Freemasonry and votes for governor, by county, New
York, 1789–1801

Majorities		Two or more lodges		Less than two lodges
		No.	%	No.
		1789		
Clinton (AF)	8	0	0	8
Yates (F)	6	4	66	2
Total	14	4	(32)	10
		1798		
Livingston (R)	10	6	60	4
Jay (F)	17	8	47	9
Total	27	14	(52)	13
		1801*		
Clinton (R)	23	14	61	9
Van Rensselaer (F)	7	3	43	4
Total	30	17	(57)	13

SOURCES: Votes from data assembled by Philip Lampi, on file at the American Antiquarian Society, Worcester, Mass.; lodges from *Transactions of the Grand Lodge of Free and Accepted Masons of the State of New York, 1816–1827* (New York, 1880).

*Lodges are calculated from 1800 data.

Table 7. Freemasonry and vote on the Constitution in Virginia, by county, 1788

	Lodges formed by				
	1788	1789–95	1796–1800	No lodge	Total
Federalist	12	7	2	19	40
Divided	3	0	1	3	7
Antifederalist (%)	1 (6)	9 (56)	5 (62)	17 (44)	32 (40)
Total	16	16	8	39	79

SOURCES: Votes from Richard R. Beeman, *The Old Dominion and the New Nation, 1788–1801* (Lexington, Ky., 1966), p. 244; lodges from Thomas S. Webb, *The Freemason's Monitor, or, Illustrations of Masonry: In Two Parts* (New York, 1802), pp. 285–86; John Dove, comp., *Proceedings of the M.W. Grand Lodge of Ancient York Masons of the State of Virginia* . . . (Richmond, 1874), pp. 55, 151, 246.

Table 8. Freemasonry and vote on the Jay Treaty in the Virginia House of Delegates, by county, 1795

	Lodges formed by				
	1788	1789–95	1796–1800	No lodge	Total
In favor	7	3	2	11	23
Divided	2	2	2	5	11
Opposed (%)	7 (44)	11 (65)	4 (50)	21 (52)	43 (53)
No vote	0	1	0	3	4
Total	16	17	8	40	81

SOURCES: Votes from Richard R. Beeman, *The Old Dominion and the New Nation, 1788–1801* (Lexington, Ky., 1966), p. 247; lodges from Thomas S. Webb, *The Freemason's Monitor, or, Illustrations of Masonry: In Two Parts* (New York, 1802), pp. 285–86; John Dove, comp., *Proceedings of the M.W. Grand Lodge of Ancient York Masons of the State of Virginia . . .* (Richmond, 1874), pp. 55, 151, 246. On the Republican Societies, see Eugene Perry Link, *Democratic-Republican Societies, 1790–1800* (New York, 1942), pp. 13–15.

Table 9. Freemasonry and vote on the Virginia Resolutions in the Virginia House of Delegates, by county, 1798

	Lodges formed by				
	1788	1789–95	1796–1800	No lodge	Total
Opposed	7	7	2	11	27
Divided	2	2	3	7	14
In favor (%)	7 (44)	8 (47)	2 (25)	22 (54)	39 (48)
No vote	0	0	1	1	2
Total	16	17	8	41	82

SOURCES: Votes from Richard R. Beeman, *The Old Dominion and the New Nation, 1788–1801* (Lexington, Ky., 1966), p. 248; lodges from Thomas S. Webb, *The Freemason's Monitor, or, Illustrations of Masonry: In Two Parts* (New York, 1802), pp. 285–86; John Dove, comp., *Proceedings of the M.W. Grand Lodge of Ancient York Masons of the State of Virginia . . .* (Richmond, 1874), pp. 55, 151, 246.

Table 10. Masonic affiliations of North Carolina representatives in Congress, 1789–1803 (1st to 7th Congresses)

	Freemasons*		All others	
	No.	Terms	No.	Terms
Federalist	6	14	5	8
Republican	4	5	17	31

NOTE: All known eighteenth-century Masons are listed by lodge in Thomas C. Parramore, *Launching the Craft: The First Half-Century of Freemasonry in North Carolina* (Raleigh, N.C., 1975), pp. 213–38; compare with representatives listed in John F. Hoadley, *Origins of American Political Parties, 1789–1803* (Lexington, Ky., 1986), pp. 199, 201, 203, 206, 208, 210, 213.

*By 1793.

Table 11. Freemasonry and popular vote for Congress in North Carolina, 1800–1816

	Counties	Counties with lodges (1802)	
		No.	%
Strongly Republican	31	11	35
Federalist, 1st quintile	16	12	75
Federalist, 2d quintile	15	4	27
Total	62	27	(44)

SOURCES: Lodges from Thomas S. Webb, *The Freemason's Monitor, or, Illustrations of Masonry: In Two Parts* (New York, 1802), p. 287; voting from James H. Broussard, *The Southern Federalists, 1800–1816* (Baton Rouge, 1978), p. 407.

Table 12. Freemasonry and vote on the Constitution in South Carolina, 1788

	No. of districts	Federalist			Antifederalist			Divided
		With lodge	No. of lodges	W/out lodge	With lodge	No. of lodges	W/out lodge	W/out lodge
Outside Charleston								
Georgetown region	3	1	1	2	0	0	0	0
Charleston region	11	1	1	8	0	0	1	1
Beaufort region	3	1	1	2	0	0	0	0
Middle country	8	1	1	3	1	1	3	0
Upcountry	8	0	0	1	1	1	5	1
Total	33	4	4	16	2	2	9	2
Charleston	1	1	11	1	0	0	0	0

SOURCES: Lodges from Albert G. Mackey, *The History of Freemasonry in South Carolina . . .* (1861; reprint ed., Charleston, S.C., 1936); Thomas S. Webb, *The Freemason's Monitor; or, Illustrations of Freemasonry: In Two Parts*, new ed. (Providence, 1805), pp. 314–16; voting data from Orin G. Libby, *The Geographic Distribution of the Vote of the Thirteen States on the Federal Constitution, 1787–1788* (Madison, Wis., 1894), p. 115.

Table 13. Freemasonry and voting in the congressional election of 1800 in South Carolina

	No. of districts	Federalist repr.			Federalist repr./ votes Republican			Republican rep.		
		With lodge	No. of lodges	W/out lodge	With lodge	No. of lodges	W/out lodge	With lodge	No. of lodges	W/out lodge
Outside Charleston										
Georgetown region	5	4	6	1	0	0	0	0	0	0
Charleston region	11	2	2	9	0	0	0	0	0	0
Beaufort region	4	2	3	2	0	0	0	0	0	0
Middle country	12	2	2	3	0	0	0	1	1	6
Upcountry	12	1	1	0	4	8	0	4	6	3
Total	44	11	14	15	4	8	0	5	7	9
Charleston	1	1	20*	0	0	0	0	0	0	0

SOURCES: Lodges from Albert G. Mackey, *The History of Freemasonry in South Carolina* . . . (1861; reprint ed., Charleston, S.C., 1936); Thomas S. Webb, *The Freemason's Monitor; or, Illustrations of Freemasonry: In Two Parts*, new ed. (Providence, 1805), pp. 314–16; election data assembled by Philip Lampi, on file at the American Antiquarian Society, Worcester, Mass.; James H. Broussard, *The Southern Federalists, 1800–1816* (Baton Rouge, 1978), p. 408.

*Approximate.

Table 14. Freemasonry and popular vote for Congress in South Carolina, 1800–1816

	No. of districts	Federalist			Republican		
		With lodge	No. of lodges	W/out lodge	With lodge	No. of lodges	W/out lodge
Outside Charleston							
Georgetown region	5	1	2	1	3	4	0
Charleston region	11	1	1	8	1	1	1
Beaufort region	4	2	3	2	0	0	0
Middle country	11	2	2	3	1	1	5
Upcountry	12	0	0	1	9	15	2
Total	43	6	8	15	14	21	8
Charleston	1	1	20*	0	0		0

SOURCES: Lodges from Albert G. Mackey, *The History of Freemasonry in South Carolina . . .* (1861; reprint ed., Charleston, S.C., 1936); Thomas S. Webb, *The Freemason's Monitor; or, Illustrations of Freemasonry: In Two Parts*, new ed. (Providence, 1805), pp. 314–16; election data assembled by Philip Lampi, on file at the American Antiquarian Society, Worcester, Mass.; James H. Broussard, *The Southern Federalists, 1800–1816* (Baton Rouge, 1978), p. 408.

*Approximate.

Table 15. Freemasonry and popular vote for Congress in Georgia, 1800–1816

	Counties	Counties with lodges (1802)		No. of lodges
		No.	%	
Republican	20	4	20	5
Federalist, 1st quintile	9	3	33	4
Federalist, 2d quintile	8	4	50	11
Total	37	11	(30)	20

SOURCES: Votes from James H. Broussard, *The Southern Federalists, 1800–1816* (Baton Rouge, 1978), p. 408; lodges from William H. Rosier and Frederick L. Pearson, Jr., *The Grand Lodge of Georgia, Free and Accepted Masons, 1786–1980* (Macon, Ga., 1983), p. 31.

Contributors
Index

Contributors

JOHN L. BROOKE, an associate professor in the Department of History at Tufts University, Medford, Massachusetts, is the author of *The Heart of the Commonwealth: Society and Political Culture in Worcester County, Massachusetts, 1713–1861* (1989) and *The Refiner's Fire: The Making of Mormon Cosmology, 1644–1844* (1994), which were awarded, respectively, the Merle Curti Award and the Bancroft Prize. He is currently examining Revolutionary settlements, print culture, and the public sphere in New York's Hudson Valley and the wider early republic, a project provisionally titled "The World of Martin Van Buren."

ANDREW R. L. CAYTON is professor of history at Miami University in Oxford, Ohio. He is the author of *The Frontier Republic: Ideology and Politics in the Ohio Country, 1780–1825* (1986) and, with Peter S. Onuf, *The Midwest and the Nation: Rethinking the History of an American Region* (1990). He is coeditor, with Jeffrey P. Brown, of *The Pursuit of Public Power: Political Culture in Ohio, 1787–1861* (1994). His most recent book is *Frontier Indiana* (1996).

JAMES H. KETTNER is professor of history at the University of California, Berkeley. He is the author of *The Development of American Citizenship, 1608–1870* (1978), winner of the Jamestown Prize for Early American History. He is currently completing an extended study of the Pleasants manumission case.

GARY J. KORNBLITH teaches American history at Oberlin College. He has published articles in *Business History Review, Journal of the Early Republic,* and other scholarly journals. He is the coauthor, with John M. Murrin, of "The Making and Unmaking of an American Ruling Class," in Alfred F. Young, ed., *Beyond the Ameri-*

CONTRIBUTORS

can Revolution (1993). Professor Kornblith is currently working on a biography of Joseph T. Buckingham, a nineteenth-century Boston printer and editor.

JOHN LAURITZ LARSON is a member of the Department of History at Purdue University and coeditor of the *Journal of the Early Republic*. He is the author of *Bonds of Enterprise: John Murray Forbes and Western Development in America's Railway Age* (1984) and "Jefferson's Union and the Problem of Internal Improvement," in *Jeffersonian Legacies*, ed. Peter S. Onuf (1993). He is finishing a book on internal improvement and the role of the state from the Revolution to the Civil War era.

MAEVA MARCUS is director of the Documentary History Project and editor of the multivolume series *The Documentary History of the Supreme Court of the United States, 1789–1800*. To date, five volumes have been published by Columbia University Press. Marcus was Visiting Professor of Law at Georgetown University Law Center from 1983 to 1987. The author or editor of a number of works in American legal and constitutional history, among them *Truman and the Steel Seizure Case: The Limits of Presidential Power* (1977) and *Origins of the Federal Judiciary: Essays on the Judiciary Act of 1789* (1992), she is currently writing a judicial biography of Louis D. Brandeis and preparing a narrative history of the judiciary in the age of Federalism.

THOMAS P. SLAUGHTER is professor of history at Rutgers University. He is the author of *The Natures of John and William Bartram* (1996), *Bloody Dawn: The Christiana Riot and Racial Violence in the Antebellum North* (1991), and *The Whiskey Rebellion: Frontier Epilogue to the American Revolution* (1986). He edited the Library of America edition of William Bartram's *Travels, and Other Writings* (1996) and *Ideology and Politics on the Eve of Restoration: Newcastle's Advice to Charles II* (1984). His current research is on "Mythic Americas," on native, African, and European imaginative constructions of the New World, c. 1450–1850, and "The Natures of the New World," on Euro-American theories of humans in nature, c. 1492–1800.

Contributors

BERNARD W. SHEEHAN is professor of history at Indiana University. He is the author of *Seeds of Extinction: Jeffersonian Philanthropy and the American Indian* (1973) and *Savagism and Civility: Indians and Englishmen in Colonial Virginia* (1980). He is currently writing a biography of George Rogers Clark.

GORDON S. WOOD is University Professor and Professor of History at Brown University. He is the author of *The Creation of the American Republic, 1776–1787* (1969) and *The Radicalism of the American Revolution* (1992). He is currently working on a volume in the Oxford History of the United States dealing with the period of the early republic, from 1789 to 1815.

Index

Abernethy, Thomas Perkins, 157, 177, 179
Adams, Abigail, 157–59
Adams, John, 50, 242, 265, 339, 348–49; and Bavarian Illuminati, 351; and Blount, William, 156, 183; criticism of, 246; election of, 161, 263; and Fries's Rebellion, 96–97, 107; and Southwest, 180
Adams, John Quincy, 188
Adams, Samuel, 251, 257, 259, 261, 290
Alabama, 188
Alexandria, Masons in, 273
Alien and Sedition Acts, 48, 276, 319, 338, 355
Alien Laws. *See* Alien and Sedition Acts
Allen, Ethan, 314
American Philosophical Society (Philadelphia), 315, 333
Ames, Fisher, 263
Ames, Nathaniel, 352
Ancient York revival, 346–47
Anderson, Benedict, 281
Andros, Edmund, 290
Anglo-Spanish War, 174
Annapolis, voluntary associations in, 285
Annapolis Convention (1786), 237
Anti-Britannic Marine Society (Charleston), 294, 309
Antifederalists, 1, 80–82, 85, 295, 301–2
Antislavery, 20–21, 136–55
Appleby, Joyce, 19, 265–66, 313
Armstrong, John, 332
Artisans, 20; political economy of, 249–72

Association of Tradesmen and Manufacturers of the Town of Boston, 251, 258
Associations: Confederation era, 294–95; Revolutionary, 294; voluntary, 284–85, 307–9, 313–16, 332–33, 344. *See also* Masonic lodges; Masons; Sons of Liberty
Associators (Pa.), 291–92
Au Glaize on the Maumee, conference at, 208
Aurora, 341, 358
Austin, Benjamin, Jr., 250–52, 255, 259–60, 263, 270–72
Austin, William, 342

Bache, Benjamin Franklin, 246, 310
Baldwin, Abraham, 33–34
Baltimore: Masons in, 347–49; political economy of artisans in, 253–54, 265; Revolutionary associations in, 294; voluntary associations in, 313
Baltimore Mechanical Co., 292
Bank of the United States, 19, 245
Banner, James M., Jr., 265–66
Barlow, Joel, 300–301, 334
Bartlett, Josiah, 351–53, 355
Baruel, Abbé, 319
Bavarian Illuminati, 276, 284, 319–22, 325, 335, 342, 348, 350–54, 357–58
Bayard, James A., 183
Becket, Thomas, 64
Bedford, Gunning, 305, 337
Beeman, Richard R., 341
Belcher, Andrew, 286
"Belcher's Apostate," 285

INDEX

Hayburn, William, 37
Hayburn's Case, 36–40
Heckewelder, John, 217
Hendrick, 219
Henry, Patrick, 20, 141, 238–39
Henry VIII, 65–66, 70, 100
Hillhouse, James, 210–11
History of American Law (Friedman), 55–56
Hodges, John, 122–23
Hohendahl, Peter, 279
Holland, James, 211
Homestead Act (1863), 23
Hooper, William, 339
Horanian Literary Society (N.Y.), 309
Horsehoe Bend, Battle of, 188
Hosmer, Stephen Titus, 335–36
House of Representatives (U.S.), and William Blount, 181–83
Houstoun, George, 330
Howe, Sir William, 76
Howland, John, 267–68
Hoxie, Frederick, 119–22
Hull, William, 187
Humane Society (N.Y.), 313
Hurst, James Willard, 54, 57–63, 71, 88
Hylton, Daniel, 43–45

Illinois, 188
Illuminati. *See* Bavarian Illuminati
Indiana, 188
Indians, 166–68, 170–71, 174, 176, 187–88, 190–222. *See also* Cherokees; Chicasaws; Chippewas; Choctaws; Creeks; Delawares; Iroquois; Miamis; Ottawas; Shawnees; Wyandots
Invalid Pensions Act (1792), 36–41
Invalid Pensions Act (1793), 40
Iredell, James, 35–36, 38–39, 95, 104–5, 111, 120, 129
Iroquois, 195–96, 198–200, 208–9, 214, 217–20; and American Revolution, 191; decline of, 193
Israel, Israel, 334

Jackson, Andrew, 162, 176, 188, 336
Jackson, James, 303, 306, 330
Jacob, Margaret C., 279
Jarvis, Charles, 250, 263
Jay, John, 45, 317; and Bavarian Illuminati, 353; and judicial review, 27, 38–39; and Masons, 332
Jay Treaty, 170, 264, 324, 338, 341–42, 352
Jefferson, Thomas, 14–16, 18–20, 24, 245, 247, 330; and Burr conspiracy, 110; and Alexander Hamilton, 310; and Indians, 191, 203–4; and judiciary, 12; and *Marbury* v. *Madison*, 52; *Notes on the State of Virginia*, 267–68; and political societies, 322–23; and Society of Cincinnati, 301; and West, 229, 231, 235
Jeffreys, George, 68–71, 104, 132
John Forbes and Co., 187
Johnson, John, 201
Johnson, Samuel, 303, 339
Johnson, Thomas, 234, 357
Johnson, William, 287
Jones, Dorothy V., 171
Joyce, William, 70
Judd, William, 334, 336
Judicial review, 25–53; of acts of Congress, 28–50; of state laws, 26–29
Judicial system, as instrument of consolidation, 11–13
Judiciary Act of 1789, 12–13, 26–27, 43, 51
Judiciary Act of 1801, 13, 49–50

Kane, John K., 130
Keating, George, 349
Kentucky, 163; Confederation era associations in, 295; Masons in, 336
Kerber, Linda K., 2
Kerr, David, 347
Kettner, James H., 21
"Key of Libberty" (Manning), 311–12, 322
Kirby, Ephraim, 334
Kirkland, Samuel, 217

Kline, Henry, 126
Knox, Henry, 15–16, 231–32; and
    Indians, 23, 201–4, 207–8,
    212–15, 218, 222
Kornblith, Gary J., 20
Koselleck, Reinhart, 278

Lafayette, marquis de, 199, 231,
    233
Lamb, John, 295, 313
Land speculation, 16, 157–63,
    168–70, 172–79
Languedoc Canal, 228–29
Larson, John Lauritz, 17
Lathrop, Joseph, 321
Laurance, John, 31, 34
Laurens, Henry, 20
Lee, Arthur, 198–200
Lee, Henry (Light-Horse Harry),
    243, 341
Lee, Richard Henry, 231
Legion of the United States, 170
Leib, Michael, 334
Leigh, Egerton, 287
Lemay, J. A. Leo, 285
L'Enfant, Pierre Charles, 4, 305–6
Leslie, John, 167
Lewis, William, 78, 99–100
Liberty Society (Ga.), 294
Liberty Tree Society (Charleston),
    294
Lincoln, Benjamin, 205, 207–8
Lipson, Dorothy Ann, 335
Lisle, Lady Alice, 68, 132
Liston, Robert, 160
Little Turtle, 209
Livingston, Edward, 332
Livingston, Henry Brockholst,
    119–22
Livingston, Robert R., 301,
    303–4, 330–31
Logan, Charles, 144–46
Logan, James, 144
London Corresponding Society,
    314
Louisiana, 161, 177–80, 185, 187
Lovat, Lord Simon, 69
Loyal Nine (Boston), 289

McGillivray, Alexander, 167,
    174–75
McHenry, James, 186

McKean, Thomas, 334
McKee, Alexander, 207
McKitrick, Eric, 164
McLaine, Archibald, 339
Maclay, William, 246
Madison, James, 8, 13–15, 18,
    238, 244–45, 247, 295; and
    Aurora, 341; and commercial
    retaliation against Great Brit-
    ain, 263–64; and Indians,
    211; and judicial review, 31–
    33, 39–40; and *Marbury* v.
    Madison, 50–51; and treason
    clause, 78–80, 83; and West,
    188, 231
Maier, Pauline: "Boston and New
    York in the Eighteenth Cen-
    tury," 256–57
Maitland, Frederick William, 66
Malcolm, Samuel B., 156
Manning, William, 18, 311–12,
    322
Mansfield, Lord, 100
Marbury, William, 50–51
Marbury v. *Madison,* 41, 50–52
Marchant, Henry, 27
Marcus, Maeva, 11
Marshall, John, 13, 305; and
    Blount conspiracy, 181; and
    judicial review, 50–52; and
    Masons, 303, 322, 340–41;
    and Pleasants case, 149,
    151–52; and treason law,
    110–13, 115–18, 126
Martin, Luther, and treason
    clause, 79, 81
Maryland: Masons in, 273,
    347–50; and navigation of Po-
    tomac River, 232–34; Sons of
    Liberty in, 292
Maryland Provisional Council of
    Safety, 294
Mason, George, and treason
    clause, 81
Masonic lodges: American Union
    Lodge, 298, 304; Ancient
    York Grand Lodge (Charles-
    ton), 343–47; Apollo Lodge
    (Troy, N.Y.), 356; Friendship
    Lodge (Charleston), 357;
    Friendship Lodge (Sunbury,
    Pa.), 302; Georgia Grand

INDEX

Masonic lodges (*cont.*)
Lodge, 306, 339; Grand
Lodge of Maryland, 273;
Grand Lodge of South Caro-
lina, 275; Hiram Lodge
(Westmoreland Co., Va.),
341; Holland Lodge (New
York), 331–32; King Solo-
mon's Lodge (Charlestown,
Mass.), 352; Lodge 22 (Alex-
andria, Va.), 273; London
Grand Lodge, 286, 290; Mas-
sachusetts Grand Lodge, 351,
353; Meridian Lodge (Water-
town, Mass.), 353; Modern
Grand Lodge (S.C.), 343,
345–47; Morning Star Lodge
(Worcester, Mass.), 350–51,
355–56; New York Grand
Lodge, 304; Pennsylvania
Grand Lodge, 299, 333; St.
Andrew's Grand Lodge (Boston), 289; St. John's Grand
Lodge (Mass.), 286, 298; St.
John's Lodge (Boston), 286;
St. John's Lodge (Hartford),
334; St. John's Lodge No. 1
(New York City), 304; Temple Lodge (Bennington, Vt.),
356; Virginia Grand Lodge,
322; Warren Lodge (N.Y.),
332; Williamsburg (Va.)
Lodge, 287; York Grand
Lodge (S.C.), 306
Masons: and American Revolution, 288–90; Ancient Rite,
287, 299; and Bavarian Illuminati, 319–22, 325, 333,
342, 348, 350–54, 357–58; in
colonial America, 286–88;
and Constitution, 302–3; and
Continental Army, 296–99,
304, 334; in England, 279; in
Europe, 286; and Federalists,
297, 303–4, 325, 328–29,
331–32, 334–41, 343–45,
347–49, 359; in Federalist
era, 304–9; in France, 278;
Modern Rite, 287, 290, 299;
and Republicans, 325–42,
344–59; in United States,
273–75, 283, 286–90, 296–

300, 302–9, 319–59; and
George Washington, 273–74,
298–99, 304, 306, 322, 327,
355–57; and Washington's
death, ceremonies for,
355–57; York Rite, 309. *See
also* tables pp. 362–77
Massachusetts: American Revolution in, 290; county conventions in, 293; Masons in, 286,
289, 298–99, 328, 350–56 (*see
also* table p. 367); voluntary
associations in, 307–9, 316
Massachusetts Charitable Me-
chanic Association, 252
Massachusetts Constitutional Soci-
ety, 251, 316
Massachusetts Spy, 308
May, Henry F., 277, 280
"Mechanics and the Jeffersonians,
The" (Young), 252–53
Mechanics Society: of Baltimore,
313; of New York City, 332
Miamis, 167–68, 209
Mid-Atlantic cities: citizenship in,
256–57; labor in, 256; popu-
lation in, 255
"Middle ground," 167, 193
Mifflin, Thomas, 333
Miller, Samuel, 332
Milton, Joyce, 56
Minervaean Society (Brookfield,
Mass.), 307–9
Mississippi River, 188; navigation
of, 165, 175–76, 179–80
Mississippi Territory, 163, 187
Mitchell, John, 121, 345; treason
trial of, 89–95, 101–4
Mobile, 176, 188
Modern Chivalry (Brackenridge),
190, 315
Monmouth's Rebellion, 68
Monroe, James, 342
Montesquieu, 6
Montfort, Joseph, 287
Montgomery, Richard, 300
Morgan, William, 327
Morris, Gouverneur, 332
Morris Robert, 16, 178, 231, 233,
243
Morse, Jedediah, and Bavarian Il-
luminati, 276, 284, 320–22,